Underwater Cultural Heritage and Ii

The UNESCO Convention on the Prote
Cultural Heritage 2001, which entered
in 2009, is designed to deal with threats to underwater cultural
heritage arising as a result of advances in deep-water technology.
However, the relationship between this new treaty and the UN
Convention on the Law of the Sea is deeply controversial.

This study of the international legal framework regulating
human interference with underwater cultural heritage explores
the development and present status of the framework and gives
some consideration to how it may evolve in the future. The central
themes are the issues that provided the UNESCO negotiators with
their greatest challenges: the question of ownership rights in
sunken vessels and cargoes; sovereign immunity and sunken
warships; the application of salvage law; the ethics of commercial
exploitation; and, most crucially, the question of jurisdictional
competence to regulate activities beyond territorial sea limits.

SARAH DROMGOOLE is Professor of Maritime Law at the University
of Nottingham.

CAMBRIDGE STUDIES IN INTERNATIONAL AND COMPARATIVE LAW

Established in 1946, this series produces high quality scholarship in the fields of public and private international law and comparative law. Although these are distinct legal sub-disciplines, developments since 1946 confirm their interrelations.

Comparative law is increasingly used as a tool in the making of law at national, regional and international levels. Private international law is now often affected by international conventions, and the issues faced by classical conflicts rules are frequently dealt with by substantive harmonisation of law under international auspices. Mixed international arbitrations, especially those involving state economic activity, raise mixed questions of public and private international law, while in many fields (such as the protection of human rights and democratic standards, investment guarantees and international criminal law) international and national systems interact. National constitutional arrangements relating to 'foreign affairs', and to the implementation of international norms, are a focus of attention.

The series welcomes works of a theoretical or interdisciplinary character, and those focusing on the new approaches to international or comparative law or conflicts of law. Studies of particular institutions or problems are equally welcome, as are translations of the best work published in other languages.

General Editors   James Crawford SC FBA
Whewell Professor of International Law, Faculty of Law, University of Cambridge

John S. Bell FBA
Professor of Law, Faculty of Law, University of Cambridge

A list of books in the series can be found at the end of this volume.

Underwater Cultural Heritage and International Law

Sarah Dromgoole

CAMBRIDGE
UNIVERSITY PRESS

University Printing House, Cambridge CB2 8BS, United Kingdom

Cambridge University Press is part of the University of Cambridge.

It furthers the University's mission by disseminating knowledge in the pursuit of education, learning and research at the highest international levels of excellence.

www.cambridge.org
Information on this title: www.cambridge.org/9781107480124

First published 2013
3rd printing 2014
First paperback edition 2014

A catalogue record for this publication is available from the British Library

Library of Congress Cataloguing in Publication data
Dromgoole, Sarah.
Underwater cultural heritage and international law / Sarah Dromgoole.
    pages cm.
ISBN 978-0-521-84231-0 (Hardback)
1. Underwater archaeology – Law and legislation.   2. Cultural property – Protection
(International law)   3. Convention on the Protection of Underwater Cultural Heritage
(2001)   4. Unesco.   I. Title.
K3791.D76 2013
344´.09409162–dc23   2013003684

ISBN 978-0-521-84231-0 Hardback
ISBN 978-1-107-48012-4 Paperback

Additional resources for this publication at www.cambridge.org/dromgoole

This book is dedicated to my parents,
Colin (E.C.B.) Dromgoole and Kathleen Mead

Contents

Preface

My interest in the legal protection of underwater cultural heritage dates back to the mid 1980s. At that time I wrote an undergraduate dissertation examining what was then the very inadequate UK domestic law on the topic. In the early 1990s, I went on to write a Ph.D. thesis building on this work, which included one chapter exploring international law on the subject. That chapter referred to the nascent legal framework for 'objects of an archaeological and historical nature' enshrined in the UN Convention on the Law of the Sea of 1982 (a treaty which only came into force a year after my doctorate was awarded in 1993).

Since that time, interest in the subject of shipwrecks and underwater cultural heritage has grown enormously and a great deal has changed from a legal perspective, not least at the international level. The Law of the Sea Convention is now a mature treaty (its thirtieth anniversary is being celebrated as I write) and is not too far from universal acceptance. A UNESCO-sponsored treaty on underwater cultural heritage is also in place, which elaborates upon the skeletal framework on the matter established in 1982. The subject-specific treaty is controversial, not least because of its complex relationship with the 1982 Convention. Nonetheless, it came into force internationally on 2 January 2009 and seems set to become an influential instrument in the years to come.

At the time of writing, the states parties to the UNESCO treaty are still in the process of working out how to implement its complex regulatory framework. Other states are reflecting on the fact that it has come into force and are actively considering their position with respect to it, or at least maintaining a 'watching brief'. This juncture therefore seems a timely one to take stock of the subject. This book endeavours to do that by reflecting on how the current international legal framework took shape, how it stands at the present time and how it may develop in the future. The discussion is arranged thematically and the principal focus is on the issues that have posed the greatest challenges for those seeking to develop a satisfactory global legal framework in this field. While the book is by no means solely about the UNESCO Convention, the Convention provides its frame of reference. One of the purposes of the book is to encourage those who have concerns about the Convention to give it some further consideration; the other is to promote greater interest in, and understanding of, the subject as a whole.

Given its fascinating nature, it is perhaps surprising that there are relatively few monographs in this subject area. The most notable is Anastasia Strati's seminal work, published in 1995, which provides an excellent analysis of the development of international law up to that time (*The Protection of the Underwater Cultural Heritage: An Emerging Objective of the Contemporary Law of the Sea*). Another valuable work is Patrick O'Keefe's handbook on the UNESCO Convention 2001, published in 2002, which provides a succinct article-by-article commentary on the Convention and affords rare personal insight into its negotiating history (*Shipwrecked Heritage: A Commentary on the UNESCO Convention on Underwater Cultural Heritage*). The present volume is designed to complement these books and to be read alongside them. As well as including copious references to these works, it also draws on the wealth of other literature on the subject that has been published over the last forty years or so. (In order to provide as many examples of state practice as possible, it draws quite extensively on two volumes of national perspectives published under my editorship: see the bibliography. In some instances, the authors or other individuals have kindly supplied updates.)

I have been keen to produce a book that will be of some practical value, as well as of academic interest, and I have therefore endeavoured to make the volume as accessible as possible to archaeologists, heritage managers and other readers who may not have a legal background. To this end, the General introduction includes sections providing some basic information about matters such as the nature and sources of international law, treaty interpretation, the background to the Law of the Sea Convention and the nature of the internationally recognised maritime zones. I have tried to avoid using technical legal jargon where possible; where it is used, I have tried to explain it.

One of the challenges of writing a book on this subject is that it cuts across a number of very different legal areas, ranging from general public international law to domestic private law. My background is in maritime law and, specifically, private maritime law. This means that my focus has tended to be on aspects of the subject that are directly maritime-related; it also means that there may be some clumsiness in my handling of matters relating to general public international law. Where this is the case, I hope that other aspects of the book may go some way to making up for it.

As far as possible the book represents the state of affairs as at July 2012.

Acknowledgements

In the course of writing this book I had the benefit of a great deal of support and assistance and I would like to express my thanks to all those named below for the help they gave me. Many are friends and colleagues in the field with whom I have collaborated over many years. Among other things, I would like to acknowledge that much of what is in this book originates in things I have learned from them, including through their own writing.

Mark Dunkley, Antony Firth, Jim Goold, Ulrike Guérin, Thijs Maarleveld, Ian Oxley, Ole Varmer and Steve Waring were all hugely generous in sharing their expertise and experience throughout this project, and their assistance was invaluable. I am indebted to Patrick O'Keefe and Lyndel Prott, not only for their support for the project, but for the enormous inspiration their own work has been to me (its influence is obvious from the text). David Freestone, Jim Nafziger, Roger Thomas and Gillian Hutchinson provided me with valuable assistance in various ways, as did my colleagues in Nottingham, Olympia Bekou, Howard Bennett, James Fawcett, David Fraser and Nigel White. Several of those named above gave up time to review draft chapters and extracts, and the feedback that I received from them, and from an anonymous reviewer, was enormously helpful. The following people also provided valuable assistance, in particular by responding with generosity to requests for information and insights on all sorts of matters: Mariano Aznar-Gómez, Piers Davies, Graham Fairclough, Nicola Ferri, Brendan Foley, Craig Forrest, Jeremy Green, John Gribble, Ole Grøn, Moritaki Hayashi, Steve Hunt, Seán Kirwan, Jan Klabbers, Erika Laanela, Lucie Lambrecht, George Lambrick, Gwénaëlle Le Gurun, Peggy Leshikar-Denton, Friedrich Lüth, Martijn Manders, Maija Matikka, Garry Momber, Fionbarr Moore, Paul Myburgh, Nessa O'Connor, Chris Pater, Tullio Scovazzi, Greg

Stemm, Andrew Tate, Chris Underwood, Mike Williams and Bob Yorke. (If I have inadvertently overlooked anyone, I sincerely apologise.)

This book almost certainly would not have seen the light of day without the support of the Leverhulme Trust. The award of a twelve-month Leverhulme Research Fellowship provided me with the sustained period of time required to really get to grips with the project. I am also greatly indebted to the School of Law at Nottingham and, in particular, my Head of School, Stephen Bailey, for supporting my Leverhulme application and granting me two further periods of study leave to enable me to complete the manuscript. Thanks are also due to Finola O'Sullivan of Cambridge University Press for her encouragement and interest in the project, as well as her considerable patience in waiting for the manuscript for much longer than could reasonably have been expected. I would also like to thank the staff of Cambridge University Press generally for their professional approach and assistance and Paul Smith for his careful copy-editing.

My greatest debt of gratitude is owed to my husband, Michael. The work on this book has been demanding and without his support in all sorts of ways I would not have managed to complete the task. His feedback on the first full version of the manuscript was invaluable.

Table of cases

European Court of Human Rights

International Court of Justice

International Tribunal for the Law of the Sea

Table of domestic legislation

Australia

Petroleum (Submerged Lands) Act 1967 265
Historic Shipwrecks Act 1976 265
Protection of Movable Cultural Heritage Act 1986 336 n. 103

Cayman Islands

Abandoned Wreck Law 1966 102

Denmark

Museum Act of 2001 253 n. 46
Law on the Contiguous Zone 2005 253 n. 46

Dominican Republic

Act No. 66/07 265 n. 97

France

Law No. 89–874 70 n. 21, 253 n. 47

Ireland

Continental Shelf Act 1968 265
National Monuments (Amendment) Act 1987 265
National Monuments (Amendment) Act 1994 101

Table of treaties and other international instruments

Abbreviations

ASA	Abandoned Shipwreck Act of 1987 (USA)
CADG	Columbus-America Discovery Group
CAHAQ	Ad Hoc Committee of Experts on the Underwater Cultural Heritage (Council of Europe)
CHM	common heritage of mankind
CMI	Comité Maritime International [International Maritime Committee]
DOALOS	Division for Ocean Affairs and the Law of the Sea (United Nations)
ECHR	European Court of Human Rights
EEZ	exclusive economic zone
G-77	Group of 77
GPS	global-positioning system
ICJ	International Court of Justice
ICOMOS	International Council on Monuments and Sites
ICUCH	International Committee on Underwater Cultural Heritage (of ICOMOS)
IFREMER	L'Institut Français de Recherche pour l'Exploitation de la Mer [French Research Institute for the Exploitation of the Sea]
ILA	International Law Association
ILC	International Law Commission
IMO	International Maritime Organisation
ISA	International Seabed Authority
ITLOS	International Tribunal for the Law of the Sea
JNAPC	Joint Nautical Archaeology Policy Committee
LOSC	UN Convention on the Law of the Sea 1982
MOD	Ministry of Defence

MOU	memorandum of understanding
NGO	non-governmental organisation
NIEO	New International Economic Order
NMSA	National Marine Sanctuaries Act of 1972 (USA)
NOAA	National Oceanic and Atmospheric Administration (USA)
OCS	outer continental shelf
OME	Odyssey Marine Exploration
PMRA	Protection of Military Remains Act (UK)
RMST	RMS *Titanic*, Inc.
ROV	remotely operated vehicle
scuba	self-contained underwater breathing apparatus
SMCA	Sunken Military Craft Act of 2004 (USA)
TOBI	Towed Ocean Bottom Instrument
UCH	underwater cultural heritage
UN	United Nations
UNCLOS I	First UN Conference on the Law of the Sea
UNCLOS II	Second UN Conference on the Law of the Sea
UNCLOS III	Third UN Conference on the Law of the Sea
UNESCO	United Nations Educational, Scientific and Cultural Organisation
WHOI	Woods Hole Oceanographic Institution

General introduction

'Underwater cultural heritage' (hereafter UCH) is the term commonly used today to mean material found underwater, generally lying on – or embedded in – the seabed, which has the potential to yield information about past human existence. This information is acquired using archaeological techniques and for this reason UCH is sometimes defined in rough terms as material of archaeological interest. Although shipwrecks are the predominant form of UCH, the term encompasses far more than just shipwrecks; equally, while there is a tendency to associate archaeology with the study of very old things, the remit of modern archaeology extends to the material remains of recent times.

Archaeological remains of all kinds, by their nature, are a finite and non-renewable resource and, for various reasons, archaeological remains located in the marine environment are regarded as a particularly valuable part of that resource. Where remains are lying on or in the seabed, the water column acts as a natural shield against human interference and the rate of natural decay is likely to be slowed by the environmental conditions. Marine sites can also offer rare (sometimes unique) insights into past human life, including into matters such as the nature and extent of trade and human interaction throughout the ages; the true course of historic naval battles and engagements; and even the daily life and movements of prehistoric man. In the case of shipwrecks, an additional value is that they may form a 'closed deposit', in other words a site containing material all in use at the same time. Such 'time-capsules' are rarely found in terrestrial archaeology and contain important information for dating purposes.

Prior to the 1950s, UCH was generally well protected from human interference by its marine environment. However, since that time the combination of a revolution in marine technology and increasing utilisation of the sea and its resources means that threats from human activities have vastly increased. Today virtually the entire global stock of shipwrecks and other UCH lying in the oceans is exposed to the possibility of human interference, deliberate or otherwise.

As in many other fields, the law has tended to respond fairly slowly and reactively to developments in relation to UCH. Nevertheless, there is now a growing body of law – at both domestic and international levels – that is designed to regulate human activity in the interests of UCH preservation. Attention to date, especially at the international level, has focused on the question of how to protect UCH from deliberate interference. In particular, the commercial exploitation of shipwrecks by those interested solely in profiting financially is a matter that has been of growing concern. For example, it has been estimated that in the last twenty years alone commercial exploitation has been responsible for the destruction of at least 345 major shipwrecks, as well as severe damage to many thousands of other sites.[1]

This extended introduction is designed primarily to provide readers (especially those who are not familiar with the subject, or do not have a legal background) with some general information they may find useful before reading other parts of the book. Section 1 provides a brief historical overview of the subject; sections 2 and 3 provide some information relating to legal matters of direct relevance; section 4 introduces the UNESCO Convention 2001; and section 5 explains the approach and structure of the book. Many of the issues raised in the General introduction are returned to in greater detail in the chapters that follow.

1.   A brief historical overview

The development of interest in UCH and its legal protection took place in two distinct phases, each of which was prompted by significant technological advances.

1.1   Early developments

The recovery of material from wrecks on the seabed is an activity that is centuries old. In the seventeenth and eighteenth centuries the 'divingbell' permitted access to wrecks lying at depths of up to eight fathoms

---

[1] Guérin, 'The 2001 UNESCO Convention on the Protection of Underwater Cultural Heritage', p. 5.

(approximately fifteen metres).[2] In the nineteenth century, the Deane brothers famously recovered guns from the *Royal George* off Spithead, Portsmouth, using a 'diving helmet and dress' that allowed them to descend to depths of more than twenty fathoms (approximately thirty-six metres).[3] At the start of the twentieth century, sponge divers using similar equipment made the first discovery of an ancient shipwreck on the seabed, a first-century BC wreck in fifty-five metres of water off the Greek island of Antikythera.[4] However, it was not until the invention of the aqualung in the 1940s, which led to widespread use of self-contained underwater breathing apparatus (scuba), that the need for some form of legal regulation of activities to afford protection to historically significant shipwrecks, and other UCH, began to be questioned.

In the period between 1950 and 1980, the rapid expansion of 'scuba-diving' in coastal waters for recreation and other purposes led to the discovery of many shipwrecks and other archaeological remains. In the absence of legal regulation, it also led to a great deal of damage to sites and dispersal of recovered artefacts. The impact of these developments was felt first, and most keenly, in the warm and archaeologically rich waters of the Mediterranean Sea, where many sites were ransacked in the 1950s and 1960s.[5] However, during the 1960s and early 1970s, other parts of the world were increasingly affected, including Australia, where four Dutch East Indiamen were discovered and plundered by treasure seekers, and the USA, where the proximity of sunken Spanish colonial-era shipwrecks to the coasts of Florida led to the emergence of treasure-hunting activity on an industrial scale. Even in the less hospitable waters of northern Europe, a spate of notorious incidents occurred. These included the ransacking of several historically significant shipwrecks off the coasts of the UK; the recovery of treasures from a number of Spanish Armada wrecks located off the west coast of Ireland; and the salvage of large numbers of gold and silver coins from the Dutch East Indiaman *Akerendam*, lying off the Norwegian coast.

---

[2] See, generally, Earle, *Treasure Hunt*.   [3] See, generally, Bevan, *The Infernal Diver*.
[4] See, generally, Weinberg *et al.*, 'The Antikythera Shipwreck Reconsidered'.
[5] A survey undertaken in 1973 reported evidence of widespread looting of Classical Age wrecks off the coast of Turkey: Bass, 'Turkey: Survey for Shipwrecks, 1973'. In the early 1980s, it was reported that, off the French Mediterranean coast, divers had reputedly 'plundered every old wreck lying above a depth of 50 metres': Marx, 'The Disappearing Underwater Heritage'. (The depth of fifty metres is significant because it is the approximate limit of standard scuba equipment.)

As discoveries were made, the archaeological potential of the seas began to be appreciated. Two defining moments in the gradual evolution of maritime archaeology into a distinct sub-branch of archaeology were the employment, in the late 1950s and early 1960s, of 'classically correct' archaeological techniques by Bass and Throckmorton to investigate sites in the Mediterranean Sea,[6] and the publication – in 1978 – of Keith Muckleroy's seminal text on maritime archaeology, which set out the principles, theories and methods of the new sub-discipline.[7] The raising of the *Vasa* in Sweden in 1961, and the *Mary Rose* in the UK in 1982, demonstrated that maritime archaeology was a subject that was not only of academic interest but also one that had the potential to engage enormous public enthusiasm as well.

During the 1960s and 1970s a number of cases arose before the admiralty courts of common law jurisdictions requiring them to adjudicate on competing claims to historic shipwrecks. In doing so they used the law of salvage and other traditional principles. These are designed to determine private rights with respect to *recent* marine casualties and encourage recovery of material without regard to its potential cultural value. However, at the same time the first domestic legislation providing protection specifically for UCH was also enacted and there was a stirring of interest at both regional (specifically European) and global levels in the question of legal protection for UCH. Among other things, this led to the inclusion of two articles addressing the matter in the UN Convention on the Law of the Sea 1982 (hereafter LOSC).

1.2   1985: A turning point

In 1985, scientists from two oceanographic institutions engaged in testing the capabilities of a new generation of deep-water submersible vehicle set for themselves a particular challenge: to locate the wreck of RMS *Titanic*. Employing deep-towed submersibles equipped with sonar imagery and video equipment, they undertook systematic search operations in an area of the North Atlantic Ocean 150 square-miles in size, situated 300 miles or so from shore. After two months of effort, they found the wreck lying at a depth of approximately 3,800 metres; two years later, around 1,800 artefacts were recovered from the site with the aid of a submersible fitted with manipulator arms.

---

[6] Bascom, 'Deepwater Archaeology', p. 263.   [7] Muckleroy, *Maritime Archaeology*.

The discovery of the *Titanic* proved to be a pivotal moment for the development of international legal protection for UCH. It represented the notional point in time when the physical protection previously afforded to UCH in the open oceans by the limitations of scuba came to an end and the question of how to protect deep-water sites lying far from shore became of some practical relevance. The discovery also sparked interest in a whole host of questions, including the ownership of the *Titanic*, its cargoes and the personal items on board; the value of the wreck in cultural and other terms; and the ethics of interfering with wreck sites, particularly where they represent major gravesites.

The *Titanic* was discovered only three years after the adoption of the LOSC and almost a decade before that treaty entered into force. However, even at this stage, there was a widespread view that the two provisions in that treaty relating to UCH did not afford adequate protection to UCH. In 1988, the International Law Association took up the task of drafting a treaty that would remedy the inadequacy.

1.3 More recent developments

The discovery of the *Titanic* marked the start of a revolution in marine technology and an era of deepwater exploration that continues to this day. In the late 1980s, sophisticated sonar equipment and remotely operated vehicles (ROVs) were used to locate the SS *Central America*, located at a depth of approximately 2,400 metres, and to recover a substantial quantity of gold from the wreck. In the mid-1990s, similar equipment was used to recover 179 tons of copper and tin ingots from the SS *Alpherat*, lying at a depth of 3,770 metres.[8] Today, there are ROVs capable of operating at depths in excess of 6,000 metres,[9] opening up access to virtually the entire ocean floor.

Although ultra-deep search and recovery operations (in waters exceeding 1,000 metres in depth) are still few and far between, similar tools and techniques are available for use in a wide range of applications

---

[8] This feat set a world record for the deepest shipwreck salvage operation, a record which may not yet have been broken (see www.bluewater.uk.com/achievements.htm). Blue Water Recoveries, the British-based company which undertook this operation, has discovered a number of deep-water shipwrecks including M/V *Derbyshire* at a depth of 4,210 metres, DKM *Bismarck* at 4,700 metres and M/V *Rio Grande* at 5,762 metres.

[9] See, for example, the capabilities of the Towed Ocean Bottom Instrument (TOBI), a deep-towed system operated by the National Oceanography Centre, Southampton (http://noc.ac.uk/research-at-sea/nmfss/nmep/tobi).

in all parts of the seas. Acoustic and magnetic imaging devices are now standard equipment for those engaged in exploring the ocean floor: side-scan and bathymetric sonar systems are employed to identify seabed protrusions and indentations; sub-bottom profilers provide cross-sectional analyses of the sub-sea strata to enable identification of material buried in sediment; and magnetometers can locate ferrous material.[10] While manned or unmanned submersibles are required to provide direct physical access to very deep parts of the seafloor, divers employing specialised gas mixtures and other sophisticated equipment now quite routinely work at depths up to and even exceeding 100 metres.[11] Since it became available for civilian use in the mid-1990s, global-positioning system (GPS) technology has become common ship-board equipment,[12] providing an indispensable tool for vessels that need to pinpoint their positions with precision, including those engaged in salvage or archaeological research in the open oceans.

The activities of an American-based marine exploration and shipwreck recovery company, Odyssey Marine Exploration (hereafter OME), illustrate how modern technology has revolutionised the field of shipwreck search and recovery. Over recent years OME has surveyed and mapped thousands of square miles of seabed and discovered hundreds of wrecks, ranging from Roman and Phoenician vessels to German U-boats and modern fishing vessels. Among its discoveries have been the eighteenth-century British warship, HMS *Victory*, in the English Channel, and the Spanish colonial-era warship, *Nuestra Señora de las Mercedes*, off the coast of Portugal. OME's activities, which are undertaken on a commercial basis but take some account of cultural values,[13] have given rise to heated debate concerning the ethics of the sale of commercially valuable cargoes from historic shipwrecks; whether it is possible to combine a profit motive with good archaeology; and whether appropriate archaeological methodology can be employed to excavate deep-water sites beyond the range of divers.

It is not just well-financed commercial organisations or oceanographic institutions that are making use of advanced technology in

---

[10] See, generally, Mather, 'Technology and the Search for Shipwrecks'.

[11] For example, in 2007, divers accessed the wreck of RMS *Carpathia* off the coast of Ireland, which lies at a depth of 156 metres: Parham and Williams, 'An Outline of the Nature of the Threat to Underwater Cultural Heritage in International Waters'.

[12] The Navstar global positioning system (GPS) was originally developed for US military use. It was made available to civilian users in 1996.

[13] See further, Chap. 6.

the context of UCH. Increasingly, marine archaeologists employ such technology in their day-to-day work. As a result, the full archaeological potential of the marine environment, especially with respect to *non-shipwreck* remains, is becoming better understood. In 2009, an Anglo-Greek archaeological team utilising digital technology was able to identify and map the layout of the streets and buildings of the submerged Bronze Age city of Pavlopetri, a site extending over 30,000 square metres of seabed.[14] Technology of the same kind has also enabled archaeologists to identify submerged land-surfaces on parts of the continental shelf that were exposed during the Ice Ages: recent discoveries by Scandinavian archaeologists of Mesolithic dwelling remains, graves and fishing structures illustrate the potential these land-surfaces have to yield unique evidence about the life of our early ancestors.[15]

Recoveries of large quantities of hand axes and the bones of mammoths and other land animals by fishermen and dredging operators working in the North Sea provide further evidence of the archaeological potential of the continental shelf, but also demonstrate that commonplace commercial activities in the marine environment have considerable potential to interfere with archaeological evidence. Trawling by fishermen, dredging for marine aggregates, pipeline- and cable-laying, and the construction of wind-farms and other installations all pose a substantial threat. As the scale and intensity of such activities increase, so does the risk of harm to UCH in all its forms.

Many states now have legislation in place to protect UCH in their coastal waters. While much of this legislation is designed to regulate deliberate human interference, increasingly it is being supplemented by measures to minimise incidental damage and destruction by general marine activities. Today, when domestic courts are called upon to adjudicate in cases relating to historic wrecks, they are showing increasing awareness of cultural values and considerations. After six years of effort, in 1994, the International Law Association (ILA) handed over to UNESCO a draft text for a treaty on UCH protection. This became the basis for the development of the Convention on the Protection of the Underwater Cultural Heritage, adopted in 2001.

---

[14] 'Lost Greek city that may have inspired Atlantis myth gives up secrets', *Guardian*, 16 October 2009.

[15] See Grøn and Mortensen, 'Stone Age in the Danish North Sea Sector'. The discoveries are apparently 'unparalleled' by dry sites.

2. Relevant branches of law

From a legal point of view, what makes this field fascinating – but at the same time complex – is that it lies at the interface between three distinct branches of law: admiralty/private maritime law, the law of the sea and cultural heritage law. These legal areas are quite different in nature and are designed to perform very different and not always compatible functions.

2.1 Admiralty/private maritime law

Admiralty law is an area of private law relating to maritime activities. As an area of private law, it governs relations between individuals or other private entities and, among other things, determines competing private rights and interests. It is administered by domestic courts and, specifically, the admiralty courts of the common law jurisdictions.

The principles applied by the early English admiralty courts were derived from classical and medieval codes originating in continental Europe; they were then developed and passed on to other common law jurisdictions, including Australia, Canada, Ireland, New Zealand, Singapore and the USA. While admiralty law is a feature of the common law world, civil law systems have their own equivalent principles for dealing with maritime disputes. However, although the common law and civil law principles have common roots, they developed along quite separate lines and operate in different ways today. In the context of UCH, it is the admiralty law of the common law world that has had the most significant impact.

Admiralty law is designed to provide certainty and predictability for private parties with respect to their dealings. It also fulfils broader public policy objectives, such as safety of life and property, and protection of the marine environment. The remit of the admiralty courts extends to the 'rescue' of maritime property in peril and the determination of rights to such property through application of the laws of salvage and 'wreck'.[16] In some jurisdictions, admiralty courts also occasionally apply the law of finds to such property. Given that admiralty law relates to trans-border activity, and ships and individuals can move about quite freely in the marine environment, there are special rules for dealing with matters of enforcement and jurisdiction.

---

[16] 'Wreck' is a technical term. See, further, Chap. 2, section 2, esp. n. 10.

The principles of modern admiralty law derive from domestic case law and statutes, but there is now also a significant body of relevant international law in the form of treaties developed under the aegis of international organisations such as the Comité Maritime International (CMI) [International Maritime Committee] and the International Maritime Organisation (IMO). Of particular pertinence in the present context is the IMO's International Salvage Convention of 1989.

2.2 The law of the sea

The law of the sea is an important sub-category of public international law, a major area of legal specialism with its own distinct principles, enforcement mechanisms and tribunals. As an area of public international law, the law of the sea is generally concerned with relations between states.

The modern law of the sea is largely a product of the twentieth century, although, like admiralty law, its roots are deep in the past. Its objective is to establish legal order over maritime space by establishing a framework of rules for determining the rights and duties of states in respect of their use of the oceans. A central feature of this framework is the division of the oceans into distinct maritime zones, each with its own specific legal regime.

Throughout its history, the law of the sea has been characterised by a tension between the concepts of 'closed seas' and 'open seas', and this tension has had a profound influence on its development. The right of a coastal state to control a narrow belt of water immediately adjacent to its shores has been accepted for centuries. However, a debate, originating in the seventeenth century and continuing to this day, concerns the extent to which the broader maritime space should be subject to national control. While the concept of open seas – embodied in the notion of freedom of the high seas – has generally tended to prevail, during the twentieth century it has been subject to a certain degree of erosion. Today, in the international arena, the debate is conducted by two opposing political groupings. The predominant interest of 'coastal states' is in preserving the integrity of their rights over their coastal waters and, at times, in extending those rights; the predominant interest of 'flag states' (or 'maritime states') is to preserve their navigational freedom so that their merchant and military fleets can move freely about the globe.

Until the twentieth century, the rules of international law of the sea had developed through the custom and practice of states. However, during that century there were a number of attempts to codify those

rules in treaty form. Most notably, the UN held three diplomatic conferences on the law of the sea. The first UN Conference on the Law of the Sea
(UNCLOS I) resulted in the four Geneva Conventions of 1958: the
Convention on the Territorial Sea and the Contiguous Zone; the Convention on the High Seas; the Convention on the Continental Shelf; and the
Convention on Fishing and Conservation of the Living Resources of the
High Seas. The second conference (UNCLOS II), in 1960, failed to produce
any agreement. The outcome of the third conference (UNCLOS III), which
began in 1973 and concluded in 1982, was the LOSC. This treaty is the
pre-eminent source of the law of the sea today.

2.2.1   UN Convention on the Law of the Sea 1982

The initial driver behind UNCLOS III was the question of governance of
the deep seabed in light of growing interest in the possibility of commercially exploiting deep seabed mineral resources. There were concerns on
the part of the developing world that industrialised states would be free
to exploit for themselves these potentially hugely valuable resources
unless a regulatory framework was put in place providing for the sharing
of the resources. Another general driver behind the Conference was the
emergence on the international scene of a large number of newly independent states whose interests were very different from those of the
maritime powers that had dominated proceedings at UNCLOS I. The new
states sought various changes to the international legal order governing
the oceans, including greater rights over the natural resources of their
offshore waters. It was concluded that a comprehensive review of the law
of the sea needed to be undertaken and that its outcome should be a
single instrument to replace the four Geneva Conventions. The ultimate
objective was to produce 'a comprehensive constitution for the oceans
that would stand the test of time'.[17]

   After fifteen years of preparatory work, including nine years of substantive negotiations, the LOSC was opened for signature at the final
session of UNCLOS III, held at Montego Bay, Jamaica, in 1982. This
mammoth treaty comprised 320 articles, set out in seventeen parts,
along with nine annexes. It created two new maritime zones; fixed the
maximum breadth of the territorial sea at twelve miles; set out rules
governing all the recognised maritime zones; created special regimes for

---

[17] See 'A Constitution for the Oceans: Remarks by Tommy B. Koh, President of the Third
   United Nations Conference on the Law of the Sea' (available at www.un.org/Depts/los/
   convention_agreements/texts/koh_english.pdf).

international straits and archipelagic states; and established three new international institutions. It also made provision for a host of other matters relating to the use of ocean space, including the nationality and status of ships; immunity of warships and other ships used on non-commercial service; protection and preservation of the marine environment; and marine scientific research.

In light of the presence of a large number of newly independent states, UNCLOS III was the largest diplomatic conference ever to have been convened. There were approximately 160 participating states, almost twice the number in attendance at UNCLOS I. These states formed themselves into a range of interest groupings. In light of the huge numerical disparity between the Group of 77 (G-77), the negotiating bloc representing the interests of developing states,[18] and the small – but powerful – bloc of maritime states, the traditional system of majority voting during the development of the text of the treaty was replaced by a novel consensus procedure. Under this procedure every effort was made to reach agreement on matters of substance by way of consensus and votes were only permitted when all efforts to reach a consensus were exhausted. Session chairs produced working texts which were amended only where the chair felt that a proposed amendment would increase support for the text as a whole. The ultimate aim of this process was to produce a 'package deal' balancing the interests of all concerned.

At the end of the negotiations, dissatisfaction on the part of the USA and a number of other industrialised states with one particular aspect of the treaty – the regime for the deep seabed established in Part XI – meant that a consensus could not be reached on the final text. In consequence, the Convention was adopted by majority vote.[19] It was not until twelve years later, in 1994, that the objections were overcome by means of an 'Implementation Agreement', which introduced modifications to Part XI; in the same year, the LOSC entered into force. In the period that followed, with the exception of the USA, all the major maritime powers and most other industrialised states ratified the Convention. At the time

[18] The G-77 is an intergovernmental organisation made up of developing states. Its objective is to promote the economic and other interests of the developing world. As its name implies, it was formed by seventy-seven states, but now has 131 members (see www.g77.org/doc). During UNCLOS III, its membership comprised approximately 120 states: Churchill and Lowe, *The Law of the Sea*, p. 228.

[19] There were 130 votes in favour, 4 against and 17 abstentions. The states voting against were Israel, Turkey, the USA and Venezuela. Among the abstentions were the German Democratic Republic, the Federal Republic of Germany, Italy, the Netherlands, Spain, the Soviet Union and the UK.

of writing, there are 162 states parties: aside from the USA, other notable non-parties are Colombia, Iran, Israel, Peru, Turkey and Venezuela. Despite the fact that the USA has yet to accede to the Convention, recent US Administrations have been strongly in favour of the treaty and of US ratification.[20] Technically, the USA remains party to all four of the Geneva Conventions; in practice, it regards most of the provisions of the LOSC as reflective of customary international law and, therefore, as binding on all states, whether or not parties to the treaty.

To understand the law of the sea in general, and the LOSC in particular, it is necessary to appreciate the politically charged nature of this area of law. The respective rights of states over the oceans have huge strategic, economic, military and security implications and are therefore matters that have a major political imperative. A key policy objective of the maritime powers is to ensure that the delicate balance of rights, jurisdiction and duties of coastal states and flag states enshrined in the LOSC 'package deal' is not eroded by state practice. Of predominant concern is the question of 'creeping jurisdiction', in other words attempts by coastal states to extend their rights and jurisdiction – either geographically or functionally – beyond the position set out in the treaty.

2.2.2   Maritime zones and related terminology

The following comments are designed to provide a brief introduction to the major maritime zones recognised by international law, as well as to some related terminology. (In this section, and throughout the book, references to miles in the context of maritime zone limits are references to nautical miles from coastal baselines.)

Territorial sea. Part II of the LOSC sets out the legal regime for the territorial sea and contiguous zone. The territorial sea is an area automatically appurtenant to a coastal state, extending up to twelve miles from coastal 'baselines'.[21] In this zone the coastal state has sovereignty,[22] but its sovereignty must be exercised in accordance with the LOSC and other rules of international law.[23] The LOSC sets out detailed rules for the establishment of baselines, but the normal baseline for measuring the breadth of the territorial sea and other zones is the

---

[20] For example, in December 2011, US Secretary of State Hillary Clinton referred to US accession to the LOSC as a 'key piece of unfinished business' (see www.gc.noaa.gov/gcil_los.html). Ratification must be approved by the US Congress, where there is a strong body of resistance to the treaty.

[21] LOSC, Arts. 2 and 3.   [22] On the notion of sovereignty, see section 3.1, below.

[23] LOSC, Art. 2(3).

low-water line.[24] With one exception, waters on the *landward* side of baselines (which may include bays and estuaries) are classified as internal waters.[25] Internal waters are treated as part of the land territory of a state,[26] the territorial sea as its maritime territory.

The contiguous zone. The contiguous zone is a zone contiguous to the territorial sea, extending no further than twenty-four miles from baselines.[27] In this zone, the coastal state may exercise the control necessary to prevent or punish infringement within its territory, or territorial sea, of its customs, fiscal, immigration or sanitary laws and regulations.[28] It can also take certain measures to control traffic in UCH.[29] Coastal states may claim a contiguous zone, but are not obliged to do so.

Archipelagic waters. Part IV of the LOSC creates a special regime which can be used by certain archipelagic states.[30] This regime permits qualifying states to draw baselines so as to enclose the islands making up the archipelago; where this is done, the maritime waters within the baselines for the most part constitute 'archipelagic waters'.[31] The archipelagic state has sovereignty over these waters, regardless of their depth or distance from the coast,[32] subject to the rights of other states set out in Part IV.

The Exclusive Economic Zone. Part V of the LOSC establishes the legal regime for the exclusive economic zone (EEZ). The EEZ was a creation of the LOSC and arose as a result of calls by some developing states to have the right to control access to fish stocks in their offshore waters. It is an area beyond and adjacent to the territorial sea,[33] extending no further than 200 miles from baselines.[34] In the EEZ, the coastal state has 'sovereign rights'[35] for the purpose of exploring and exploiting, conserving and

---

[24] LOSC, Art. 5.

[25] LOSC, Art. 8(1). The exception is in relation to archipelagic waters: see below.

[26] The term 'inland waters' is generally used to refer to internal waters that do not have a maritime character, including lakes, rivers and canals.

[27] LOSC, Art. 33(2).   [28] LOSC, Art. 33(1).   [29] LOSC, Art. 303(2).

[30] The term 'archipelagic state' is defined by the Convention to mean 'a State constituted wholly by one or more archipelagos and may include other islands': Art. 46(a). Not all states falling within this definition are able to take advantage of the special regime in Part IV. To do so, they must be able to meet the technical requirements for the drawing up of archipelagic baselines outlined in Art. 47 of the treaty.

[31] As well as being able to draw up 'archipelagic baselines' enclosing the islands making up the archipelago, archipelagic states are also entitled to draw baselines around each of the islands following the normal rules. Bays and estuaries enclosed within these baselines will constitute internal waters, not archipelagic waters.

[32] LOSC, Art. 49(1).   [33] LOSC, Art. 55.   [34] LOSC, Art. 57.

[35] On the meaning of sovereign rights, see, further, Chap. 7, section 3.4.

managing the natural resources of the waters superjacent to the seabed, and of the seabed and its subsoil, as well as other related rights and jurisdiction.[36] Like the contiguous zone, a coastal state has a right to claim an EEZ, but is not obliged to do so.[37]

The continental shelf. The emergence of the continental shelf as a legal (or 'juridical') zone was prompted, in some measure, by the Truman Proclamation of 1945, in which the USA unilaterally asserted rights over the natural resources of the seabed and subsoil of its continental shelf.[38] By the time of UNCLOS I, other states had claimed rights of a similar kind. The 1958 Geneva Convention on the Continental Shelf enshrined the notion that a coastal state has rights over this submarine area and its natural resources, and made provision with respect to the nature and extent of those rights. The legal regime for the juridical continental shelf is now set out in Part VI of the LOSC. This defines the continental shelf as follows:

the seabed and subsoil of the submarine areas [of a coastal State] that extend beyond its territorial sea throughout the natural prolongation of its land territory to the outer edge of the continental margin, or to a distance of 200 nautical miles from the baselines from which the breadth of the territorial sea is measured where the outer edge of the continental margin does not extend up to that distance.[39]

This means that, in principle, all coastal states have a juridical continental shelf extending to at least 200 miles from baselines,[40] including states whose physical continental margin does *not* extend to that distance. However, where a coastal state has a continental margin that extends further than 200 miles, its juridical continental shelf will extend to the outer edge of the continental margin.[41] States with a continental margin

---

[36] LOSC, Art. 56(1).
[37] If the coastal state claims both a contiguous zone and an EEZ, the contiguous zone will fall within the EEZ and will therefore be subject to Part II *and* Part V of the LOSC.
[38] Proclamation No. 2667 of 28 September 1945, 64 *Fed. Reg.* 48,701. There had been one or two earlier claims of a similar nature, but the assertion of such rights by the USA, given its political weight, was particularly influential.
[39] Art. 76(1). Rules for determining the outer limit of the continental margin are set out in Art. 76(4)–(6).
[40] Clearly, special provision needs to be made for states with coastlines facing each other that are less than 400 miles apart: see Art. 83. (Art. 83 is one of a number of provisions in the treaty that cater for delimitation of maritime borders in the case of states with opposite or adjacent coasts.)
[41] The continental margin comprises the submerged prolongation of the land mass of the coastal state (Art. 76(3)). This submerged land mass has three elements: a 'shelf', a

extending further than 200 miles are known as 'broad-margin' states and the area of continental margin *beyond* 200 miles is commonly referred to as the outer continental shelf (OCS). In contrast to the contiguous zone and the EEZ, the juridical continental shelf exists *ipso facto* and *ab initio* without the need for the coastal state to claim it.[42] Part VI of the LOSC affords the coastal state sovereign rights for the purpose of exploring and exploiting the natural resources of the continental shelf.[43] Bearing in mind that the continental shelf comprises only the seabed and subsoil and *not* the water column superjacent thereto, the natural resources referred to are primarily mineral resources and, in particular, oil and gas. However, they also include other non-living resources and living organisms closely associated with the seabed and subsoil.[44]

Where the coastal state claims an EEZ, the EEZ will coexist with the continental shelf to a distance of 200 miles and Parts V and VI – which are designed to dovetail – will apply in tandem to the area from twelve to 200 miles. The legal regime for the OCS, as well as in the area from twelve to 200 miles in circumstances where no EEZ is declared, is governed by Part VI and also Part VII relating to the high seas.

The high seas. The high seas regime, set out in Part VII of the LOSC, applies to all parts of the sea that are not included in the EEZ, the territorial sea or the internal waters of a state, or in the archipelagic waters of an archipelagic state.[45] The high seas are open to all states[46] and '[n]o State may validly purport to subject any part of the high seas to its sovereignty'.[47] Part VII sets out a non-exhaustive list of high seas 'freedoms', which include freedom of navigation and freedom of fishing.[48] These must be exercised with due regard for the interests of other states in their own exercise of the high seas freedoms.[49]

The Area. Part XI of the LOSC establishes the legal regime for the international seabed 'Area'. Like the EEZ, the Area is a creation of the LOSC. The Area comprises 'the seabed and ocean floor and subsoil thereof, beyond the limits of national jurisdiction'.[50] The phrase 'beyond the limits of national jurisdiction' means the seabed and subsoil beyond

---

'slope' and a 'rise'. The juridical continental shelf therefore does not equate to the geomorphological feature known as the continental shelf.
[42] *North Sea Continental Shelf Cases* [1969] ICJ Reports 3, at 23.   [43] LOSC, Art. 77(1).
[44] See LOSC, Art. 77(4). See, further, Chap. 7, section 3.4.   [45] LOSC, Art. 86.
[46] LOSC, Art. 87(1).   [47] LOSC, Art. 89.
[48] LOSC, Art. 87(1). The freedom of fishing is subject to certain provisions relating to the conservation and management of the living resources of the high seas.
[49] LOSC, Art. 87(2).   [50] LOSC, Art. 1(1)(1).

the limits of the juridical continental shelf. Like the continental shelf, the Area comprises the seabed and subsoil, not the superjacent water column, which is subject to the high seas regime in Part VII. Part XI (as amended by the 1994 Implementation Agreement) sets out an elaborate framework regulating activities relating to the exploration and exploitation of the mineral resources of the Area.

Three terms that are quite commonly used with respect to maritime waters are 'inshore waters', 'offshore waters' and 'international waters'. These terms are not referred to in the LOSC. However, they are generally used to mean, respectively: waters landward of the territorial sea limit; waters between the territorial sea limit and the outer limit of the juridical continental shelf; and all waters beyond the territorial sea limit. Where the terms are used in this book, these are the meanings intended.

2.3   Cultural heritage law

In contrast to admiralty law and the law of the sea, cultural heritage law is a legal area that has modern roots and is still at a relatively nascent stage of development. It includes elements of public and private law, as well as domestic and international law. In the context of this book, it is the public and international law aspects of the subject which are of most direct relevance and the following comments relate to these aspects.

Cultural heritage law is concerned with the protection of cultural heritage in the broad public interest. To date, much of the debate in this field has centred on the questions of exactly what should be protected and what 'protection' should entail. As a result, the notions of 'cultural heritage' and 'protection' are in constant flux. In its earliest stages of development, the focus of cultural heritage law was on preserving the most obvious manifestations of cultural heritage, including historic buildings and monuments, and archaeological sites and objects. Today, there is a much broader view of what merits protection and the notion of protection itself is now recognised to encompass a range of possibilities (from 'preservation in aspic' to 'managed change and decline'). Increasingly, a resource-based approach is taken to the subject and law, policy and practice with respect to cultural heritage is sometimes integrated with that for the natural environment.

Inevitably, the development of international law in this field has been influenced by national approaches and experiences. Significant distinctions between the approach and experience of states with a common law tradition and those with a civil law tradition can be a particular source of tension. Many of these distinctions derive from fundamentally different attitudes to the treatment of private property rights and to the balance to be drawn between public, and private, rights and interests. In Europe, these distinctions have been compounded by stark differences in the scale of the task of protecting the remains of the past between the north and the south of the continent. Nonetheless, there are a growing number of treaties and other legal instruments designed to set international standards for the protection of cultural heritage.

The organisation responsible for the development of many of these instruments is UNESCO, a specialised agency of the UN. It was founded at the end of the Second World War to promote international cooperation among its member states in the fields of education, science and culture. The UNESCO Convention on the Protection of the Underwater Cultural Heritage 2001 is part of an expanding portfolio of legal instruments developed by UNESCO as part of its culture brief. The earliest treaty in this portfolio was the 1954 Hague Convention for the Protection of Cultural Property in the Event of Armed Conflict; one of the most recent was the Convention for the Safeguarding of the Intangible Cultural Heritage 2003. Two other instruments in the portfolio that have had a major global impact are the 1970 Convention on Illicit Trade in Cultural Property and the 1972 World Heritage Convention.[51]

At a regional level, an organisation that has been particularly active in the field of cultural heritage is the Council of Europe. The Council, founded in 1949, has among its aims the promotion of legal standards, cultural cooperation and the development of Europe's cultural identity. At the time of writing, it has forty-seven member states across the continent of Europe. The Council of Europe has been responsible for several initiatives related to UCH and has played a significant role in the development of international law in this area.

3.   A few observations on international law

The following observations relate to aspects of international law which are of particular significance in the context of this book. They are designed primarily to assist readers who are non-lawyers.

---

[51] The formal titles of these treaties are the UNESCO Convention on the Means of Prohibiting and Preventing the Illicit Import, Export and Transfer of Ownership of Cultural Property and the UNESCO Convention Concerning the Protection of the World Cultural and Natural Heritage.

3.1   Sovereignty and jurisdiction

Two interrelated concepts of major significance in the field of international law are sovereignty and jurisdiction. It is difficult to discuss these concepts in the abstract because they mean different things in different contexts. Nonetheless, a few introductory words should be said about them.

According to Lowe:

> The purpose and role of every State is to control activities within its borders so far as possible, or more accurately to ensure that activities within its borders are not regulated by another State. That idea is expressed in international law through the concept of sovereignty.[52]

As this quotation suggests, a state has sovereignty *inside* its territorial borders. Sovereignty indicates that a state has unchallengeable power over the territory and persons within that territory; however, that power may be subject to limitations under international law, for example in certain circumstances where the property or subjects of *other* states are located within the territory. One such limitation – which is placed on the sovereignty of the state with respect to its *maritime* territory (the territorial sea and archipelagic waters) – is the right of innocent passage of foreign-flagged ships.[53]

Jurisdiction has been referred to as 'an aspect of sovereignty'.[54] It encompasses the power to prescribe laws ('legislative jurisdiction') and the power to enforce laws ('enforcement jurisdiction'). These two powers frequently, but not always, go hand-in-hand. In areas over which a state has sovereignty, it has the most extensive form of jurisdiction, sometimes referred to as full or 'plenary' jurisdiction. This form of jurisdiction can be contrasted with more limited jurisdictional rights which may be enjoyed by a state in areas *beyond* its territorial borders. The sovereign rights of a state over the natural resources of its continental shelf and EEZ are an example of such rights. These rights are limited *geographically* to the seaward extent of the continental shelf and EEZ, and they are limited *functionally* to purposes connected with the natural resources of those zones.

There are various bases on which states may exercise jurisdiction beyond their territory. Some of these bases arise from general principles of international jurisdiction and some from principles related to

---

[52] Lowe, *International Law*, p. 138.   [53] See, further, Chap. 7, section 3.2.
[54] Brownlie, *Principles of Public International Law*, p. 299.

maritime jurisdiction specifically.[55] In the context of this book, an important example of extra-territorial jurisdiction is the jurisdiction that a state has over its flag vessels. This form of jurisdiction is known as flag state jurisdiction. It is based on the notion that the authorisation to fly the flag of a state effectively confers on a vessel the nationality of the state.[56] On the high seas, ships are subject to the *exclusive* jurisdiction of their flag state, save for in exceptional circumstances.[57] Curiously, in recent years little consideration has been given to the question of whether the jurisdiction of the flag state extends to the *wreck* of a flagged vessel. However, there appears to be a general assumption that it does not.[58]

3.2   Sources of international law

There are a number of sources of international law. However, the main ones – and the ones of greatest relevance to the subject matter of this book – are international treaties and international custom.

3.2.1   Treaties

Treaties (or conventions) are agreements between two or more states that are intended by their parties to be binding upon them in international law. The binding nature of a treaty is based on the notion of consent. Therefore, in principle, a treaty is only binding on the states

---

[55] For further discussion, see Chap. 7, sections 2 and 3.

[56] See, further, Chap. 7, section 2.2. (It should be noted that '[t]he view that a ship is a floating part of state territory has long fallen into disrepute': Brownlie, *Principles of Public International Law*, p. 318.)

[57] LOSC, Art. 92(1). The same principle applies to the EEZ in so far as it is not incompatible with Part V of the LOSC: LOSC, Art. 58(2).

[58] According to Churchill and Lowe, the 'persistence of flag State jurisdiction over wrecks' is a 'problematic question': Churchill and Lowe, *The Law of the Sea*, p. 152. Commentators appear divided on the question of whether there may have been a customary rule of international law in the first half of the twentieth century to the effect that flag state jurisdiction persisted even after a vessel had sunk, as well as on the question of whether the 1958 Geneva Convention on the High Seas had the effect of overturning any such rule (see, for example, Caflisch, 'Submarine Antiquities and the International Law of the Sea', pp. 21–2, including accompanying footnotes, and p. 25 n. 81; cf. Nafziger, 'Finding the Titanic', p. 345; ILA, Queensland Conference (1990), International Committee on Cultural Heritage Law, First Report, p. 7). The rejection of proposals at UNCLOS III for flag states to have exclusive jurisdiction over wrecks outside territorial waters largely seems to have ended debate about the matter in the post-UNCLOS III era (although O'Connell – writing soon after the LOSC was adopted – appeared to leave the matter open: O'Connell, *The International Law of the Sea*, Vol. II, p. 911). For related discussion (in the context of sunken warships), see Chap. 4, section 2.1.

that are parties to it.[59] A state which is not a party to a treaty is known as a 'third State':[60] a treaty 'cannot, by its own force, impose an obligation on a third State, nor modify in any way the legal rights of a third State without its consent'.[61]

The main source of legal rules relating to treaties is itself a treaty, the Vienna Convention on the Law of Treaties 1969. It contains rules relating to matters such as the conclusion, application, operation and amendment of treaties. Two specific aspects of these rules that are of particular relevance to this book are the relationship between treaties relating to the same subject matter and treaty interpretation.

The relationship between treaties relating to the same subject matter. The question of the application of successive treaties relating to the same subject matter is of some significance in the present context given that the LOSC deals in part with the same subject matter as the UNESCO Convention 2001. The general rules on this matter are set out in Article 30 of the Vienna Convention. Among other things, this provides:

> 2. When a treaty specifies that it is subject to, or that it is not to be considered as incompatible with, an earlier or later treaty, the provisions of that other treaty will prevail.
> 3. When all the parties to the earlier treaty are parties also to the later treaty but the earlier treaty is not terminated or suspended ... the earlier treaty applies only to the extent that its provisions are compatible with those of the later treaty.
> 4. When the parties to the later treaty do not include all the parties to the earlier one:
>   (a) as between States parties to both treaties the same rule applies as in paragraph 3;
>   (b) as between a State party to both treaties and a State party to only one of the treaties, the treaty to which both States are parties governs their mutual rights and obligations.

These rules are residual in nature[62] and this means that a treaty may itself set out its relationship with other treaties. In fact, both the LOSC and the UNESCO Convention do this. The provision they make in this regard is discussed in detail later.[63]

---

[59] However, if the provisions of a treaty are reflective of customary international law, they will be binding on all states: see, further, section 3.2.3, below.

[60] See Vienna Convention on the Law of Treaties 1969, Art. 2(1)(h).

[61] Aust, *Modern Treaty Law and Practice*, p. 256. See, further, Vienna Convention 1969, Arts. 35 and 36.

[62] Aust, *Modern Treaty Law and Practice*, p. 227.   [63] See, in particular, Chap. 8, section 2.

Treaty interpretation. Much of this book is about treaty law (the substantive provisions of treaties). In order to understand the meaning of treaty provisions, one needs to be aware that there are established rules of treaty interpretation. The key rules are set out in Articles 31 and 32 of the Vienna Convention.

Article 31(1) sets out the general rule on interpretation:

A treaty shall be interpreted in good faith in accordance with the ordinary meaning to be given to the terms of the treaty in their context and in the light of its object and purpose.

Paragraph 2 of Article 31 makes it clear that the 'context' of a treaty includes the whole of the text and its preamble and annexes, as well as any agreement or instrument concerning the treaty which was made, or agreed to, by all the parties. Together with the context, and the object and purpose of the treaty, Article 31(3) provides that account shall also be taken of:

(a) any subsequent agreement between the parties regarding the interpretation of the treaty or the application of its provisions;
(b) any subsequent practice in the application of the treaty which establishes the agreement of the parties regarding its interpretation;
(c) any relevant rules of international law applicable in the relations between the parties.

While usually it is the ordinary meaning of a term or phrase that one seeks to establish, according to Article 31(4), '[a] special meaning shall be given to a term if it is established that the parties so intended'.

According to Article 32:

Recourse may be had to supplementary means of interpretation, including the preparatory work of the treaty and the circumstances of its conclusion, in order to confirm the meaning resulting from the application of article 31, or to determine the meaning when the interpretation according to article 31:

(a) leaves the meaning ambiguous or obscure; or
(b) leads to a result which is manifestly absurd or unreasonable.

This article makes it clear that recourse to the preparatory work and the circumstances of the conclusion of the treaty is a *supplementary* means of interpretation only.

Treaty interpretation is a delicate matter. It requires an appropriate balancing of consideration of three elements: the text of the treaty; the object and purpose of the treaty; and the intentions of the parties as evidenced by the preparatory work, the circumstances of the conclusion of the treaty and subsequent agreements and practice of states parties.[64] The ascertainment of the intention of the parties through the preparatory work is the aspect of treaty interpretation that can be most problematic. This is particularly the case for treaties like the LOSC and the UNESCO Convention 2001. Both were the subject of long and politically contentious negotiations. In neither case is there a full official record of the negotiations and in both the device of deliberate textual ambiguity was used to facilitate agreement on the most contentious issues. In such circumstances, recourse to the preparatory work to determine the intention of the parties is of limited assistance.[65]

3.2.2   Customary international law

Aside from treaty law, the other main source of international law is international custom. This can be defined as a practice of states that is generally recognised to be obligatory. It is important to note that there are *two* requisite elements:

(i)   there must be a practice, which is both general and consistent; and
(ii)   that practice must be generally accepted as law.

The second element is referred to as *opinio juris*. It requires a belief on the part of states that their conduct – or the conduct of other states – is legally obligatory, rather than undertaken for other reasons, such as diplomatic courtesy. Sources of evidence of international custom are many and various: they include official statements made by government legal advisers, or in press releases and official documentation; domestic statutes; and international and domestic judicial decisions and related pleadings.[66]

Customary law, like treaty law, is based on the notion of consent. If a customary rule is to be 'opposable' to a state, that state must be taken to have consented to the rule.[67] Assent may be presumed through acquiescence. However, where a state persistently objects to an emerging rule, it will not be bound by that rule.[68]

---

[64] See Aust, *Modern Treaty Law and Practice*, p. 231.
[65] See Churchill and Lowe, *The Law of the Sea*, pp. 460–1; O'Keefe, *Shipwrecked Heritage*, pp. 33–4.
[66] See Lowe, *International Law*, pp. 42–6.
[67] It should be noted that there are certain so-called 'peremptory' rules of customary international law from which no derogation is permitted because they are regarded as logical or moral imperatives: see Lowe, *International Law*, pp. 58–60. These rules are of little relevance in the present context.
[68] The role that consent plays in the formation of customary international law, and the related notions of acquiescence, persistent objection and opposability, are complex and

3.2.3   The relationship between customary international law and treaties

An international treaty may be designed to codify pre-existing customary rules of international law, to progressively develop international law by creating new rules, or to do both. Where a treaty creates new rules, those rules will be binding only on the parties to the treaty, unless practice in accordance with the conventional rule becomes so general and consistent as to produce a customary rule of international law binding on states whether or not they are parties to the treaty.

In practice, it is relatively rare for treaty provisions to be mirrored by customary international law (or, as Lowe puts it, to have a 'parallel existence').[69] This is because it will be difficult to show the requisite *opinio juris* (that state practice is conducted because of a belief that it is required by *custom*, rather than by treaty obligation).[70] However, the LOSC is an example of a treaty where most of its rules are widely regarded as representative of customary international law.[71] Its purpose was both to codify pre-existing customary law and to progressively develop international law. As far as the latter was concerned, the consensus process that formed the basis of the treaty negotiation led to a situation where the development of the treaty text, and of customary law, during UNCLOS III went hand-in-hand in such a way that many of its rules were reflected in customary law by the time of the adoption of the treaty.[72] Other rules of the treaty have become part of customary international law since that time. As a result of the remarkable consensus that has built up around the LOSC, it is widely regarded as 'the benchmark against which state actions are judged in the law of the sea'.[73]

4.   UNESCO Convention on the Protection of the Underwater Cultural Heritage 2001

The LOSC provides the general international legal framework within which activities in the marine environment are conducted. Among other things, it sets out the rights, jurisdiction and duties of coastal states and

---

controversial matters. For further discussion in the context of the law of the sea, see Churchill and Lowe, *The Law of the Sea*, pp. 8–11. For a more detailed discussion of the formation of customary international law generally, see Lowe, *International Law*, pp. 36–63.

[69] Lowe, *International Law*, p. 86.   [70] See *ibid.*, pp. 84–6.

[71] The 1969 Vienna Convention on the Law of Treaties is another example.

[72] See Lowe, *International Law*, pp. 83–6; see also Harrison, *Making the Law of the Sea*, pp. 51–9.

[73] Harrison, *Making the Law of the Sea*, p. 56.

flag states in the various maritime zones. It also includes two articles – Articles 149 and 303 – that provide for UCH. These articles establish a duty on states to protect UCH, and to cooperate for that purpose.[74] They also make some specific provision for UCH located in the contiguous zone and in the Area.[75] That provision is limited and widely regarded as inadequate to deal with circumstances in which UCH located anywhere in the marine environment is vulnerable to human interference.

The UNESCO Convention on the Protection of the Underwater Cultural Heritage 2001 is the international community's response to this inadequacy and to concerns about the increasing incidence of commercial exploitation of shipwrecks. It is the product of thirteen years of preparatory work, including four years of formal negotiations, and its purpose is to afford a comprehensive legal regime for UCH in all maritime zones and one which will ensure that this important aspect of cultural heritage is preserved for the benefit of the whole of humanity. At the core of the Convention is a complex regime that enables states – working individually and collectively – to regulate activities in international waters. The primary objective of this regulation is to ensure that any intentional interference with UCH sites is undertaken in accordance with internationally accepted archaeological principles and standards of behaviour. The archaeological principle that is central to the treaty's framework and ethos is that there should be a presumption in favour of preservation *in situ* until such time as intervention is justified for scientific or protective purposes.

The general principles and objectives of the UNESCO Convention 2001 are rooted in law and practice related to cultural heritage. However, the fact that the treaty is designed to regulate activities at sea means that it does not fall purely within the sphere of cultural heritage law, but is also a part of the law of the sea. Its hybrid character means that it has the potential to impact on matters of general oceans governance which are of far greater political import for many states than the matter of heritage protection. This helps to explain why the gestation period of the Convention was almost as long as that for the LOSC and also why the Convention is such a politically controversial instrument.

From the outset, those involved in the drafting of the new treaty knew a number of contentious issues would need to be satisfactorily addressed if the initiative was to have any prospect of achieving a universally acceptable outcome. Foremost among these was the question of precisely

---

[74] LOSC, Art. 303(1).   [75] LOSC, Art. 303(2) and Art. 149 respectively.

how the Convention would relate to the LOSC, given the pre-eminent status of that treaty. More specifically, how would it approach the matter of coastal state jurisdiction in the EEZ and on the continental shelf given that, under the LOSC, that jurisdiction is firmly tied to the matter of natural resource exploration and exploitation? Another area of difficulty was the question of the material scope of application of the new treaty: in other words, how was UCH to be defined for the purposes of the treaty? This question was problematic at a general level, given differing national approaches and views on the matter, and it was also problematic with respect to one very specific question: should sunken warships be included in the conventional framework? While such wrecks may be of great historical significance, they also give rise to issues of considerable political sensitivity. Other areas where there were serious differences of view in the international community related to the relationship between the new treaty and private maritime law. It was recognised that a potential 'deal-breaker' was the question of how the Convention dealt with the law of salvage and the related law of finds: should they be excluded from application to UCH, or should they continue to play a role? A related question was the approach the Convention should take to the commercial exploitation of UCH: in particular, should the regime permit some participation by commercially motivated parties in activities on UCH sites? A further important question was: where there are identifiable ownership rights in UCH, how should they be dealt with?

Despite the challenges faced, there was considerable political commitment to the process and many of those involved in the negotiations worked tirelessly to find acceptable compromises on the core areas of contention. Inevitably, the traditional tension characterising the law of the sea played an important part in the overall political dynamic. Although the maritime powers accepted the need for action, their overriding concern was to ensure that the new treaty did not prejudice their wider political imperatives: they therefore resisted pressure from the G-77 and other states for coastal states to be given direct jurisdiction over UCH on the continental shelf. Mirroring the process at UNCLOS III, the chair of the formal sessions played a vital role in the development of the text and in facilitating compromise on areas of difficulty. However, the eventual outcome also mirrored that at UNCLOS III. A consensus could not be reached on the wording of a number of key provisions and the negotiations concluded with a majority vote. A substantial proportion of those present (and, by the end of the negotiations, there were a large number of states present)[76] voted in favour of the Convention, but a small minority either abstained, or voted against, including the USA and a number of other maritime powers.[77] These states had concerns about two particular aspects of the text. First, they regarded the regulatory framework for the continental shelf and EEZ established by the Convention as prejudicial, or at least potentially prejudicial, to the 'package deal' enshrined in the LOSC; secondly, they were dissatisfied with the Convention's treatment of sunken warships.

The UNESCO Convention entered into force internationally on 2 January 2009, three months after the deposit of the twentieth instrument of ratification.[78] At the time of writing, it has forty-one states parties.[79] These states are engaged in establishing institutional structures and other arrangements for the implementation of the Convention and, as yet, there has been little state practice under its regime. At the present time none of the maritime states listed above has ratified the Convention. The particular significance of this fact is that the regulatory regime the Convention establishes is heavily reliant on flag state jurisdiction and the participation of these states is crucial if the regime is to be fully functional and effective.

5. The approach and structure of this book

This book is concerned with the relationship between UCH and international law, and with the many and varied influences which have shaped that relationship. At present and for the foreseeable future there are essentially two parallel international legal regimes in place relating to UCH protection: the UNESCO conventional regime and the general international legal framework outside that regime, which is governed largely by the LOSC. For this reason the book does not focus solely on the

[76] At the fourth and final meeting, almost ninety states were represented: see Garabello, 'The Negotiating History of the Convention on the Protection of the Underwater Cultural Heritage', p. 91.
[77] For voting details, see Chap. 1, section 3.1.2. (It is worth comparing these details with those for the states that voted against the LOSC or abstained from the vote in 1982: see n. 19, above.)
[78] As required by Art. 27.
[79] Albania, Argentina, Barbados, Benin, Bosnia and Herzegovina, Bulgaria, Cambodia, Croatia, Cuba, Democratic Republic of the Congo, Ecuador, Gabon, Grenada, Haiti, Honduras, Iran, Italy, Jamaica, Jordan, Lebanon, Libya, Lithuania, Mexico, Montenegro, Morocco, Namibia, Nigeria, Palestine, Panama, Paraguay, Portugal, Romania, Saint Kitts and Nevis, Saint Lucia, Saint Vincent and the Grenadines, Slovakia, Slovenia, Spain, Trinidad and Tobago, Tunisia and Ukraine.

UNESCO Convention. Nonetheless, it uses the Convention as a prism through which to explore the subject as a whole. In particular, it takes as its focal points the issues that posed the greatest challenges at the UNESCO negotiations. These issues lie at the heart of the subject and at the heart of the book.

The first two chapters are essentially introductory in nature. Chapter 1 outlines the evolution of international law in this area from the genesis of Articles 149 and 303 of the LOSC to the adoption of the UNESCO Convention. Chapter 2 explores how these treaties and other legal instruments have defined UCH in order to establish their material scope of application. Chapters 3 to 6 examine in turn a number of the core areas of contention: the question of ownership rights and other types of interest in UCH; the status of sunken warships; the application of salvage law and the law of finds; and commercial exploitation. The general background to each of the issues is explored, as well as the approach taken by general international law and by the UNESCO Convention. The thorniest question of all – jurisdiction – is dealt with in two chapters: Chapter 7 considers the matter of the rights, jurisdiction and duties of states with respect to UCH under general international law and Chapter 8 examines the jurisdictional mechanisms established by the UNESCO Convention. Chapters 9 and 10 give some consideration to aspects of the UNESCO Convention's regime that have not otherwise been addressed, including questions relating to the practical and technical implementation of the Convention. The final section of the book reflects on the future prospects for international law in this field.

Unless the context indicates otherwise, the abbreviation 'UCH' is used to refer to underwater cultural heritage broadly defined and the expression 'general international law' is used to mean the international legal framework outside the UNESCO conventional regime.

1 The evolution of international law on underwater cultural heritage

1. Introduction

Since the 1950s and the dawning of awareness of the potential cultural significance of shipwrecks and other forms of UCH, there have been a number of international initiatives designed to provide such material with legal protection. Some have been more successful than others, but they have all contributed in one way or another to the international legal position that exists today.

This chapter charts the development of international law in this field from the earliest initiatives through to the adoption of the UNESCO Convention on the Protection of the Underwater Cultural Heritage 2001.[1] It plots the development of interest in, and approaches to, the matters that became focal points of contention during the UNESCO negotiations, focusing in particular on the central questions of coastal state jurisdiction and the application of salvage law. It also traces the emergence of increasingly sophisticated approaches to UCH protection and management as appreciation of the cultural value of UCH grew and marine archaeological theory and practice developed. Changing perceptions of the threats posed to UCH over the five decades in question are also noted.

The subject matter of this chapter has already been extensively covered in academic literature and therefore the treatment here is relatively brief and intended primarily to provide a backdrop for the discussion that comes in later chapters. To give some sense of attitudes prevailing at key moments in the evolution of the subject, the language of contemporary reports and commentaries is sometimes adopted.

---

[1] This chapter is not concerned with international agreements made for the protection of specific wreck sites, or for the protection of UCH in specific regional seas. These are discussed in a number of later chapters.

2. Initiatives preceding the UNESCO Convention 2001

In its early phases, the development of international law in this field took place through two separate processes: one at a global, and the other at a regional, level. The processes overlapped in their timing by six years and therefore each was in some measure influenced by the other. As will be seen, both had a profound influence on the shape and content of the UNESCO Convention 2001.

2.1   UN Convention on the Law of the Sea 1982 (LOSC)

The first notable reference to UCH in an international forum was in 1956. It was made in the preparatory report for UNCLOS I produced by the UN's International Law Commission (ILC).[2] This report included seventy-three draft articles, along with a commentary on each. The articles formed the basis for the text of the Geneva Conventions of 1958 and the commentary provided a basis for the interpretation of those treaties.[3]

In its report, the ILC accepted the notion already emerging in customary international law that a coastal state could exercise control and jurisdiction over the continental shelf for the purpose of exploring and exploiting its natural resources. However, its acceptance of the notion came with the explicit proviso that the rights should be exercised for that sole purpose and should not affect the freedom of the high seas any more than is 'absolutely unavoidable'.[4] It enshrined the notion in draft Article 68 and used the formulation 'sovereign rights' to refer to the rights concerned. In its commentary on draft Article 68, the ILC declared:

It is clearly understood that the rights in question do *not* cover objects such as wrecked ships and their cargoes (including bullion) lying on the seabed or covered by the sand of the subsoil.[5]

---

[2] The ILC was established by the UN General Assembly in 1948 for the purpose of promoting the codification and progressive development of international law. It comprises a permanent body of thirty-four independent experts on international law: see, further, Boyle and Chinkin, *The Making of International Law*, pp. 171 *et seq.*

[3] The ILC report is accorded considerable weight in light of its carefully considered nature and the fact that it was the product of professional independent expertise 'illuminated by the observations of governments': Churchill and Lowe, *The Law of the Sea*, p. 15.

[4] Report of the International Law Commission to the General Assembly, 11 UN GAOR Supp. (No. 9), UN Doc A/3159 (1956), reprinted in (1956) *Yearbook of the International Law Commission*, Vol. II, pp. 295–6.

[5] *Ibid.*, Vol. II, p. 298. Emphasis added.

This statement made it clear that the ILC was firmly of the view that shipwrecks were not encompassed within the sovereign rights of the coastal state on the continental shelf and therefore should not be regarded as natural resources in this context.

Draft Article 68 became Article 2(1) of the Geneva Convention on the Continental Shelf. In light of the ILC's pronouncement, it became generally accepted that the sovereign rights of coastal states over natural resources referred to in that article could not be interpreted as extending to shipwrecks. This conclusion was to have a profound impact on the development of international law with respect to UCH.

The issue of UCH next came to international attention in 1968. In that year the UN General Assembly established the Committee on the Peaceful Uses of the Sea-Bed and the Ocean Floor Beyond the Limits of National Jurisdiction (known as the Sea-Bed Committee) to undertake the preparatory work for a new treaty which would establish a legal regime for the deep seabed. The Sea-Bed Committee was charged with drawing up a list of subjects that should be included within that regime. Thanks to Greece, a state deeply concerned about the plight of UCH in the Mediterranean Sea,[6] the topic of 'Archaeological and Historical Treasures' was on the final list approved by the Sea-Bed Committee in 1972.[7]

UNCLOS III began in 1973 and its business was divided between three main committees. Given its starting point, UCH initially fell within the remit of the First Committee, which was concerned with the deep seabed regime. However, towards the end of the negotiations, it was recognised that efforts also needed to be made to address UCH in more general terms and to deal with the more pressing issue of finding a means of controlling activities arising closer to shore. The matter was therefore raised in the Second Committee, which was concerned with the regimes for zones other than the deep seabed, including the continental shelf and the EEZ.

The outcome of the deliberations was the inclusion in the LOSC of two, separately negotiated, provisions relating to UCH.

2.1.1 Article 149

The text of Article 149 originated in proposals made by Greece and Turkey in 1972 and 1973, and developed through several stages. A draft article modifying the proposals appeared in a negotiating text prepared by the Chairmen of all three Committees and the Conference

---

[6] See General introduction, section 1.1, above.
[7] See, further, Strati, *The Protection of the Underwater Cultural Heritage*, p. 297.

President in 1975.[8] Further substantial modifications were then under-taken in the First Committee and a revised article appeared in a subse-quent negotiating text of 1976.[9] The form of that article remained virtually unchanged in all subsequent texts. By the end of this gestation period, the substance of the original proposals had been considerably emasculated.

Article 149 provides:

All objects of an archaeological and historical nature found in the Area shall be preserved or disposed of for the benefit of mankind as a whole, particular regard being paid to the preferential rights of the State or country of origin, or the State of cultural origin, or the State of historical and archaeological origin.

Article 149 is located in Part XI of the LOSC, which establishes the regime for the Area, in other words the deep seabed and subsoil thereof beyond the limits of national jurisdiction.[10] Part XI sets out a highly technical frame-work for the management of the Area and its resources. It declares both to be the 'common heritage of mankind'[11] and provides that activities relat-ing to the resources of the Area must be carried out for the benefit of mankind as a whole.[12] It establishes an institution called the International Seabed Authority (ISA), to undertake the management process.

At least two points about Article 149 are clear from the text of the Convention read alongside the negotiating history. First, objects of an archaeological and historical nature found in the Area are *not* part of the resources of the Area. These are defined restrictively to include mineral resources only.[13] Therefore, despite the fact that such objects are to be preserved or disposed of 'for the benefit of mankind as a whole', they are not encompassed within the common heritage of mankind (CHM) principle enshrined in Part XI. Secondly, it is clear that the functions of the ISA, the body set up by Part XI, are limited to matters related to the exploration and exploitation of the mineral resources of the Area. The body is accorded no direct role in respect of objects of an archaeological and historical nature.

On other matters relating to Article 149, there is far less clarity. It is unclear how old an object must be to qualify as being of 'an archaeological

---

[8] The Informal Single Negotiating Text. See UN Doc A/CONF.62/WP.8, UNCLOS III Off. Rec. Vol. IV, p. 137.

[9] The Revised Single Negotiating Text. See UN Doc A/CONF.62/WP.8/Rev.1/Part I, UNCLOS III Off. Rec. Vol. V, p. 125.

[10] LOSC, Art. 1(1)(1).   [11] LOSC, Art. 136.   [12] LOSC, Art. 140(1).

[13] LOSC, Art. 133(a).

and historical nature'; it is also unclear what the precise nature is of the preferential rights referred to in the article, as well as which states have such rights. Even more importantly, the article does not address the question: if the ISA is not responsible for implementing the objective set out in the article, then who is? The negotiating history of the article provides some indicators about these matters, but they are far from decisive.

2.1.2   Article 303

Article 303 of the LOSC originated in a proposal made by Greece in 1979, in the Second Committee, that the sovereign rights of the coastal state in respect of both the continental shelf and the EEZ be extended to include rights regarding the discovery and salvage of any 'object of purely archaeological or historical nature on the seabed and subsoil'.[14] Later the same year, Greece revised its proposal, the amended form referring only to the continental shelf.[15] This version gained support from six further states.[16] However, it soon became clear that it would not achieve consensus: in sessions in 1980 it met with opposition from three maritime states, namely the USA, the UK and the Netherlands.[17] That opposition was predicated on the following chain of argument:

[the proposal] granted the coastal state rights over its continental shelf which were unrelated to the latter's natural resources and thus might pave the way for other exceptions, favouring creeping jurisdiction and, ultimately, lead to a regime of full coastal state sovereignty over the continental shelf.[18]

A counter-proposal made by the US for a general duty to be imposed on states to protect archaeological and historical objects found in the marine environment led to a debate over the extent of the waters to which such a duty should apply. During that debate, Greece argued for full coastal state jurisdiction over UCH to the 200-mile limit;[19] the USA

---

[14] Caflisch, 'Submarine Antiquities and the International Law of the Sea', p. 16.

[15] According to Caflisch, in light of the definition of the continental shelf adopted in the draft of Art. 76(1), reference to the EEZ was 'unnecessary'. Under that definition, the continental shelf was at least as broad as the EEZ and the assumption was that archaeological and historical objects will only be found on or in the seabed, not in the water column: *ibid.*, p. 17 n. 58. (For the reason why the UNESCO Convention 2001 opted to refer to both the continental shelf and the EEZ, see Chap. 8, n. 45.)

[16] Cape Verde, Italy, Malta, Portugal, Tunisia and Yugoslavia.

[17] Caflisch, 'Submarine Antiquities and the International Law of the Sea', p. 17.

[18] *Ibid.*

[19] Nordquist suggests that the notion of using a 200-mile limit probably originated in an initiative of the Council of Europe in 1978 (on which, see section 2.2.1, below): Nordquist, Rosenne and Sohn, *United Nations Convention on the Law of the Sea 1982*, Vol. V, p. 159 n. 2.

responded by proposing a text based on the combination of a general duty and some limited control in the twelve- to twenty-four-mile zone.[20] Ultimately, the US proposal was adopted, on the basis that it was 'closer to a compromise' than any of the other proposals on the table.[21]

Article 303 provides:

1. States have the duty to protect objects of an archaeological and histor-ical nature found at sea and shall cooperate for this purpose.

2. In order to control traffic in such objects, the coastal State may, in applying article 33, presume that their removal from the sea-bed in the zone referred to in that article without its approval would result in an infringement within its territory or territorial sea of the laws and regulations referred to in that article [i.e. customs, fiscal, immigration or sanitary regulations].

3. Nothing in this article affects the rights of identifiable owners, the law of salvage or other rules of admiralty, or laws and practices with respect to cultural exchanges.

4. This article is without prejudice to other international agreements and rules of international law regarding the protection of objects of an archaeological and historical nature.

Article 303 is located in Part XVI of the Convention, which is headed 'General Provisions'.[22] Its location in that part is assumed to mean that – with the exception of paragraph 2, which relates specifically to the contiguous zone – the article applies generally and is not geographically restricted. The effect of this is that the duty on states in paragraph 1

[20] According to Oxman, Vice Chairman of the US delegation, '[t]he real focus of concern [was] the area immediately adjacent to the territorial sea' and '[t]he main issue was the policing of [this] area'; 'the vast seaward reaches of the economic zone and continental shelf were really not relevant to the problem': Oxman, 'The Third United Nations Conference on the Law of the Sea', p. 240. Strati has suggested that these assertions were politically motivated and did not reflect reality: see Strati, *The Protection of the Underwater Cultural Heritage*, pp. 343–4. However, it is possible they may have been at least partly influenced by the conventional wisdom that ancient seafarers sailed close to the coast and avoided the open sea (a view challenged by recent discoveries: see, for example, N. Paphitis, 'Roman shipwrecks found nearly a mile deep', *Associated Press*, 21 June 2012).

[21] Nordquist, Rosenne and Sohn, *United Nations Convention on the Law of the Sea 1982*, Vol. V, p. 159. For further discussion of the circumstances surrounding this crucial compromise, see Caflisch, 'Submarine Antiquities and the International Law of the Sea', pp. 17–19; Strati, *The Protection of the Underwater Cultural Heritage*, pp. 162–5; Hayashi, 'Archaeological and Historical Objects under the United Nations Convention on the Law of the Sea', pp. 294–5.

[22] After the USA made the proposal for a duty of protection to apply to the marine environment generally the issue was transferred from the Second Committee (whose business included the regimes for the continental shelf and EEZ) to the Informal Plenary of the Conference.

applies to all sea areas, as does the saving for the rights of identifiable owners, the law of salvage and other matters set out in paragraph 3. The negotiating history of the article also makes it clear that the coastal state is afforded no rights in respect of UCH on the continental shelf or in the newly created EEZ and – by virtue of paragraph 2 – only limited competence in respect of the removal of UCH in the twelve- to twenty-four-mile contiguous zone.[23]

The precise nature of the jurisdictional competence afforded to coastal states by paragraph 2 is far from clear. The lack of clarity is, in part, because of the complex wording of the provision, which includes a legal fiction[24] and a cross-reference to another article. In part, it is also because the wording was deliberately ambiguous. The USA, the UK and the Netherlands wished to avoid a formal extension of coastal state jurisdiction over UCH beyond the twelve-mile territorial limit; Greece and the co-sponsors of the Greek proposals wished to provide a means of controlling the removal of UCH in the twelve- to twenty-four-mile zone. The wording accommodates both objectives.[25]

In 1989, Nordquist suggested that the meaning of paragraphs 3 and 4 of Article 303 was 'self-explanatory'.[26] However, this is not entirely the case. Article 303(3) is clearly a saving provision in respect of 'the rights of identifiable owners, the law of salvage or other rules of admiralty, or laws and practices with respect to cultural exchanges',[27] but the impact it has on the application of other provisions is uncertain. In particular, it is unclear what its relationship is with Article 303(2), and also with Article 149 (given that Article 303(3) is of general geographical application). Is the effect of Article 303(3) that the laws of salvage and other

---

[23] The contiguous zone is a zone contiguous to the territorial sea extending no further than twenty-four miles from baselines: LOSC, Art. 33.

[24] A good definition of a legal fiction is '[t]he assumption by the law that a particular assertion is true (even though it may not be) in order to support the functioning of a legal rule': *Webster's New World Dictionary* (2006).

[25] For discussion of Art. 303(2), see Chap. 7, section 3.3.

[26] Nordquist, Rosenne and Sohn, *United Nations Convention on the Law of the Sea 1982*, Vol. V, p. 161. This volume is one of a series, produced over a number of years, under the general editorship of Myron Nordquist. The series provides an article-by-article commentary on the LOSC. In the words of Churchill and Lowe, it 'enjoys an unusual authority on the subject': Churchill and Lowe, *The Law of the Sea*, p. 27.

[27] The reference in Art. 303(3) to laws and practices with respect to cultural exchanges reflects the fact that international cultural exchanges have long been regarded as of benefit to humanity and have been promoted by instruments in the cultural heritage field. It makes clear that protective measures should not inhibit legitimate exchanges of this kind. See, further, Strati, *The Protection of the Underwater Cultural Heritage*, pp. 174–5.

rules of admiralty override the protective objectives of those provisions? And, assuming it does apply to Article 149, how do the rights of identifiable owners interact with the preferential rights referred to in that provision? Article 303(4) is also unclear: in particular, does it mean that Article 303 is 'without prejudice' only to *pre-existing* international agreements and rules of international law regarding the protection of objects of an archaeological and historical nature,[28] or is it also without prejudice to agreements made at a later date?

2.1.3   An 'incomplete' regime

Thanks to the efforts of a small group of states (motivated, for the most part, by a desire to find a means of regulating the recovery of UCH situated in the Mediterranean Sea), the LOSC includes some limited provision relating to UCH protection. However, even before the text of the treaty was finalised, that provision was the subject of considerable criticism.

While there are many aspects of Articles 149 and 303 that are open to criticism, the core problems are the following. As far as Article 149 is concerned, the fundamental problem is its failure to designate an agency to put into practice the protective principle it enshrines: as Caflisch pointed out in his seminal article of 1982, this failure deprives the principle of 'all real significance'.[29] As far as Article 303 is concerned, a view expressed by Caflisch that the duties set out in paragraph 1 of that article are 'far too general and vague to have any significant normative content'[30] is widely shared and the need to resort to a 'constructive ambiguity' in paragraph 2 – the only provision in the LOSC affording a concrete mechanism to control interference with UCH *beyond* territorial limits – is a self-evident flaw. On the face of it, the saving for salvage law in paragraph 3 of Article 303 is an active encouragement to the unregulated recovery of UCH: Scovazzi, a leading commentator, has characterised this provision as an 'invitation to looting'.[31] However, the most glaringly obvious problem with the two articles taken together – and one noted by virtually every commentator on the subject – is that they appear to leave a particular geographical 'gap' in the provision they afford. That gap relates to the continental shelf *beyond* the contiguous zone; in other words, to the area of the continental shelf from

---

[28] For example, the 1970 UNESCO Convention on Illicit Trade in Cultural Property.
[29] Caflisch, 'Submarine Antiquities and the International Law of the Sea', p. 29.
[30] *Ibid.*, p. 20.
[31] See, for example, Scovazzi, 'The Protection of Underwater Cultural Heritage', p. 125.

twenty-four miles to the outer limit of the juridical continental shelf (which forms the boundary with the Area). This geographical area – which is at least 176 miles in breadth and, in the case of broad-margin states, potentially much more extensive[32] – falls outside the scope of application of the zonal-specific provisions in Article 303(2) and Article 149. Instead, it is subject only to the general provisions set out in Article 303, paragraphs 1 and 3. As a result, deliberate interference with UCH in the gap for the most part is governed by the general rules of the LOSC. In essence, this means that the principle of freedom of the high seas applies to the search for and recovery of UCH and the only state with competence to control such activity (at least, to do so effectively) is the flag state of the ship engaged in the activity.[33]

Without doubt the regime for UCH established by the LOSC is 'complicated and not complete'.[34] Despite there being a question-mark over whether Article 303(4) was in fact intended to refer only to agreements antecedent to the LOSC, it has been widely interpreted as extending an invitation to a competent international organisation to elaborate upon, and complete, 'this incipient new branch of law'[35] in a subject-specific instrument.

2.2   Developments within the Council of Europe

In January 1977, during a debate on progress at UNCLOS III (which was mid-way through its term at that point), the matter of UCH and, more especially, the problem of 'illicit exploration' of shipwrecks by 'skin divers', was raised in the Parliamentary Assembly of the Council of Europe.[36] Wrecks around the shores of Europe, it was pointed out, represented 'unique historical records' of the European cultural heritage.[37] Recognising that it was unlikely that the treaty under

---

[32] See Chap. 7, n. 92.

[33] The states of nationality of individuals on board the ship also have jurisdiction to take action to control the activities of their own nationals. However, in practice, the exercise of such jurisdiction will not be as effective as the exercise of jurisdiction by the flag state of the vessel involved.

[34] Nordquist et al., United Nations Convention on the Law of the Sea 1982, Vol. VI, p. 230.

[35] Ibid., Vol. V, p. 162.

[36] See the speech of John Roper, for the UK, in Council of Europe, Parliamentary Assembly debate on the UN Conference on the Law of the Sea, 28th Ordinary Session, Official Report, 24 January 1977 (AS (28) CR 20, 20th Sitting).

[37] Ibid. 'Like tombs, they are closed deposits frozen at a moment of time when the ship goes down. But what is not generally realised is that objects under water very often are preserved in a way in which objects in earth are not preserved. They are maintained at

negotiation at UNCLOS III would be in place quickly, the Assembly instructed its Committee on Culture and Education to embark on a study of the subject.[38]

2.2.1   The Roper Report and Recommendation 848 (1978)

In 1978, the Committee published its findings in a report.[39] The report included an explanatory memorandum by the rapporteur, John Roper, the then Vice Chairman of the Committee, and two separate reports prepared by expert consultants on archaeological and legal aspects. It also incorporated a formal Recommendation, entitled 'Recommendation 848 on the Underwater Cultural Heritage'. The report, widely referred to as the Roper Report, was one of the first detailed studies concerning UCH and its legal protection,[40] and it proved to be hugely influential.

A 'striking fact' which had apparently emerged from the study was that there was 'very considerable interest' in UCH in Europe, as well as further afield.[41] The Report commented that '[t]he fast-growing public enthusiasm for the sport of underwater diving is matched by increasing appreciation of the importance of the historical and archaeological material found underwater, as also by the increasing activity of trained archaeologists and those legislating in the field'.[42]

The Report identified as the 'main danger' to UCH intentional human interference by both professional and amateur treasure hunters, an activity which it referred to as 'modern piracy'.[43] In its view, the lack of recognition of underwater archaeology as a valid scientific discipline and the fact that there were few specialist marine archaeologists had left the material remains of the past located in the marine environment exposed. This meant that '[c]ommercial interests, a refinement of salvage operators, [had] intervened and sub-aqua enthusiasm for sunken treasures [had] been awakened'.[44] The Report went on to note that proper

---

constant humidity. Perhaps it is not generally realised that leather and timber are better preserved under water, in a wreck, than in any other way.'

[38] See Order No. 361 (1977) and Council of Europe, Parliamentary Assembly, 28th Ordinary Session, Official Report, 24 January 1977 (AS (28) CR 20, 20th and 21st Sittings).

[39] Parliamentary Assembly of the Council of Europe, 'The Underwater Cultural Heritage: Report of the Committee on Culture and Education (Rapporteur: Mr. John Roper)', Doc. 4200-E, Strasbourg, 1978.

[40] To the author's knowledge the only earlier study relating to law and UCH was published by Crane Miller in 1973: Crane Miller, *International Law and Marine Archaeology*. A more general study of UCH had been published by UNESCO in 1972: *Underwater Archaeology: A Nascent Discipline*.

[41] Doc. 4200-E, 1978, p. 3.   [42] *Ibid.*, p. 4.   [43] *Ibid.*, p. 6.   [44] *Ibid.*, p. 7.

archaeology in the marine environment was hugely expensive and emphasised that interference should not take place until the technical expertise and facilities were in place to ensure that the work was undertaken appropriately.[45] In his report, the expert archaeological consultant, David Blackman, pointed out that, once a site had been located and a pre-disturbance survey conducted,

[t]he next stage *may* be *excavation*, but I should stress that it is too often assumed that excavation must automatically follow. The best means of preserving an underwater site is to leave it where it is.[46]

An analysis of the legislation of European states undertaken by the legal consultants Lyndel Prott and Patrick O'Keefe made it clear that domestic legislation relating to UCH was varied and inadequate and, more importantly, generally did not apply *beyond* the territorial sea.[47] The Roper Report concluded that progress on the matter could be made at a European level and that such progress might eventually form the basis of wider international agreement.[48] Although the focus of attention at the time was on the Mediterranean Sea, it concluded that the experiences and interests of most European states were sufficiently similar 'to suggest that recommendations for action in the member states of the Council of Europe may meet with some success'.[49] Recommendation 848 on the Underwater Cultural Heritage urged member states of the Council of Europe to review their domestic legislation and, where necessary, revise it in order to comply with a number of minimum requirements.

These minimum requirements for national legislation, laid out in an annex to the Recommendation, were based on recommendations made by Prott and O'Keefe. Three of the requirements proved to be of particular significance with respect to the future direction of international legal protection for UCH. They were:

ii   Protection should cover all objects that have been beneath the water for more than 100 years ...

. . .

iv   National jurisdiction should be extended up to the full 200 mile limit ...
v.   Existing salvage and wreck law should not apply to any items protected under ii and iv above.

---

[45] *Ibid.*, p. 6.   [46] *Ibid.*, p. 36. (Emphasis in original.)
[47] *Ibid.*, p. 49. This conclusion was based on an analysis of the legislation of European states undertaken by Lyndel Prott and Patrick O'Keefe (Doc. 4200-E, 1978, Appendix III).
[48] *Ibid.*, p. 3.   [49] *Ibid.*

In their report, Prott and O'Keefe had concluded that the application of traditional salvage and wreck laws to UCH was inappropriate because these laws encouraged the unregulated recovery of material.[50] They had also recommended the adoption of the age criterion of 100 years to identify the objects subject to the scheme of protection (an approach, they pointed out, was taken by some Scandinavian legislation). In their view, such a criterion should have the effect of reducing the impact of the salvage law exclusion and thereby avoiding 'severe hardship' for salvors.[51]

The Roper Report recognised that the proposal for an extension of national jurisdiction was the most controversial of the recommendations.[52] According to the Report:

[t]he reasoning behind the proposal [was] the need to allocate responsibility for cultural remains that are ... accessible in waters outside existing territorial limits

and

to plan ... for protecting what is apparently out of reach but may soon be in danger as a result of technological developments.[53]

The reference to 'the full 200-mile limit' was a reference to the new concept of an exclusive economic zone, then under development at UNCLOS III.[54] Prott and O'Keefe used the term 'cultural protection zone' to refer to the proposed zone, a term devised to emphasise that the purpose of the zone was *cultural protection*, not economic exploitation; therefore, while the zone could be regarded as 'analogous' to the EEZ, it was clearly distinguishable from both the EEZ and the continental

---

[50] At the time Recommendation 848 was drawn up, Art. 303 of the LOSC had not yet been conceived. Therefore, there was nothing to indicate that this proposal might be out of step with subsequent developments at UNCLOS III.

[51] Doc. 4200-E, 1978, p. 70.   [52] *Ibid.*, p. 17.   [53] *Ibid.*

[54] *Ibid.* The selection of a zone coterminous with the 200-mile EEZ, rather than the continental shelf, was determined at least in part because of the circumstances in the Mediterranean Sea, where the physical continental shelves are narrow in breadth and therefore use of the continental shelf would not have covered the whole of the sea. Prott and O'Keefe pointed out that if the continental shelf was chosen as the limit, at least half of the Mediterranean Sea would be excluded from the protective framework: *ibid.*, p. 66. (Presumably this calculation was made on the basis of the definition of the continental shelf under the 1958 Geneva Convention on the Continental Shelf, which was 'the seabed and subsoil ... adjacent to the coast but outside the area of the territorial sea, to a depth of 200 metres or, beyond that limit, to where the depth of the superjacent waters admits of the exploitation of the natural resources of the said areas': Art. 1.)

shelf.[55] What was being proposed was that coastal states should have full jurisdictional competence (both legislative and enforcement jurisdiction) over UCH out to 200 miles.

Acknowledging that there might be difficulty implementing the proposed zone simply through a process of unilateral extensions of coastal state jurisdiction,[56] the Roper Report suggested that the proposed cultural protection zone could be adopted through a European treaty.[57] In their report, Prott and O'Keefe suggested that if such a zone was widely adopted by European states, it could become the basis for the formation of a rule of customary international law.[58]

Recommendation 848, which was adopted by the Parliamentary Assembly of the Council of Europe in October 1978, included a recommendation to the Committee of Ministers that it draw up a European convention on the protection of UCH, open to all of the Council of Europe's member states and also to other states bordering on seas in the European area.[59]

2.2.2   Draft European Convention 1985

In 1979 the Council of Europe's Committee of Ministers decided to accept the recommendation of the Parliamentary Assembly that it draw up a European treaty on UCH and set up an Ad Hoc Committee of Experts (CAHAQ) to undertake the task. CAHAQ held six plenary meetings between 1980 and 1985.

A draft European Convention on the Protection of the Underwater Cultural Heritage was finalised in March 1985 and submitted to the Committee of Ministers for approval. However, in light of objections by Turkey to the provisions relating to the territorial scope of the Convention, the draft was never adopted.[60] The final text and all related documents remain confidential and publicly unavailable. Nevertheless, an earlier version of the draft was declassified to allow for consultation by

---

[55] Prott and O'Keefe, *Law and the Cultural Heritage*, Vol. I, pp. 100–1.

[56] Note was taken of the fact that, in 1976, Australia had exerted legislative jurisdiction over UCH on its continental shelf and that Norway also exercised some relevant controls in this area: Doc. 4200-E, 1978, p. 56. These, and other, unilateral extensions of jurisdiction with respect to UCH are discussed further in Chap. 7, section 4.1.

[57] Doc. 4200-E, 1978, p. 17.   [58] *Ibid.*, p. 57.   [59] Recommendation 848, 1(a).

[60] At the time, the Council of Europe operated a treaty adoption system under which it was possible for one state to block the signature-opening process: see Polakiewicz, *Treaty Making in the Council of Europe*, p. 25.

interested parties.[61] The following comments are based on the declassified version, but draw on further insights from other official documents on file with the author.

In its preamble, the draft Convention acknowledged 'the importance of the underwater cultural heritage as an integral part of the cultural heritage of mankind'; the need for 'more stringent supervision to prevent ... clandestine excavation'; and the fact that such excavation would cause 'irremediable loss of [the] historical significance' of the heritage 'by destroying [its] environment'. It also recognised that the treatment of UCH required the application of scientific methods, appropriate techniques and equipment, and highly qualified professional expertise.[62] The material scope of application of the draft Convention was broadly defined to include 'all remains and objects and any other traces of human existence located entirely or in part in the sea', which were to be considered as being part of UCH and to constitute 'underwater cultural property' for the purposes of the Convention.[63] In line with Recommendation 848, underwater cultural property 'being at least 100 years old' would qualify for protection.[64]

The draft Convention provided that 'Contracting States shall ensure as far as possible that all appropriate measures are taken to protect underwater cultural property *in situ*'[65] and 'shall require that discoverers of underwater cultural property leave this property, as a principle, where it is situated'.[66] It therefore adopted the principle of protection *in situ* which was becoming increasingly established in

---

[61] DIR/JUR (84) 1, Strasbourg, 22 June 1984. The Draft Convention, as released, constitutes the version adopted by the Ad Hoc Committee of Experts on the Underwater Cultural Heritage (CAHAQ) on the occasion of its fifth meeting, held in Strasbourg, 19–23 March 1984. The confidential character of the text was waived by decision of the Committee of Ministers taken by their 374th meeting at Deputies level (14–22 June 1984). As is the general practice with Council of Europe treaties, the draft Convention was accompanied by an Explanatory Report (also declassified). These explanatory reports are not intended to provide an authoritative interpretation of the treaty, but rather to facilitate the application of its provisions: Polakiewicz, *Treaty Making in the Council of Europe*, pp. 26–7. They can be treated as part of the context of the treaty for the purposes of treaty interpretation: see General introduction, section 3.2.1, above.

[62] Draft Convention, declassified version. The preamble of the final text had fewer and less-detailed clauses than those of the declassified version.

[63] Art. 1(1).

[64] Art. 1(2). Although the draft Convention adopted a 100-year threshold for its application, the provision was formulated somewhat differently from that in Recommendation 848 because it referred to the age of the material rather than the length of time it had been underwater. For further discussion, see Chap. 2, section 3.2.2.

[65] Art. 3(1).   [66] Art. 6(2).

land archaeology.[67] Authorisations to carry out survey, excavation or recovery operations could be granted, but only on the basis of 'scientific considerations'.[68] As far as recovered artefacts were concerned, the draft Convention acknowledged the archaeological principle of 'association of finds' and the need to ensure that, as far as possible, material is conserved in a manner facilitating its study and public display.[69] Contracting states were required to ensure that 'all discoveries of underwater cultural property be reported without delay to their competent authorities, whether the property has been removed from its place of discovery or not'[70] and also to provide for 'official registration' of known underwater cultural property and new discoveries.[71] There were further provisions designed to promote training in underwater archaeological investigation and excavation methods, and in techniques for conservation,[72] as well as appreciation of UCH and awareness of the need to protect it.[73] Other significant features of the draft Convention included a duty on contracting states to co-operate in the protection of UCH,[74] including with respect to illegally recovered or illegally exported UCH,[75] and provision for the establishment of a permanent body – a 'Standing Committee' – to keep the implementation of the Convention under review.[76]

Despite the fact that the draft Convention had its origins in Recommendation 848, it did not adopt that instrument's approach to national jurisdiction and the application of salvage and wreck laws. Instead, it followed the approach of the LOSC. The influence of UNCLOS III is hardly surprising given that the final versions of Articles 149 and 303 had been more or less settled by the time CAHAQ started its work.

Rather than providing for the exclusion of the application of salvage and wreck laws, the draft Convention echoed Article 303(3) of the LOSC:

Nothing in this Convention affects the rights of identifiable owners, the law of salvage or other rules of maritime law, or laws and practices with respect to cultural exchanges.[77]

---

[67] The precise origins of the principle are hard to trace and the extent to which it was an established tenet of archaeology in the early 1980s is unclear. However, at an international level, reference was made to the principle in the 1956 UNESCO Recommendation on International Principles Applicable to Archaeological Excavations (which applies in principle to marine archaeology as well as terrestrial archaeology). See para. 8 of that instrument. For further discussion of the principle, see Chap. 9, section 3.2.

[68] Art. 5(2).   [69] Art. 10(1).   [70] Art. 6(1).   [71] Art. 7(1).   [72] Art. 4.

[73] Art. 10(2).   [74] Art. 9.   [75] Art. 12.   [76] Art. 16.   [77] Art. 2(7).

The only difference of note between this provision and Article 303(3) is its replacement of the reference to 'rules of admiralty' with 'rules of maritime law', presumably to make it explicit that the saving applied to *any* relevant rules of private maritime law, not simply those administered by the admiralty courts of the common law world.[78]

On the question of the extent of national jurisdiction over UCH, it seems that three options were considered: to limit the territorial scope of application of the Convention to the twelve-mile territorial sea; to adopt an approach based on the continental shelf or on the 200-mile EEZ; or to adopt an approach based on the contiguous zone.[79] It appears that the second of these options was rejected by several states on the basis that it had been superseded by the developments at UNCLOS III (and indeed had been rejected in that forum). The third option – which could be regarded as the compromise option – garnered the broadest support. The draft Convention therefore adopted a reformulated version of the legal fiction device in Article 303(2).[80]

Despite the decision to use the contiguous zone as the basis for the territorial scope of application of the Convention, the continental shelf beyond that limit was not entirely ignored. A further provision relating to coastal state jurisdiction was set out in Article 2(5).[81] This stated:

Each Contracting State, in the exercise of its jurisdiction over the exploration for and exploitation of the natural resources of its continental shelf, shall take appropriate measures for the protection of underwater cultural property in accordance with the objectives of this Convention.

This provision was prompted by the practice of certain states (notably Greece and Norway) to make it a requirement that oil and gas contractors working on the continental shelf report archaeological discoveries

---

[78] In light of the lack of consensus over the provisions in respect of jurisdiction (which also appear in Art. 2 of the declassified version of the draft Convention), the draft Explanatory Report makes no comment on Art. 2 and therefore provides no insight into this provision.

[79] Leanza, 'The Territorial Scope of the Draft European Convention on the Protection of the Underwater Cultural Heritage', p. 127.

[80] According to Leanza, CAHAQ considered at least five different wording formulations for this provision: *ibid*. The formulation adopted in the relevant provisions of the declassified version of the draft Convention (Art. 2(2)–(3)) attempted to avoid at least some of the fiction of Art. 303(2) by referring to the infringement of the *cultural property laws* of the state, rather than its customs, fiscal, immigration and sanitary laws and regulations. A different formulation was adopted in the final text: for details, see Strati, *The Protection of the Underwater Cultural Heritage*, pp. 170–1.

[81] In the final draft, this provision became Art. 17, but the text remained the same.

made in the course of their work.[82] In linking the taking of measures to protect UCH with a coastal state's jurisdiction over the natural resources of the continental shelf, Article 2(5) managed to avoid raising concerns about creeping jurisdiction.

Turkey's dissatisfaction with the provisions on jurisdiction related to the potential difficulties of their application in the eastern Aegean Sea, given its dispute with Greece over maritime boundaries in that area. It objected to the use of the contiguous zone as the basis for the territorial scope of application of the Convention and maintained the view that the continental shelf was the 'only logical and viable' approach because it would plug the gap in the provision made by Articles 149 and 303 of the LOSC.[83] Out of the sixteen member states represented at the final meeting of CAHAQ,[84] it seems that only Turkey objected to the final text of the Convention and to its adoption and opening for signature.

It has to be said that there is some irony in the fact that a technical issue regarding delimitation between the two states that had first brought the question of UCH to international attention caused the derailment of the first attempt to produce a specific international treaty in the field. Nevertheless, despite its failure, the Council of Europe's initiative made a vital contribution to the evolution of international law in the area. It demonstrated that there was recognition at a political level, certainly within Europe, of the need for a treaty framework to afford protection to UCH in extra-territorial waters; it laid extremely valuable groundwork for such a framework, especially with respect to aspects unrelated to jurisdiction; and it demonstrated that acceptable compromises could be reached on areas of contention such as salvage law. It also provided a stark forewarning that the jurisdictional question could prove to be a major obstacle to achieving a comprehensive protective regime in the post-UNCLOS III era.

2.2.3   Valletta Convention 1992

The abandonment of the draft European Convention in the mid-1980s marked the end of the Council of Europe's attempts to create a treaty dedicated to UCH. However, it did not mark the end of that

[82] The practice of Norway in this respect had been noted by Prott and O'Keefe in their survey of national practice for the Council of Europe in 1978: see Doc. 4200-E, 1978, pp. 56 and 120. For further discussion of the practice and its legitimacy in international law, see Chap. 7, section 4.1.
[83] Minority statement made by the Turkish expert, on file with the author.
[84] Austria, Cyprus, Denmark, France, Federal Republic of Germany, Greece, Ireland, Italy, the Netherlands, Norway, Portugal, Spain, Sweden, Switzerland, the UK and Turkey.

organisation's interest in furthering the protection of UCH. In the late 1980s, it began work on revising a relatively old treaty, the European Convention on the Protection of the Archaeological Heritage 1969. The original 1969 Convention applied only implicitly to UCH. Among the motivations for revising the text was the recognition that – given the apparently irresolvable deadlock on the 1985 draft treaty – the matter of UCH was one that still needed to be addressed. The revised text therefore explicitly included UCH within its scope.

The European Convention on the Protection of the Archaeological Heritage (Revised) 1992 was opened for signature in Valletta, Malta, in 1992; thereafter it became known as the Valletta Convention. Its core aim is 'to protect the archaeological heritage as a source of the European collective memory and as an instrument for historical and scientific study'.[85]

According to its Explanatory Report, the revised treaty 'stands as testimony to the evolution of archaeological practice throughout Europe'.[86] Certainly during the two decades following the adoption of its predecessor, there had been a number of significant changes. First of all, as the Explanatory Report acknowledges, there had been a 'major switch' from investigating the archaeological heritage through excavation and recovery to the use of more sophisticated and less intrusive techniques. Excavation was now regarded as a final, and by no means inevitable, stage in the process of archaeological investigation. The Convention recognises that excavation is essentially a destructive activity[87] and enshrines a preference for the protection of the archaeological heritage *in situ*.[88] Secondly, perceptions of the archaeological heritage had become much more sophisticated and had moved away from an object-centred approach to one that recognised that the *context* in which an object was found was equally important in terms of the information about the past it could elicit.[89] Thirdly, a wider range of threats to the archaeological heritage were perceived. While the original 1969 treaty had been addressed purely at dealing with illicit and clandestine excavations, those responsible for drafting the Valletta Convention had in mind a broad range of threats: 'major planning schemes, natural risks, clandestine or unscientific excavations and insufficient public awareness'.[90] The focus had shifted from the question of how to treat

---

[85] Art. 1(1).
[86] Explanatory Report, p. 1. For the status of the Explanatory Report, see n. 61, above.
[87] See wording of Art. 3(ii).   [88] See Arts. 4(ii) and 5(iv).
[89] See, further, Chap. 2, section 3.2.3.   [90] Preamble.

objects and sites *after* their chance discovery, to the question of how to manage the archaeological heritage in its entirety.

The Valletta Convention requires that each state party has in place procedures for the authorisation of excavation and other archaeological activities that ensure that such activities are conducted scientifically and that non-destructive methods of investigation are applied wherever possible.[91] In one of the first indications of how the question of commercial exploitation of UCH was likely to be treated in the context of international protective regimes, the Explanatory Report makes clear that excavations 'made solely for the purpose of finding precious metals or objects with a market value should never be allowed'.[92] Among other things, the Convention also makes provision for the maintenance of an inventory of the archaeological heritage;[93] mandatory reporting of chance discoveries;[94] the integrated conservation of the archaeological heritage within the planning process;[95] public financial support for archaeological research and conservation;[96] facilitation of the collection and dissemination of scientific knowledge;[97] promotion of public awareness and access;[98] prevention of the illicit circulation of archaeological material;[99] and monitoring of the application of the Convention.[100]

The Convention defines the 'archaeological heritage' broadly to include 'all remains and objects and other traces of mankind',[101] 'whether situated on land or underwater',[102] so long as those elements meet three criteria.[103] One of those criteria is that the elements 'must be located *in any area within the jurisdiction of the parties*'.[104] Clearly this includes the territorial sea. However, it also provides leeway for individual states parties to interpret the scope of their jurisdiction more widely. On this point, the Explanatory Report provides:

the actual area of State jurisdiction depends on the individual States and in respect of this there are many possibilities. Territorially, the area can be

---

[91] Art. 3.   [92] Explanatory Report, p. 8.   [93] Art. 2(i).   [94] Art. 2(iii).
[95] Art. 5.   [96] Art. 6.   [97] Art. 7.   [98] Art. 9.   [99] Art. 10.   [100] Art. 13.
[101] Art. 1(2).   [102] Art. 1(3).
[103] For details of all three criteria, see Chap. 2, section 3.2.3.
[104] Valletta Convention, Art. 1(2)(iii). Emphasis added. The 1969 Convention did not refer to its territorial scope of application. However, as Strati points out: 'in light of the nature of the measures adopted, which assume the undiscretionary authority and the exclusive competence of contracting States, it would be reasonable to conclude that it applies only to archaeological objects found within national territories' (Strati, *The Protection of the Underwater Cultural Heritage*, p. 78); in other words, it would include archaeological remains in the territorial sea, but not those beyond that limit.

coextensive with the territorial sea, the contiguous zone, the continental shelf, the exclusive economic zone or a cultural protection zone.

Noting that some member states of the Council of Europe restrict their jurisdiction over UCH to the territorial sea, while others extend it to the continental shelf,[105] the Explanatory Report makes clear that the Convention recognises and reflects these differences of state practice, without 'indicating a preference' for one or the other.[106] Under the terms of the Convention, states parties are therefore free to determine the extent of the maritime areas under national jurisdiction to which they will apply the Convention.

By not making the choice for states parties, those drafting the treaty neatly side-stepped the issue which had derailed the 1985 draft European Convention. Their tactic ensured that their initiative could achieve broad support from the member states of the Council of Europe, including those that took a 'coastal state' or 'flag state' perspective. Significantly, Turkey and Greece were among its original signatory states, as were France, Germany, the Netherlands and the UK.

The Valletta Convention has proved to be a remarkably successful treaty. It came into force in 1995 and has been widely ratified and implemented by states across the continent of Europe.[107] It is regarded by European archaeologists and heritage managers as an important and effective standard-setting instrument.[108] From a UCH perspective, the specific inclusion of sites, objects and other remains situated underwater within its scope of application afforded valuable formal recognition of the fact that UCH is of no less importance than its terrestrial counterpart and should be treated on a par. However, the 'seamless' approach taken to remains situated on land and underwater means that the provisions of the Convention do not address the unique circumstances of heritage

---

[105] Apart from the practice of Norway and Greece, already noted, within the European context, Spanish cultural heritage legislation enacted in 1985 applied to material on the continental shelf, and the remit of Irish national monuments legislation was extended to the furthest extent of the continental shelf in 1987: see, further, Chap. 7, section 4.1.

[106] Explanatory Report, p. 6.

[107] At the time of writing, the Valletta Convention has been ratified by forty-two of the forty-seven member states of the Council of Europe, including the UK, the Netherlands, France, Germany, Greece, Ireland, Italy, Portugal and Spain.

[108] Having said that, its approach is becoming dated and it is gradually being superseded by a new generation of standard-setting instruments sponsored by the Council of Europe. These include the European Landscape Convention 2000 and the Framework Convention on the Value of Cultural Heritage for Society 2005, both of which apply in general terms to UCH.

situated in the marine environment. In particular, implementation of many of the treaty's provisions relies upon the traditional 'town and country' planning system, but in the marine zone equivalent planning systems are still a rarity.[109] The Convention also does little to address the core area of difficulty with respect to the protection of UCH: the need for regulatory mechanisms to control activities targeting UCH in extra-territorial waters. Given that its provisions are framed from the perspective of the needs of the terrestrial heritage, its focus is on a broad range of threats, rather than on the specific problem of activities targeting the heritage and it gives states parties merely the *option* of applying its provisions extra-territorially. As a result, state practice in this regard is variable depending on national attitudes to the jurisdictional question.[110] Furthermore, the Valletta Convention is in nature only a regional instrument and therefore does nothing to directly assist the protection of UCH more globally.[111]

3. The UNESCO initiative

By the mid-1980s it was becoming clear that major strides were being made in the field of marine technology, particularly with respect to the development of submersibles capable of reaching great depth. The discovery of the *Titanic* in 1985 – and the subsequent recovery of a large number of artefacts from the site[112] – provided powerful evidence of the potential for the application of this technology for shipwreck search and recovery operations. If there had been doubt about the threat to UCH lying in the open oceans a decade or so previously,[113] there was no room for doubt now: it was manifestly evident that UCH located anywhere on the continental shelf, or indeed on the deep seabed, was vulnerable to deliberate human interference.

---

[109] On this, see, further, Chap. 10, section 3.

[110] This statement is based on anecdotal evidence of state practice. To the author's knowledge, no comprehensive survey has been undertaken of the practice of the states parties to the Valletta Convention with respect to extra-territorial application.

[111] Before leaving consideration of relevant Council of Europe initiatives, note should be made of Council of Europe Recommendation 1486 on Maritime and Fluvial Cultural Heritage (2000) (Doc. 8867), which was adopted by the Committee of Ministers on 18 July 2001. This Recommendation, incorporated in a report produced by Edward O'Hara, the rapporteur for the Parliamentary Assembly's Committee on Culture and Education, contained several recommendations relating to UCH. These were informed by the initiative then taking place within the UNESCO forum (see below) and were broadly aligned with its fundamental principles.

[112] See General introduction, section 1.2, above.   [113] See n. 20, above.

In 1985, the prevailing international law on the subject was somewhat uncertain. Although it seemed likely that the LOSC would gain sufficient ratifications to enter into force, it had yet to do so.[114] While many of its provisions may have been representative of customary international law,[115] this certainly could not be said of either Articles 149 or 303. Nonetheless, it was recognised that these articles had a 'symbolic importance' and could not be ignored.[116] In particular, Article 303(1) placed a duty on states to protect UCH and to cooperate for that purpose, and Article 303(4) appeared to anticipate that such cooperation could manifest itself in the form of a global treaty to plug gaps in the LOSC regime. UNESCO was the obvious international organisation with competence to take up this task. However, the initiative that eventually led to the UNESCO Convention 2001 had its origins in another quarter.

3.1   Background and process

3.1.1   Groundwork by the International Law Association

In 1988, the International Law Association[117] took up interest in the subject of UCH protection. Aware that the Council of Europe's recent attempt to produce a treaty in this field had reached an impasse, and recognising a growing sense within the international community generally that something needed to be done to provide satisfactory protection for UCH, the ILA's newly established Committee on Cultural Heritage Law decided to take on as its first task the preparation of a new draft convention on UCH.[118]

The ILA produced a skeleton draft in 1990,[119] and then two further drafts, one in 1992[120] and one in 1994.[121] The 1994 draft was adopted at

---

[114] At the end of 1987, the LOSC had thirty-four states parties, almost all of which were G-77 members. Sixty ratifications were required for it to enter into force (LOSC, Art. 308). It did so on 16 November 1994. See, further, General introduction, section 2.2.1, above.

[115] See General introduction, section 3.2.3, above.

[116] ILA, Queensland Conference (1990), International Committee on Cultural Heritage Law, First Report, p. 10.

[117] The ILA is a private body comprising individuals with an interest in international law. The Association's main objectives are the study, clarification and development of international law. These objectives are pursued through the work of specialised international committees overseen and endorsed by general biennial conferences.

[118] During its work, the ILA Committee consulted with a broad range of experts: see O'Keefe and Nafziger, 'Report', p. 417 n. 2.

[119] See ILA, Queensland Conference (1990), International Committee on Cultural Heritage Law, First Report, Appendix I.

[120] See ILA, Cairo Conference (1992), International Committee on Cultural Heritage Law, Report and Draft Convention for Consideration at the 1992 Conference.

[121] For the 1994 ILA Draft Convention with article-by-article commentaries, see O'Keefe and Nafziger, 'Report', pp. 404–17.

the ILA's 66th Conference in Buenos Aires that year. This draft (here-after 1994 ILA Draft) was then forwarded to UNESCO for consideration and became the 'blueprint for the development of' the UNESCO Convention 2001.[122]

The ILA Committee drew on, and was influenced by, the experience of the Council of Europe: the Chairman of the ILA's Cultural Heritage Law Committee, Patrick O'Keefe, has referred – in particular – to the debt that the 1994 ILA Draft owed to the 1985 draft Convention.[123] Like that instrument, the ILA text adopted a broad definition of UCH and a 100-year threshold for material to qualify for protection under its regime.[124] However, on the two other core issues – salvage law and coastal state jurisdiction – the 1994 ILA Draft departed from the approach of the earlier treaty initiative and instead adopted an approach more reflective of its forebear, Recommendation 848. On salvage law, the ILA text provided for its non-applicability to material falling within the scope of application of the Convention.[125] On coastal state jurisdiction, it made provision which would have allowed a state party to opt to establish a 'cultural heritage zone' in an area beyond its territorial sea up to the outer limit of its continental shelf.[126] Where a state party did establish such a zone, it would be required to take measures to ensure that activities within the zone affecting UCH complied with certain minimum standards to be set down in a Charter annexed to the Convention.[127]

Given that the approach of the 1985 draft Convention on salvage law and jurisdiction had been influenced by the LOSC, how did the ILA Committee regard the relationship between that treaty and its own proposals? Its decision to exclude the application of salvage law appears to have been made on the basis that the saving provision for the law of salvage in Article 303(3) of the LOSC did not preclude later instruments

---

[122] O'Keefe, *Shipwrecked Heritage*, p. 23.   [123] *Ibid.*, p. 22.   [124] 1994 ILA Draft, Art. 2(1).

[125] *Ibid.*, Art. 4.

[126] *Ibid.*, Arts. 1(3) and 5. It may be recalled (see n. 54, above) that the 200-mile limit was selected by Recommendation 848 because the continental shelf as defined by the 1958 Geneva Convention on the Continental Shelf would have been inadequate to cover the whole of the Mediterranean Sea. However, this problem did not arise with the definition of the continental shelf under the LOSC.

[127] A suggestion that consideration should be given to the development of guidelines for the conduct of archaeological activities in the form of a 'code of practice', which might be attached to a treaty instrument, was made by Prott and O'Keefe in the Roper Report: see Council of Europe Doc. 4200-E, 1978, p. 48. On the subsequent development of the 'Charter', see, further, section 3.1.3, below.

from modifying or excluding salvage law.[128] On the jurisdiction question, it seems that giving states the option to establish a cultural heritage zone over the continental shelf was regarded as justifiable on the following premise:

There is no rule of international law that prohibits a matter discussed during the negotiations for one convention and rejected being raised in negotiations for a later convention, particularly where the latter is more specific.[129]

The *optional* approach to extended jurisdiction was clearly influenced by the approach of the Valletta Convention. The success of that initiative suggested that such an approach was a way of reconciling two diametrically opposing viewpoints: the view that '[i]t would be meaningless to simply repeat the provisions of the [LOSC] ... without bringing any improvements'[130] and the view that there should be no extension of coastal state jurisdiction beyond the position enshrined in the LOSC.[131]

O'Keefe has pointed out that there was a 'fundamental difference in purpose' between the Council of Europe's draft Convention and the ILA draft.[132] The territorial scope of application of the Council of Europe's instrument was never intended to extend further than the limits of national jurisdiction. The ILA draft, on the other hand, was designed to deal with international waters generally, including the area beyond national jurisdiction. In doing this, it addressed the fact that because Article 149 of the LOSC provides no means of fulfilling the objective it sets out, the 'gap' in jurisdictional provision created by the LOSC in practice extends to *include* the Area, as well as the continental shelf beyond twenty-four miles. The ILA draft therefore made use of general principles of international jurisdiction, specifically the nationality and territorial principles,[133] in order to provide some means of deterring activities in this area that were

---

[128] See O'Keefe, 'The Buenos Aires Draft Convention on the Protection of the Underwater Cultural Heritage Prepared by the International Law Association', p. 101.

[129] *Ibid.*, p. 99.

[130] A view expressed by Italy during the ILA meetings: *ibid.* Italy's position is interesting because it had taken a similar position to the maritime powers with respect to coastal state jurisdiction until the late 1990s. However, its position on the matter changed as a result of activities by a US team of archaeologists (with US naval assistance in the form of a nuclear-powered submarine), at Skerki Bank, a deepwater feature located on important trading routes off the coast of Scilly and rich in shipwrecks. For a note of this policy change, see O'Keefe, *Shipwrecked Heritage*, p. 27.

[131] O'Keefe, 'The Buenos Aires Draft Convention on the Protection of the Underwater Cultural Heritage Prepared by the International Law Association', p. 99.

[132] *Ibid.*, p. 95.   [133] On these principles, see, further, Chap. 7, section 2.

inconsistent with the Charter. A state party was required to prohibit its nationals and vessels under its flag from engaging in such activities in respect of any area not within a cultural heritage zone or territorial sea of another state party;[134] it was also required to prohibit the use of its territory in support of such activities.[135] Where material brought into the territory of a state party had been retrieved in a manner contrary to the Charter, provision was made for its seizure.[136]

3.1.2   The UNESCO process

Cognisant of the ILA's work, in 1993, UNESCO took up the matter and began to consider the possibility of developing a new international instrument for the protection of UCH. At its 141st Session in 1993, the UNESCO Executive Board called on the Director-General of UNESCO to undertake a study into the feasibility of drafting such an instrument.[137] The study was prepared by the UNESCO Secretariat and presented to the 146th Session of the Executive Board in 1995.[138]

The feasibility study concluded that the situation beyond the territorial sea was, in its word, 'critical':[139]

At the present time there is literally no object which cannot be located and explored on the sea-bed. Sophisticated equipment can pinpoint any anomaly on the sea-bed, and advanced technology enables the lifting of objects. This technology, pioneered for the exploration of natural resources, is now in use by salvors. The cost of this technology is dropping rapidly and can be used by 'treasure hunters' whose interest is solely in the recovery of commercially valuable material, without regard to the proper methodology of archaeological excavation.[140]

Noting that shipwrecks in coastal waters had already been the subject of 'severe looting', it made the point that much of the UCH that remained unexplored was on the outer continental shelf or on the deep seabed; it also noted that deep-water shipwrecks are of 'particular importance' since for 'various chemical and biological reasons' they are likely to be exceptionally well preserved. In its view, the application of salvage law encouraged removal of material for commercial purposes and therefore promoted damage to, and destruction of, UCH.[141]

---

[134] 1994 ILA Draft, Art. 8.   [135] Ibid., Art. 7.   [136] Ibid., Art. 10.
[137] Resolution 5.5.1, para. 15.
[138] UNESCO Secretariat, 'Feasibility Study for the Drafting of a New Instrument for the Protection of the Underwater Cultural Heritage', presented to the 146th Session of the UNESCO Executive Board, Paris, 23 March 1995, Doc. 146 EX/27.
[139] Ibid., para. 29.   [140] Ibid., para. 11.   [141] Ibid., para. 32.

Noting the LOSC's provisions for UCH, the study concluded that these were 'not adequate'.[142] Moreover, since the 'general thrust' of the LOSC was not related to UCH protection, it also concluded that it would not be appropriate to deal with the inadequacy 'by way of amendment or Protocol to' the LOSC.[143] It pointed out that, when consulted by the ILA about a possible treaty on UCH, the response of other international organisations had been one of disinterest: the UN Division for Ocean Affairs and the Law of the Sea (DOALOS) did not reply;[144] the IMO indicated that it was interested only in wrecks that posed a hazard to navigation; and the CMI indicated that it was not directly interested in the topic.[145]

The feasibility study identified three 'major issues' that would need to be resolved: first, issues relating to jurisdiction, not simply the extent of coastal state jurisdiction in respect of UCH, but also the question of how to control activities on the deep seabed beyond the limits of national jurisdiction; secondly, the place of salvage law; and thirdly, the adoption of archaeological standards by which to judge the appropriateness of activities.[146]

The overall conclusion of the study was that it would be feasible to elaborate an instrument for the protection of UCH. However, at its meeting in May 1995, the UNESCO Executive Board decided that more time was required for examination of the issues, particularly those relating to jurisdiction.[147] At the 28th Session of the UNESCO General Conference which took place in October/November 1995, it was evident that all member states (to whom both the 1994 ILA Draft and the feasibility study had been circulated) regarded the matter as one of major concern.[148] The Director-General was therefore invited to organise, in consultation with the UN and the IMO, a meeting of experts in archaeology, salvage and jurisdictional regimes to consider the matter further. At this meeting, in May 1996, it was unanimously

---

[142] Ibid., para. 42.   [143] Ibid.

[144] DOALOS, the Secretariat for the LOSC, did cooperate with UNESCO at a later stage. However, its position was awkward because of questions regarding the relationship between the two treaties. For contrasting perspectives on this matter, see Blumberg, 'International Protection of Underwater Cultural Heritage', pp. 502–3 and O'Keefe, Shipwrecked Heritage, p. 29.

[145] UNESCO, Feasibility Study, para. 18. See also O'Keefe, 'International Waters', p. 231.

[146] UNESCO, Feasibility Study, para. 21.

[147] See Clement, 'Current Developments at UNESCO Concerning the Protection of the Underwater Cultural Heritage', p. 311.

[148] Ibid., p. 312.

accepted that there was a need for a convention and this was reported back to the 29th Session of the UNESCO General Conference in October 1997. The Conference invited the Director-General to prepare a first draft.

A preliminary draft text based on the 1994 ILA Draft, but amended in light of comments by states and by the meeting of experts, was published in 1998.[149] This draft (hereafter 1998 UNESCO Draft) was then discussed at two meetings of government-nominated experts. The first took place in June/July 1998 and the second in April 1999. A revised draft, adopted by the participants at the second meeting, formed the basis for work at a third meeting held in July 2000, but was not formally amended at that meeting.[150] The Director-General of UNESCO made it clear that a fourth meeting, scheduled for March/April 2001, was to be the last meeting before a text was finalised.[151] At that meeting, attention focused on a Single Negotiating Text produced by the Chairman.[152] At this stage, there were three particular issues on which agreement still needed to be reached: the core questions of coastal state jurisdiction and salvage law, and a further issue: sunken warships.

The potential for the issue of sunken warships to cause difficulties in the creation of an international legal regime for UCH was a matter that had come to light when the ILA was laying its groundwork for the treaty. A number of the major maritime states maintain that the sovereign immunity of warships and other state vessels and aircraft continues after they have been wrecked at sea and that, consequently, no one may interfere with such wrecks without the express consent of the flag state. This claim is disputed by other states. Given the political sensitivity of the issue, and the desire to avoid becoming mired down in it, the 1994 ILA Draft had simply excluded sunken warships and other state vessels and aircraft from its scope of application. This approach was also followed by the 1998 UNESCO Draft. However, commentators pointed out that such exclusion would seriously undermine the entire purpose of the new treaty because sunken warships form an important component of UCH. Efforts were therefore made to

---

[149] Doc. CLT-96/Conf.202/5, April 1998. For a discussion of this draft, see Dromgoole and Gaskell, 'Draft UNESCO Convention on the Protection of the Underwater Cultural Heritage 1998'. The text of the 1998 draft, along with explanatory comments, can be found appended to that article.

[150] Doc. CLT-96/CONF.205/5 Rev. 2, July 1999. This draft was a working text and will not be considered further here.

[151] See O'Keefe, *Shipwrecked Heritage*, p. 30.   [152] *Ibid.*

include state vessels and aircraft within the scope of the Convention, but to make special provision which would take account of the status claimed for them by some flag states.

By the end of the scheduled period for the fourth meeting, an acceptable compromise had been found on the salvage law question. However, no agreement had been reached on the other two outstanding issues. The meeting was therefore extended by a further six days in July 2001.[153] Despite this extension and efforts to accommodate the concerns of flag states, compromise formulas with respect to the wording of the provisions relating to coastal state jurisdiction on the continental shelf and in the EEZ, and sunken warships, could not be found. As a result, the Chairman's Single Negotiating Text, with amendments, was put to a vote and adopted by forty-nine votes in favour, four against and eight abstentions. On 29 October 2001, at the 31st Session of the UNESCO General Conference, a recommendation that the Text be adopted was debated by Programme Commission IV. Amendments were proposed by several of the maritime states and rejected. The Text was then approved by ninety-four votes in favour to five against, with nineteen abstentions.[154] On 2 November 2001, the Text was formally adopted in plenary session by eighty-seven votes in favour,[155] four against[156] and fifteen abstentions.[157] On 6 November 2001, it was signed by the Director-General of UNESCO and the President of the General Conference and opened for accession.[158]

First-hand commentaries on the negotiations make it clear that they were characterised by tensions with respect to both substantive and

---

[153] The time constraints imposed by UNESCO and its handling of other procedural matters at the end of the negotiations upset a number of the participating states, especially those who were unsatisfied with the text. See the Statements on Vote of the Netherlands, Turkey and the UK, reproduced in Camarda and Scovazzi, *The Protection of the Underwater Cultural Heritage*, pp. 424–5, 432 and 432–3. See also the Statement on Vote by Greece set out in Strati, 'Greece' (2nd edn), pp. 118–20. On the US viewpoint, see Blumberg, 'International Protection of Underwater Cultural Heritage', p. 503 n. 17.

[154] The extra vote against was accounted for by the USA, whose contra-vote was recorded.

[155] No formal record was kept of those states voting in favour. The varying numbers of votes in favour, and abstentions, on the different voting occasions were accounted for partly by the fact that not all states were present on each occasion and partly by some states shifting their positions.

[156] Russian Federation, Norway, Turkey and Venezuela.

[157] Brazil, the Czech Republic, Colombia, France, Germany, Greece, Iceland, Israel, Guinea-Bissau, the Netherlands, Paraguay, Sweden, Switzerland, Uruguay and the UK.

[158] UNESCO's treaty-making procedures do not include a process whereby states can indicate by signature their consent to be bound prior to (but also subject to) the deposit of their instrument of adherence: see, further, O'Keefe, *Shipwrecked Heritage*, p. 141.

procedural matters.[159] Inevitably, the most fundamental area of dispute was the question of coastal state jurisdiction, with the majority of participants supporting an extension of coastal state jurisdiction on the continental shelf in the interests of UCH protection and a vocal minority opposing such an extension. Arguments about the question of compatibility with the LOSC (whether the proposals were compatible or not, and also whether they *needed* to be compatible, or not) were used by both sides to support their positions.

Among those states that failed to vote in favour of the Convention were a number of maritime states. Russia and Norway voted against the Convention; France, Germany, the Netherlands and the UK abstained. The USA did not have a vote because it was not a member of UNESCO at the time. However, it too expressed serious reservations about the final Text. All of these states were dissatisfied with the provisions relating to coastal state jurisdiction on the continental shelf and in the EEZ, and several were also dissatisfied with the provisions with respect to sunken warships.[160] Nonetheless, in statements made at the end of the negotiations, they also made it clear that they strongly supported the Convention's general principles and objectives and were disappointed that their concerns had not been overcome.[161]

Notably, two other states that abstained, or voted against the Convention, were Greece and Turkey. The fact that the Convention did not provide full and direct coastal state jurisdiction over UCH on the continental shelf (in other words, turn the continental shelf into a 'cultural protection zone') was a bitter disappointment for Greece after its long campaign on this issue. Having accepted compromises on salvage law and commercial exploitation, it clearly considered it a step too far to accept the concessions that had been made with respect to coastal state jurisdiction.[162] It was also dissatisfied with the concessions made with

---

[159] See, for example, O'Keefe, who provides a fascinating account of the intense efforts made by participants at the fourth meeting to reach consensus, as well as of the politics of the negotiations: *Shipwrecked Heritage*, pp. 25–32. See also Garabello, 'The Negotiating History of the Convention on the Protection of the Underwater Cultural Heritage'; Espósito and Fraile, 'The UNESCO Convention on Underwater Cultural Heritage', pp. 204–9.

[160] France, Germany, Russia, the UK and the USA.

[161] See Statements on Vote for all the relevant maritime states with the exception of Germany, reproduced in Garabello and Scovazzi, *The Protection of the Underwater Cultural Heritage*, pp. 239–53.

[162] Not without reason, Greece regarded the provisions with respect to the continental shelf and EEZ as over-complicated and difficult to enforce: see the Statement on Vote by Greece set out in Strati, 'Greece' (2nd edn), pp. 118–20.

respect to warships.[163] The opposition of Turkey centred on the fact that it is not a state party to the LOSC and therefore had issues with respect to the technical relationship between the two treaties.[164]

3.1.3 Development and status of the Annex

A major contribution of the ILA's Committee on Cultural Heritage Law to the development of the UNESCO Convention was its recognition at an early stage in its work that there was a need for a set of archaeological standards to govern activities directed at UCH.[165] Such standards would provide guidance for the competent national authorities in making a judgement about whether or not activities were acceptable and would also ensure uniformity of practice. In 1991, the ILA Committee had called on a newly established scientific committee of the International Council on Monuments and Sites (ICOMOS)[166] to assist with the drafting of such standards.

The ICOMOS International Committee on the Underwater Cultural Heritage (ICUCH) embarked on the task of preparing a set of principles, or 'Charter', to be appended to the draft treaty[167] and the eventual outcome of the process was the International Charter on the Protection and Management of Underwater Cultural Heritage, which was adopted by the 11th General Assembly of ICOMOS in Sofia, Bulgaria, in 1996.[168] The UNESCO Convention includes an Annex which is closely based on this Charter.

An important question for the ILA Committee and, later, also for the UNESCO negotiators, was the relationship that the benchmark standards should have with the treaty itself. Such a question is not uncommon in treaty-making. Should the standards have the same status as the treaty, or a lesser legal status, in other words that of a non-binding code of practice to which the treaty simply refers? If the standards were to be

---

[163] *Ibid.* The Greek concern on this issue related not only to the provisions in the Convention relating to sunken warships but also to a provision (Art. 13) relating to operational warships: see, further, Chap. 8, n. 101.
[164] See Turkey's Statement on Vote, reproduced in Camarda and Scovazzi, *The Protection of the Underwater Cultural Heritage*, p. 432.
[165] O'Keefe, *Shipwrecked Heritage*, p. 21.
[166] ICOMOS is 'an international non-governmental organisation of professionals, dedicated to the conservation of the world's historic monuments and sites': see www.icomos.org.
[167] For details of the process, see Grenier, 'The Annex', pp. 111–12.
[168] The International Charter on the Protection and Management of Underwater Cultural Heritage 1996 supplements the ICOMOS Charter for the Protection and Management of Archaeological Heritage 1990.

afforded treaty status, should they be incorporated in the main text of the treaty, or in an annex? The option most generally favoured during the UNESCO negotiations was to give the standards binding force through some form of incorporation in the treaty. However, this then gave rise to the question of amendment. The process of treaty amendment is notoriously difficult and time-consuming, and the standards are intended to reflect prevailing good practice. If they were to be an integral part of the treaty, how could it be ensured that they keep pace with changing archaeological theory and practice? The 1994 ILA Draft allowed for ICOMOS to make revisions to the appended 'Charter' from time to time, permitting states parties effectively to 'opt-out' from amendments to which they did not consent.[169] However, as pointed out by O'Keefe, one difficulty with this approach is that over the course of time different states parties may end up applying different standards.[170] It became apparent too that the notion that a non-governmental organisation such as ICOMOS could make revisions binding on states parties, even with some provision for opt-out, would be unacceptable to some states.

The position taken by the Convention on this matter is as follows:

> The Rules annexed to this Convention form an integral part of it and, unless expressly provided otherwise, a reference to this Convention includes a reference to the Rules.[171]

This means that the 'Rules' in the Annex to the UNESCO Convention are not just a code of practice or guidelines, but have the status of binding treaty provisions. No special provision is made for the revision of the Annex and, instead, it is subject to the general amendment procedures applicable to the rest of the Convention.[172]

The significance of the Annex for the Convention as a whole is difficult to overstate. The Rules in the Annex are not simply an integral part of the Convention in a technical sense; they are integral to its entire spirit and ethos.[173] This is illustrated by the fact that a number of the fundamental principles of the Convention are simply reiterations of the general principles of the annexed Rules. Given that these Rules derived from

---

[169] 1994 ILA Draft, Art. 15. See also 1998 UNESCO Draft, Art. 24, which followed the approach of the 1994 ILA Draft but made provision for the formal notification of states parties of revisions.

[170] O'Keefe, 'Protecting the Underwater Cultural Heritage', p. 302.

[171] UNESCO Convention, Art. 33.

[172] See UNESCO Convention, Art. 32. For a discussion of the amendment procedures, see Chap. 10, section 6.

[173] See Grenier, 'The Annex', p. 120.

the ICOMOS Charter,[174] it is clear that the work of ICOMOS – a body with professional expertise in the heritage sector – had a profound influence on the final shape of the Convention.

At the conclusion of the UNESCO negotiations, the Annex was widely praised, including by those states unable to support the Convention as a whole. At the time, a number indicated that they would adopt, or at least consider adopting, the Rules in their national law and practice.[175]

3.2   The UNESCO Convention 2001: overview

The UNESCO Convention 2001 is a substantial and technically complex treaty. The main body of the text contains thirty-five articles and the Annex includes an additional thirty-six Rules. The conventional regime is governed by a number of overarching objectives and general principles. These are enunciated in Article 2 and in Part I of the Annex, and referred to in the preamble and other parts of the text.

The treaty 'aims to ensure and strengthen the protection of underwater cultural heritage'[176] and its overall objective is the preservation of UCH 'for the benefit of humanity'.[177] The preamble recognises that cooperation between states, other organisations and interested parties 'is essential' for the protection of UCH[178] and the principle that 'states parties shall cooperate in the protection of underwater cultural heritage' – set out in Article 2(2) – is a cornerstone of the Convention.[179]

As far as its material scope of application is concerned, in general terms the Convention follows the approach of the 1994 ILA Draft. 'Underwater cultural heritage' is defined broadly to include 'all traces of human existence having a cultural, historical or archaeological character which have been partially or totally underwater, periodically or continuously, for at least 100 years'.[180] Arguments made by certain states that the definition should include a criterion based on 'significance' were rejected. On two specific aspects of its material scope, the Convention does not follow the ILA approach. First, in order to avoid

---

[174] During the governmental expert meetings, some modifications were made to the language adopted by the Charter in order to reflect the conventional status of the Annex and a few amendments of a more substantive nature were made for political reasons. See Garabello, 'The Negotiating History of the Convention on the Protection of the Underwater Cultural Heritage', pp. 183–92; see also O'Keefe, *Shipwrecked Heritage*, p. 152.

[175] See, for example, the Statements on Vote by France and Norway reproduced in Camarda and Scovazzi, *The Protection of the Underwater Cultural Heritage*, pp. 427 and 430.

[176] Art. 2(1).   [177] Art. 2(3).   [178] Preambular clause 10.   [179] Art. 2(2).

[180] Art. 1(1)(a).

potentially difficult questions relating to the rights of identifiable owners, the 1994 ILA Draft applied only to UCH 'which has been lost or abandoned'.[181] The difficulty of defining the notion of abandonment led to this approach being dropped and the final text of the Convention says nothing about ownership rights, private or public. However, it does recognise that some states may have a special interest in certain UCH and caters for this interest by introducing a novel concept: the notion that states may have a 'verifiable link' to UCH. Secondly, unlike the 1994 ILA Draft, the Convention applies to sunken warships and other state vessels and aircraft, but makes specific provision for them which varies according to the maritime zone in which they are located.

An important distinction drawn by the Convention is between two forms of activities affecting UCH: those that are 'directed at' UCH and those 'incidentally affecting' UCH. Activities 'directed at' UCH are defined to mean 'activities having underwater cultural heritage as their primary object and which may, directly or indirectly, physically disturb or otherwise damage underwater cultural heritage'.[182] Activities 'incidentally affecting' UCH, on the other hand, are defined to mean 'activities which, despite not having underwater cultural heritage as their primary object or one of their objects, may physically disturb or otherwise damage underwater cultural heritage'.[183] The Convention focuses on controlling the former, although it also includes some significant provision with respect to the latter. The bulk of the conventional framework is designed to ensure that activities 'directed at' UCH are undertaken in accordance with the archaeological benchmark standards enshrined in the Annex.

Parts II–XIV of the Annex include detailed rules covering all aspects of archaeological project management, including: project design, funding and timetable; the competence and qualifications of the project team; conservation and site management; reporting and dissemination of results; and curation of project archives. The Convention adopts the fundamental archaeological principle that remains should be protected *in situ* wherever possible and provides that preservation *in situ* must be considered as the 'first option' before activities directed at UCH are allowed or engaged in.[184] Activities directed at UCH may be authorised only in a manner consistent with the protection of that heritage[185] and shall not adversely affect that heritage more than is necessary to achieve

---

[181] 1994 ILA Draft, Art. 2(1).   [182] Art. 1(6).   [183] Art. 1(7).   [184] Art. 2.
[185] Rule 1.

the objectives of the project.[186] Non-destructive techniques and survey methods must be used in preference to recovery of objects.[187] If excavation or recovery is deemed necessary 'for the purpose of scientific studies or for the ultimate protection' of the UCH, the methods used must be as non-destructive as possible.[188] Where UCH is recovered, it must be deposited, conserved and managed in a manner that ensures its long-term preservation.[189] States parties must ensure that proper respect is given to all human remains located in maritime waters[190] and activities directed at UCH must therefore avoid the unnecessary disturbance of human remains or venerated sites.[191] In line with the overall objective that humanity should reap the benefit of the protective regime, non-intrusive access to observe or document *in situ* UCH is encouraged.[192] Furthermore, the project archives – including any recovered UCH – as far as possible must be kept together and intact in a manner that is available for both professional and public access.[193]

As the experience of the Council of Europe demonstrated, attempts to exclude the application of salvage law to UCH in the text of a binding international instrument will meet with political resistance from some common law states. The final text of the UNESCO Convention replaced the clear-cut exclusion of salvage law in the 1994 ILA Draft with a compromise provision. This severely curtails – but does not totally exclude – the application of salvage law and the related law of finds.

A central tenet of the Convention is its commitment to the principle that there should be no commercial exploitation of the archaeological heritage. The centrality of this principle to the initiative arose in part from the deep international concern about increasing levels of commercial exploitation and, in part, from the input of ICOMOS. The view that commercial exploitation is fundamentally incompatible with the protection and management of archaeological heritage is one that is deeply held by much of the international heritage community. However, the question of whether or not the treaty scheme should allow some room for the involvement of commercially motivated organisations was a contentious one. The US delegation, in particular, was of the view that it should. Ultimately, a compromise was struck. The principle that there should be no commercial exploitation is set down in a simple and unqualified form in Article 2(7). However, it is

---

[186] Rule 3.   [187] Rule 4.   [188] Rule 4.   [189] Art. 2(6).
[190] Art. 2(9). (Human remains are encompassed within the definition of UCH in Art. 1(1)(a).)
[191] Rule 5.   [192] Art. 2(10).   [193] Rule 33.

elaborated upon in Rule 2 of the Annex and this incorporates two carefully delimited provisos to the general principle.

In the interests of ensuring the uniform application of the annexed Rules to all areas of the sea, provision is made for each of the recognised maritime zones, *including* the territorial sea and other areas under coastal state sovereignty.[194] However, at the heart of the treaty are the provisions with respect to the continental shelf and EEZ, and the Area. Articles 9 and 10 create a complex regulatory framework for the continental shelf and EEZ, which involves a reporting and notification procedure, and the taking of various forms of protective action by states parties, acting alone and in concert. In attempting to create a formula acceptable to flag states, Articles 9 and 10 incorporate a number of constructive ambiguities[195] and accord a special role to a 'Coordinating State', which may or may not be the coastal state. The provisions in Articles 11 and 12, which relate to the Area, reflect the form – if not the entire substance – of Articles 9 and 10.

As a supplement to the provisions relating to each of the maritime zones, Articles 14, 15 and 16 oblige states parties to make use of the territorial and nationality principles of jurisdiction to counter activities that are contrary to the Convention. This reflects a view expressed by the ILA Committee that a 'responsible regime of control must, *at a minimum*, apply accepted general principles of international jurisdiction'.[196] Evidence of the ILA's influence is also found in Articles 17 and 18, which require states parties to impose sanctions for the violation of measures taken to implement the Convention, including the seizure of UCH where it has been recovered contrary to the terms of the Convention.

Underpinning the entire treaty framework is the principle that states parties must cooperate in the protection of UCH. The all-important regulatory regimes it creates for the continental shelf and EEZ, and the Area are dependent upon states parties sharing information and taking collaborative and coordinated action. The Convention also establishes a more general framework for cooperation, information-sharing and

---

[194] Art. 7. Art. 8 makes provision for the contiguous zone. When ratifying the Convention, or at any time thereafter, states may choose to declare that the Rules shall apply to inland waters too: see Art. 28.

[195] Ambiguity is also used as a device in Art. 3, which sets out the relationship between the Convention and the LOSC.

[196] ILA, Cairo Conference (1992), International Committee on Cultural Heritage Law, Report and Draft Convention for Consideration at the 1992 Conference, p. 13. Emphasis added.

mutual assistance by states parties for the purposes of UCH protection, and envisages that – over time – participating states will develop broad-ranging collaborative efforts on a whole host of matters, including investigation, excavation, documentation, conservation, study and presentation of UCH,[197] and training.[198] Furthermore, states parties are encouraged to enter into formal bilateral, regional or other multilateral agreements, or to develop existing agreements, for the preservation of UCH, provided such agreements are 'in full conformity' with the Convention and do not 'dilute its universal character'.[199]

The treaty does not create a permanent body, such as the ISA, to implement the Convention on behalf of states parties, nor one that might review its implementation, such as the Standing Committee proposed in the 1985 draft European Convention. Instead, implementation is left to the states parties themselves,[200] with the assistance of a Secretariat within UNESCO.[201] Provision is made for a Meeting of States Parties to be convened on a regular basis and for that Meeting to decide on its own functions and responsibilities.[202] The influence of the LOSC is clear in some of the procedural aspects of the Convention. As with the LOSC, reservations to the Convention are prohibited (unless expressly provided for)[203] and the provision made for the settlement of disputes incorporates the complex compulsory dispute settlement machinery in the LOSC.[204] Also, the process of amending the treaty is onerous and reflects, to some extent, the amendment procedures enshrined in the LOSC.

4. Concluding remarks

Of the three 'major issues' identified by the 1995 UNESCO feasibility study as needing to be satisfactorily addressed by a new international instrument on UCH, two were dealt with successfully. The compromise the UNESCO Convention 2001 enshrines on the question of salvage law is politically acceptable and the standards set out in its Annex by which the appropriateness of activities must be judged appear to be universally supported by states. Indeed, the Annex is undoubtedly the Convention's greatest achievement to date. However, there remain two stumbling blocks in the way of the Convention becoming a fully effective global

---

[197] Art. 19.   [198] Art. 21.   [199] Art. 6.
[200] Each State Party must establish competent authorities, or reinforce existing ones, to ensure the proper implementation of the Convention: Art. 22.
[201] Art. 24 makes provision for the Secretariat for the Convention.   [202] Art. 23.
[203] Art. 30.   [204] Art. 25.

regime: the old chestnut of coastal state jurisdiction and the relatively new concern relating to the treatment of sunken warships. Although the device of constructive ambiguity has been deployed successfully in the field of UCH protection on a number of occasions to accommodate differing viewpoints, with respect to these issues the tactic appears to have failed (at least so far) to achieve its objective.

2 Defining underwater cultural heritage

1. Introduction

How one should go about defining the subject matter of a legal instrument designed to afford protection to an aspect of the cultural heritage, in other words determine the material scope of application of that instrument, depends upon the nature of the protective measures that are proposed. If the instrument will affect and, in particular, restrict human activities, then clearly an appropriate balance needs to be struck between the restriction imposed and the benefit derived from the restriction. In the context of archaeological remains lying *in situ*, a proposal effectively to *prohibit* human interference (apart from in circumstances such as force majeure or necessity) is likely to be applied only to material of exceptional significance; on the other hand, a broadly framed definition would be quite appropriate for an instrument that merely requires the reporting of discoveries. The most common approach, lying somewhere between these two extremes, is the imposition of a system for the authorisation of activities to ensure that they are conducted appropriately. In this case, it might be regarded as appropriate to apply the measure to a broad range of material but then to take account of the particular significance of the material when determining whether or not authorisation is granted, and on what terms.

What, then, is UCH and how should it be defined? If one takes the modern general term 'underwater cultural heritage' and considers its meaning at a basic level, it is clear that it could encompass a very broad range of tangible things.[1] The word 'heritage' implies that something

---

[1] Although the focus of this book (and the focus of the UNESCO Convention 2001) is on the protection of tangible aspects of UCH, it should be noted that the notion of intangible cultural heritage is by no means irrelevant in the context of UCH. For example, indigenous cultures may regard certain marine and freshwater sites and spaces as having

has a value or quality which is worthy of protection so that it can be passed on to future generations; the word 'cultural' suggests something that is related to human beings; and the word 'underwater' implies something that is, or at least *was*, located underwater. As technology has advanced and gradually opened up marine areas to the possibility of human investigation, perceptions about the nature and worth of UCH have changed and developed. Shipwrecks, by virtue of their number and physical mass, are the main constituent of UCH: for this reason, and also because they tend to be the target of treasure hunters and souvenir seekers – and give rise to some unique and complex legal issues – attention often focuses upon them. However, UCH comprises far more than just shipwrecks. In coastal areas, a wide range of evidence may be found of human occupation over millennia, ranging from primitive fish-traps and shell-middens to the remnants of harbours and settlements that have become submerged over time.[2] On parts of the continental shelf, submerged prehistoric land-surfaces exist, the archaeological potential of which is only now really beginning to be appreciated.[3] On the deep ocean floor, along with shipwrecks, other forms of UCH are likely to be aircraft wrecks and the remains of space technology that have fallen into the sea.[4] In fresh waters, such as lakes and rivers, a wide range of remains may be found, including

---

spiritual or other special significance. On an international level, there is increasing interest in the safeguarding of cultural spaces of this sort, as well as in the broader notion of safeguarding landscapes, including seascapes. See, for example, the UNESCO Convention for the Safeguarding of the Intangible Cultural Heritage 2003 and two Council of Europe treaties, the European Landscape Convention 2000 and the Framework Convention on the Value of Cultural Heritage for Society 2005. A suggestion that 'sites with spiritual associations for indigenous peoples' be included in the definition of UCH for the purposes of the UNESCO Convention 2001 was rejected: see O'Keefe, *Shipwrecked Heritage*, p. 162. Nonetheless, such sites may benefit from the Convention's scheme: see, further, Chap. 9, n. 71.

[2] One example of a submerged settlement is the Iranian port of Siraf, much of which is now submerged, which has a history dating back 1,100 years: *Tehran Times*, 23 July 2012. Garabello refers to three potential causes of such submergence: Bradyseism (earth movements caused by volcanic activity), erosion and earthquake: Garabello, 'The Negotiating History of the Convention on the Protection of the Underwater Cultural Heritage', p. 103.

[3] For example, an extensive area surrounding the British Isles and covering much of the North Sea was dry land during the last Ice Age and is now the subject of intense archaeological interest: see, generally, Gaffney, Fitch and Smith, *Europe's Lost World*.

[4] The ocean floor is littered with space debris of varying degrees of cultural significance. For example, in 2012 it was reported that the engines from the Apollo 11 space mission in 1969 had been located 4,270 metres below the surface of the Atlantic Ocean: 'Jeff Bezos plans to recover Apollo 11 engines from Atlantic seabed', *Guardian*, 31 March 2012.

vessels, vehicles[5] and aircraft, isolated objects that may have been lost or discarded, and ancient lake-dwellings and burial sites.

This chapter traces the development of approaches to defining subject matter in international legal instruments which afford, or were designed to afford, protection to UCH. In the first section, it looks at the approach of early domestic legislation, which inevitably had an influence on later international approaches; in the second, it considers the approach of international instruments which preceded and influenced the development of the UNESCO Convention 2001; and in the third, it examines the approach taken by the UNESCO Convention itself.

Very often the definitions of subject matter employed in heritage laws include two types of criteria. One sets out the type of subject matter that is *capable* of being afforded protection by the legislation; the other limits the scope of the definition by reference to some value, or other factor indicative of value, which determines what is to be protected *in fact*.[6] For example, if one takes the phrase employed by Articles 149 and 303 of the LOSC to define their subject matter – 'objects of an archaeological and historical nature' – the word 'objects' describes the subject matter that is capable of being covered and the words 'of an archaeological and historical nature' describe the value that objects must possess in order to be covered in fact. Quite often, rather than expressing the value by a description in this way (or, in some cases, as well as doing so) instruments adopt a temporal criterion as an indication of value, for example by applying to objects 'that have been underwater for at least 100 years'. The terms 'definitional criteria' and 'selection criteria' have been proposed to distinguish the two aspects of a definition and this terminology is employed in this chapter.[7]

2. The approach of early domestic legislation

The need for domestic legislation to control human activities in order to avoid damage to, or destruction of, UCH started to become appreciated in the 1950s and 1960s, when scuba-diving first became a popular

---

[5] An unusual example of such a vehicle was a rare Bugatti car which was recovered from Lake Maggiore in Switzerland in 2009, seventy-three years after it was apparently dumped in the water by an irate tax inspector: see '€260,500 paid for Bugatti in the lake', *Independent*, 25 January 2010.

[6] This distinction was identified by Thomas: see Thomas, 'Heritage Protection Criteria'.

[7] See *ibid*. Thomas was writing in the specific context of UK heritage protection legislation. In this chapter, the use of the terms has been adapted to suit the international context. In particular, the selection criteria of the legislation analysed by Thomas did not include temporal elements and instead always entailed a subjective judgement of value.

activity.[8] Some states already had general cultural protection laws in place that were designed to protect terrestrial archaeological remains but extended to marine, as well as inland, waters. This was the case for a number of the states bordering the Mediterranean, such as Greece and Turkey. The legislation of these states made provision for the protection of all material deemed to be encompassed within the broad notions of 'antiquities' or 'monuments'.[9] These terms were not defined, but were interpreted as meaning remains of ancient origin. In other parts of the world, initially the only applicable legislation with respect to interference with material in the marine environment was designed with rather different objectives in mind than cultural heritage protection. In a number of common law states, the only relevant law was general maritime law designed to deal with recent maritime casualties. Provision was made for the salvage of maritime property and the determination of rights to recoveries of 'wreck'[10] on the basis of principles originating centuries ago.[11] In Scandinavia and other parts of northern Europe, there were equivalent systems of ancient origin relating to wreck or 'finds' of monetary value.[12] In neither system was there any means for *restraining* the recovery of material; on the contrary, the law positively encouraged such recovery by rewarding it.

In the 1960s and 1970s, a number of states introduced specific legislation to regulate interference with wreck sites in their coastal waters. After the spectacular recovery of the seventeenth-century warship *Vasa* in Sweden in 1961, Finland, Norway, Sweden and Denmark all put in place legislation to protect shipwrecks; in each case, the legislation adopted a temporal cut-off point for protection. In the case of the first three, a 100-year cut-off was used; the Danish legislation used 150

---

[8] See General introduction, section 1.1, above.

[9] For discussions of the legislation of Greece and Turkey, see Strati, 'Greece' (1st edn), pp. 66–75 and Blake, 'Turkey', pp. 172–7.

[10] The term 'wreck' is defined differently in different states, but for statutory purposes is generally defined widely to encompass the hull of a vessel, its fixtures, fittings, cargo and stores, and any other articles carried on board. See Dromgoole, 'A Note on the Meaning of "Wreck"'.

[11] The scheme for wreck and salvage law set out in the UK Merchant Shipping Act 1894 was followed by a number of jurisdictions, including Ireland, Australia, New Zealand and South Africa. For an outline of the early origins of the principles enshrined in the Act, see Dromgoole and Gaskell, 'Interests in Wreck', pp. 178–80.

[12] See, generally, Braekhus, 'Salvage of Wrecks and Wreckage'.

years.[13] In the UK, in response to a number of high-profile incidents resulting in serious damage to historically significant shipwrecks, the Protection of Wrecks Act 1973 was enacted. By virtue of this statute, sites of wrecked vessels which are deemed to be of 'historical, archaeological or artistic importance' may be designated for protection.[14] In 1976, the Australian Commonwealth Historic Shipwrecks Act was introduced in the wake of the discovery of four Dutch East India Company vessels off the coast of western Australia. This Act, in its original form, provided for the protection of shipwrecks and associated relics of 'historic significance'.[15]

In the second half of the 1980s, there was a new wave of activity by national legislatures and new approaches to the material scope of legislation started to emerge, including a gradual shift away from the focus on shipwrecks. In 1985, Australia amended its Historic Shipwrecks Act to introduce protection for all shipwrecks and associated relics that are at least seventy-five years old (from the date of wrecking), and including the possibility of specifically declaring younger shipwrecks for protection.[16] In 1986, South Africa amended its national monuments legislation, providing blanket protection for all wrecks over fifty years of age and prohibiting interference with, or disturbance of, such wrecks without authorisation.[17] In the USA, after it became apparent that the application of ordinary maritime law to shipwrecks of historical significance could result in patently inappropriate outcomes, federal legislation to protect shipwrecks was introduced. The US Abandoned Shipwreck Act of 1987 applies to 'a vessel or wreck, its cargo, and other contents', provided it is abandoned by its owner.[18] 'Abandonment' – a selection criterion – is not defined by the Act.[19] In the same year, in the light of events surrounding the discovery of a number of Spanish Armada wrecks, Ireland extended its general monuments legislation to include provision for wrecked vessels, as well as archaeological objects

---

[13] For discussion of the Finnish, Norwegian and Swedish legislation, see Matikka, 'Finland', pp. 47–51; Kvalø and Marstrander, 'Norway', p. 219; and Adlercreutz, 'Sweden', pp. 299–300.

[14] See, further, Dromgoole, 'United Kingdom', pp. 321–6. The 1973 Act remains in force and unamended at the time of writing.

[15] Jeffery, 'Australia' (1st edn), pp. 5–7.

[16] *Ibid.*, p. 7.

[17] Forrest, 'South Africa', p. 252. The National Monuments Act of South Africa has since been replaced by the National Heritage Resources Act 1999. See *ibid.*, pp. 254 *et seq.*

[18] On the Abandoned Shipwreck Act, see, further, Chap. 5, sections 3.4.1 and 3.4.2.

[19] On the concept of abandonment, see, further, Chap. 3, section 2.3.

more generally, lying on the seabed, provided they were over 100 years old or alternatively qualified as being of 'archaeological, historical or artistic importance'.[20] In 1989, France introduced new and innovative legislation which moved from a system based on offering some protection to wrecks of archaeological, historical or artistic interest, to one based on protecting a much broader category of 'maritime cultural assets'.[21] This concept is defined widely to include 'deposits, wrecks, remains or in general all assets of prehistoric, archaeological or historical interest'.[22]

For the most part, the legislation referred to above was designed to protect material from intentional human interference and it did this by establishing systems requiring the authorisation of activities. Generally speaking, there were three different approaches to the structure of the legislation: in some jurisdictions, the same provisions applied 'seamlessly' to both terrestrial and marine remains; in some, specific provision for UCH was included in general monuments legislation; and in others, an instrument specifically dedicated to UCH was enacted. Depending on the structure of the legislation, the nature of the waters covered tended to vary: where general monuments legislation extended to cover the marine zone, it usually applied in any event to inland waters as well; on the other hand, provisions designed specifically with UCH in mind tended to apply to marine waters only. A fundamental dichotomy was also apparent in the nature of the protection on offer: some of the laws provided for the designation of specific sites that had some special value or significance; others provided for 'blanket' protection of all remains categorised as antiquities or monuments, or qualifying under a temporal criterion. Occasionally (for example, under the Australian legislation as amended), a combination of both methods was used. Another quite striking difference reflected the attitudes taken to the question of how old something must be in order to merit protection. These reflected national historical backgrounds. At one end of the spectrum, for Greece and Turkey the focus of concern inevitably was on their immense wealth of monuments and artefacts from ancient times. At the other end of the spectrum, the first vessel to be declared as 'historic' under the Australian Historic Shipwrecks Act was a twentieth-century Japanese submarine, *I-124*, which sank in 1942.[23]

---

[20] See O'Connor, 'Ireland' (1st edn), p. 89.
[21] Law No. 89-874. See Le Gurun, 'France' (lst edn), pp. 45–6.   [22] *Ibid.*, p. 45.
[23] The *I-124* was the first vessel to have been sunk by the Royal Australian Navy in the Second World War.

3.   The approach of international initiatives preceding the UNESCO Convention 2001

As discussed in Chapter 1, the UNESCO Convention 2001 was the culmination of an evolutionary process in the development of international law in the field of UCH protection taking place over more than four decades. In the following sections, the approaches to defining UCH taken by the international initiatives which preceded the UNESCO Convention are given some consideration.

3.1   The Law of the Sea Convention 1982

The notion that the LOSC should make some provision for the protection of UCH originated at a time when the discipline of marine archaeology was in its infancy, and the focus of international attention was on the plight of UCH in the Mediterranean Sea. Article 149 – the first of the two relevant articles in the Convention to be drafted – was prompted by a proposal by Greece which led to UCH being included in the UN Sea-Bed Committee's list of topics to be dealt with by the legal regime envisaged for the deep seabed. The Greek proposal referred to 'Archaeological and Historical Treasures' and this expression was adopted in the list itself.[24] By the first substantive session of UNCLOS III in 1974, the text on the table referred to 'objects of an archaeological and historical nature'.[25] Both Articles 149 and 303 use this phrase and it appears to have the same meaning in both articles.

The fact that the word 'objects' was incorporated in the definition of the subject matter of Articles 149 and 303 is perfectly understandable given the nature of the discoveries made in the Mediterranean in the period leading up to UNCLOS III. It was not only ancient wrecks and submerged coastal structures that had been discovered, but also many isolated objects, including ancient bronze and marble statues, as well as scattered items of ancient cargoes, including *amphorae*, metal ingots and pottery sherds.[26] Nonetheless, it seems odd that the word 'objects' was used as the *sole* definitional criterion since it does not seem entirely apt to describe fixed structures, or ancient wrecks that may well have largely disintegrated or become embedded in sand or mud.

---

[24] Strati, *The Protection of the Underwater Cultural Heritage*, p. 297.

[25] *Ibid.*, pp. 298–9.

[26] See Strati, 'Greece' (1st edn), pp. 65–6; Blake, 'Turkey', pp. 169–70. In some cases, the number of objects associated with a wreck cargo ran into hundreds or even thousands: see Blake, *ibid.*

Unless it is established that the parties to an international agreement intended a term to have a special meaning, which is not the case here, a term must be interpreted in good faith in accordance with its ordinary meaning in the context in which it is found and in light of the treaty's object and purpose.[27] The ordinary meaning of the word 'object' is a material thing and the word is generally associated with a thing that is movable. One might therefore question whether something that was originally a fixed, immovable, structure can qualify as an object. In civil law systems, such structures are likely to be characterised in legal terms as immovable property and in common law systems, as real property and associated 'fixtures'. A ship, when afloat, would constitute movable property (or, in common law, a form of personal property known as a 'chattel'); therefore, when afloat, the word 'object' to describe a ship does not seem inappropriate. Once sunk, this becomes more questionable. Whether a sunken hull continues to be treated legally as movable property (or a chattel) is a matter that varies between jurisdictions.[28] However, from a purely practical perspective, once it starts to disintegrate, or becomes incorporated into the seabed (thereby becoming difficult or even impossible to move in one piece or in sections), the word 'site' rather than 'object' would seem to be more appropriate. Nevertheless, in light of the object and purpose of Articles 149 and 303, and the context of the term as found therein, there is no reason to doubt that a broad interpretation was intended that would encompass fixed structures and shipwrecks. The fact that the word 'object' was the only word used may be simply a reflection of prevailing assumptions. In particular, it seems likely that it was assumed that what needed to be protected was material only once it had been discovered and that the obvious way to protect such discoveries was to recover them, rather than leaving them *in situ*.[29]

In order to fall within the scope of Articles 149 and 303, objects must be 'of an archaeological and historical nature'. This phrase represents the selection criterion. The word 'nature' is very broad in scope compared with other words sometimes employed in the selection criteria

---

[27] See Vienna Convention on the Law of Treaties 1969, Art. 31(1) and (3). On the rules on treaty interpretation more generally, see General introduction, section 3.2.1, above.

[28] See Prott and O'Keefe, *Law and the Cultural Heritage*, Vol. I, pp. 182 and 308–9, which discusses the interesting English case of *Elwes* v. *Brigg Gas Co.* (1886) 33 ChD 562 and a US case that followed it, *Allred* v. *Biegel* (1949) 219 SW 2d. 665.

[29] The wording of Arts. 149 and 303 indicates that such assumption may have been made. Art. 303(1) refers to objects 'found' at sea and Art. 149 to objects 'found' in the Area. In the case of the latter, provision is made for their preservation or 'disposal'.

of protective instruments. Words such as 'importance', 'significance', 'value' or 'interest' all introduce a limitation of some kind based on a value judgment, whereas the word 'nature' does nothing to limit the objects to which the articles apply. The limiting factor in the phrase therefore can only be the words 'archaeological and historical'. Although these words are frequently employed to describe the subject matter of protective legislation, it seems that during UNCLOS III no consideration was given to definitions in other contexts.[30] In commenting on the selection criteria in Articles 149 and 303, O'Keefe has pointed out that '[t]he adjective "archaeological" really has no meaning because archaeology is a process and not a description'. He went on to explain this further by saying: '[o]bjects cannot have an archaeological nature. What the drafters ... probably meant were objects which might, through the medium of archaeological interpretation, prove to be of value to humankind'.[31] There can be little disagreement with this, or indeed with O'Keefe's comment on the adjective 'historical': '[a]n object of an "historical nature" is obviously one which is associated with the history of humankind'.[32] In practice, the core uncertainty about the selection criterion used in Articles 149 and 303 is the question: when is an object too *young* to qualify?

Oxman, Vice-Chairman of the US delegation to UNCLOS III famously and controversially argued that the legislative history of the LOSC suggested that the term 'archaeological and historical nature' should be interpreted as covering only material that is 'many hundred of years old' and was not intended to apply to 'modern objects whatever their historical interest'.[33] He went on to suggest:

[I]t may be that if a rule of thumb is useful for deciding what is unquestionably covered ... the most appropriate of the years conventionally chosen to represent the start of the modern era would be 1453: the fall of Constantinople and the final collapse of the remnants of the Byzantine Empire. Everything older would clearly be regarded as archaeological or historical. A slight adjustment to 1492 for applying the article to objects indigenous to the Americas, extended perhaps

---

[30] Oxman, 'Marine Archaeology and the International Law of the Sea', p. 364.

[31] O'Keefe, *Shipwrecked Heritage*, p. 17.

[32] *Ibid.* The legislative history indicates that the word 'and' should be read as disjunctive, in other words that the 'and' should be read as an 'or' (see the intervention of the Tunisian delegation referred to below).

[33] See Oxman, 'Marine Archaeology and the International Law of the Sea', p. 364, quoting observations made by Oxman at the negotiations.

to the fall of Tenochtitlán (1521) or Cuzco (1533) in those areas, might have the merit of conforming to historical and cultural classifications in that part of the world.[34]

In making this statement, Oxman appears to have been influenced, at least in part, by the drafting history of Article 303 which shows that a reference to 'objects of historical origin' was added to the term 'archaeological objects' at the insistence of the Tunisian delegation, which felt that the expression 'archaeological objects' might not be broad enough to cover Byzantine relics.[35] Not only Oxman, but all those involved in the drafting process, would also have been influenced by the attitudes and approaches of the Mediterranean states more generally, including Greece and Turkey, whose domestic legislation was designed to protect the treasures of antiquity, in other words the period prior to the Middle Ages.

It is not surprising to find that, in making his assertion, Oxman was also influenced by the possibility that 'an unduly liberal reading of the term' 'could prejudice certain rights and principles that states were unwilling to yield' in the negotiations,[36] a reference to concerns about the expansion of coastal state powers on the continental shelf. As some justification for his restrictive view, he referred to the fact that Article 303 – by virtue of paragraph 3 – 'expressly does not affect the law of salvage'.[37] However, it hardly seems necessary to draw a cut-off several *centuries* ago in order to clearly distinguish between material subject to the law of salvage and material subject to protective provisions.[38] Moreover, the fact that Article 303(3) includes not only a saving for salvage law but also one for the rights of identifiable owners could be used to make precisely the opposite argument: why make such a saving if it is virtually inconceivable that the material in question could be subject to identifiable ownership rights?[39]

In any event, even before the text of the LOSC was finalised, doubt was expressed as to whether the articles were limited in the way Oxman

---

[34] Oxman, 'The Third United Nations Conference on the Law of the Sea', p. 241 n. 152.
[35] *Ibid.*   [36] Oxman, 'Marine Archaeology and the International Law of the Sea', p. 364.
[37] *Ibid.*
[38] Indeed, Strati has argued that a 100-year cut-off would be 'a reasonable time limit' to determine the scope of salvage law: Strati, *The Protection of the Underwater Cultural Heritage*, p. 173. Whether it is necessary clearly to separate the scope of salvage law and the scope of Art. 303 is in fact questionable: see, further, Chap. 5, section 3.1.
[39] On the question of establishing ownership rights in UCH, see, further, Chap. 3, section 2.2.

suggested. Caflisch, for example, asserted: 'It is far from certain ... that [Oxman's] very restrictive interpretation will prevail'.[40] Today, with the benefit of several decades of subsequent state practice to draw on, it is absolutely apparent that it has not.[41] While there has been little if any state practice with respect to Article 149, a substantial body of state practice has developed with respect to Article 303. A growing number of states are utilising the provision in paragraph 2 of that article with respect to removal of UCH from the contiguous zone and there is no evidence that it is being limited to material that is centuries old.[42] Similarly, there appears to be no such limitation with respect to practice that can be regarded as implementation of the duty to protect UCH, and to cooperate for that purpose, set out in paragraph 1 of Article 303. For example, as discussed above, there are several examples in domestic legislation of the use of 100-year thresholds for protection and, in some cases, more recent ones. Furthermore, Australia is far from alone in regarding specific twentieth-century sites as worthy of protection on account of their historical significance. Under the UK Protection of Wrecks Act, an early aircraft carrier and several early submarines have been designated for their historical significance.[43] In France, in 1994, a court at first instance determined that the *François Kléber*, a warship lost during the First World War, was eligible to be designated as a maritime cultural asset under French heritage legislation.[44] In Oxman's own nation, the USA, one of the most famous wreck sites on the National Register of Historic Places is the USS *Arizona*, lost at Pearl Harbor

---

[40] Caflisch, 'Submarine Antiquities and the International Law of the Sea', pp. 8–10.

[41] Art. 31(3) of the Vienna Convention on the Law of Treaties provides that account must be taken of 'any subsequent practice in the application of the treaty which establishes the agreement of the parties regarding its interpretation'. Aust has referred to subsequent practice as 'a most important element' of treaty interpretation: Aust, *Modern Treaty Law and Practice*, p. 241.

[42] On state practice in this respect, see Chap. 7, section 3.3.

[43] One of the submarines is the *Holland No. 5*, launched in 1902, one of a class of submarines used by the British Admiralty to assess the potential of such vessels as weapons. It had been adapted to include the then novel concept of a periscope to allow surface vision when the vessel was submerged. See www.english-heritage.org.uk/discover/maritime/map.

[44] Le Gurun, 'France' (1st edn), pp. 47–8. The court came to its conclusion on the basis that sunken warships from the Great War were 'patently connected' with the notion of a maritime cultural asset because they were 'remains of a glorious and tragic event of the history of [the] country'. Interestingly, the court also concluded that the same could not be said for the *Saracen*, a cargoship, despite the fact that it sank at the same time and in the same circumstances: *ibid*.

in 1941.[45] Indeed, there is no doubt that the USA now accepts that relatively recent remains fall within the scope of Article 303. In the late 1990s the USA was primarily responsible for the drafting of an international agreement to protect the *Titanic* (then less than 100 years old), the agreement referring in its preamble specifically to Article 303 as a relevant provision.[46] In 2001, a US Presidential Policy statement also stated, in the general context of sunken state vessels, aircraft *and* spacecraft: 'international law encourages nations to preserve objects of maritime heritage wherever located for the benefit of the public'.[47] Although the most prominent example of implementation by the international community of the duty to cooperate to protect UCH – the UNESCO Convention 2001 – uses a 100-year cut-off, a rule of thumb of fifty years is not out of line with general state practice.[48]

A distinction between the subject matter of Articles 149 and 303 is that Article 149 explicitly applies to *all* objects of an archaeological and historical nature, whereas the provisions of Article 303 apply to such objects generally and do not refer to 'all'. In fact, this distinction is a logical extension of the content of the articles. It would be impractical to oblige states to protect, and to cooperate to protect, all such objects found anywhere at sea and equally nonsensical to require them to regulate the removal of all such objects in the contiguous zone when they are not *required* to regulate removal in that zone, but merely given the option to do so. On the other hand, there is no logical reason to limit the aspirational protective objective enshrined in Article 149, or the preferential rights of states of origin referred to in that article.

---

[45] According to Varmer, although the relevant statute – the National Historic Preservation Act of 1966 – does not include a cut-off period for its scope of application, 'a 50-year rule of thumb for consideration of significance has developed as a matter of practice': Varmer, 'United States' (2nd edn), p. 375.

[46] The Agreement was negotiated by four states: the USA, the UK, France and Canada. For further discussion, see Chap. 7, section 4.3.

[47] Statement on United States Policy for the Protection of Sunken Warships, 19 January 2001, Weekly Compilation of Presidential Documents, 22 January 2001. On this statement, see, further, Chap. 4, section 2.2.

[48] An early draft of the provision that became Art. 149 specifically referred to material that was 'more than fifty years old'. Although this paragraph was dropped, it indicates that some of the negotiators had in mind a much less restrictive interpretation than that of Oxman. During the UNESCO negotiations, the US delegation suggested that a threshold of fifty years be adopted, which would have aligned the Convention with its domestic practice: see, further, section 4.2.1, below.

3.2   The Council of Europe initiatives

Over the course of the second half of the twentieth century, perceptions about the subject matter worthy of protection through general cultural heritage legislation evolved considerably, as did views about how that protection should be effected. A wider range of cultural values were gradually recognised and there was a trend towards a resource-based approach where the focus was on the management of the entire resource, rather than on the identification and preservation of select elements. These changes were reflected in both national and international heritage protection legislation and inevitably fed through to instruments relating to UCH specifically.

3.2.1   Recommendation 848 (1978)

The term 'underwater cultural heritage' was adopted for the first time in an international instrument in the title of the Council of Europe's Recommendation 848, which was incorporated in the Roper Report of 1978.[49] However, although Recommendation 848 related explicitly to 'the underwater cultural heritage', it did not attempt to define the phrase, nor was it referred to in the minimum legal requirements set out in the Recommendation. Instead, they referred in quite general terms to underwater objects and sites.[50]

Among the minimum requirements laid down by Recommendation 848 was the following:

[p]rotection should cover all objects that have been beneath the water for more than 100 years, but with the possibility of discretionary exclusion of less important objects (or less important antiquities) once they have been properly studied and recorded, and the inclusion of historically or artistically significant objects of more recent date.[51]

In considering this requirement, it needs to be borne in mind that Recommendation 848 was a non-binding instrument designed to encourage member states of the Council of Europe to adopt minimum standards in respect of their national legislation. As such, there was no need to establish precise criteria for the subject matter to which it referred (although there may have been some assumption that it related, at least

---

[49] Parliamentary Assembly of the Council of Europe, 'The Underwater Cultural Heritage: Report of the Committee on Culture and Education (Rapporteur: Mr. John Roper)', Document 4200-E, Strasbourg, 1978. For the background to the Roper Report and Recommendation 848, see Chap. 1, section 2.2.1.

[50] Recommendation 848 (1978) Annex, i.   [51] Recommendation 848 (1978) Annex, ii.

primarily, to man-made material).[52] What the Recommendation did do, however, was to specify a temporal cut-off point. This was at the suggestion of Prott and O'Keefe, the expert legal consultants. Their recommendation that the period that should be chosen was 100 years was influenced by the approach of Finland, Sweden and Norway, which all used this period as the threshold for their legislation protecting shipwrecks. While that legislation varied in the approach taken to how that cut-off was measured (in Finland and Sweden the 100-year period was taken from the date of the ship's loss; in Norway from the date of the ship's construction), the approach of Recommendation 848 – taking the length of time that objects had been 'beneath the water' – has the advantage that the same cut-off is likely to apply to all associated objects. In the case of a shipwreck assemblage, which is likely to comprise not only the hull of the ship and its fixtures and fittings, but also cargoes, personal effects and other items on board, this is clearly important since all these items may have widely differing dates of manufacture.

One of the most significant of the minimum legal requirements laid down by Recommendation 848 was the exclusion of salvage and wreck laws from application to material falling within its scope. Where such an exclusion is proposed, it is important that it is clear when it applies. A temporal criterion establishes a clear dividing line between material subject to the ordinary rules of private maritime law and that subject to heritage law; in the view of Prott and O'Keefe, the period of 100 years would avoid an undue effect on salvors.[53] The use of a temporal cut-off also avoids the need for subjective value judgments: it carries with it an implicit assumption that *all* material falling within the cut-off is of sufficient value in historical, archaeological or other cultural terms to be worthy of protection and, equally, that material that has been underwater for a shorter period is not of such value. On the other hand, a cut-off is inherently arbitrary. Recommendation 848 ameliorated this arbitrariness by its provision for discretionary *inclusion* of material that had been underwater for less than 100 years and for the discretionary *exclusion* of material that had been underwater for more than this time.

The preamble to Recommendation 848 '[s]tressed the essential unity of land and underwater archaeology', and the central thrust of the

---

[52] The report of the expert legal consultants made several references to man-made material and recommended 'a scheme of protection of all man-made items' underwater for more than 100 years: see Document 4200-E, Strasbourg, 1978, p. 62.

[53] *Ibid.*, p. 70.

Roper Report was that UCH should be treated as equal to terrestrial archaeology and that, where possible, a 'seamless' approach should be taken. In cases where a state's legislative provisions for UCH were separate and distinct from those for its terrestrial heritage, Recommendation 848 provided:

There should be no loopholes in the system of protection. The definition of underwater objects and sites should extend up to what was covered by land antiquities legislation.[54]

This requirement raises several important, interrelated, questions which those responsible for drafting any instrument for the protection of UCH should take into account. One question relates to the meaning of 'underwater'. While the term 'underwater cultural heritage' is frequently used to refer to cultural heritage located specifically in the marine zone, cultural material is also located in *inland* waters, such as lakes and rivers.[55] Furthermore, whether material qualifies as 'underwater' relates not only to the *nature* of the waters in which it is located, but also to the *degree to which it is submerged by water*. Areas may be periodically flooded, particularly tidal areas along the coast or in estuaries.[56] Recommendation 848 highlights that all material qualifying as cultural heritage needs to be afforded equal protection and care must be taken to ensure that there are no 'loopholes' through which material may fall.[57] While the Recommendation did not state a preference for whether remains in inland waters should be protected by the same legislative provisions as those in marine waters, in their report Prott and O'Keefe pointed out that special circumstances affecting cultural heritage in the marine zone need to be taken into account, such as difficulties of enforcing legislation

---

[54] Recommendation 848 (1978) Annex, i.

[55] For states that have many inland lakes and rivers, this question is particularly important. For example, in Poland there have been numerous discoveries in inland waters, including a ninth-century statue of the pagan deity Swiatowid which is regarded as one of the most important heritage finds ever made in the country: see, further, Kowalski, 'Poland', p. 230.

[56] The wreck of the Dutch East Indiaman, the *Amsterdam*, which lies on the foreshore at Hastings in the UK, is accessible on foot at low tide.

[57] An example of remains that appear to fall through such a 'loophole' in national legislation are the 'Purton Hulks'. These are a group of eighty-one barges and other working vessels that lie derelict on the foreshore of the River Severn in the UK. Campaigners who have sought to have them legally protected have faced difficulties because they do not fall comfortably within the present scheme of heritage legislation. See 'Purton Hulks – maritime history sunk by neglect', *Daily Telegraph*, 18 October 2008.

in the marine environment and the application of laws (notably salvage and wreck laws) that are not applicable on land.[58]

3.2.2   Draft European Convention 1985

The approach to the definition of subject matter taken by the Council of Europe's 1985 draft European Convention on the Protection of the Underwater Cultural Heritage was somewhat different from that of Recommendation 848.[59] At least in part, this reflected the fact that it was designed to be a binding instrument and therefore needed to define its material scope with precision.

Article 1 of the draft Convention provided:

1. For the purposes of this Convention all remains and objects and any other traces of human existence located entirely or in part in the sea, lakes, rivers, canals, artificial reservoirs or other bodies of water, or in tidal or other periodically flooded areas, or recovered from any such environment, or washed ashore, shall be considered as being part of the underwater cultural heritage, and are hereinafter referred to as 'underwater cultural property'.
2. Underwater cultural property being at least 100 years old shall enjoy the protection provided by this Convention. However, any Contracting State may provide that such property which is less than 100 years old shall enjoy the same protection.[60]

Although the draft Convention used the term 'underwater cultural heritage' in its title, and in general references to its subject matter, the alternative phrase 'underwater cultural property' was employed as the technical term to refer to material falling within its scope. The draft Explanatory Report accompanying the draft Convention indicates that the term 'underwater cultural *property*' was chosen because 'it was more comprehensive than the term "object", which might be deemed to include only movable goods and not immovable property'.[61] However, it does not explain why the word 'property', rather than 'heritage', was chosen. The term 'cultural property' had been used by a number of previous international instruments in the field, most notably two of

[58] Council of Europe Doc. 4200-E, 1978, p. 61.

[59] For the background to the draft European Convention, see Chap. 1, section 2.2.2.

[60] As in Chap. 1, the version of the draft Convention and Explanatory Report referred to is the declassified version of 1984. However, Art. 1 of the draft Convention is the same in both the declassified version of the draft Convention and the final text. With only one exception (referred to below), the comments on Art. 1 are the same in both versions of the draft Explanatory Report.

[61] Explanatory Report, p. 12. (Emphasis in the original.)

UNESCO's treaties, the 1954 Convention for the Protection of Cultural Property in the Event of Armed Conflict and the 1970 Convention on Illicit Trade in Cultural Property. On the other hand, a third UNESCO treaty, the 1972 World Heritage Convention, employed the term 'cultural heritage'. As Prott and O'Keefe have pointed out, the word 'property' is laden with connotations that are inappropriate in the context of an instrument designed to protect cultural material.[62] Among other things, it implies ownership and, hence, control by an owner. At least in common law systems, ownership as a legal concept carries with it rights which are not necessarily compatible with the public interest in heritage protection, including the rights to exploit, to alienate and to exclude others.[63] The word 'heritage', on the other hand, is imbued with the notion of stewardship and the sense that something requires special care so that it can be passed on to future generations. Possibly the fact that the draft Convention specifically reserved the rights of identifiable owners[64] influenced its use of the word 'property' rather than 'heritage'. In any event, today the term 'cultural heritage' is generally favoured, especially for instruments designed to afford protection to remains which lie *in situ*.[65]

The definitional criterion for 'underwater cultural property' set out in Article 1(1) of the draft European Convention was 'all remains and objects and any other traces of human existence'. This is an almost identical phrase to one used by an earlier Council of Europe treaty, the 1969 European Convention on the Protection of the Archaeological Heritage.[66] The phrase reflects not only the broadening of perceptions of UCH, and of the archaeological heritage more generally, but also recognition that it was important to have a definition that encompassed all material worthy of protection. The phrase left no room for doubt that it was capable of covering not only objects and other remains that are man-made, but remains of *any nature* that evidence human existence. This would include human remains (for which the word 'object' seems inappropriate), the bones of butchered animals, and natural materials that were used or affected by humans (such as preserved ancient

---

[62] See, generally, Prott and O'Keefe, '"Cultural Heritage" or "Cultural Property"?'

[63] For further discussion of ownership rights in the context of UCH, see Chap. 3.

[64] See Chap. 1, section 2.2.2.

[65] There is still a tendency to use the term 'cultural property' in the context of illicit trade in cultural material and export licensing, where questions relating to ownership are much more likely to arise.

[66] In Art. 1 of the 1969 Convention, a disjunctive 'or' was used rather than a conjunctive 'and'. On this Convention, see, further, section 3.2.3, below.

pollen or seeds from cultivated plants). Interestingly, the draft Explanatory Report emphasises that the expression 'any other traces of human existence' was intended to embrace 'geographical features of historical significance'.[67] Although no guidance is given as to exactly what was in mind, it seems that the drafters may have anticipated the growth of interest in submerged prehistoric land-surfaces which has taken place in more recent decades.[68] In line with Recommendation 848, the draft Convention also took an all-embracing approach to the notion of 'underwater', providing for the protection of material 'located entirely or in part in the sea, lakes, rivers, canals, artificial reservoirs or other bodies of water, or in tidal or other periodically flooded areas' and also for that *recovered* from any such environment, or washed ashore.

Although the draft Convention did not follow the approach of Recommendation 848 in excluding salvage law, nonetheless it adopted its approach of using a temporal criterion of 100 years as its selection criterion (though for some unknown reason basing the cut-off on age, rather than length of time underwater). Contracting states were given discretion to afford protection to material less than 100 years old, for example by setting a lower age limit or a criterion of intrinsic cultural value,[69] but not to exclude older material. Probably as an acknowledgement that some states in Europe might have been more comfortable with the application of a criterion of intrinsic cultural value with respect to *all* material falling within the scope of the draft Convention, not simply that *less* than 100 years old, the Explanatory Report stated:

Although the article does not expressly include a criterion of historical or archaeological significance, the word 'cultural' itself makes clear that, in implementing the obligations laid down by the Convention, Contracting States will be able to adopt criteria of cultural value.[70]

This statement indicated that the competent national authorities of contracting states would be able to take account of the significance of

---

[67] Explanatory Report, p. 12.
[68] For further discussion of this point, see section 3.2.3, below. Although it seems that these drowned landscapes had been known about for decades (see Gaffney, Fitch and Smith, *Europe's Lost World*, chap. 1), interest in them only really developed in the 1990s and 2000s when advances in remote-surveying technology opened up the possibilities for investigating their archaeological potential.
[69] See Explanatory Report, p. 12.
[70] Interestingly, this statement appeared only in the final version of the Explanatory Report, not the declassified version.

material, even that *over* 100 years old, in determining whether or not to grant authorisation for interference and, if so, on what terms.

3.2.3   Valletta Convention 1992

The 1969 European Convention on the Protection of the Archaeological Heritage was superseded by a revised treaty in 1992. The Valletta Convention, as the revised version is known, relates to the archaeological heritage generally, including UCH.[71]

The way the Valletta Convention defines 'the archaeological heritage' is quite complex. In Article 1, it defines what it refers to as the 'elements' of this heritage. The phrase used to establish the definitional criteria is 'all remains and objects and any other traces of mankind'.[72] Article 1(3) makes it clear that included within this description of subject matter are 'structures, constructions, groups of buildings, developed sites, moveable objects, monuments of other kinds as well as their context, whether situated on land or under water'.[73] The list was not intended to be exhaustive.[74] To be subject to protection by the Convention, these elements of the archaeological heritage are required to meet certain selection criteria. All of the following criteria must be met: (i) the elements must come from 'past epochs'; (ii) their preservation and study must 'help to retrace the history of mankind and its relation with the natural environment'; and (iii) the main sources of information about them must be excavations or discoveries and other methods of research.[75] These criteria could be regarded simply as a way of spelling out in more specific terms the notion that the elements must be of an archaeological and historical nature.

The approach taken by the Valletta Convention to defining subject matter is easier to understand if one considers its roots. The original 1969 Convention used the term 'archaeological objects' to refer to its subject matter and defined those objects to include 'all remains and objects, or any other traces of human existence, which bear witness to epochs and civilisations for which excavations or discoveries are the

---

[71] For the background to the Valletta Convention, see Chap. 1, section 2.2.3.

[72] Art. 1(2).

[73] Art. 1(3). The seamless approach of the Valletta Convention with respect to UCH and terrestrial heritage meant that there was no need to include provision relating to remains that are only partially underwater, or only periodically so.

[74] Explanatory Report, p. 5.

[75] See Art. 1(2), and also the Explanatory Report. A final criterion requires that the elements must be 'located in any area within the jurisdiction of the parties': on this, see Chap. 1, section 2.2.3.

main source or one of the main sources of scientific information'. The definition of the subject matter of the revised Convention is clearly designed to build on the original notion but to refine it, in particular to emphasise that it is not just objects that are important, but 'any evidence, of whatever nature, that can throw light on the past of mankind'.[76] In making the refinements, it seems that there were two points in particular which the drafters sought to emphasise. First, mere remnants, or traces, of human existence may be as important as objects. The Explanatory Report gives as an example a discolouration in soil: this discolouration may be all that remains of a former wooden structure but it may yield a great deal of information about that structure.[77] Another example would be an ancient human footprint preserved in mud: such footprints can provide a great deal of valuable information about the way of life of our prehistoric ancestors.[78] Secondly, and of fundamental archaeological importance, the *context* in which an object or other element of the archaeological heritage is found is as important as the object or element itself.[79] The context, in other words the physical surroundings, may be man-made or natural, or a combination of both. In itself it is an important information source, not only about the history of mankind but also – as the Valletta selection criteria make clear – about the relationship over time between mankind and the natural environment. An object entirely dissociated from its context may have relatively little, or even no, value as a source of archaeological information; where the context is also preserved, or at least recorded, it is likely to add considerably to the overall knowledge that can be gleaned.

The expression 'any other traces of mankind' is a reformulation of the phrase 'any other traces of human existence' adopted by the original 1969 Convention and followed by the 1985 draft European Convention. Unlike the draft Explanatory Report accompanying the 1985 draft Convention, the Valletta Convention's Explanatory Report does not explicitly state that the expression was intended to include 'geographical features of historical significance'. However, there is no reason to doubt that it does, at least in so far as such features do directly evidence human existence, or provide the immediate context for such evidence. The core requirement is that there 'must be something, even a trace, which comes

---

[76] Explanatory Report, p. 5.   [77] *Ibid.*
[78] See, for example, Gaffney, Fitch and Smith, *Europe's Lost World*, pp. 63–4, which discusses the significance of Mesolithic human footprints preserved in the silt of the Severn Estuary, UK.
[79] See Explanatory Report, p. 5.

from past human existence'.[80] To illustrate this point, one can take the example of a pit, found in a prehistoric drowned land-surface, which contains evidence indicating that it was used as a Mesolithic hearth site or oven.[81] In such a case, it seems that not only charred material in the pit, such as stones and flints, but also the pit itself, whether hewn, or a natural feature, would fall within the definition.[82] On the other hand, natural environmental deposits in the general area of the pit – despite the fact they may date from Mesolithic times and have considerable archaeological potential – would not be covered.[83] Nor would the preserved remains of Mesolithic-period flora and fauna – even though they too may well provide general clues as to what early humans may have cultivated or eaten – unless it is clear they had some direct association with humanity.

One notable distinction between the approach of the Valletta Convention and that of the earlier Council of Europe instruments on UCH is that it does not use an age criterion. As far as age is concerned, it simply requires that remains be from 'past epochs'. Although technically this appears to exclude the remains of the present epoch (giving rise to questions about when that epoch commenced), in practice and given that many modern archaeologists now prefer to regard time as a continuum, rather than as divided into distinctive periods, the factor that is more likely to influence decisions about what is and is not included is whether or not the preservation and study of the remains will 'help to retrace the history of mankind and its relation with the natural environment'. The attitude of competent national authorities to this question is likely to vary considerably across the continent of Europe.

The Valletta Convention is a wide-ranging instrument designed to deal with a range of threats to the archaeological heritage.[84] The way that its definition of archaeological heritage is framed, and the wording of

---

[80] Ibid.

[81] At least one such pit, dug into the ground and used to hold heated flints and stones, has been found at the Bouldnor Cliff prehistoric submerged site off the Isle of Wight, UK: personal communication with Garry Momber, 14 August 2012.

[82] Where the pit was a natural feature, rather than hewn, one might question whether it would form a 'trace of mankind' or part of the context. However, presumably it would fall within the notion of a 'developed site' for the purposes of Art. 1(3) and would therefore constitute a 'trace of mankind' for the purposes of the Valletta Convention.

[83] Archaeologists would argue that the environmental deposits in the immediate vicinity of the pit provide relevant context and therefore would fall within the definition. In the end this would be a matter for the judgment of the competent heritage authority.

[84] See Chap. 1, section 2.2.3.

its provisions more generally,[85] give contracting states some flexibility in determining how to implement its terms. Furthermore, as an instrument addressing the archaeological heritage generally, rather than UCH specifically, it makes no reference to salvage law or other laws that apply exclusively in the marine environment. Therefore, there was no need for a clear dividing line to be drawn between the scope of these laws and that of the treaty.

4.   The approach of the UNESCO Convention 2001

The UNESCO Convention 2001 is a very different instrument from the Council of Europe's Valletta Convention. Among other things, it relates to UCH specifically and it focuses on addressing one particular threat: treasure hunting and other unregulated activities that target UCH, especially in the open oceans. In light of this, the question of the application of salvage law was a central one and – while the UNESCO treaty does not exclude salvage law – it does severely curtail its application to UCH falling within its scope.[86] However, despite the differences between the two treaties, the UNESCO Convention's definition of UCH draws on that of the Valletta Convention, and also that of the Council of Europe's earlier UCH initiatives. In large part, this was thanks to the initial groundwork laid by the ILA.

Article 1(1) of the UNESCO Convention defines the term 'underwater cultural heritage' as follows:

(a) 'Underwater cultural heritage' means all traces of human existence having a cultural, historical or archaeological character which have been partially or totally underwater, periodically or continuously, for at least 100 years such as:
  (i) sites, structures, buildings, artefacts and human remains, together with their archaeological and natural context;
  (ii) vessels, aircraft, other vehicles or any part thereof, their cargo or other contents, together with their archaeological and natural context; and
  (iii) objects of prehistoric character.
(b) Pipelines and cables placed on the seabed shall not be considered as underwater cultural heritage.
(c) Installations other than pipelines and cables, placed on the seabed and still in use, shall not be considered as underwater cultural heritage.

---

[85] See, for example, Art. 3, which relates to the authorisation of archaeological activities.
[86] See, further, Chap. 5, section 4.

To ensure an all-inclusive approach (in other words, taking on board the point made in 1978 by the Council of Europe's Recommendation 848 regarding 'loopholes' in the system of protection), Article 1(1)(a) provides that material 'partially or totally underwater, periodically or continuously, for at least 100 years' falls within the definition. This wording ensures that cultural material in coastal and inter-tidal areas is covered by the Convention's regime, a matter which is likely to become of growing significance given predictions of the impact of climate change upon sea levels.[87]

Although the Convention was designed with the regulation of activities in the marine zone in mind, a number of states called for inland waters to be covered. As a result, provision is made that, '[w]hen ratifying ... [the] Convention or at any time thereafter, any state ... may declare that the Rules shall apply to inland waters not of a maritime character'.[88]

4.1   Definitional criteria

In a number of respects the wording of paragraph (a) of Article 1(1) is reminiscent of that in both the draft European Convention 1985 and the Valletta Convention 1992, although it has been further refined. The definitional criterion is now simply: 'all traces of human existence'. Like the Valletta Convention, a non-exclusive list is provided with the aim of ensuring that there is no room for doubt that all types of sites and objects, movable and immovable material, and human remains are included within the definition, as well as their archaeological and natural context.

For the first time, aircraft are referred to explicitly. It sometimes seems to be overlooked in literature relating to UCH that many thousands of military and civil aircraft have been lost at sea (and in inland waters) in the period since the first engine-powered aircraft flight by the Wright brothers in 1903. Today the potential for sunken aircraft to be of historical and archaeological interest – for example, because of their association with specific events or individuals, or because they are

---

[87] Recent discoveries of material in the Polar regions related to the activities of early explorers give rise to a further point of interest in relation to the question of what 'underwater' means in the context of the UNESCO Convention. For example, a stock of whisky belonging to Ernest Shackleton was found embedded in ice near the South Pole in 2010. Would a similar find embedded in ice in the Arctic Ocean qualify (assuming it fell within the 100-year threshold)? In light of the object and purpose of the Convention, the all-embracing nature of the definition in Art. 1(1)(a) and the fact that ice is merely frozen water, there seems no reason why such finds would, or should, be excluded.

[88] Art. 28.

rare examples of particular types of aircraft – is widely recognised and there is increasing interest in the subject of aviation archaeology, especially with respect to losses during the First and Second World Wars.[89] Although examples of specific sunken aircraft sites protected by national heritage laws remain rare,[90] one notable example is the airship USS *Macon*, lost in the Pacific in 1935, which was added to the US National Register of Historic Places in 2010. As each year passes, increasing numbers of aircraft will fall within the scope of the Convention and therefore they are likely to become an increasing focus of attention.[91]

Another type of remains explicitly referred to in Article 1(1)(a) are 'objects of prehistoric character'. Again the intention seems to be simply to make it absolutely clear that an object dating from prehistoric times can qualify as a 'trace of human existence'. However, as with the Valletta Convention, the fact that an object, or indeed any material remains, dates from prehistoric times is not in itself enough to mean that it falls within the scope of the Convention. It must represent a trace of human existence, or form part of the context for such traces.[92] Therefore natural material such as sediments, peat and fossilised fauna and flora dating from prehistoric times will only be covered to the extent that they are directly associated with evidence of human existence.[93] During the UNESCO negotiations, a number of states raised the possibility of the inclusion of prehistoric landscapes, or indeed natural sites, more

[89] See, for example, English Heritage, *Military Aircraft Crash Sites: Archaeological Guidance on their Significance and Future Management* (available at www.english-heritage.org.uk/publications/military-aircraft-crash-sites). Early draft texts for the treaty excluded sunken state-owned or state-operated vessels and aircraft used for non-commercial purpose from the scope of application of the Convention. However, this exclusion was later dropped: see, further, Chap. 4, section 3.1.

[90] One of the reasons for this is that some states have protected such remains by legislation principally designed for other purposes, for example, the UK PMRA 1986 and the US SMCA. On these statutes, see Chap. 4, section 2.2.

[91] At the time of writing, it seems that aircraft parts have been found in the South Pacific which could be remains from the Lockheed Electra flown by Amelia Earhart, the pioneering US aviator, during her doomed attempt to become the first woman to fly around the globe in 1937. Although it will be more than two decades before this aircraft falls within the scope of the Convention, it is clearly one that has great historical significance.

[92] The fact that paragraph (iii) of Art. 1(1)(a) does not explicitly include the words 'together with their archaeological and natural context', in line with paragraphs (i) and (ii), appears to be a drafting oversight.

[93] See, further, section 3.2.3, above.

generally.[94] However, it seems that these ideas were not pursued because the management regime envisaged for material falling within the scope of the Convention would not necessarily afford appropriate protection for such areas.[95]

Paragraphs (b) and (c) of Article 1(1) contain two specific *exclusions* from the scope of application of the Convention, one in respect of pipelines and cables, and the other in respect of installations more generally. There is a vast – and rapidly multiplying – quantity of man-made equipment on the seabed which is in use for all sorts of purposes and the exclusion of such material from the scope of the Convention was almost certainly a necessary step. Not all of this equipment would be excluded from its scope merely by virtue of the 100-year cut-off and hence there was a need for some specific provision in this regard. On the face of it, it might seem unclear why the Convention should draw a distinction between pipelines and cables on the one hand, and other types of installation on the other, explicitly excluding the former, *whether or not in use*, but the latter only where still in use. However, the pipeline and cable industry has been used to a privileged position for its infrastructure and activities under international law of the sea[96] and it seems that the cable industry, in particular, was keen to remain in control of the removal of its old infrastructure.[97] Installations on the seabed other than pipelines and cables may well be of a military nature, or related to the exploration or exploitation of natural resources, or marine scientific research.[98] While one would imagine that most such installations still in use would be less than 100 years old, it is not inconceivable that some may fall over the 100-year threshold. Article 1(1)(c) makes it clear they

---

[94] See the explanatory comments on Art. 1 of the 1998 UNESCO Draft which form part of UNESCO Doc. CLT-96/Conf.202/2, April 1998 (reproduced in the appendix to Dromgoole and Gaskell, 'Draft UNESCO Convention on the Protection of the Underwater Cultural Heritage 1998').

[95] *Ibid.*

[96] Protection was provided for submarine cables under international treaty law as early as 1884 and the LOSC accords a privileged status to both cables and pipelines.

[97] O'Keefe, *Shipwrecked Heritage*, p. 45. Some of this cabling may be made of metal, such as copper, which is commercially valuable.

[98] The term 'installation' is not defined by the Convention. The LOSC refers to cables, pipelines and installations, but it also refers to 'structures' and 'equipment'. According to Wegelein, the term 'structure' may be regarded as synonymous to 'installation' and the term 'equipment' connotes something that is employed for a particular purpose and then removed, in contrast to an 'installation' which is intended to remain in place permanently or at least for an extended period of time: see Wegelein, *Marine Scientific Research*, p. 138.

would not be affected by the Convention. On the other hand, if they are no longer in use, they will fall within the definition of UCH.

4.2   Selection criteria

At least on the face of it, the definition of UCH set out in Article 1(1) of the UNESCO Convention includes two selection criteria. One is based on the objective consideration of whether material has been underwater for at least 100 years and the other on the subjective consideration of whether material has 'a cultural, historical or archaeological character'.[99]

4.2.1   The temporal criterion

The UNESCO Convention's adoption of a 100-year threshold for its material scope of application is in line with the Council of Europe's 1985 draft European Convention, which followed the approach of Recommendation 848 (1978) and some national laws. However, unlike the draft European Convention, the UNESCO Convention does not include any provision enabling a state to *include* remains which have been underwater for less than that length of time[100] and, equally, there is no provision enabling a state to *exclude* from the treaty framework material which has been underwater for over 100 years.[101]

The adoption of the 100-year cut-off is a very significant limitation upon the scope of the Convention. It has the effect of excluding from the treaty framework a great deal of material of potential historical and archaeological significance. In particular, although the material remains of the First World War will soon start to be covered, it will be several decades before those from the Second World War will be afforded protection. Oddly, perhaps, it does not seem that the question of the temporal criterion was the subject of a great deal of debate during the UNESCO negotiations.[102] For this reason it is difficult to gauge the extent to which the cut-off was regarded simply as part of a pragmatic compromise with the salvage industry rather than as some indication

---

[99] Early drafts of the Convention followed the approach of the US Abandoned Shipwreck Act of 1987 by using abandonment as a selection criterion. However, this approach was later dropped. See, further, Chap. 3, section 3.2.1.

[100] According to Garabello, this was because of concerns about the potential application of the Convention to recently wrecked military craft: Garabello, 'The Negotiating History of the Convention on the Protection of the Underwater Cultural Heritage', p. 105 n. 31.

[101] See the related discussion in section 4.2.2, below.

[102] Garabello, 'The Negotiating History of the Convention on the Protection of the Underwater Cultural Heritage', p. 105.

that – as a matter of principle – twentieth-century remains are some-how undeserving of protection. Certainly it seems that some states proposed more recent thresholds. For example, Poland proposed that all wrecks before 1945 be included[103] and the USA proposed a cut-off of fifty years.[104]

As a device for resolving issues relating to private commercial interests (not only those of salvors, but also of identifiable owners), 100 years does seem to be an appropriate threshold for application of the treaty regime. While undoubtedly there are remains that have been underwater for less than 100 years which are of interest to archaeologists, equally there will also be remains that have been underwater for more than that time which are of interest to commercial parties.[105] Furthermore, many relatively modern wrecks give rise to other issues besides those of either a cultural or a commercial nature. For example, many are gravesites where close relatives may still be alive, and many wartime wrecks are also hazardous in one way or another. The establishment of a 100-year threshold meant that the negotiators avoided becoming embroiled in such issues.[106]

4.2.2   The character criterion

To constitute UCH for the purposes of the UNESCO Convention, not only must material have been underwater for at least 100 years, but also it must have 'a cultural, historical or archaeological character'. This selection criterion was inserted in the text at a relatively late stage of the negotiations.[107]

---

[103] See the explanatory comments on Art. 2 of the 1998 UNESCO Draft which form part of UNESCO Doc. CLT-96/Conf.202/2, April 1998 (reproduced in the appendix to Dromgoole and Gaskell, 'Draft UNESCO Convention on the Protection of the Underwater Cultural Heritage 1998').

[104] See Varmer, 'United States', p. 107. The US proposal (which was supported by the UK) combined the cut-off with a significance criterion: see, further, section 4.2.2, below.

[105] For example, the Salvage Association of London – which represents private interests – has on its records, and maintains an interest in, marine casualties dating back to 1860. See, further, Chap. 3, section 2.2.

[106] The Convention does not envisage that material falling within its scope may pose a hazard. However, while the majority of wrecks that are environmental or other hazards date from the twentieth century, the fact that a wreck sank earlier than this does not necessarily mean that it will not be hazardous. Furthermore, as time passes, more and more twentieth-century wrecks will fall within the conventional framework. On this matter, see, further, Chap. 4, Concluding remarks.

[107] For a detailed discussion of the debate on this issue, see Garabello, 'The Negotiating History of the Convention on the Protection of the Underwater Cultural Heritage', pp. 106–9.

The question of whether or not the definition of UCH should include a criterion based on the *significance* of material had been a matter of considerable debate during the negotiations and indeed was one of the issues that threatened an overall consensus. Traditionally, common law countries have tended to take a selective approach to the protection of heritage assets generally, selecting for protection those assets considered of particular significance; civil law states, on the other hand, have tended to adopt a more expansive – protectionist – approach, affording protection for all heritage sites or assets over a certain age, or deemed to qualify as 'antiquities' or 'monuments'.[108] However, in the specific context of UCH, systems based on so-called 'blanket' protection have become increasingly favoured internationally and are now used even by some common law states (notably Australia). An important advantage of the blanket system is that legal protection is in place *before* new sites are discovered; by contrast, where a system is based on designation of specific sites of significance, a newly discovered site will need to have its significance assessed before it can be granted legal protection. Making such an assessment takes time, and physical intervention, perhaps extensive, is likely to be required.[109] To include a significance criterion *alongside* a temporal criterion would potentially undermine the advantage of the blanket approach. It would also introduce a subjective element and thereby open up the possibility that different national authorities would interpret the notion of significance in very different ways, jeopardising the overall aim of a universal standard.

On the face of it, the fact that material over 100 years underwater must have a 'cultural, historical or archaeological character' to qualify as UCH for the purposes of the Convention indicates that the proponents of a significance criterion won the argument. However, the word 'character' – initially mooted in an effort to find a compromise on the issue – has more in common with the word 'nature' (used in Articles 149 and 303 of the LOSC) than it does with the word 'significance', or commonly used alternatives such as 'importance', 'value' or 'interest'. As O'Keefe has argued, it is doubtful whether the character criterion does anything over and above the 100-year time-limit to restrict the

---

[108] See section 2, above.

[109] It seems that this was the reason why the 1994 ILA Draft did not include a significance criterion: see O'Keefe, 'The Buenos Aires Draft Convention on the Protection of the Underwater Cultural Heritage Prepared by the International Law Association', p. 97. While some interference may also be required to establish the length of time material has been underwater, it is likely to be less than that required to determine significance.

scope of the definition since virtually *anything* over 100 years underwater may be said to have cultural, historical or archaeological character.[110] Therefore, the insertion of the character formula in practice does not appear to provide states with any discretion to exclude material that is over 100 years underwater from the conventional regime on the ground that they regard it as of little or no significance.[111]

The two states particularly exercised by the question of significance were the USA and the UK. For the USA, it seems that the compromise 'character' formula, enshrined in the final text, would have been acceptable 'as part of an otherwise broadly acceptable package'.[112] The main reason for this would appear to be that relevant US domestic legislation – while framed around the notion of significance – is applied in such a way that there is a virtual presumption that material over fifty years of age *is* historically significant.[113] For this and other reasons it is not thought that the legislation would require amendment, as far as its material scope of application is concerned, to be consistent with the treaty.[114]

The position in the UK is not so straightforward. In its formal Statement on Vote at the end of the negotiations, outlining the reasons for its failure to vote in favour of the Convention, the UK made the following comment:

[T]he text obliges signatory states to extend the same very high standards of protection to all underwater archaeology over 100 years old. It is estimated that there are probably about 10,000 wreck sites on the seabed under the United Kingdom's territorial sea and it would neither be possible nor desirable to extend legal protection to all of them. The United Kingdom believes that it is better to focus its efforts and resources on protecting the most important and unique examples of underwater cultural heritage. It would simply be impossible to enforce the application of the rules in the Annex to every one of the thousands of wreck sites.[115]

---

[110] O'Keefe, *Shipwrecked Heritage*, p. 43.

[111] Even where a system of blanket protection is in place, marine heritage managers are likely to take account of significance in making decisions about the management of a protected site. For example, the level of significance of a site may determine the degree of access permitted to the site by recreational divers, or the role permitted to amateur archaeologists in any archaeological intervention at the site. Under the conventional regime, there is some scope for applying differential management strategies of this kind under the annexed Rules, but it is relatively limited. See, generally, Chap. 9.

[112] Blumberg, 'International Protection of Underwater Cultural Heritage', p. 498 and text of n. 23.

[113] See Varmer, 'United States' (2nd edn), pp. 374–6.   [114] *Ibid.*

[115] See the UK's Statement on Vote, reproduced in Camarda and Scovazzi, *The Protection of the Underwater Cultural Heritage*, pp. 432–3. In an earlier statement made by one of the

It is clear from the statement that, in the view of the UK, the 'character' criterion adds nothing by way of limitation to the 100-year threshold. It is also clear that the main concern for the UK relates to its ability to fulfil the duty that the Convention imposes on states parties to ensure that the Rules annexed to the Convention are applied to activities directed at UCH in the *territorial sea*.[116] Under the UK Protection of Wrecks Act 1973 approximately sixty wreck sites in the territorial sea are designated for protection on account of their 'historical, archaeological or artistic importance' and a handful of other UCH sites are afforded protection under other legislation. The concern of the UK is not only that it would need to overhaul its legislation, but also – given the fact that the UK's coastal waters are peculiarly rich in shipwrecks[117] – that it would be costly to afford protection to *all* UCH sites dating back more than 100 years.[118]

5. Concluding remarks

'Underwater cultural heritage' is now the internationally accepted phrase used to refer to historical and archaeological material in the marine zone. In general usage, it has no specific temporal limit. For the purposes of the UNESCO Convention 2001, the term applies only to material that has been underwater for at least 100 years. The fact that *all* material over this threshold falls within the scope of the Convention appears to be problematic only for the UK.[119] However, the fact that the Convention does not protect material that has been underwater for

UK's delegates, it seems that reference was made to the possibility that the number of wreck sites around the coasts of the UK could possibly amount to 'half a million': see Garabello, 'The Negotiating History of the Convention on the Protection of the Underwater Cultural Heritage', p. 108 n. 37.

[116] Art. 7(2).

[117] The density of shipwrecks in the territorial waters adjacent to England in particular is thought 'likely to be amongst the highest in the world': Roberts and Trow, *Taking to the Water*, p. 5. In terms of diversity, too, the resource may be 'potentially without equal elsewhere in the world': Oxley, 'Making the Submerged Historic Environment Accessible', p. 87.

[118] It is possible that these concerns are based on some misunderstanding of the notion of blanket protection and could be alleviated: see, generally, Firth, 'Underwater Cultural Heritage Off England'; see also Dromgoole, 'Reflections on the Position of the Major Maritime Powers with Respect to the UNESCO Convention on the Protection of the Underwater Cultural Heritage 2001', p. 7.

[119] It should be noted, however, that private commercial interests in some other jurisdictions are also unhappy with the lack of a significance criterion: see, further, Chap. 5, section 4.4.

less than 100 years means that there are many remains of historical and archaeological significance that fall outside its protective regime.[120] In particular, the material legacy of the Second World War will be excluded for years to come. From a purely pragmatic standpoint, this may have been a sensible outcome; from the point of view of principle, however, it has to be said that it is seriously out of line with the holistic approach of modern heritage thinking and general state practice.

---

[120] It is open to states to take action, individually or collectively, to protect younger material. However, in international waters the action that can be taken under general international law is limited. One possibility is an inter-state agreement, such as that negotiated in respect of the *Titanic*. Article 6 of the Convention explicitly encourages such agreements: see, further, Chap. 10, section 2.

3 Ownership and other interests in underwater cultural heritage

1. Introduction

Ownership is regarded as the *'greatest possible interest in a thing which a mature system of law recognises'*[1] and an owner's interest is legal, in the sense that it is enforceable in law. Throughout the field of cultural heritage protection there are tensions between ownership rights and the requirements of cultural heritage management, and the area of UCH is no exception. The role of the law is to try to achieve an appropriate balance between the rights of owners and the need to protect heritage values. Traditionally, states with a common law system have tended to pay considerable regard to the private rights of the owner and to take a restrictive approach with respect to protective measures they have put in place; states with a civil law background, on the other hand, have tended to favour public – cultural – interests over private interests and generally have taken a more protectionist approach.[2] Indeed, civil law systems often provide for assets deemed to comprise part of the cultural heritage to be taken into state ownership, regarding this as the best way to afford them protection.

The complexity of the notion of ownership and the fact that there are fundamental differences of attitude and approach internationally

---

[1] Honoré, 'Ownership', p. 108 (emphasis in original). By 'a thing' is meant property. Under the common law, the two main categories of property are personal property and real property (land). The nearest civil law equivalent is the distinction between movable and immovable property. (For the application of these terms to UCH, see Chap. 2, section 3.1.) Ownership must be distinguished from possession. A party who has possession of property has a possessory title to that property and thereby an enforceable legal interest. However, this interest is limited and must be distinguished from the full title of the owner. An example of a possessory title is that acquired by a salvor in possession of a wreck site. See, further, Chap. 5, section 2.1.

[2] See, further, Chap. 2, section 2.

to that notion means those tasked with drafting international treaty provisions in the field of cultural heritage protection may find the question of ownership particularly challenging. Sometimes, they may conclude that it is best to 'sweep it under the carpet' by not referring to it at all, instead leaving it as a matter to be governed solely by applicable domestic law. At the same time, given that the subject matter of such treaty provisions is not simply 'property' but is also 'heritage', they may bestow some formal recognition on interests that are broader than, or entirely different from, those of owners. In the context of UCH, the question of ownership generally has greater practical significance than it does in the context of terrestrial archaeological heritage and the relevant international law also explicitly recognises a number of other rights and interests whose incidents are far from being fully understood. Among other things, questions may arise about the extent to which they are legally enforceable, as well as about their interaction with the rights of identifiable owners in circumstances where such rights continue to persist.

This chapter is split into three parts. The first part considers ownership rights in the context of UCH, exploring how they may be acquired, legally established and lost under domestic law. The second part examines the approach taken to ownership rights by both the LOSC and the UNESCO Convention 2001. The final part considers other types of interest recognised by these two treaties and explores the relationship between these interests and identifiable ownership rights.

2.   Ownership

In the common law, ownership is sometimes said to afford the owner with a 'bundle of rights' over the property in question. These include the right to control, including the right to exclude others; the right to alienate (that is, to sell, or otherwise transfer title); the right to exploit; and the right to destroy. Each of these rights has the potential to run counter to notions of heritage management, two central tenets of which are that associated finds should be kept intact as a collection, and that access to that collection should be possible for researchers and the general public. It is therefore common for domestic law to circumscribe ownership rights to ensure that heritage values are protected; in some cases, such rights may even be expropriated.

In the context of UCH, the question of ownership has arisen mainly in respect of shipwrecks. Issues arise concerning not just the ownership of the vessel (hull, fixtures and fittings), but also of the cargo, and personal possessions of passengers and crew.[3] It is usually the cargo that will be the most commercially valuable part of a wreck and in some exceptional cases the values involved are (at least potentially) enormous.[4] This factor has made the question of ownership rights in the UCH context significant and, at times, contentious.[5] In respect of UCH other than shipwrecks, the issue of ownership arises much less frequently, either because the remains are too ancient for ownership to be traceable and/or because they have no commercial or other value that might invoke an ownership claim. For these reasons, the following discussion focuses on the ownership of shipwrecks.[6]

2.1 Acquisition of ownership rights

There are many ways in which ownership in sunken vessels and associated artefacts may be acquired. In the case of older wrecks that have been lost for some time, one means of acquiring ownership is through succession in title from the original owner. The inheritance of rights in this way may be personal,[7] or corporate.[8] Ownership rights may also be

---

[3] In principle, questions could also arise concerning the ownership of human remains associated with a wreck. Whether a dead body can constitute property has been the subject of considerable debate: see, for example, Magnusson, 'Proprietary Rights in Human Tissue', pp. 27–34. For some consideration of the implications of treating human remains as capable of ownership in the context of shipwrecks, see Dromgoole and Gaskell, 'Interests in Wreck', pp. 159–60.

[4] Estimates of the commercial value of the 500,000 or so coins recovered from the Spanish warship *Mercedes* have been in the region of £300 million: see, for example, 'Treasure hunters ordered to hand over £300m booty from sunken ship', *The Times*, 5 June 2009. However, estimates of this kind can sometimes prove to be very wide of the mark (see the case of the *Central America* below). Newspaper reports that the sunken British warships HMS *Sussex* and HMS *Victory* may each have been carrying cargoes worth a billion pounds or more have yet to be substantiated.

[5] While occasionally there are finds of great commercial value on land, such as the huge hoard of Roman and Celtic coins unearthed by metal detectorists in the Channel Islands in 2012 (see 'Roman and Celtic coin hoard worth up to £10m found in Jersey', *BBC Online News*, 26 June 2012), generally such finds are of ancient origin and there is no possibility of tracing ownership rights.

[6] In the future, questions relating to the ownership of sunken aircraft and associated material are likely to arise with increasing frequency in the context of cultural heritage law, policy and practice. Generally, the same principles will apply as for shipwrecks.

[7] For example, it seems that a direct lineal descendant of the original owner may have claimed ownership of the wreck of the *Resurgam*, the first mechanically powered submarine: Fletcher-Tomenius and Williams, 'The Protection of Wrecks Act 1973', p. 626. The *Resurgam* is located off the north coast of Wales (and designated under the UK Protection of Wrecks Act 1973). On the establishment of such rights, see section 2.2, below.

[8] For example, hypothetically, the corporate successor of the White Star Line, original owner of the *Titanic*, could claim ownership of the hull of the liner, and its fixtures and fittings: see, further, section 2.2, below.

purchased, or acquired through donation.[9] Those that recover a wreck may occasionally acquire ownership too, either through an *in specie* salvage award, or through application of the law of finds.[10] Another group whose ownership rights are of some significance are insurers. Under marine insurance law, in paying out for a total loss, insurers become entitled to take over the interest of the owner or other assured in whatever may remain of the subject matter insured.[11] Since marine insurance was formally established by the early seventeenth century, in considering the ownership of vessels and cargoes dating from this period onwards the question of whether or not the property was insured is a factor that needs to be borne in mind.[12]

Just as private individuals and companies may acquire ownership rights in wrecked vessels and cargoes, so may states. Again, it is possible that a state may have inherited rights. A number of maritime states claim that title to sunken warships (unless captured or surrendered in war)[13] persists until such time as it is expressly relinquished[14] and several of these states have asserted rights even in respect of vessels that are centuries old. For example, the UK recently asserted rights in respect of HMS *Sussex* (lost in 1694) and HMS *Victory* (lost in 1744),[15] and Spain did so in respect

---

[9] On several occasions, the UK's Ministry of Defence, acting on behalf of the Crown, has gifted title to historically significant sunken warships to charitable trusts. For example, HMS *Victory* (predecessor of Nelson's flagship) was gifted to such a trust in 2012.

[10] For an explanation of these methods of acquiring ownership, see Chap. 5. (It should be noted that acquisition of ownership by a salvor is generally rare and must be distinguished from the much more common situation where a salvor acquires only a possessory title.)

[11] See, for example, the UK Marine Insurance Act 1906, s. 79(1). Marine insurance law is complex and arcane, and establishing the rights of an insurer is a matter that requires considerable care. For a detailed discussion of the rights of insurers to sunken vessels and cargoes, see Dromgoole and Gaskell, 'Interests in Wreck', pp. 168–78.

[12] One particularly famous case of an early casualty in which Lloyd's of London had an interest is the *Lutine*, which sank in 1799 with over £1 million of *specie* on board. For details, see *ibid.*, p. 171.

[13] The *Lutine* is an example of a vessel claimed as prize (twice): see *ibid.*, p. 156. The dispute between Lloyd's (as insurer) and the Dutch Government (whose claim was based on prize) as to rightful ownership of the *specie* on board was eventually settled: see *ibid.*, pp. 156–7.

[14] See, further, section 2.3, below. On sunken state vessels and aircraft generally, see Chap. 4.

[15] In the case of HMS *Sussex*, the UK government entered into a controversial 'partnering agreement' with the US ocean exploration and shipwreck recovery company, Odyssey Marine Exploration (OME), for the recovery of a cargo of 10 tonnes of gold coins reputedly on board. In the case of HMS *Victory*, the government paid a salvage reward to OME in respect of two large cannon recovered from the site. For further discussion with respect to these wrecks, see Chap. 6, sections 2.2.2 and 4.3.

of the warship *Mercedes* (see below). States may also benefit from rights of succession to corporations, one notable example being the Dutch government's ownership of the assets – including wrecks – of the Dutch East India Company.[16] Another way in which states may have acquired ownership of wrecked vessels and cargoes is through war risk insurance. Many wrecks of merchant shipping casualties of the First and Second World Wars will be owned by states that paid out under war risk insurance schemes. The UK's Department for Transport, for example, exercises rights of title in respect of nearly 5,000 such casualties.[17]

A question of some interest concerns the rights of ex-colonies vis-à-vis those of their former colonial powers. This question arose recently in the case of the Spanish naval frigate *Mercedes*, which sank in 1804. In 2007, approximately 594,000 (mainly silver) coins and other artefacts were recovered from the site, 100 miles west of the Straits of Gibraltar, by Odyssey Marine Exploration (OME), a commercial company engaged in ocean exploration and shipwreck recovery. In the ensuing salvage proceedings initiated by OME in a US district court (and eventually determined by the Eleventh Circuit Court of Appeals), Spain asserted a claim to the vessel and its contents, including the coins, on the basis that the *Mercedes* was a sovereign-owned Spanish vessel, subject to sovereign immunity.[18] Peru interceded to claim ownership, co-ownership, or an equitable share of the *specie*, citing as one of the bases for its claims the controversial concept of state succession.[19] It argued that the coins had

---

[16] The Batavian Republic, a predecessor of the Kingdom of the Netherlands, took over the assets and liabilities of the Dutch East India Company when it was liquidated in 1795: see, further, Maarleveld, 'The Netherlands', pp. 163–5. The UK government may also hold ownership rights in wrecks of East India Company vessels, although its title is disputed by India and Pakistan: see Dromgoole and Gaskell, 'Interests in Wreck', pp. 155–6.

[17] In 2009, the UK government asserted ownership rights in respect of two of these wrecks, RMS *Laconia* and SS *Cairnhill*, both British merchant vessels lost during the First World War, by filing Statements of Interest in salvage law actions which had been initiated in the US federal admiralty courts. More recently, it entered into salvage contracts with OME for the recovery of shipments of silver on board two other wartime merchant casualties, the SS *Gairsoppa*, lost in 1941 and the SS *Mantola*, lost in 1917. Both wrecks lie in deep water off the Irish coast. (In July 2012, OME reported that it had recovered approximately forty-eight tonnes of silver from the *Gairsoppa*.)

[18] *Odyssey Marine Exploration, Inc.*, v. *Unidentified, Shipwrecked Vessel*, 675 F. Supp. 2d 1126 (MD Fla. Dec. 22, 2009); *aff'd*, 657 F.3d 1159 (11th Cir. (Fla.) Sept. 21, 2011); *cert. denied*, 132 S. Ct. 2379 (US May 14, 2010). The case is discussed in greater detail, in the context of the claim to sovereign immunity, in Chap. 4, section 2.3.2.

[19] Among other things, Peru cited the Vienna Convention on Succession of States in Respect of State Property, Archives and Debts 1983, which has yet to come into force and is politically deeply contentious, in support of its argument that the notion of state

been created from ore mined in territory that is now part of modern-day Peru, and had also been minted in that territory.[20] Spain counter-argued that what mattered was the express and agreed terms of cession made at the time of independence, which did not include property that was then outside the territory of Peru (including that sunk at sea).[21]

Domestic heritage legislation sometimes provides for states to acquire ownership of wrecks in their coastal waters. The legislation may provide for the acquisition of wrecks which are, or appear to be, ownerless. For example, the Irish National Monuments (Amendment) Act 1994 provides for state ownership of 'any archaeological object found in the state ... where such object has no known owner at the time when it was found'.[22] In Norway, the Cultural Heritage Act of 1978 provides for state ownership of vessels more than 100 years old, together with the cargo and other associated objects, 'when it seems clear under the circumstances that there is no longer any reasonable possibility of finding out whether there is an owner, or who the owner is'.[23] More rarely, legislation may be expropriatory in nature. The South African National Heritage Resources Act 1999 declares that 'all archaeological objects ... are the property of the State',[24] archaeological objects being defined to include wrecks of vessels and aircraft, and associated cargo and other items, which are older than sixty years or which the state heritage agency regards as worthy of preservation.[25] As Forrest has pointed out, the fact that the statute does not address the issue of prior ownership rights and therefore appears to extinguish them is likely to be problematic.[26] Among other things, questions about the payment of compensation may arise.[27] The South African legislation is also unusual in that it appears to assert ownership over material found not just in the territorial sea but also in the contiguous zone.[28]

---

succession should apply: *The Republic of Peru's Response to the Kingdom of Spain's Motion to Dismiss or for Summary Judgment*, 17 November 2008, pp. 27–8. Aside from Spain and Peru, twenty-five individuals, mainly claiming to be descendants of individuals with cargo aboard the *Mercedes*, also came forward with claims.

[20] See 675 F. Supp. 2d 1126, 1146, n. 24.

[21] For further discussion of the case, see section 4.1.2, below.

[22] For further details, see O'Connor, 'Ireland' (2nd edn), pp. 134 *et seq.* O'Connor points out that '[t]he definition of 'archaeological object' ... is very broad and encompasses objects of all periods': *ibid.*, p. 135. See, further, Long, *Marine Resources Law*, pp. 559–60.

[23] Kvalø and Marstrander, 'Norway', pp. 221–2.   [24] NHRA, s. 35(2).   [25] NHRA, s. 2(ii)(c).

[26] Forrest, 'South Africa', p. 260.   [27] See, further, section 2.4, below.

[28] As Prott and O'Keefe have pointed out, within state territory – including the territorial sea – a state has the power 'to vest ownership in any juristic person, including ... itself': Parliamentary Assembly of the Council of Europe, 'The Underwater Cultural Heritage: Report of the Committee on Culture and Education (Rapporteur: Mr John Roper)',

Domestic legislation providing for state ownership of wrecks or material from wrecks for reasons other than to protect cultural value is also
quite common. For example, the UK Merchant Shipping Act 1995 makes
provision for the Crown to assume title to unclaimed wreck, effectively
codifying the sovereign's traditional common law prerogative in this
regard.[29] Despite the original intention of the provision being to provide
income for the Exchequer, in recent times the Crown has forgone
any financial interest in material of historical significance.[30] In other
jurisdictions, too, maritime laws originally enacted for purposes other
than cultural heritage protection and providing for state ownership are
increasingly being administered in ways that may aid the protection of
cultural interests. For example, the Abandoned Wreck Law enacted in
1966 by the Cayman Islands vests ownership rights in wrecks that have
been on the seabed for more than fifty years in the state and provides for
the sharing of the value of recovered wreck between the salvor and the
government of the Cayman Islands. However, it seems that for many years
the government has denied salvage applications from treasure hunters.[31]

2.2   Establishment of ownership rights

It will be apparent from the foregoing discussion that the fact that property
has sunk to the bottom of the sea does not mean that the owner loses its
rights.[32] Indeed, even if a vessel has been lying at the bottom of the sea for
centuries, generally there is no presumption of a loss of title. Unless the
property has been subject to some form of lawful expropriation,[33] or has
been abandoned by its owner,[34] the ownership rights will continue to persist.

Document 4200-E, Strasbourg, 1978, p. 55. Whether or not a state has the power to
interfere with ownership rights in material found in the contiguous zone is a more
controversial question: see, further, Chap. 7, sections 3.3 and 3.5.

[29] See, further, Dromgoole and Gaskell, 'Interests in Wreck', pp. 178–82. Part IX of the
1995 Act, relating to wreck and salvage, largely re-enacts Part IX of the 1894 Act of the
same name. The question of whether the Crown or the finder has title to unclaimed
wreck recovered from international waters has been determined in favour of the finder:
The Lusitania [1986] QB 384.

[30] See, further, Dromgoole, 'United Kingdom', p. 320.

[31] See Leshikar-Denton and Luna Erreguerena, *Underwater and Maritime Archaeology in Latin
America and the Caribbean*, pp. 222–3. An initiative to replace the 1966 Act with new,
heritage-based, legislation appears to have lost momentum: personal communication
with Peggy Leshikar-Denton, 5 August 2012.

[32] According to Prott and O'Keefe, '[i]t is possible to state categorically that in no
jurisdiction does a shipowner lose title to a vessel when it sinks': Prott and O'Keefe, *Law
and the Cultural Heritage*, Vol. I, p. 318.

[33] On the question of expropriation, see section 2.4, below.

[34] On abandonment, see section 2.3, below.

The question of whether or not ownership rights exist in wrecks that have some cultural significance arises most frequently in the context of treasure salvage litigation taking place in the forum of the US federal admiralty courts.[35] Should anyone – a state, corporation or an individual – wish to assert ownership rights in the property that is the subject of the salvage action, it will need to come before the court. To be able to establish its claim, several hurdles will need to be cleared. These will include establishing the identity of the original owner and demonstrating a direct line of succession from that party through to the claimant.[36] It may also need to deal with the question of whether the ownership rights have been lost at some point, for example by some form of transfer or by abandonment. Where the claimant is an insurer, there are likely to be even more hurdles to overcome: among other things, it will be necessary to establish that the original insurer exercised its entitlement to take over the benefit of the property assured.[37]

Clearing these hurdles successfully can be extraordinarily difficult, even in respect of quite recent casualties. The circumstances in respect of the *Titanic*, lost in 1912, illustrate the problems that may be faced. The hull, fixtures and fittings were insured for £1 million and the insurance claim for an actual total loss was met in full.[38] However, there were many signatures on the Lloyd's underwriting slip and – even in so far as these are decipherable – most of the interests they represent can no longer be identified. There are also questions about whether rights in the *Titanic* were in fact taken up by the underwriters and, assuming they were, whether the vessel was under-insured, in which case the successor-in-title to the original owner, White Star Line, may retain some rights.[39] Another case in point is the SS *Central America*. This sidewheel steamer was carrying consignments of gold from Panama to New York in 1857, when she sank off South Carolina. After the vessel was found in 1989, the salvage company, Columbus-America Discovery

---

[35] For an explanation of why the cases tend to arise in the US courts, and a detailed discussion of the application to UCH of the law of salvage and the associated law of finds, see Chap. 5.

[36] On the question of the establishment of succession in title with respect to private individuals, see, further, below.

[37] See, further, Dromgoole and Gaskell, 'Interests in Wreck', pp. 168–70.

[38] *Ibid.*, pp. 172–3.

[39] The chain of succession would appear to lead to the Carnival Corporation (via Kvaerner, Trafalgar House and Cunard). In the long-running salvage action concerning the *Titanic* in the US federal admiralty courts (see, further, Chap. 5, section 3.4.3), no one has claimed ownership of the hull.

Group, initiated a salvage action. Reports that the gold on board might be worth up to $1 billion[40] led to a number of insurance companies and representatives of insurance interests coming forward to claim that they had paid out on cargo insurance policies. However, they had considerable difficulty proving their claims because they were only able to rely on contemporary newspaper reports, rather than official records, that they had insured the consignments and paid out on the loss.[41]

The Salvage Association of London maintains detailed records of maritime losses around the world dating back to 1860 and represents private interests in these casualties. In the case of vessels and their cargoes *pre-dating* that year, generally it will only be states, rather than private entities, that will have any chance of overcoming the hurdles to establishing an ownership claim. In recent years, Spain has intervened in salvage actions concerning historic vessels and cargoes on several occasions, motivated by a desire to protect both its cultural heritage and the sanctity of its sunken gravesites. On the first occasion, its claims to ownership of the naval frigates *Juno* (lost 1750) and *La Galga* (lost 1802) were upheld in a landmark decision in 2000 by the Fourth Circuit Court of Appeals (the *Sea Hunt* case).[42] In 2011, the Eleventh Circuit upheld Spain's claim to the frigate *Mercedes* (lost 1804) and its cargo of coins.[43] The outcome in both of these cases demonstrates that the assertion of state rights can prove to be an effective way of protecting cultural interests.

Ownership claims may be made well in advance of all the facts regarding the identity of a wreck (let alone the case in support of the ownership claim itself) being fully assembled. However, before

---

[40] See Kellam J. in the remand hearing: *Columbus-America Discovery Group, Inc.* v. *Unidentified, Wrecked and Abandoned Sailing Vessel*, 1993 WL 580900, 15 (ED Va. Nov. 18, 1993). The eventual bullion value was approximately $21 million, while the costs of the salvage company (awarded 90 per cent) were almost $30 million.

[41] *Columbus-America Discovery Group* v. *Atlantic Mutual Insurance* Co., 974 F.2d 450 (4th Cir. 1992). Despite the absence of official records, it was held by the Fourth Circuit Court of Appeals that several of the insurers had not abandoned their interests. On remand back to the district court, it was held that the salvors were entitled to approximately 90 per cent of the proceeds of sale, with the remainder to go to insurers who could prove title. See, generally, O'Keefe, 'Gold, Abandonment and Salvage'. On the rights of insurers, and whether or not they had abandoned those rights, see also the more recent case of *Yukon Recovery* (below).

[42] *Sea Hunt, Inc.*, 47 F. Supp. 2d 678 (ED Va. 1999), *aff'd in part, rev'd in part*, 221 F.3d 634 (4th Cir. 2000), *cert. denied*, 531, US 1144 (2001). See, further, section 2.3, below.

[43] *Odyssey Marine Exploration, Inc.*, v. *Unidentified, Shipwrecked Vessel*, 675 F. Supp. 2d 1126 (MD Fla. Dec. 22, 2009); *aff'd*, 657 F.3d 1159 (11th Cir. (Fla.) Sept. 21, 2011); *cert. denied*, 132 S. Ct. 2379 (US May 14, 2010). For further discussion, see Chap. 4, section 2.3.

ownership rights can be established, the identity of the sunken vessel must be determined. In some cases this can be done with, at least relative, ease.[44] For example, a warship may have been known to be carrying highly distinctive cannon and one or more of those cannon may have been discovered.[45] However, in other cases the identity may be much more difficult to determine: for example, if – like the *Mercedes* – a vessel had exploded under enemy fire.[46] One difficulty for the owner-ship claimant is that physical evidence at the wreck site usually will be entirely within the salvor's control and yet it may not be in the salvor's interests for the identity to be established. Questions may then arise about the level of disclosure that the salvor is required to make to the court.

Ownership claims by private individuals to a ship, cargo or personal possessions based on succession in title are rare and there appear to be no examples of such claims having been formally established by a court of law.[47] The fact that a claimant is a direct descendant of the original owner (even the closest, or only known, descendant) does not mean that they would necessarily have inherited the property: this is a question that a court would almost certainly wish to explore.[48]

---

[44] A vessel's identity is only likely to be established after at least some level of intervention and in many cases very extensive intervention will be required. In some cases, of course, the identity will never be established.

[45] For example, this appears to have been the case with the (sunken) British warship, HMS *Victory*. Despite the fact that the wreck was situated at a location somewhat different from where it might have been expected, two distinctive bronze cannon recovered from the site were identified as having originated from Admiral Sir John Balchin's 'first rate' warship.

[46] In the case of the *Mercedes*, the wreckage was 'strewn in an area a few football fields square': 675 F. Supp. 2d 1126, 1136. Although the salvor argued that the site could possibly represent an amalgamation of shipwrecks, or might not represent a shipwreck at all, Magistrate Judge Pizzo concluded that the presence of at least one of two distinctive bronze cannon at the site was 'highly probative of the vessel's identity': 675 F. Supp. 2d 1126, 1135 n. 8. The Eleventh Circuit, taking into account all the factual circumstances, concurred with the conclusion that the site was that of the *Mercedes*: 657 F.3d 1159, 1174.

[47] In the case of the *Mercedes*, the claims of individuals to ownership of some of the private cargoes on board the ship were not determined during the US federal litigation. See, further, Chap. 4, section 2.3.2.

[48] The author has not discovered any instances of such claims being established 'to the satisfaction of the receiver' under the UK Merchant Shipping Act 1995, s. 239(1), or equivalent provisions in other jurisdictions. However, succession in title alone is unlikely to satisfy the UK's Receiver of Wreck, who would require 'compelling' evidence of ownership: personal communication with Alison Kentuck, Receiver of Wreck, 31 July 2012.

2.3 Abandonment of ownership rights

It appears to be a matter of general acceptance that ownership rights are not lost merely through the sinking of a vessel: instead, for the owner to lose its rights it must be shown that it has either transferred those rights, for example through a treaty of cession, or has abandoned them.[49] For abandonment to occur, the mere physical abandonment of a ship (typically by the crew in the face of imminent peril) is not sufficient;[50] instead, there must also be some form of positive *intention* on the part of the owner to relinquish its rights of ownership. Such intention may be express, or may be inferred from the circumstances.

A difficult question is the extent to which one can ascertain an intention to abandon through mere lapse of time and failure to take action. Where a wreck has been lying neglected on a beach for many years, one might well draw the conclusion that ownership rights have been abandoned. If a claimant did come forward in such circumstances, it might find it difficult to refute the circumstantial evidence of an intention to abandon. On the other hand, in circumstances where a ship sank in deep water far out to sea and its location has been discovered only recently, or salvage has been impossible or economically unfeasible, can it really be said that the owner has demonstrated a positive intention to abandon its rights merely through its failure to take action? While different jurisdictions take different approaches to this question, it is clear that – in the absence of an *express* abandonment – an inference of abandonment will not be lightly drawn.

In the case of sunken warships and other state vessels engaged on public service, the position on abandonment is somewhat different from that for ordinary commercial vessels. A number of maritime powers, including France, Germany, Japan, Russia, Spain, the UK and the USA, take the firm position that ownership rights in such sunken vessels cannot be abandoned unless there has been *express* relinquishment: until such time, they insist that these wrecks remain the property of the flag state.[51] Express relinquishment of rights may have occurred through

---

[49] The question of the abandonment of ownership rights is very different from the question of the abandonment of liabilities, for example for environmental pollution. See, generally, Dromgoole and Forrest, 'The Nairobi Wreck Removal Convention 2007 and Hazardous Historic Shipwrecks'.

[50] However, the state of mere physical abandonment does have some significance in salvage law: see, further, Chap. 5, section 2.1.

[51] See the formal statements to this effect in Federal Register, Vol. 69, No. 24, 5 February 2004, discussed further in Chap. 4, section 2.2. For more detailed discussion of the position of sunken state vessels (and aircraft), see generally Chap. 4.

treaty. For example, in the *Sea Hunt* case the question of whether Spain
had relinquished its rights under the 1763 Definitive Treaty of Peace
signed by France, Great Britain and Spain was a point at issue in respect
of the Spanish frigate *La Galga*.[52]

In US litigation relating to the salvage of historic wrecks, the question
of abandonment is frequently central to determining the rights of
the salvor. The federal admiralty courts have shown themselves reluctant to make a finding of abandonment, especially where the owner
(even more particularly, a sovereign state) comes forward to make a
claim. A substantial body of case law has grown up since the 1970s
relating to the question of abandonment. Initially, salvors were inclined
to argue that a wreck *had* been abandoned, in order that they could claim
ownership under the law of finds;[53] however, after the enactment of the
US Abandoned Shipwreck Act of 1987 (ASA), in cases where the Act
applied, they shifted their strategy to arguing that a wreck had *not* been
abandoned and that they were therefore entitled to a reward under the
law of salvage.[54] In the landmark *Sea Hunt* case, the central question
before the court was whether Spain had abandoned its ownership rights
in the two galleons *Juno* and *La Galga*. Unusually for a case that related
to the ASA, it was the salvage company that was seeking to rely on
abandonment.[55] The Fourth Circuit Court of Appeals was impressed
that Spain had come before the court to claim its rights and took

[52] *Sea Hunt, Inc.*, 47 F. Supp. 2d 678, 688–90 (ED Va. 1999). The trial judge's finding of
express abandonment of *La Galga* under the 1763 Treaty was reversed by the Fourth
Circuit Court of Appeals: 221 F.3d 634 (4th Cir. 2000). The Fourth Circuit emphasised the
need for 'clear and convincing' evidence of express abandonment and concluded that
the wording of the treaty was not clear enough. On this case, see, further, Chap. 4,
section 2.3.2. The question of whether shipwrecks were ceded by this treaty has also
been considered in respect of French vessels lying off the Canadian coast: see Le Gurun,
'France' (2nd edn), pp. 93–4.
[53] This approach proved successful in the landmark *Treasure Salvors* case, concerning the
Spanish treasure galleon, *Atocha*. See *Treasure Salvors* v. *The Unidentified Wrecked and
Abandoned Sailing Vessel* 569 F.2d 330 (5th Cir. 1978). Spain did not assert a claim in this
case. See, further, Chap. 5, section 3.4.1.
[54] Under the ASA, the USA asserts title to any abandoned shipwreck that is embedded in
the submerged lands of a state or is located on the submerged lands of a state and is
included in, or deemed eligible for inclusion in, the National Register of Historic Places.
That title is then automatically transferred to the relevant state. Wrecks deemed to be
'abandoned', a term not defined by the Act, therefore become public property, rather
than the property of the finder. See, further, Chap. 5, section 3.4.2.
[55] In this case, the state of Virginia had asserted ownership of the wrecks under the ASA
and had issued the salvor, Sea Hunt, with a permit allowing it to recover artefacts.
The permit included provision for the state and Sea Hunt to share any proceeds. See,
further, Chap. 4, section 2.3.2.

particular account of this fact. It held that where a previous owner claims long-lost property involuntarily taken from its control, the law will be 'hesitant' to find abandonment.[56] If the owner comes forward, abandonment by express acts must be shown for it to lose its rights. This, it was said, reflected the longstanding admiralty law rule that when articles are lost at sea the title of the owner remains. While the Fourth Circuit placed some emphasis on the fact that the claimant was a sovereign state, and that it was acting to protect the sanctity of its military gravesites, there is nothing in the decision to suggest that these facts were decisive. It seems, therefore, that a similar position would be taken even in the case of non-state owners. Indeed, the authority relied upon by the court was the *Columbus-America* case, which involved private claimants.[57] The Fourth Circuit affirmed that '[a]n inference of abandonment is permitted only when no owner appears'.[58] At the same time it confirmed the position taken by Spain, the USA and other states that an *express* abandonment was required in the case of warships and other state vessels.[59]

An interesting case relating to the question of when abandonment may be inferred from the circumstances is *Yukon Recovery* v. *Certain Abandoned Property* (2000).[60] This case related to the question of which of two salvors was entitled to exclusive rights to recover a cargo of gold on a vessel that had sunk in 1901. A 'pure salvor' seeking exclusive rights to the site argued that a competing 'contract salvor' had no rights because the insurance company with whom it had made the contract had previously abandoned the property.[61] The Ninth Circuit Court of Appeals concluded that the fact that 'extremely primitive, although

[56] 221 F.3d 634, 641 (4th Cir. 2000), citing *Columbus-America*, 974 F.2d 450, 467–8 (4th Cir. (Va.) Aug. 26, 1992).

[57] See section 2.2, above.

[58] 221 F.3d 634, 641, citing *Columbus-America*, 974 F.2d 450, 465.

[59] 221 F.3d 634, 643. In the same year, but just prior to the Fourth Circuit's decision in the *Sea Hunt* case, the Eleventh Circuit Court of Appeals also showed itself reluctant to accept evidence of abandonment in the case of the TBD-1, a US Navy torpedo bomber that crashed off the Florida coast in 1943 during a training flight: *International Aircraft Recovery, LLC* v. *Unidentified, Wrecked and Abandoned Aircraft*, 218 F.3d 1255 (11th Cir. 2000), *cert. denied*, 121 S. Ct. 1079 (2001). Evidence that the plane had been struck from the Navy's inventory of active planes was not enough to establish abandonment.

[60] *Yukon Recovery LLC* v. *Certain Abandoned Property*, 205 F.3d 1189 (9th Cir. (Alaska) 2000); *cert. denied*, 531 US 820, 121 S. Ct. 62 (2000).

[61] Salvage may or may not be undertaken under contract. A 'pure salvor' is one who undertakes salvage without being contracted to do so. On this, and the question of competing salvors, see, further, Chap. 5, section 2.1.

ingenious' technology was available in 1934 to enable the recovery of two-thirds of the vessel's hull did not mean that the insurance company had abandoned its rights to the gold because it had not made use of that technology to recover the gold. Instead it concluded that '[i]t is only by virtue of modern technological advances that the current salvage attempt is within the realm of possibility'.[62]

What becomes of property that *is* abandoned? Two distinctive approaches may be discerned. In some jurisdictions, abandoned property becomes the property of the state, either by virtue of sovereign prerogative or by statute. In other jurisdictions, property that has been abandoned will be *res nullius*, in other words, ownerless, and will remain so until such time as a finder reduces it to his or her possession.[63] The former approach is sometimes known as the 'English' rule and the latter as the 'American' rule (in light of the pre-ASA position that title to abandoned wrecks vested in the finder, the position which remains the case for non-ASA cases). As between the two approaches, a system based on the 'English' rule is likely to be preferable from a cultural heritage standpoint because it avoids operation of the 'finders keepers' principle.

While domestic legislation providing for state ownership of abandoned property is sometimes advantageous from a cultural heritage perspective, potentially it can lead to problems in respect of property in which *other* states have, or at least claim, an ownership interest. For example, under Finnish antiquities legislation, the wreck of a ship that sank more than 100 years ago and that lies within the Finnish territorial limit belongs to the Finnish state if it can be inferred from external circumstances that it has been abandoned by its owner.[64] In 1999, the wreck of the *Vrouw Maria* was discovered in the outer archipelago off Turku. This Dutch merchant vessel, which sank in 1771 en route from Amsterdam to St. Petersburg, was believed to have been carrying valuable artworks bought at auction on behalf of Catherine the Great. In 2005, in a salvage action brought by the finders, the Turku Court of Appeal held that the wreck had been clearly abandoned and that it belonged to the state of Finland.[65] However, in 2008, it was reported that Russia – successor in title to the property of the Russian Empire,

---

[62] 205 F.3d 1189, 1194.   [63] On the law of finding, see Chap. 5.

[64] For details of the Finnish legislation, see Matikka, 'Finland', pp. 47 *et seq.*

[65] For details of this action, see *ibid.*, pp. 52–4. See also, Chap. 5, section 3.3. (After this decision, the finders took the case to the European Court of Human Rights. For a discussion of the points at issue, see Chap. 5, section 3.3.)

including that of Catherine the Great – had shown an interest in the prospect of recovery of the paintings.[66] As in this case, where the conclusion appears to have been reached that the best way forward is to seek to reach agreement to collaborate over the future management of the wreck, such conflicts may ultimately prove to be resolvable only through diplomacy and cooperation.[67]

An example of the successful resolution of conflicts of this kind can be found in the approach of Australia and the Netherlands in the case of the four Dutch East Indiamen located off the coast of Western Australia. After the discovery of these wrecks, political tensions arose between Australia and the Netherlands concerning the question of ownership. The Netherlands claimed ownership on the basis that it was the successor in title to the Dutch East India Company, but Australia was of the view that the wrecks had been impliedly abandoned through lapse of time and inaction.[68] Ultimately the dispute was resolved when the two states entered into a bilateral agreement providing for the disposition of artefacts recovered from the sites. The Agreement Between the Netherlands and Australia Concerning Old Dutch Shipwrecks of 1972 provides for the transfer of 'all the rights, title and interest' of the Netherlands to the wrecks and for the sharing of artefacts between the Netherlands, Australia and the State of Western Australia.[69] It acknowledges that the Netherlands was 'successor to the property and assets' of the Dutch East India Company but not that it had title to the wrecks. Instead it refers to the 'continuing interest' of the Netherlands in articles recovered therefrom, 'particularly for historical and other cultural purposes'.[70]

[66] These may have been packed in leaden containers sealed with wax, in which case they may be in a good state of preservation: see 'Russia to raise shipwreck containing Catherine the Great's treasures', *Daily Telegraph*, 18 November 2008.
[67] As at the end of 2010, a formal agreement had yet to be reached, but all states with an interest – Finland, Russia, the Netherlands and Sweden (the last because it holds relevant historical archives) – had been involved in discussions at political level: personal communication with Maija Matikka, 21 December 2010.
[68] O'Keefe, *Shipwrecked Heritage*, p. 68.
[69] The Agreement is enshrined in Schedule 1 to the Australian Commonwealth Historic Shipwrecks Act 1976. In Schedule 2, the four vessels are listed: *Batavia, Vergulde Draeck (Gilt Dragon), Zuytdorp* and *Zeewyk*. While in the past the sharing of the artefacts was undertaken by physically splitting up the collection and holding it in separate locations, in 2010, the Dutch holding was returned to Australia. In the future, the collection will be shared by means of an online database: see, further, Chap. 9, n. 46.
[70] On the Agreement, see, further, Chap. 10, section 2. See also Prott and O'Keefe, *Law and the Cultural Heritage*, Vol. I, pp. 318–19; Jeffery, 'Australia' (1st edn), pp. 3–5. According to Maarleveld, the Agreement itself 'is nothing more than a deed of transfer of ownership

2.4 The circumscription or expropriation of ownership rights by heritage legislation

In circumstances where private ownership rights persist, there is considerable potential for conflicts to arise between the owner's wishes with respect to their property and the aims and objectives of heritage legislation. This potential is exemplified by a fairly recent case relating to RMS *Lusitania*. The liner sank off the Irish coast in 1915 after a German U-boat attack and ownership rights to the hull and its appurtenances were purchased from the war risks insurer by a group of private individuals in 1967. One of these individuals, Bemis, later bought out his co-owners. In 1995, the wreck site was designated as a restricted area under Irish national monuments legislation and in 2001 Bemis applied for a licence under that legislation to undertake an intrusive investigation of the wreck. In 2007, the Irish Supreme Court upheld a ruling at first instance that concluded that a decision by the Irish culture ministry to refuse Bemis a licence was *ultra vires*, void and of no effect.[71] Although the case turned on matters of statutory interpretation and procedure, it seems to have been accepted – at least by the judge at first instance and the culture ministry – that the property rights of the applicant *were* a relevant consideration in determining the outcome of the licence application.[72]

The fact that the property rights should have been taken into account in determining whether or not a licence was issued does not necessarily mean that a licence would have to be issued, or that any licence that was issued could not be made subject to conditions which would curtail the owner's rights. An earlier decision of the Irish Supreme Court relating to the ownership of a hoard of treasure confirmed the principle that the state is entitled to regulate the exercise of private property rights for the 'common good' arising from the protection of cultural heritage.[73] Although the decision is regarded as a landmark in Irish law for other

---

on the condition of shared benefits' but nevertheless it has formed the basis for decades of cooperation with respect to the management of the wrecks: Maarleveld, 'The Netherlands', p. 165, incl. n. 24.

[71] *Bemis* v. *Minister for Arts, Heritage, Gaeltacht and the Islands* [2007] 3 IR 255.

[72] For the interesting judgment at first instance, see *Bemis* v. *Minister for Arts, Heritage, Gaeltacht and the Islands* [2005] IEHC 207. While one of the three judges in the Supreme Court agreed that the owner's rights were a relevant consideration (see Fennelly J. at p. 260), the majority decision on this point was that the Court should not pronounce on this issue.

[73] *Webb* v. *Ireland* [1988] IR 353.

reasons,[74] the 'common good' principle on which it is based is an extension of a fundamental principle of international law that 'no one shall be *arbitrarily* deprived of his property'.[75] It is common for states to circumscribe the property rights of owners in the interests of cultural heritage protection,[76] in other words to restrict an owner's ability to exercise full ownership rights, including the rights to exclude others, to alienate and to destroy. What matters is that this is not done arbitrarily and an appropriate balance is struck between public and private interests.[77]

Occasionally (for example, as appears to be the case with the South African National Heritage Resources Act 1999),[78] heritage legislation may amount to a 'taking' of property, in other words, deprivation of title. To be a lawful 'taking', or expropriation, just compensation is likely to be required.[79] However, in the more common situation where heritage legislation deals with the question of property rights by providing for the deeming of abandonment after a certain period of time, it seems likely that in most circumstances this would be regarded as merely an interpretation of the general notion of abandonment, not as a taking.[80]

---

[74] It established a principle at common law that the state, not the finder, was the owner of archaeological finds which had no known owner. The principle was later codified in the National Monuments (Amendment) Act 1994 (see section 2.1, above). For further discussion, see O'Connor, 'Ireland' (2nd edn), pp. 131–4.

[75] Universal Declaration of Human Rights, Art. 17(2). Emphasis added. See also the European Convention on Human Rights, First Protocol, Art. 1. This issue is considered again, in the context of the possessory rights of salvors and finders, in Chap. 5, section 3.3.

[76] On this, see Prott and O'Keefe, '"Cultural Heritage" or "Cultural Property"?', p. 310.

[77] In the specific context of application of Art. 1 of the First Protocol to the European Convention on Human Rights, the key factor appears to be that there must be proportionality between the restriction imposed on the owner's rights and the public benefit derived from that restriction. On this provision, see, further, Chap. 5, section 3.3. Where the curtailment of rights is so severe that it amounts to a deprivation of title, compensation will be payable: see below.

[78] See section 2.1, above.

[79] Compensation for the taking is likely to be required under domestic constitutional laws. Where the property of a foreigner is involved, public international law will require 'prompt, adequate, and effective' compensation: see Brownlie, *Principles of Public International Law*, p. 533. In some circumstances, the taking of the property of a foreigner will also give rise to questions under private international law as well. For a general discussion of the question of taking, see Prott and O'Keefe, *Law and the Cultural Heritage*, Vol. III, Chap. 8.

[80] See, for example, Prott and O'Keefe, *Law and the Cultural Heritage*, Vol. I, p. 193; Council of Europe Doc. 4200-E, 1978, pp. 55 and 68. But see also section 3.2.1, below.

3. Treatment of ownership rights by international law

One of the most difficult issues facing the drafters of any international legal instrument designed to afford protection to UCH is deciding how to deal with existing rights of ownership. Clearly there are a whole host of potential conflicts that might arise between the rights of owners (particularly, but not necessarily, the rights of private owners) and the demands of cultural heritage protection.

Prima facie, the most straightforward way to avoid any potential conflict would be to find a means of taking ownership rights out of the picture altogether. One option would be to adopt an approach whereby all UCH over, say, 100 years underwater, is *deemed* to be abandoned. However, in light of the fact that valuable commercial interests in shipwrecks dating from 1860 are still documented and traceable, such a measure is likely to be politically unpalatable to states that traditionally favour private interests. An alternative approach would be to limit the scope of the protective measures to material that *is* abandoned. However, unless the concept of abandonment is defined by the instrument, the US experience with the ASA suggests that problems will arise; equally, the drawing up of a definition of abandonment is likely to pose its own difficulties.[81] If either of the above options was followed, questions would arise regarding the status of the abandoned property. Clearly the 'American' rule – whereby finder becomes keeper – would be inappropriate, but there would also be difficulty in applying the 'English' rule that abandoned property falls into public ownership. Some states have political and philosophical objections to the notion of state ownership and many states would be concerned about potential liabilities that might arise.[82] There would also be questions about *which* particular state should become the owner given the multitude of potential scenarios that would arise in the context of an instrument applicable to extra-territorial waters. The fact that different states have very different approaches to the concept of property, and to the balance to be drawn between private property rights and the public interest, would make reaching an international consensus on issues such as these immensely difficult.

---

[81] See section 3.2.1, below.

[82] For example, in circumstances where a wreck poses a navigational or pollution hazard. For detailed discussion of such hazards, see Dromgoole and Forrest, 'The Nairobi Wreck Removal Convention 2007 and Hazardous Historic Shipwrecks'.

3.1 Ownership and the Law of the Sea Convention 1982

Of the two articles relating to UCH in the LOSC, only one refers explicitly to the question of ownership.

Article 303(3) provides:

Nothing in this article affects the rights of identifiable owners, the law of salvage or other rules of admiralty, or laws and practices with respect to cultural exchanges.[83]

The precise effect of this provision is hard to fathom. Certainly it is not an attempt to exclude or abolish the rights of identifiable owners; equally, it does not provide that states *must* recognise ownership rights, or give them priority over heritage protection objectives, when they implement the provisions to which this paragraph applies.

Article 303(3) applies to other paragraphs of Article 303: namely, paragraph 1, which imposes a general duty on states to protect UCH found at sea and to cooperate for that purpose, and paragraph 2, which makes specific provision in respect of UCH found in the contiguous zone.[84] It also appears to apply to Article 149, the other provision in the LOSC addressing UCH. As pointed out in Chapter 1, the reason for this is that the provisions of Article 303 – with the exception of paragraph 2 – are generally assumed to apply to all sea areas by virtue of the fact that Article 303 is located in Part XVI of the treaty (headed 'General Provisions').[85] In fact, in light of this, Article 149 tends to be regarded as a specific application of the duty to protect set out in Article 303(1).[86]

The saving in Article 303(3) makes it clear that the duty under paragraph 1 and the control mechanism in paragraph 2 do not, *in themselves*, have the effect of interfering with, or expropriating, the rights of identifiable owners.[87] Instead, in circumstances where these provisions apply, the question of ownership rights will be one that falls to be determined by the applicable domestic law. As seen above, this may deal with such rights in a variety of ways.[88] As far as the impact of

---

[83] Emphasis added.

[84] It is irrelevant to the 'without prejudice' clause in Art. 303(4).

[85] See Chap. 1, section 2.1.2. Interestingly, an early draft of Art. 149 specifically recognised ownership rights. See, further, section 4.1.1, below.

[86] See, further, Chap. 7, section 3.5.

[87] For a detailed discussion of the operation of these provisions, see Chap. 7, sections 3.1 and 3.3. As far as 'the law of salvage and other rules of admiralty' are concerned, see Chap. 5, section 3.1.

[88] The position of South Africa with respect to the contiguous zone is particularly interesting. On this, see, further, Chap. 7, section 3.3.

Article 303(3) on Article 149 is concerned, a factor that needs to be taken into account is that article's recognition of other interests in UCH. The interaction between these interests and possible ownership rights therefore needs to be taken into account.[89]

A question that arises from time to time is the extent to which Article 303(3) may affect, and fetter, later international agreements in the field. It can be argued that any attempt to create a subsequent treaty relating to UCH is a specific application of the duty to protect in Article 303(1) and is therefore subject to Article 303(3). This could mean that a subsequent treaty should not itself interfere with ownership rights but leave the matter to be determined by national laws. However, account must also be taken of Article 303(4). This provides:

This article is without prejudice to other international agreements and rules of international law regarding the protection of objects of an archaeological and historical nature.

Assuming, as most commentators have done, that the 'other international agreements and rules of international law' referred to in this paragraph include treaties that are concluded subsequent to, as well as antecedent to, the LOSC, then it would seem that Article 303(3) has no effect on the freedom of the negotiators of a subject-specific treaty on UCH to deal with ownership rights in whatever way they see fit.

3.2   Ownership and the UNESCO Convention 2001

3.2.1   Background

In 1978, Prott and O'Keefe, the expert legal consultants appointed to advise the Council of Europe's Committee on Culture and Education on the formulation of recommended minimum requirements for domestic laws on UCH, advocated state ownership of all material that had been underwater for more than 100 years.[90] They believed this would enable the competent heritage authority to determine the fate of the material without delay and uncertainty.[91] However, the proposal was not incorporated in the minimum requirements laid down by Recommendation 848. The 1985 draft European Convention also made no attempt to interfere with private ownership rights by providing for state ownership,

---

[89] See, further, section 4.1, below.
[90] Council of Europe Doc. 4200-E, 1978, p. 68.   [91] Ibid.

or otherwise, and instead adopted a saving provision along the lines of that in Article 303(3) of the LOSC.[92]

In the early stages of the development of a draft for what would become the UNESCO Convention 2001, the approach pursued by the ILA and, in turn, initially by UNESCO, was to follow the lead of the US statute, the ASA, by applying the Convention only to material that had been abandoned.[93] However, the failure of that statute explicitly to define abandonment had resulted in considerable uncertainty and litigation before the US courts and it was therefore recognised that – in order 'to stabilize expectations'[94] – the Convention would need to provide a definition.

The definition adopted by the 1998 UNESCO Draft, which followed that of the 1994 ILA Draft, specified two sets of circumstances when abandonment would be 'deemed' to have taken place: first, where an owner had not taken action in respect of its property within twenty-five years of the availability of technology making the action possible; and secondly, where such technology was not available, after the lapse of a period of fifty years since the owner last asserted an interest.[95] This definition was open to criticism on a number of grounds.[96] One of the most significant of these grounds is that an owner could argue that its position over a period of time had been adopted on the basis of the then prevailing domestic law. The application of a recently devised formula for abandonment would therefore amount to a retrospective taking of property rights, for which it would be entitled to compensation. Rather than stabilising expectations, it seemed that the provision had the effect of doing precisely the opposite: upsetting expectations that may have been established years in the past.

Apart from the difficulties involved in drawing up a clear and workable definition of abandonment, another serious impediment to the

---

[92] Art. 2(7) of the declassified version of 1984 (the same provision was incorporated in the final text, but in a different article). As far as ownership rights are concerned, the only difference between this provision and Art. 303(3) of the LOSC was that while Art. 303(3) provides that nothing in the article will affect the rights of identifiable owners the 1985 provision made it clear that nothing in the whole of the Convention would affect those rights.

[93] The 1994 ILA Draft also applied to UCH that had been 'lost': see Art. 2(1). The word 'lost' is highly ambiguous and it may have been for this reason that it was later dropped.

[94] O'Keefe and Nafziger, 'Report', p. 406, citing a commentary on the 1994 ILA Draft.

[95] 1998 UNESCO Draft, Art. 1(2). See also 1994 ILA Draft, Art. 1(2).

[96] See Dromgoole and Gaskell, 'Draft UNESCO Convention on the Protection of the Underwater Cultural Heritage', pp. 180–3. See also Bederman, 'The UNESCO Draft Convention on Underwater Cultural Heritage', pp. 334–8.

original approach of the ILA and UNESCO was that it caused problems with respect to its application to sovereign vessels and aircraft. As outlined above, the USA and a number of other maritime states take a robust line on the question of ownership of such craft and insist that title can be lost only through *express* relinquishment. In recognition that any provision in a treaty having the effect of interfering with this principle would be unacceptable to these states, the early drafts excluded such vessels and aircraft from their scope of application.[97] However, the consequence of this exclusion was that a large and important component of UCH then fell outside the treaty's protective regime. The early drafts also provided no guidance in respect of the status of property that *was* deemed to be abandoned: would one of the 'English' or 'American' approaches be adopted, both problematic, or might the material be held in some manner for the benefit of humankind, in light of the overall objective of the initiative? The latter outcome – while in some senses principled – does not sit comfortably with domestic law approaches to property and, ultimately, any problems *would* need to be addressed by domestic law. In any event, given all these difficulties, at the Second Meeting of Government Experts in 1999, the attempt to apply the instrument only to UCH that had been abandoned was dropped.

3.2.2   Approach of the UNESCO Convention and its implications

In light of the difficulties in trying to deal with the matter 'head-on', the UNESCO Convention makes no reference to ownership at all. In the absence of any guidance from the treaty, the assumption must be that ownership rights will continue to exist in material falling within the scope of the Convention unless the applicable domestic law provides otherwise.

Leaving ownership as a matter to be determined by national laws was the pragmatic way forward. Not only did it facilitate the inclusion of warships within the scope of the Convention, but also the negotiation process as a whole. The approach means that national heritage authorities and, ultimately, national courts will have to deal with any ownership claims that might arise with respect to material falling within the definition of the Convention. The balancing of the rights of the owner with the public interest – as represented by the Convention's principles and protective framework – will be a very similar exercise to that undertaken under pre-conventional legislative frameworks. However, implementation

[97] 1994 ILA Draft, Art. 2(2); 1998 UNESCO Draft, Art. 2(2).

of the treaty framework – which requires, among other things, that preservation *in situ* be considered as the first option; that any activities directed at UCH may only be undertaken for limited reasons and in compliance with the annexed Rules; and that any recoveries must be kept together and intact as a collection in a manner that is available for professional and public access – inevitably will result in a substantial interference with any owner's rights. Unlike the position under some domestic legislation, there is little room for any allowances to be made to take account of the owner's wishes. Where the interference is such that it amounts to a deprivation of title, compensation is likely to be payable and there seems to be little that a state party can do to avoid this. Where the treaty's provisions for the seizure of material are triggered, particular problems can be envisaged.[98]

One needs to bear in mind that it is only UCH that has been underwater for at least 100 years that falls within the scope of the Convention. This threshold, in itself, can be regarded as a compromise between heritage protection interests and the interests of owners.[99] Nonetheless, in light of the Salvage Association's records of losses dating back to 1860, it is quite possible that private interests may come forward to claim commercially valuable cargoes to which the Convention applies and, as the years pass and more documented losses fall within the 100-year threshold, such claims are likely to become increasingly common.

As the UK government has demonstrated on a number of occasions in recent years,[100] states may also be interested in asserting ownership rights in shipwreck cargoes of commercial value. Given that they may have some chance of establishing an ownership interest in UCH *pre-dating* the mid nineteenth century, the question of state ownership under the conventional regime is likely to be particularly significant. Fundamentally there is no distinction in kind between state ownership and private ownership. However, states will have a wider range of motivations for asserting their rights: sometimes it will be for financial benefit, but sometimes it will be to protect the cultural value of the site or its sanctity as a gravesite. For obvious reasons, difficulty in reconciling their interests with the scheme of the Convention is most likely to arise in the first instance.[101] Where a state owner has ratified the Convention,

---

[98] See Art. 18. For discussion, see Chap. 9, section 5.1.
[99] See Chap. 2, section 4.2.1.   [100] See nn. 15 and 17, above.
[101] For a discussion of the question of a reconciliation between the *non-financial* interests of states in their sunken property and the principles and rules of the Convention, see

it will of course be duty bound to abide by the principles of the Convention and to cooperate with other states. It is therefore in circumstances where *non*-states parties claim ownership that difficulties are particularly likely to arise. Nonetheless, such states will need to give consideration to the nature and extent of the duty under Article 303(1) of the LOSC to protect UCH and to cooperate for that purpose. Most states are a party to the LOSC and, even where they are not, they should reflect on the extent to which the duty in Article 303(1) may now represent the position under customary international law.[102] Ultimately, just as is the case now, it seems likely that in most cases disputes will be resolved through diplomatic channels.

4. Other interests recognised by international law

The LOSC and the UNESCO Convention 2001 both formally recognise other types of interest in UCH besides those of an owner.

4.1   *Interests recognised by the Law of the Sea Convention 1982*

Article 149 of the LOSC provides:

All objects of an archaeological and historical nature found in the Area shall be preserved or disposed of *for the benefit of mankind as a whole, particular regard being paid to the preferential rights of the State or country of origin, or the State of cultural origin, or the State of historical and archaeological origin.*[103]

This article, located in Part XI of the treaty, applies only to material found on the deep seabed beyond the limits of national jurisdiction.[104] It explicitly refers to two forms of interest: that of 'mankind as a whole' and that of states (or countries) with 'preferential rights' by virtue of the fact that they are places of 'origin'.

4.1.1   Interests of mankind

In providing that '[a]ll objects of an archaeological and historical nature found in the Area shall be preserved or disposed of *for the benefit of mankind as a whole*', what does Article 149 actually mean?

Chap. 4, section 3.3. For a discussion of the question of commercial exploitation *by* states, see Chap. 6, section 3.4.

[102] See, further, Chap. 7, section 3.1. It should also be noted that many states have expressed support for the general principles of the Convention, especially the Rules in the Annex, even if they have reservations about other aspects of the Convention.
[103] Emphasis added.   [104] See LOSC, Art. 1(1).

The legal regime for the Area set out in Part XI provides that '[t]he Area and its resources are the *common heritage of mankind*'[105] and that '[a]ctivities in the Area shall ... be carried out for the benefit of mankind as a whole'.[106] However, for the purposes of the LOSC, the 'resources' of the Area comprise only the mineral resources of the Area[107] and 'activities' in the Area are only activities relating to the exploration and exploitation of those mineral resources.[108] Therefore, cultural material found on the deep seabed – despite the fact it could be characterised as a resource of the Area – falls outside the 'common heritage of mankind' (CHM) concept enshrined in Part XI. Nonetheless, there can be little doubt that the aspirational objective expressed in Article 149 – that UCH found in the Area shall be dealt with for the benefit of mankind as a whole – was influenced in some measure by the approach Part XI takes to mineral resources.

Much has been written about the CHM concept.[109] It has commonly arisen in respect of areas or spaces that have yet to be appropriated by any state or entity and the concept is characterised by certain basic elements.[110] One of the most fundamental of these elements is that the space and its resources are not to be subject to appropriation by either public or private entities. A sharing of the benefits – usually *economic* benefits – by all people and not simply those that have the ability to access the area and exploit the resources is another key feature. A third element is that the administration of the space and its resources is undertaken by an agency of some kind on behalf of mankind. The CHM concept first came to international attention in 1967[111] and to date its most concrete manifestations have been in the Moon Treaty 1979[112] and the LOSC. In the LOSC, the regime established under Part XI was designed to provide for the sharing of the economic benefits of polymetallic nodules and other minerals located on or in the deep seabed.

[105] LOSC, Art. 136. Emphasis added.   [106] LOSC, Art. 140.
[107] LOSC, Art. 133(a).   [108] LOSC, Art. 1(1)(3).
[109] For a good starting point, see Baslar, *The Concept of the Common Heritage of Mankind in International Law*.
[110] See Joyner, 'Legal Implications of the Concept of the Common Heritage of Mankind', pp. 191–2.
[111] On 1 November 1967, the Maltese Ambassador to the UN, Avid Pardo, famously proposed in a speech to the UN General Assembly that the resources of the deep seabed beyond the limits of national jurisdiction should be used in the 'interests of mankind': see Churchill and Lowe, *The Law of the Sea*, p. 226.
[112] More formally known as the Agreement Governing the Activities of States on the Moon and other Celestial Bodies 1979.

Part XI makes provision for activities in the Area to be managed by the International Seabed Authority (ISA), which acts on behalf of mankind.[113]

At the time of UNCLOS III, a notion related to the CHM concept had also started to emerge in the context of cultural heritage. The 1954 Hague Convention for the Protection of Cultural Property in the Event of Armed Conflict provides that damage to cultural property is regarded as 'damage to the cultural heritage of all mankind'[114] and the 1972 World Heritage Convention provides that cultural – and natural – heritage of 'outstanding universal value' needs to be preserved as part of 'the world heritage of mankind as a whole'.[115] The variations in the relevant language formulations in these, and later, heritage instruments suggest that the notion they employ is looser than the CHM concept,[116] but nonetheless its characteristics are broadly similar. However, rather than envisaging a sharing of *economic* benefits, the notion envisages the sharing by humanity of broader – non-economic – benefits deriving from protective measures, as well as the sharing of *responsibility* for ensuring that such measures are put in place notwithstanding the economic and technical disparities that arise on a national and regional basis. The notion that the resource is an inheritance, to be cared for on behalf of future generations, plays a prominent role in this context and, again, as with the more formal CHM concept, there may be an agent of some kind that acts in the interests of mankind, often characterised as a steward or custodian. For example, in the case of the World Heritage Convention, this agent is the World Heritage Committee.[117]

Article 149 gives expression to the notion that UCH is a matter of public interest and assumes that mankind *as a whole* has an interest in all such material. In this respect the provision takes an 'internationalist' rather than 'nationalist' perspective:[118] UCH found in the Area – whatever

---

[113] LOSC, Art. 137(2).

[114] Hague Convention 1954, preamble. See, further, O'Keefe, *The Protection of Cultural Property in Armed Conflict*, pp. 94–5.

[115] World Heritage Convention 1972, preamble. See, further, Francioni, *The 1972 World Heritage Convention*, pp. 15–16.

[116] It certainly comes with less philosophical baggage. See the discussion of the influence of the New International Economic Order (NIEO) on the CHM concept in Joyner, 'Legal Implications of the Concept of the Common Heritage of Mankind', pp. 192–3.

[117] Detailed provision for the Committee is set out in Arts. 8–14 of the World Heritage Convention.

[118] Merryman distinguished two approaches to cultural material and used the terms 'cultural nationalism' and 'cultural internationalism' to refer to these approaches: see Merryman, 'Two Ways of Thinking About Cultural Property' and 'Cultural Property Internationalism', essays republished in Merryman, *Thinking about the Elgin Marbles*, chaps. 3 and 4 respectively.

its origins – is regarded as of common interest to *all* states and to *all* mankind, not simply to those connected to its place of origin. The objective of the article is that mankind as a whole should benefit from its preservation or disposal. However, a serious deficiency of Article 149 is that it makes no provision for a steward to act on behalf of mankind to ensure that this objective is met.

As previously noted,[119] there is an implication from the wording of Article 149 (the fact that it refers to 'objects' which are to be 'preserved or disposed of') that it does not envisage that UCH will remain *in situ*, but rather that after discovery it *will* be recovered and brought ashore. If recovered objects are to be preserved for mankind as a whole, as a starting point one might suppose that they would be deposited in a publicly accessible museum, or similar institution. However, one of the curious features of Article 149 is that it includes the words 'or disposed of', thereby at least appearing to imply that not *all* material falling within its scope need be retained in perpetuity. In so far as the reference to disposal might include sale and dispersal, this seems to run counter to notions of stewardship and inheritance. Furthermore, if ownership rights can persist (and the fact that Article 303(3) appears to apply to Article 149 indicates that this *is* the case),[120] how do these rights interact with the interests of mankind? The fact that Article 149 provides that '*[a]ll* objects of an archaeological and historical nature found in the Area *shall be* preserved or disposed of for the benefit of mankind as a whole'[121] certainly suggests that ownership rights – at least in so far as these are held by *private* interests[122] – should be subordinated to, and restricted in, the public interest. In itself, this simply reflects the position under much domestic heritage legislation. However, if the limitation amounts to a taking, one question that manifests itself is: who would be responsible for the payment of compensation?

4.1.2 Preferential rights of states (or countries) of origin

Despite the absence of sovereignty implicit within the CHM notion proper, in its articulation of a legal regime for UCH in the Area Article 149 refers to the 'preferential rights' of certain states and

---

[119] See Chap. 2, section 3.1.

[120] See section 3.1 above. An early draft of the provision that became Art. 149 included the following paragraph: 'The recovery and disposal of wrecks and their contents more than 50 years old found in the Area shall be subject to regulation by the Authority *without prejudice to the rights of the owner thereof*': ISNT, art. 19, para. 1. Emphasis added. While this wording was dropped, it may perhaps provide an indication of the intention of the drafters in this respect.

[121] Emphasis added.   [122] On the rights of states, see section 4.1.2, below.

requires that 'particular regard' must be paid to these rights when determining the fate of material.

The fact that Article 149 refers to the preferential rights of *three* different categories of state – 'the state or country of origin', 'the state of cultural origin', and 'the state of historical and archaeological origin' – does not mean that these terms should be seen as discrete alternatives. The negotiating history of the provision suggests that these terms overlap with one another and do not have exclusive meanings.[123] The presence of all three formulas means that there is a broad basis for states to claim preferential rights and a wide variety of possible scenarios may be covered, including situations where one state has succeeded to another, or where several countries share, or shared, the same culture. As O'Keefe has pointed out, reference to 'country' provides for the fact that the concept of a state is of relatively recent origin;[124] and it may also help to deal with situations where states have split up. The fact that UCH originated in a certain place – for example, a vessel was built in, sailed from, or flew the flag of, a particular state – does not mean that that state is, or ever was, the *owner*. On the other hand, a state of origin could also have ownership rights in a vessel or cargo, depending on the circumstances. The range of states who may be in a position to claim preferential rights under Article 149 will therefore be broader than those in a position to claim ownership rights, but also seems likely to encompass all such states.

Does Article 149 envisage that more than one state can hold a preferential right to any particular object? Certainly the fact that it enshrines three different formulas for qualifying states widens the potential for more than one state to be in a position to *claim* a preferential right. Arend has proffered the example of a Roman ship, built in North Africa in 200 AD, arguing that Italy might claim to be the state of cultural origin, but pointing out that Libya might also have a claim as the state now possessing the territory in which the ship was built.[125] If both are capable of holding preferential rights to which 'particular regard' must be paid, which takes priority? The position becomes even more complex in the case of constituent parts of a shipwreck assemblage, where in some cases many states may be able to claim to

---

[123] See Strati, *The Protection of the Underwater Cultural Heritage*, p. 308.
[124] O'Keefe, *Shipwrecked Heritage*, p. 19.
[125] Arend, 'Archaeological and Historical Objects', p. 800 n. 106.

be a state of origin. Clearly there is considerable room for disputes to arise between various claimants and also some prospect that associated artefacts could eventually be dispersed.

Competing claims by states, citing Article 149, are no longer merely hypothetical. In the case of the *Mercedes*, Peru argued that its right to the *specie* on board the vessel was superior to that of Spain because 'the property physically, culturally and historically originat[ed] in Peru'.[126] In making this claim, Peru set some store by Article 149 (despite the fact that Peru conceded that it is not a party to the LOSC and that the site of the *Mercedes* is not located in the Area).[127] Spain, for its part, claimed that it – not Peru – would qualify as the state of origin for the purposes of Article 149 because at the time the *specie* 'originated' the territory in which it originated was part of Spain.[128]

What is the nature of the 'right' referred to in Article 149? Whether the article assumes that such rights were pre-existing, or whether it creates new rights, is unclear, but in any event the fact that it refers to the interest as a 'right' suggests that it is legally enforceable. However, what does the right entail? The fact that states or countries of origin are given *preferential* status and that *particular regard* must be paid to their rights, suggests that these rights take – at least some – priority over other interests recognised by Article 149.[129] Therefore, although Article 149 takes an internationalist approach through its recognition of the

[126] 675 F. Supp. 2d 1126, 1145 (MD Fla. Dec. 22, 2009).   [127] 675 F. Supp. 2d 1126, 1146.
[128] *Kingdom of Spain Reply to Claimant Republic of Peru Response to Spain's Motion to Dismiss or for Summary Judgment*, 26 January 2009, p. 8. For a number of reasons, the Magistrate Judge, Pizzo J., did not regard Peru's argument as 'persuasive': 675 F. Supp. 2d 1126, 1147. He concluded that it was outside the jurisdiction of the court to determine a dispute between the two sovereign states and that the dispute was 'best resolved through direct negotiations between the two and not in this forum': 675 F. Supp. 2d 1126, 1148. The District Judge, Merryday J., adopted Judge Pizzo's report and recommendation, and agreed that the court did not have jurisdiction to litigate conflicting claims of ownership to the cargo. However, at the same time, he also praised a statement made to the court by John Norton Moore, Professor of Law at the University of Virginia School of Law, articulating Peru's claims, and recognised 'the appeal of the legal principles Professor Moore advances and the responsiveness of those principles to considerations of justice in resolving a dispute between Peru and Spain': 675 F. Supp. 2d 1126, 1129.
[129] The concept of 'preferential rights' had been adopted in the context of international law of the sea prior to the LOSC in respect of the preferential rights of coastal states in fishing: see Strati, *The Protection of the Underwater Cultural Heritage*, p. 305 (referring to the *Fisheries Jurisdiction Cases* of 1974). In that context, '[t]he characterisation of the coastal State's rights as preferential implie[d] a certain priority': see *ibid.*

interests of mankind, a nationalist tendency may prevail when the article is taken as a whole. The impact of this could be that recovered artefacts would be returned to the state of origin, should it so wish, but in such an eventuality that state would need to take heed of the interests of mankind as a whole when determining how the material is then 'preserved or disposed of'. Generally speaking, one would assume that this means that the material should be kept in a publicly accessible institution. This would mean that, while the nationals of the state concerned clearly would be favoured in terms of access, in principle there would still be physical access for all. Material needs to be kept *somewhere*, and modern technology, particularly the Internet, would facilitate 'virtual access' on a global scale and also assist the process of finding appropriate accommodations in circumstances where a number of states claimed preferential rights to parts of an archaeological assemblage.

In light of the *preferential* status conferred upon states or countries of origin, their interests are also likely to prevail over the rights of owners unable to claim such status. Since it seems unlikely that a state with ownership rights would not qualify as a state of origin, such owners are likely to be private entities. Again, where the owner is effectively deprived of title, compensation may be payable and the obvious party to pay in this case would be the claimant state.

4.2   Interests recognised by the UNESCO Convention 2001

In the preamble to the UNESCO Convention, it is acknowledged that a wide range of individuals and organisations, including archaeologists, divers, scientific and professional organisations, and the 'public at large', are interested in UCH and that cooperation between these groups is essential if UCH is to be properly protected.[130] The Convention then goes on to give formal recognition to two particular interest groups, which may be regarded as collective representations of these more specific groups and entities. As discussed above,[131] ownership rights are not referred to in the Convention; therefore it must be presumed that they persist unless the applicable national law provides otherwise.

---

[130] See preambular clause 10. A reference to salvors in an early draft of this clause was later removed. See, further, Chap. 6, section 4.1.
[131] See section 3.2.

4.2.1   Interests of humanity

The core general principle and objective of the UNESCO Convention is set out in Article 2(3):

States Parties shall preserve underwater cultural heritage *for the benefit of humanity* in conformity with the provisions of this Convention.[132]

In contrast to the LOSC, where the equivalent principle applies only to material found in the Area, in the UNESCO Convention it applies to *all* UCH falling within the scope of the Convention, whatever its location.

The principle set out in Article 2(3) is reinforced by a number of the clauses of the Convention's preamble. These clauses give some indication of the way in which humanity's interest is perceived:

Acknowledging the importance of underwater cultural heritage as an integral part of the cultural heritage of humanity and a particularly important element in the history of peoples, nations, and their relations with each other concerning their common heritage,

...

Noting growing public interest in and public appreciation of underwater cultural heritage,

...

Convinced of the public's right to enjoy the educational and recreational benefits of responsible non-intrusive access to *in situ* underwater cultural heritage, and of the value of public education to contribute to awareness, appreciation and protection of that heritage, ...

Bearing in mind that the core archaeological principle underlying the UNESCO Convention is preservation *in situ*, the emphasis here – in contrast to that of Article 149 of the LOSC – is on promoting public access, appreciation and enjoyment of UCH *in situ* on the seabed.[133]

As seen above, one of the features of the 'common heritage' notion is that there is usually a 'steward' of some kind that can act on behalf of humanity. One controversial aspect of the UNESCO Convention is that it does not establish a specific institution for this purpose. However, the framework of the Convention is such that it is clear that the states parties – acting cooperatively – take on this role.[134] In its adoption of

---

[132] Emphasis added. In the 1994 ILA Draft and the 1998 UNESCO Draft the equivalent provisions (which referred to the 'benefit of humankind') were the only provisions accorded the status of a 'General Principle': see Art. 3 in both.

[133] For further discussion of the question of public access to UCH *in situ*, see Chap. 9, section 4.

[134] See, for example, Art. 2(3). See also, more generally, Chaps. 8–10.

the benefit of humanity notion as its core general principle, the UNESCO Convention adopts an internationalist standpoint. In fulfilling their duties under the Convention, states parties must act in the interests of humanity as a whole, not simply those of their own nationals.[135] Nonetheless, like Article 149 of the LOSC, the UNESCO Convention recognises that the nationals of one or more states may have a greater *connection* with particular components of UCH than humanity more generally and, where they do, may have a particular interest in outcomes under the Convention's protective scheme (see below). Where ownership rights persist under the applicable national law, the framework of the Convention is such that the interests of 'humanity' will inevitably take precedence.[136]

4.2.2   Interests of states with a verifiable link

The UNESCO Convention introduces a novel type of interest in UCH: that of states with a *verifiable link*, 'especially a cultural, historical or archaeological link'. It uses this concept in a number of contexts, some of which give the linked state the option of participating in decision-making about, and protection of, the UCH in question.

The inspiration for the notion of 'linked' states (as distinct from the notion of states of 'origin'), may have come from the Council of Europe's 1985 draft European Convention, which made reference to states having a 'particular interest'.[137] The 1994 ILA Draft and the 1998 UNESCO Draft both referred in their preambles to the 'State or States … having an historical or cultural link' with the heritage, although the preambular reference to any notion of this sort was later dropped. The concept of 'linked' states is much broader and more embracing than the notion – enshrined in Article 149 of the LOSC – of states or countries of 'origin', and the existence of a qualifying link should be less difficult for a state to

[135] Generally speaking, domestic heritage legislation governing UCH does *not* draw distinctions between UCH originating in the jurisdiction concerned and UCH originating elsewhere. China's is one exception: see, generally, Fu, 'China (including Taiwan)', esp. pp. 36–7. Fu suggests that if China ratified the Convention its position in this respect could be accommodated through the 'verifiable link' notion, discussed below.
[136] See section 3.2.2, above.
[137] Art. 9 of the declassified draft (on which, see Chap. 1, section 2.2.2). It is possible that the decision to include such a reference in the draft European Convention was in turn influenced by the 1972 Agreement between the Netherlands and Australia Concerning Old Dutch Shipwrecks. This referred to the 'continuing interest' of the Netherlands in articles recovered from the Dutch East Indiamen off the coast of Australia 'particularly for historical and other cultural purposes': see section 2.3, above.

demonstrate than the rather narrow and ill-defined notion of being a place of 'origin'.[138] For example, in the case of the *Titanic*, it seems likely that the UK, France, Ireland and the USA would all be able to establish that they had a verifiable link to the wrecked *hull*,[139] even though certainly the USA and perhaps even France and Ireland would find it harder than the UK to establish that they were states of *origin*. The precise formulation of the verifiable link concept used in the Convention also suggests that there is at least potential for a state to argue that it has a qualifying and verifiable 'link' that is something *other than* cultural, historical or archaeological.[140]

As a matter of principle, it seems appropriate that there should be relatively broad criteria for establishing an interest in UCH that may permit a state to participate in determining the future of that UCH. In essence, the criteria *should* be capable of encompassing all those states that feel a strong sense of identification with a particular site or recovered artefact. Unlike the concept of a preferential right under Article 149, there is no doubt that the UNESCO Convention envisages that more than one state may have a verifiable link to any particular site or object and thereby reflects historical and political realities. As the *Mercedes* case illustrates, the notion of 'origin' has the potential to be

[138] However, not everyone takes the same view. The verifiable link notion was cited as one of the reasons why Greece chose to abstain from voting in favour of the Convention: see Strati, 'Greece' (2nd edn), p. 119. Strati comments that 'in Greece's view, the terminology ... is no more helpful than the obscure formula employed by article 149': *ibid.*, pp. 125–6.

[139] The *Titanic* was a British-built ship and flew the British flag; she was lost during a voyage between the UK and the USA. Many of the passengers were British or American. The UK and the USA therefore have the strongest historical links to the vessel. However, the liner called at Queenstown in County Cork, Ireland, and a number of those who lost their lives were Irish; she also called at Cherbourg, France, and L'Institut Français de Recherche pour l'Exploitation de la Mer (IFREMER), a French government-sponsored organisation, was involved in her discovery.

[140] The precise expression 'verifiable link, especially a cultural, historical or archaeological link' is used consistently in the Convention (see Arts. 6(2), 7(3), 9(5), 11(4), 18(3) and (4)). Unless the possibility of some other type of link is open, it is difficult to understand why wording such as 'verifiable cultural, historical or archaeological link' was not used. O'Keefe argues that '[c]ultural and historical aspects of a link would always have been an essential component of any attempt to establish a "verifiable link"' but suggests that there may be other 'connecting factors' as well that contribute to the link: O'Keefe, *Shipwrecked Heritage*, p. 70. See, further, *ibid.* Arguably, an emotional attachment of some sort to the UCH in question is a minimum requirement. For example, it seems unlikely that a state could claim a 'verifiable link' on the basis that a wreck poses a hazard to its coastline or other interests, or that it simply lies in its general geographical vicinity.

highly divisive, particularly where former colonial relationships are involved. On the other hand, it is unlikely that either Spain or Peru would fail to be able to establish a verifiable link to both the *Mercedes* and her cargo of coins and, in fact (as will be seen below), there would be no *incentive* for states to compete with one another to claim the status, or to draw distinctions between particular components of an archaeological assemblage in a way that might prejudice its archaeological integrity.

So, what exactly does the status of being a 'linked' state entail? The Convention refers to states with a verifiable link in five specific contexts:

(i) Such states may be invited to join bilateral, regional or other multilateral agreements for the preservation of UCH.[141]

(ii) Such states should be informed of the discovery of identifiable state vessels and aircraft in the territorial sea or archipelagic waters of a state party.[142]

(iii) Any state party that has such a link may declare its interest in being consulted regarding UCH located in the EEZ or on the continental shelf of another state party.[143]

(iv) Any state party that has such a link may declare to the Director-General of UNESCO its interest in being consulted regarding UCH found in the Area.[144]

(v) States with such a link shall be notified by a state party if it has seized UCH that has been recovered in a manner not in conformity with the Convention.[145] The seizing state must then determine the disposition of the seized UCH taking into account various factors including the interests of states with a verifiable link.[146]

An important point of contrast with Article 149 is that the interests of states with a verifiable link are nowhere referred to as a 'right'. When one considers the specific contexts set out above, it is clear that 'soft' language has been chosen and that the Convention affords 'linked' states few enforceable rights. A state with a verifiable link to a particular site has no right to participate in an inter-state agreement relating to a site in which it has an interest; simply it 'may' be invited to participate in such an agreement.[147] It has no right to be informed of the discovery of a warship or other state craft in the territorial sea or archipelagic waters of

---

[141] Art. 6(2).   [142] Art. 7(3).

[143] Art. 9(5). Art. 10(3) imposes a duty on the coastal state, once so notified, to consult in certain defined circumstances.

[144] Art. 11(4). Art. 12(2) provides that the Director-General shall invite all such states to consult.

[145] Art. 18(3).   [146] Art. 18(4).   [147] Art. 6(2).

another state; simply it 'should' be informed of such discovery;[148] and, in respect of discoveries in other waters, even such limited exhortation is absent. 'Hard' language is used only in the context of seizure: a state 'shall' be notified if UCH in which it has an interest is seized.[149] However, even here the right to be informed leads to nothing further than to having its interests taken into account when the seizing state determines the disposition of the UCH. The seizing state has the power to determine that disposition and the interests of any linked states are just one of the factors that must be taken into account when it does so.

It is worth noting that in contexts (i), (ii) and (v) above, the wording of the relevant provisions suggests that there is no barrier to *non*-states parties claiming verifiable link status and benefiting from their terms. In contexts (iii) and (iv), on the other hand, only states that are party to the Convention will have the opportunity to benefit. One reason for the distinction appears to be that in the two sets of circumstances set out in (iii) and (iv) it is envisaged that states with a verifiable link will not only be 'consulted' about the future of the UCH in question, but will also participate directly in the Convention's management regime. Clearly, such participation would be inappropriate for non-states parties. To what extent a link must be 'verified' by the claimant state – be it a state party, or otherwise – and who is to determine that it is so verified is unclear. However, it seems unlikely that claims will be often challenged, particularly where made by states parties, since all states parties are duty bound to cooperate. There seems more likelihood of disputes arising in cases where *non*-states parties that declare a verifiable link express views about the fate of a site – or the deposition of the site archive – that do not accord with those of interested states parties. The fact that a state has a verifiable link gives it no priority status, however, and if its views conflict with the principles and Rules of the Convention, it is inevitable they will be sidelined.

As with the preferential rights recognised in Article 149, it seems that a state may claim to have a verifiable link that falls short of ownership. Equally, it is difficult to conceive of circumstances when a state with ownership rights would not qualify as a state with a verifiable link. A state may therefore find the notion useful in circumstances where it owns a wreck, but that wreck does not qualify as a 'state vessel' (or 'state aircraft') for the purposes of the Convention.[150] Whether a state should

---

[148] Art. 7(3).   [149] Art. 18(3).
[150] See Art. 1(8). See, further, Chap. 4, section 3.2.

not be able to claim a verifiable link where it expressly abandoned ownership at some point in the past, possibly many decades or even centuries ago, is an interesting question. Arguably this should not affect its claim: the sense of identification with the wreck will still be there.[151]

In view of the very limited rights afforded by the Convention to states with a verifiable link, the benefit to be derived from declaring such a link will depend largely upon the degree to which states parties fulfil their duty to cooperate to protect UCH.[152] However, cooperation should be forthcoming given that it is central to the whole ethos of the Convention, as well as imperative for the effective operation of its regulatory framework. In practice, the verifiable link concept could prove to be a powerful tool in diffusing the political and historical tensions that can emerge between states when dealing with the discovery of UCH.[153] Rather than competing with one another to claim the strongest legal interest, any state (at least any state party) that identifies with a particular site should have a reasonable expectation of having its views taken into account whatever the circumstances. Under the conventional framework there is no reason to determine which state is technically the owner, or for any acknowledgement by one state of the ownership rights of another. This approach reflects the practice in many cases today, where the concept of shared, or mutual, heritage is increasingly gaining ground and forming the basis for agreement and collaboration.[154]

In contrast to the preferential rights of states or countries of origin, recognised in Article 149 of the LOSC, the notion of states with a verifiable link is in fact about states bearing *responsibility* for the heritage, not about claiming rights over it. In particular, by speaking up and declaring an interest in UCH located on the continental shelf and in the EEZ,

---

[151] Although Australia was of the view that the Netherlands had abandoned (impliedly) its ownership rights in the Dutch East Indiamen located off Australia, nonetheless it acknowledged the 'continuing interest' of the Netherlands in the 1972 Agreement between the two states. In considering whether abandonment by a *private* owner would destroy the possibility of that owner's state of nationality claiming a verifiable link, O'Keefe concludes that '[t]he better view would be that the link should not be affected by the actions of a private party': see O'Keefe, *Shipwrecked Heritage*, p. 70.

[152] In this respect, it should be noted that the states parties to the UNESCO Convention will not merely have a duty to cooperate with other states parties, but also – by virtue of Art. 303(1) of the LOSC – with non-states parties as well.

[153] For example, one particular area where such tensions arise is in relation to UCH found in the territorial sea. See, further, Chap. 4, section 2.2.

[154] See, further, Chap. 4, section 3.3.

or in the Area, a state will be taking on some collective responsibility for ensuring that the Convention's protective framework is properly implemented. Indeed, as will become evident later,[155] the Convention's regulatory framework for these maritime zones is heavily reliant on states taking such responsibility.[156]

4.2.3   Preferential rights of states of cultural, historical or archaeological origin

The drafters of the UNESCO Convention were keen to ensure that the Convention's provisions in respect of the Area, set out in Articles 11 and 12, dovetailed as far as possible with Article 149 of the LOSC. Indeed, these provisions should be viewed as an elaboration of that provision.[157] The regime set out in these articles therefore takes account of the preferential rights referred to in Article 149. Under Article 11(4), any state party with a verifiable link may declare its interest in being consulted in respect of UCH found in the Area, 'particular regard being paid to the preferential rights of states of cultural, historical or archaeological origin'. Under Article 12(2) all those states parties that declare an interest under Article 11(4) will be invited to consult on how best to protect the site, but, according to Article 12(6), 'particular regard shall be paid to the preferential rights of states of cultural, historical or archaeological origin'.

The UNESCO Convention's regime in respect of the Area will be discussed in Chapter 8.[158] Nonetheless, there are various points that can be noted at this stage. First, a different – simpler – formulation for states with preferential rights is adopted. Secondly, the fact that the interests of states with a preferential right by virtue of their being a state of origin must be given 'particular regard' suggests that they will be afforded the same level of priority as they are under Article 149. Finally, Article 12(6) makes it clear that the preferential rights of *non*-states parties to the UNESCO Convention will be recognised.

---

[155] See, further, Chap. 8, sections 3.4, 3.5 and 4.
[156] Maarleveld has warned that '[t]he network of links encapsulated in a site ... is so complex, and may be so extremely extensive, that [the concept] risks diluting into "everyone responsible, no one taking responsibility"': Maarleveld, 'Drama, Place and Verifiable Link', p. 105.
[157] Art. 11(1) provides that states parties are responsible for protecting UCH in the Area 'in conformity with this Convention *and* Article 149 of the [LOSC]'. Emphasis added.
[158] See Chap. 8, section 3.5.

5. Concluding remarks

While the UNESCO Convention 2001 takes an internationalist stand-point, and its fundamental objective is the preservation of UCH for the benefit of humanity as a whole, in its creation of the new concept of states with a 'verifiable link' it also takes account of the fact that some sections of humanity will feel a strong sense of attachment to particular UCH and will wish to have some input into its future management. A verifiable link transcends the notion of ownership and helps to ensure that UCH is treated as 'heritage' and, as such, in accordance with inter-nationally accepted archaeological principles, rather than simply as 'property' that the owner is free to treat as it chooses. By declaring a link to UCH located in the geographical areas that are the focal points of attention for the Convention – the continental shelf and EEZ, and the Area – a state party, in essence, will be assuming a stewardship role with respect to that UCH on behalf of humanity as a whole. The concept of 'linked' states is a powerful one and it has a potential that goes far beyond the bounds of the 2001 Convention. Indeed, it is already being taken up more widely, particularly by archaeologists who regard it as a means of overcoming the practical difficulties caused when states resort to claiming, and competing with one another for, exclusive legal rights.[159] Nonetheless, the mindset of states naturally is to think in terms of their own national interests and therefore it can be envisaged that this is one of the areas of the Convention that has particular potential to give rise to disputes.

As far as private ownership rights are concerned, although occasion-ally they may be established with respect to UCH falling within the scope of the Convention, the experience of domestic heritage law suggests that, generally speaking, this should not be seriously problematic.

---

[159] See, generally, Maarleveld, 'Drama, Place and Verifiable Link' and 'The Maritime Paradox: Does International Heritage Exist?'.

4 Sunken warships and other state vessels and aircraft

1. Introduction

A significant proportion of UCH comprises sunken warships and other government-owned (or operated) vessels and aircraft that were engaged in war, or other public service, at the time of loss. Warships, in particular, by their very nature may have played an important – and sometimes defining – role in historical events and the wreck sites of such vessels may represent potent national symbols and memorials. They can therefore have exceptional cultural significance. Aside from the wrecks of pre-twentieth-century warships, such as the *Vasa*, HMS *Victory* and the *Mercedes*, the historical and archaeological significance of famous twentieth-century battleships such as USS *Arizona*, HMS *Hood* and the *Bismarck*, along with many thousands of other military vessels and aircraft lost during the First and Second World Wars, is increasingly recognised.

The question of interference with sunken warships and other state craft is a matter of great political sensitivity.[1] In many cases, the loss of such craft will have involved many human fatalities and the primary concern of states very often will be to preserve the sanctity of the site and to ensure that any human remains are afforded appropriate treatment. Whether or not the loss was as a result of war, these sites will represent the gravesites of those whose lives were lost in the service of their country. Some warships may also have been carrying commercially valuable shipments and these may be regarded as potentially recoverable financial assets. In the case of relatively recent wrecks, there may have been information or equipment on board which is still of a sensitive

---

[1] The expression 'state craft', which is common in American usage, is used in this chapter and elsewhere in this book to cover vessels and aircraft (and, potentially, even spacecraft) in public service at the time of loss.

nature, or unexploded ordnance, oil and other material which may be best left undisturbed. Increasingly, flag states are also recognising – and seeking to protect – the historical and archaeological value of their sunken state craft, especially those that pre-date the twentieth century. A further point, sometimes overlooked, is that the assertion of interest in *sunken* warships, whatever their age, can be a means whereby a flag state reinforces its sovereign rights over its *operational* warships.

In light of these interests, those states that have – or had in the past – substantial naval fleets operating around the world are concerned to ensure that no one interferes with their sunken state craft without their express authority. This includes possible interference by private salvage companies and divers, as well as by other states.[2] To ensure this objective is met, these states make two claims in respect of their sunken state craft. First, they claim that their title to such craft continues until such time as it is expressly relinquished.[3] Secondly, they claim that such craft are entitled to sovereign immunity and, as such, are subject to the exclusive jurisdiction of the flag state. It is important to draw a careful distinction between these two claims: the first relates to the question of ownership; the second to the question of jurisdiction. Nonetheless, they are closely interrelated. In particular, the second claim may well be contingent on the first.[4]

The state that has been most vocal in arguing that the recovery of sunken warships is subject to a different set of rules from those applying to private merchant vessels is the USA.[5] However, a number of other states, including Russia, Japan, France, Germany, Spain and the UK, take a similar position. The firm line taken by these states in this regard is

---

[2] As far as one can tell, incidents of unauthorised intervention by other states appear to be few and far between. One of the most famous was when the US *Glomar Explorer* deepwater recovery vessel recovered part of a Soviet submarine in international waters in 1974. Another example, which only recently came to light, was the recovery by China of HMS *Poseidon*, a British submarine, during the Cultural Revolution: 'China admits secretly salvaging British submarine HMS Poseidon', *Daily Telegraph*, 14 November 2009. In 2002, there were reports that the American and Israeli navies, acting jointly, had attempted to recover a Second World War Italian submarine, *Sciré*, off Haifa: see Garabello, 'Sunken Warships in the Mediterranean', p. 185. However, the USA and Israel argued that the interference was accidental. In practice, incidents of interference by private salvage companies and divers are far more common.

[3] See, further, Chap. 3, section 2.3.

[4] See, further, section 2.1, below. It should be noted that a state may have ownership rights in vessels that are unable to qualify for immunity. See section 2.1, below.

[5] The recovery of merchant vessels is subject to the ordinary rules of salvage: see, generally, Chap. 5.

.thing that must be taken into account by those seeking to draft an rnational instrument providing protection for UCH.

This chapter is split into two sections. The first examines the position of sunken state craft under general international law and the second explores the treatment of such craft by the UNESCO Convention 2001.

2. Sunken state craft: general international law and state practice

To what extent is the position taken by the USA and other flag states in respect of their sunken state craft a reflection of general international law? To address this question, it is necessary to consider the status of sunken warships under treaty law and then to give some consideration to modern state practice with regard to such craft.

2.1 Sunken state craft and the principle of sovereign immunity

It is a long-standing rule of international law, now enshrined in Articles 95 and 96 of the LOSC, that warships and other ships 'owned or operated by a state and used only on government non-commercial service'[6] have 'complete immunity from the jurisdiction of any state other than the flag state'[7] when sailing on the high seas.[8] This principle also extends to such vessels sailing in the EEZ of another state 'in so far as [it] is not incompatible' with the provisions relating to the EEZ set out in Part V of the LOSC[9] and, it seems, also in the territorial sea of another state, provided that the rules of innocent passage are respected.[10] In Migliorino's words, the effect of immunity is that the vessels 'are not to be stopped, detained, seized or in any way subject to aggressive action by a foreign ship'.[11] In light of this immunity, such vessels are generally excluded from the scope of application of international maritime conventions, including the Salvage Convention 1989.[12] The principle of

---

[6] LOSC, Art. 96.   [7] LOSC, Arts. 95 and 96.

[8] See the equivalent provisions in Arts. 8(1) and 9 of the 1958 Geneva Convention on the High Seas. See also the Brussels Convention for the Unification of Certain Rules Concerning the Immunity of State-Owned Ships 1926 and its Additional Protocol of 1934. Note can also be made of Art. 16 of the UN Convention on the Jurisdictional Immunities of States and their Property 2004 (not yet in force).

[9] LOSC, Art. 58(2).

[10] See LOSC, Art. 32. See, further, Oxman, 'The Regime of Warships under the United Nations Convention on the Law of the Sea', p. 818.

[11] Migliorino, 'The Recovery of Sunken Warships in International Law', p. 250.

[12] 1989 Convention, Art. 4(1). See also Art. 25 on state-owned cargoes. On the application of the 1989 Salvage Convention to wrecks generally, see Chap. 5, section 3.2.

immunity also extends to state aircraft and spacecraft.[13] In line with the 'restrictive theory' of sovereign immunity, whereby immunity is confined to circumstances in which a state acts *as a state*, immunity extends only to state craft that are engaged in *non-commercial* service.[14] Government-owned ships operated for commercial purposes are subject to the same treatment as privately owned merchant ships.

Whether or not the principle of sovereign immunity continues to apply to a state craft after it has *sunk* is a more controversial question. Pre-UNESCO conventional law, including the LOSC, does not address this issue.[15] Indeed, one of the recognised gaps in the LOSC is in respect of the status of wrecks generally. A number of academic commentators have argued that immunity does *not* continue after a warship has sunk. The basis for their argument is that – once sunk – a warship is no longer a warship, and a ship no longer a ship.[16] As such, they are no longer subject to flag state jurisdiction and therefore no longer retain their immunity. This argument leads to the conclusion that the flag state, *qua* flag state,[17] cannot prohibit a salvage attempt by another state or private operator. However, Strati has pointed out that there is another 'school of thought' on the matter that takes the view that sunken vessels *do* retain their status as ships.[18] The primary difficulty with this argument is that it would apply to sunken ships of all kinds, whether or not in non-commercial service, leading to the conclusion that *all* wrecks

---

[13] See Fox, *The Law of State Immunity*, pp. 181–4. See also Art. 3(3) of the UN Convention on the Jurisdictional Immunities of States and their Property 2004 (not yet in force).

[14] On the restrictive doctrine of state immunity, see, generally, Fox, *The Law of State Immunity*, chap. 9.

[15] Informal proposals to include specific provision on the recovery of sunken warships in the LOSC did not find their way into the Convention: for details, see Migliorino, 'The Recovery of Sunken Warships in International Law', pp. 246–9. The UN Convention on the Jurisdictional Immunities of States and their Property 2004 (not yet in force) also fails to address the issue.

[16] The argument is that a ship is no longer a ship because it is no longer capable of navigation. As far as warships specifically are concerned, reference is usually made to Art. 29 of the LOSC, which suggests that – to be a 'warship' – a ship must be 'under . . . command' and 'manned', conditions which are only possible while it is operational. See, for example, Caflisch, 'Submarine Antiquities and the International Law of the Sea', p. 22 n. 74; Migliorino, 'The Recovery of Sunken Warships in International Law', p. 251. For a list of further references, see Strati, *The Protection of the Underwater Cultural Heritage*, p. 235 n. 28.

[17] Where the flag state is also the owner of the craft, it may be able to prohibit salvage *qua* owner. See, further, section 2.3.2, below.

[18] Strati, *The Protection of the Underwater Cultural Heritage*, p. 220. See *ibid.*, p. 235 n. 29 for references.

would retain the exclusive jurisdiction of their flag on the high seas.[19] The consequence of this would be that the flag state (*qua* flag state) could prohibit salvage of *any* of its wrecks on the high seas, whether state vessels or not. From the perspective of cultural heritage protection, this would be an invaluable mechanism for controlling unwanted salvage activities. However, it is certainly not the generally accepted position.[20] For this reason, the claim that immunity continues after the sinking of a state vessel on the basis that such vessels retain their status as ships is unconvincing.

Another, more promising, avenue for arguing that sunken state craft retain immunity is to base the argument for immunity on the fact that such craft are state *property*. As outlined above, states have a wide range of reasons for maintaining an interest in warships and other state vessels after their sinking and these interests are not confined merely to recent casualties. There are therefore legitimate reasons for affording such property indefinite immunity. There is certainly some academic support for this argument,[21] and, as far as one can tell, it does appear to be the basis relied upon by the flag states for their immunity claims.[22] However, this basis for arguing that a sunken vessel is entitled to immunity is not entirely unproblematic. Forrest, for example, questions whether the immunity applies to long-lost vessels which, he argues, no longer fulfil a governmental function.[23] Also, this justification for immunity does not explain why some states claim that vessels on public service but *not* in state ownership at the time of sinking are sovereign immune.[24]

---

[19] A proposal to this effect put forward by the Soviet Union to UNCLOS III was not taken forward: see Migliorino, 'The Recovery of Sunken Warships in International Law', p. 247. The justification behind flag state jurisdiction on the high seas is that someone needs to have jurisdiction over ships plying the high seas and the obvious state is the flag state. If a ship has sunk and is no longer capable of navigation, at least from a traditional point of view there was no longer any need for anyone to have jurisdiction over it. Circumstances are, however, different now that deepwater recovery is feasible.

[20] See General introduction, above, n. 58. Curiously, perhaps, it seems that this question was not debated to any degree during the UNESCO negotiations.

[21] For a cogent analysis, see Eustis III, 'The *Glomar Explorer* Incident', pp. 178–81. See also Rubin, 'Sunken Soviet Submarines and Central Intelligence'.

[22] See, further, section 2.2, below.

[23] Forrest, 'An International Perspective on Sunken State Vessels as Underwater Cultural Heritage', p. 45.

[24] See, further, section 2.2, below.

2.2 State practice in respect of sunken state craft

One or two high-profile incidents in the 1970s and early 1980s brought the question of the status of sunken warships to international attention.[25] However, it has been the more recent advances in underwater technology – together with growing interest by states in protecting these wrecks because of their cultural value – that have led to the development of a considerable body of state practice in respect of such wrecks.

The UK appears to have been the first state to legislate specifically to protect sunken state craft when it enacted the Protection of Military Remains Act in 1986. This statute was enacted in light of heightened public concern about the sanctity of maritime war graves following the Falklands campaign of 1982. While the primary aim of the Act was to protect the sanctity of military gravesites, historical significance is included among the (non-statutory) designation criteria. This rather complex Act protects vessels and aircraft lost while 'in military service', affording automatic protection to any aircraft which crashed while in military service and providing for the designation of specific sites of wrecked vessels and aircraft, as well as the designation of named vessels.[26] Protection is afforded to craft located in both the UK territorial sea and in international waters.[27] In the interests of international comity, the Act offers some protection to military craft of other states, and several German U-boats lying in the UK territorial sea have been designated.[28]

It is when the remains of a military craft of one state are found in the territorial sea of another state that political sensitivities are most likely to arise. There is a clear tension between the sovereignty of a coastal state over its territorial sea and the notion that a wreck is sovereign immune and therefore subject to the exclusive jurisdiction of the flag state.[29]

---

[25] The first was the *Glomar Explorer* incident in 1974, referred to in n. 2, above. A second incident in 1980, which caused diplomatic tension between Japan and the Soviet Union, was the attempted salvage by a Japanese company of the *Admiral Nakhimov*, a Tsarist cruiser: see Aznar-Gómez, 'Legal Status of Sunken Warships', p. 73.

[26] The latter provision is useful where the location of the vessel is unknown. For further details of the Act, see Dromgoole, 'United Kingdom', pp. 329–35.

[27] On the application of the statute in international waters, see, further, Chap. 7, section 2.2.

[28] For a list of all designated vessels and sites, see the schedules to the Protection of Military Remains Act 1986 (Designation of Vessels and Controlled Sites) Order 2012 (2012, No. 1110).

[29] Under Art. 2(3) of the LOSC, the sovereignty of the coastal state is exercised 'subject to this Convention and to other rules of international law'. This is a reference primarily to

Although flag states are disinclined to admit, at least publicly, that there
may be some question about the extent of immunity of a wreck in these
circumstances, they do appear to concede that it is the coastal state that
ultimately has the right to control access.[30] However, the extent to
which the flag state has a right to be advised, or consulted, in advance
of interference, let alone to prohibit that interference, is a question that
is deeply controversial.

There are undoubtedly many examples of situations where coastal
states have initiated contact with flag states concerning sunken warships
located in their territorial seas.[31] Contact is usually made in circumstances where the coastal state wishes to take some action in respect of
a wreck. This action may range from simply affording it protection
under its heritage legislation to issuing a permit to allow excavation or
recovery, or intervening directly in circumstances where a wreck poses
an obstacle or other hazard. Contact may be made with the flag state
merely as a matter of information, or in order actively to involve that
state in decision-making. It is difficult to discern any consistency of
practice and inevitably the motive for making contact in each case is
unclear: it could be the belief that there is a legal obligation to contact
the flag state; on the other hand, it could be simply for reasons of
diplomatic courtesy, or because of uncertainty over the international
legal position.

In practice, matters are usually resolved diplomatically and sometimes
conclude with an exchange of notes, memorandum of understanding, or
other formal agreement.[32] The approach these agreements take to the
question of acknowledgement of the respective rights of the flag state
and the coastal state varies. An interesting early example of such an

---

the rules on innocent passage set out in Part II of the treaty. However, it can hardly be
said that a *wreck* is in innocent passage and, as discussed below, there is uncertainty as to
what the 'other rules of international law' referred to might be.

[30] See, for example, Roach and Smith, *United States Responses to Excessive Maritime Claims*,
pp. 475–6. See also Neyland, 'Sovereign Immunity and the Management of United States
Naval Shipwrecks', p. 3.

[31] For example, in 2005, the UK's Foreign Office, at the request of maritime agencies,
contacted the German government 'to advise them of the possible removal' of the First
World War U-boat *UB38*, which had become a navigational hazard in the Dover Strait. It
seems that the German authorities 'responded in a positive vein with the proviso that
the U-boat was not to be brought above the surface and was not to be destroyed'. See
Trinity House *Horizon*, 11 (winter 2008). For a list of less-recent examples, see Migliorino,
'The Recovery of Sunken Warships in International Law', pp. 253–4.

[32] The legal status of these agreements varies and only some will be legally binding. See,
generally, Aust, *Modern Treaty Law and Practice*, chap. 3.

agreement was that between the UK and Italy in 1952 in respect of HMS *Spartan*, which sank in Anzio Bay, Italy, in 1944. The agreement enabled the Italian authorities to remove the wreck for scrap, but provided for the handing over to the UK of various items, including documents, cyphers and cypher machines, cash, and human remains. The terms of this agreement are quite explicit concerning the respective rights of the two states concerned:

> Whenever the removal of the wrecks of British warships [lying in or adjacent to Italian territorial waters] is considered necessary, the Italian Government shall advise Her Majesty's Government before initiating the salvage operations, in case Her Majesty's Government intend to proceed with these operations themselves within the limit and under the conditions which shall be determined by the Italian Maritime authorities.[33]

The Italian government therefore undertook to *advise* the British government before interference took place, but – in so far as salvage operations were to be undertaken by the British government – that government recognised that its operations would be subject to Italian control.[34]

Another, more recent, example of an agreement concerning British warships located in the territorial sea of another state is the Memorandum of Understanding (MOU) of 1997 between Britain and Canada regarding Sir John Franklin's ships, HMS *Erebus* and HMS *Terror*, lost on an expedition in the Northwest Passage in 1847. This includes the following term:

> Britain, as owner of the wrecks, hereby assigns custody and control of the wrecks and their contents to the Government of Canada ... In so doing, Britain does not waive ownership or sovereign immunity ... but accepts that any site investigation, excavation or recovery ... will be under Canada's control.[35]

---

[33] Exchange of Notes constituting an agreement between the Government of the United Kingdom of Great Britain and Northern Ireland and the Government of Italy regarding the salvage of HMS *Spartan*, Rome, 6 November 1952, term (6).

[34] It seems that Italy takes a similar view on the ownership and sovereign immunity of its sunken warships as that taken by Britain and other flag states. For example, in 2005, it appears to have reacted to press reports that Croatian cultural authorities were involved in plans to explore two Italian warships, *Palestro* and *Re d'Italia*, lying in the Croatian territorial sea, by asserting its rights through diplomatic channels. The vessels had been lost during the battle of Vis (Lissa) between Austria–Hungary and Italy in 1866. (The author thanks Tullio Scovazzi for providing this information.)

[35] Memorandum of Understanding between the Governments of Great Britain and Canada pertaining to the shipwrecks HMS *Erebus* and HMS *Terror* (5, 8 August 1997), reproduced in Garabello and Scovazzi, *The Protection of the Underwater Cultural Heritage*, pp. 263–4.

It seems that the MOU was initiated by Canadian heritage authorities, which had plans to search for the remains of the vessels.[36] As with an earlier agreement with South Africa concerning HMS *Birkenhead*,[37] the MOU with Canada makes provision for the reverential treatment of human remains and the offering to Britain of significant artefacts, and also provides for the equal sharing of any gold recovered (not considered to be in private ownership) between the two governments.

Two further agreements of interest were those negotiated between France and the US in respect of their sunken state craft, the CSS *Alabama* and *La Belle*. These agreements explicitly recognise the sites as of historical and archaeological importance and provide for cooperation regarding their protection and scientific study. Initially, the discovery in 1984 of the wreck of the CSS *Alabama*, which sank off Cherbourg in 1864, led to considerable tension between France and the USA, which was resolved only after several years of negotiations.[38] In the agreement eventually reached in 1989, there is provision that '[n]either Party shall take measures adversely affecting the wreck or its associated artefacts without the *agreement* of the other Party'.[39] In 2003, a reciprocal agreement was reached between France and the USA regarding Cavelier de la Salle's vessel, *La Belle*, an auxiliary vessel of the French Navy sunk in 1686 off Texas. This agreement provides that '[t]he French Republic has not abandoned or transferred title of the wreck of *La Belle* and continues to retain title'.[40] A media note issued by the US State Department to announce the agreement stated:

[36] 'Search for Sir John Franklin's Ships', New Parks North Press Release, March 1998. Despite repeated attempts by the Canadian government to locate the *Erebus* and the *Terror* since the conclusion of the MOU, the wrecks have yet to be found.

[37] Exchange of Notes between the Government of the United Kingdom of Great Britain and Northern Ireland and the Government of the Republic of South Africa Concerning the Regulation of the Terms of Settlement of the Salvaging of the Wreck of HMS *Birkenhead*, Pretoria, 22 September 1989, reproduced in Garabello and Scovazzi, *The Protection of the Underwater Cultural Heritage*, pp. 259–60.

[38] For details, see O'Keefe, *Shipwrecked Heritage*, p. 77. See also Roach, 'France Concedes United States Has Title to CSS *Alabama*'.

[39] Emphasis added. Agreement between the Government of the United States of America and the Government of the French Republic Concerning the Wreck of the CSS *Alabama* (Paris, 3 October 1989), reproduced in Garabello and Scovazzi, *The Protection of the Underwater Cultural Heritage*, pp. 261–2.

[40] Agreement between the Government of the United States of America and the Government of the French Republic Regarding the Wreck of *La Belle* (Washington, 31 March 2003), reproduced in Garabello and Scovazzi, *The Protection of the Underwater Cultural Heritage*, pp. 265–6. On these agreements, see, further, Chap. 10, section 2. Interestingly, it seems that the French government has established a Commission that gives preliminary consideration

The Agreement ... highlight[s] U.S.–French common interests and cooperation in regard to ownership, research, preservation and display of historic sunken warships, and the effective transmission of our joint history to future generations.[41]

By the time of this second agreement, it was clearly recognised that a cooperative approach to the management of sites of this kind is the most constructive way forward.[42]

Two further recent cases of some interest once again concern British warships. The first relates to HMS *Fantome*. This vessel was reportedly carrying items ransacked by British troops from the White House in Washington when it sank in 1814 off the coast of Canada. In 2005, press reports that a private salvage operator had obtained a licence from the Nova Scotian provincial government to excavate a site believed to be the *Fantome* resulted in representations by the UK to Canada.[43] Following this intervention, the Nova Scotian authorities rejected an application by the salvor for renewal of the licence on the basis that they were unable to issue a permit that would authorise the disturbance of a sunken warship of another sovereign state without that state's *express consent*. The second case involves HMS *Sussex*, a seventeenth-century British warship reputed to have been carrying ten tons of gold coins when she was lost. The site believed to be that of the *Sussex* is located in disputed waters off Gibraltar. In 2002, the UK entered into a controversial agreement with Odyssey Marine Exploration (OME) for the recovery of the gold.[44] However, as a result of intervention by Spanish heritage authorities, the recovery operations were put on hold. The contrasting approaches taken by the UK government to these two historic warships is striking. The case of the *Sussex* provides an unusual example of a situation where the flag state – rather than wishing to *preclude* interference by others – has sought to undertake that interference itself in the face of opposition by a coastal state concerned to protect the cultural value of the site.

---

on a case-by-case basis to matters relating to the discovery of French warships in foreign waters and its findings then feed into any decisions taken by the Ministries of Defence, Culture and Foreign Affairs: see Le Gurun, 'France' (2nd edn), p. 91.

[41] 'US–France "La Belle" Agreement Signed', US Department of State Media Note, Washington, DC, 1 April 2003.

[42] The agreement relating to *La Belle* was followed by an exchange of diplomatic notes on 12 February 2004 between the USA and Japan with respect to a Japanese Type A mini-submarine discovered off Pearl Harbor in 2002. Among other things, it was agreed that the US would protect 'the interests of the Government of Japan and its citizens' in the wreck.

[43] The US State Department also made representations.

[44] On this agreement, see, further, Chap. 6, section 2.2.2.

US policy concerning sunken state craft has been formally set out and reiterated on a number of occasions. Of particular note is the Presidential Statement on US Policy for the Protection of Sunken Warships of 2001, which was a response to growing concern about the increasing accessibility of sunken craft to treasure hunters and salvors (and may also have been prompted, at least in part, by the then ongoing negotiations for a UCH treaty at UNESCO). The Statement continues to represent US policy and its substantive elements are worth quoting in full:

[T]he United States retains title indefinitely to its sunken State craft unless title has been abandoned or transferred in the manner Congress authorized or directed. The United States recognizes the rule of international law that title to foreign sunken State craft may be transferred or abandoned only in accordance with the law of the foreign flag State.

Further, the United States recognizes that title to a United States or foreign sunken State craft, wherever located, is not extinguished by passage of time, regardless of when such sunken State craft was lost at sea.

International law encourages nations to preserve objects of maritime heritage wherever located for the benefit of the public.

Those who would engage in unauthorized activities directed at sunken State craft are advised that disturbance or recovery of such craft should not occur without the express permission of the sovereign and should only be conducted in accordance with professional scientific standards and with the utmost respect for any human remains.

The United States will use its authority to protect and preserve sunken State craft of the United States and other nations, whether located in the waters of the United States, a foreign nation, or in international waters.

There are several points in this Statement that are worthy of note. The first is that there is no explicit reference to the principle of sovereign immunity; instead, emphasis is laid on the persistence of title. Secondly, the Statement is designed, in part, to put salvors on notice that the express permission of the sovereign, *qua owner*, to disturb such sites is required. Thirdly, the Statement applies to state craft of *any* age and seeks to reinforce the view that title to such craft is not extinguished by the passage of time, regardless of how long ago the craft was lost.[45] Fourthly,

---

[45] Interestingly, this represented a change from earlier policy which drew a distinction between warships sunk in the near and the distant past. Until as recently as 1980, the US distinguished vessels sunk 'in the near past' (citing the Second World War as an example) from those sunk in the more distant past (citing the seventeenth and eighteenth centuries), stating that title to the latter 'would, of course, still be determined

the USA makes it clear that it will 'use its authority' (presumably meaning whatever authority it has available to it under international law) to protect sunken state craft, including those of *other* nations, wherever located. Finally, the Statement accords recognition to the heritage value of such wrecks without drawing any distinctions with respect to age. By referring to the encouragement international law gives to nations to preserve objects of maritime heritage wherever located, it appears to be making an oblique reference to Articles 149 and 303 of the LOSC.

The terms of the Presidential Statement of 2001 were legislatively codified in the US Sunken Military Craft Act (SMCA) of 2004.[46] As well as reiterating the previously stated policy regarding title,[47] the SMCA affords protection to US sunken military craft[48] wherever located and to foreign sunken military craft within the internal waters, territorial sea and contiguous zone of the USA.[49] It also encourages the development of bilateral and multilateral agreements in respect of such craft.[50] Three fundamental aims of this statute appear to be: (i) to prevent unauthorised disturbance; (ii) to give clear notice of policy and practice to potential salvors and others; and (iii) to encourage reciprocal treatment of US state craft located in the waters of other states. Again, the emphasis is on title, rather than on the notion of immunity.

The policy of the USA, and a number of other flag states, was formally set out in statements published in the US Federal Register in 2004. The common feature of all the statements is their insistence that there should be no interference with sunken state craft without *express consent*. The statements of France, Germany and the UK – as well as referring to title – all expressly state that sunken state craft are entitled to sovereign immunity; the statements of Japan, Russia, Spain and the USA, on the other hand, make no reference to the concept of immunity and rely on the persistence of title. Whether this reflects any real difference of

by the more conventional interpretation of abandonment of that period': Letter from US Department of State to Maritime Administration, dated 30 December 1980, reprinted in US Department of State, 8 *Digest of US Practice in International Law* 999, 1004 (1980). The fact that the policy had been changed was confirmed by US Ambassador David Balton in his submission in support of Spain in the *Mercedes* case.

[46] Public Law No. 108-375.   [47] See SMCA, sec. 1401.

[48] The term 'sunken military craft' for the purposes of the Act includes sunken military vessels, aircraft, spacecraft and their associated contents: see SMCA, sec. 1408(3).

[49] According to Varmer, '[t]he provisions [of the SMCA] extend the jurisdiction of the US to the maximum degree possible, consistent with the notion that sovereign vessels carry their sovereign status with them and that a coastal state can regulate activities within its waters': Varmer: 'United States', p. 369.

[50] SMCA, sec. 1407.

viewpoint is debatable. The fact that emphasis was laid on the persistence of title could simply reflect a collective view that the immunity of sunken state craft derives from the fact that such craft are state property. As Forrest has pointed out:

immunity can only pertain to a state vessel if the state does indeed still own that vessel. … If a state abandons ownership of a state vessel, the principle of sovereign immunity will not apply.[51]

However, it is curious to note that the three statements which make reference to sovereign immunity also are the only ones that explicitly cover craft which were 'owned *or operated*' at the time of sinking.[52] It is unclear what the justification is for the claim that vessels are sovereign immune which were on non-commercial service at the time of sinking, but *not* in state ownership at that time.[53]

2.3 Treatment of sunken state craft by the US federal admiralty courts

One area of state practice of some significance in the present context is US federal admiralty court decision-making in cases involving the recovery of material from sunken state craft. Whenever a state has come before these courts to assert its rights in such craft, these rights have been consistently upheld.[54] Of particular note (in part because they were determined by two different US federal court circuits) are two recent cases involving historic warships of Spain that are now regarded as landmark decisions. In both, the claims of the Kingdom of Spain (with statements of support from the US government) were upheld. In one case the claim was based on ownership *simpliciter*; in the other on sovereign immunity. According to Aznar-Gómez, these

---

[51] Forrest, 'An International Perspective on Sunken State Vessels', p. 42.
[52] Emphasis added.
[53] It is interesting to note a comment in the conference report accompanying the bill which became the SMCA, which says that the provisions of the bill 'would clarify the circumstances under which such sunken craft, entitled to sovereign immunity *when they sank*, remain the property of the flag state until officially abandoned'. Emphasis added. See also the comment by Robert Blumberg, then Attorney-Advisor for the US State Department, that the SMCA 'clarifies that sunken military vessels and aircraft – both US and foreign – located in US waters that *were* entitled to sovereign immunity remain property of their flag States unless expressly abandoned': 'International Protection of Underwater Cultural Heritage', p. 500. Emphasis added.
[54] See *Hatteras, Inc.* v. *The USS Hatteras*, 1984 AMC 1094 (SD Tex. 1981), *aff'd*, 698 F.2d 1215 (5th Cir. 1982); *US* v. *Steinmetz*, 763 F. Supp. 1293 (DNJ 1991), *aff'd*, 973 F.2d 212 (3rd Cir. 1992), *cert. denied*, 113 S. Ct. 1578 (1993); *International Aircraft Recovery, LLC* v. *Unidentified, Wrecked and Abandoned Aircraft*, 218 F.3d 1255 (11th Cir. 2000), *cert. denied*, 121 S. Ct. 1079 (2001). For the most recent cases, see, further, below.

cases effectively 'close' the US admiralty courts to claims by salvors against non-abandoned sunken state craft.[55]

2.3.1   The *Juno* and *La Galga* (*Sea Hunt*) (2000)

This case related to two Spanish naval frigates, *La Galga* and the *Juno*. Both were wrecked off the coast of Virginia after encountering hurricanes, the former in 1750 and the latter in 1802. In the case of *La Galga*, most of the crew and passengers survived; in the case of the *Juno*, at least 413 lives were lost. A commercial salvage operator, Sea Hunt, Inc., was issued with a permit by the state of Virginia to search for the wrecks and, when found, Virginia claimed title to them under the Abandoned Shipwreck Act of 1987 (ASA).[56] When Spain learnt that a permit for commercial exploitation had been awarded, it issued a diplomatic note of protest.[57] Despite this protest, intervention at the site went ahead and Sea Hunt initiated an *in rem* salvage action in the district court in Norfolk.[58]

The case turned on the question of ownership and the rights of the owner in the case of unwanted salvage. The salvor argued that the vessels had been abandoned by their owner and that it was entitled to recover artefacts by virtue of the permit issued by the state of Virginia. The Fourth Circuit Court of Appeals found in favour of Spain in respect of both vessels.[59] It held, emphatically, that express abandonment was the governing standard because the owner, Spain, had asserted its title.[60] It also concluded that neither vessel had been expressly abandoned by Spain, reversing a finding of the district court that Spain had expressly abandoned *La Galga* when it entered into the 1763 Definitive Treaty of Peace between France, Great Britain and Spain. In that treaty Spain had transferred most of its New World territories to Great Britain. However,

---

[55] Aznar-Gómez, 'Treasure Hunters, Sunken State Vessels and the 2001 UNESCO Convention on the Protection of Underwater Cultural Heritage', p. 218.

[56] Under the ASA, the USA asserts title to any abandoned shipwreck that is embedded in the submerged lands of a state or is located on the submerged lands of a state and is included in or deemed eligible for inclusion in the National Register of Historic Places. That title is then automatically transferred to the relevant state. See 43 USC 2105(a) and (c). The permit provided for the proceeds of salvage to be split between Sea Hunt and Virginia: 'Spain Wins Right to Protect Sunken Vessels', Covington and Burling Press Release, 9 August 2000.

[57] 'Spain Wins Right to Protect Sunken Vessels', Covington and Burling Press Release, 9 August 2000.

[58] *Sea Hunt, Inc.* v. *Unidentified, Shipwrecked Vessel or Vessels*, 47 F. Supp. 2d 678 (ED Va. 1999), *aff'd in part, rev'd in part*, 221 F.3d 634 (4th Cir. 2000), *cert. denied*, 531 US 1144 (2001).

[59] 221 F.3d 634.   [60] 221 F.3d 634, 640–1. See, further, Chap. 3, section 2.3.

in the absence of specific reference to vessels or shipwrecks in the treaty's terms of cession, the Fourth Circuit concluded that the terms of the treaty did not provide the 'clear and convincing evidence' of express abandonment that was required. It went on to hold that, as owner, Spain was entitled to prohibit unauthorised salvage[61] and ordered the salvor to return to Spain artefacts removed from the site.

There were three specific factual circumstances that clearly impressed the Fourth Circuit, although none appears to have been decisive. First of all, the court was impressed with the fact that Spain wished to protect the sanctity of its maritime gravesites;[62] secondly, some reliance was placed upon the 1902 Treaty of Friendship and General Relations between the USA and Spain in arguing that an express abandonment standard was appropriate;[63] and thirdly, the fact that the ownership claim in this case was being made by a sovereign state, and was formally supported by other sovereign states,[64] also carried weight. However, there is nothing to suggest that the sovereign status of the owner of the *Juno* and *La Galga* was in any sense determinative and, in fact, the central support for application of the express abandonment standard came from the *Columbus-America* case, which had involved private claimants.[65] The decision therefore appears to have potentially wide application.

It was partly as a result of the outcome of this case that the SMCA was enacted in 2004.[66] One of the purposes of this federal statute is to ensure the uniform application across the federal court system of the

[61] The Fourth Circuit affirmed the finding of the district court that '[i]t is the right of the owner of any vessel to refuse unwanted salvage': see 221 F.3d 634, 647, n. 2. Indeed, the court seemed to think that it was enough that the salvor knew before bringing the action that the vessel was a sovereign ship and that the sovereign 'might' make a claim of ownership and decline salvage: 221 F.3d 634, 647, n. 2.

[62] In fact, only one of the wrecks, the *Juno*, is a significant gravesite.

[63] Specifically, Art. X of that treaty, which provides: 'In cases of shipwreck, damages at sea, or forced putting in, each party shall afford to the vessels of the other ... the same immunities which would have been granted to its own vessels in similar cases'. See 221 F.3d 634, 642. It seems that this treaty is unique among US treaties of friendship, commerce and navigation in referring specifically to shipwrecks: Statement of Interest, US State Department, 18 December 1998, para. 13.

[64] Apart from the support of the US, as *amicus curiae*, the UK also issued a diplomatic note supporting Spain's assertion that the terms of the 1763 Treaty could not be interpreted as involving an express abandonment of *La Galga*: 'Spain Wins Right to Protect Sunken Vessels', Covington and Burling press release, 9 August 2000.

[65] See Chap. 3, section 2.3.

[66] Another case of significance, decided at much the same time, was *International Aircraft Recovery, LLC* v. *Unidentified, Wrecked and Abandoned Aircraft*, 218 F.3d 1255 (11th Cir. 2000), *cert. denied*, 121 S. Ct. 1079 (2001). See, further, Chap. 5, section 3.4.4.

principles arising out of this case, especially the express abandonment standard, with respect to sunken military craft, and the notion that the sovereign owner can refuse salvage.[67] Among other things, the statute protects the sunken state craft of foreign states located landward of the twenty-four-mile US contiguous zone by making it clear that no person may engage in, or attempt to engage in, unauthorised activity directed at such craft.[68]

2.3.2   The Mercedes (2011)

In 2007, the US ocean exploration and shipwreck recovery company, Odyssey Marine Exploration (OME) discovered a shipwreck in international waters roughly 100 miles west of the Straits of Gibraltar. It gave the wreck the code name 'Black Swan'. Approximately 594,000 coins, mainly of silver, and a number of small artefacts were recovered from the site and flown into the jurisdiction of the US district court in Tampa, Florida; an *in rem* salvage action was then initiated by OME.[69] The Kingdom of Spain came forward to assert that the vessel was the *Nuestra Señora de las Mercedes*, a Spanish frigate that had exploded with great loss of life in 1804 in a 'pivotal' engagement with a British squadron.[70] As such, Spain claimed that the vessel was a sovereign immune Spanish warship and, for this reason, the case should be dismissed on the ground that the court did not have subject matter jurisdiction.

In 2009, the Magistrate Judge, Mark Pizzo, issued a report and recommendation in favour of Spain. Judge Pizzo concluded, on the balance of evidence, that the wreck *was* the *Mercedes*[71] and, as such, was 'unquestionably' the property of Spain.[72] Under the US Foreign Sovereign Immunities Act (FSIA) of 1976, which sets out the basis for US court jurisdiction over foreign states, a foreign state and its property are

---

[67] See US Department of the Navy, 'Talking Points on the Sunken Military Craft Act', 28 March 2009 (available at www.history.navy.mil).

[68] SMCA, sec. 1402(a). In the case of such craft, the law of finds shall not apply in any event and no salvage rights or awards shall be granted without the express permission of the foreign state concerned: SMCA, sec. 1406(c) and (d).

[69] *Odyssey Marine Exploration, Inc.* v. *Unidentified, Shipwrecked Vessel*, 675 F. Supp. 2d 1126 (MD Fla. Dec. 22, 2009); *aff'd*, 657 F.3d 1159 (11th Cir. (Fla.) Sept. 21, 2011); *cert. denied*, 132 S. Ct. 2379 (US May 14, 2010).

[70] 675 F. Supp. 2d 1126, 1130. The engagement, which became known as the Battle of Cape Saint Mary, was 'pivotal' because it led, in part, to Spain declaring war against Britain and entering into the Napoleonic Wars as a French ally: 657 F.3d 1159, 1173. For a detailed outline of the history of the *Mercedes*, see 657 F.3d 1159, 1171–3.

[71] On the question of its identity, see, further, Chap. 3, section 2.2.

[72] 675 F. Supp. 2d 1126, 1139.

presumptively immune from the jurisdiction of the US courts unless an exception applies.[73] Judge Pizzo concluded that none of the exceptions put forward by OME was applicable and, consequently, the court was 'without jurisdiction to adjudicate the claims against Spain's property'.[74] He recommended that OME be directed to return the recovered items to Spain.[75] Later the same year, both the report and recommendation were adopted in their entirety by the District Judge, Steven Merryday. OME announced immediately that it would appeal to the Eleventh Circuit Court of Appeals.[76] In 2011, the Eleventh Circuit upheld the decision of the district court, ruling that the evidence before the district court supported the determination that the wreck was the *Mercedes*; that, as such, it was immune from arrest; and that the district court did not err when it ordered the release of the recovered items to the custody of Spain.[77]

In contrast to the *Sea Hunt* case, this case was argued by Spain not on the basis purely of its ownership rights, but rather on the basis that the shipwreck was immune from suit. According to Magistrate Judge Pizzo, the success of the salvor's claims against the *res* 'hinged on the wreck's identity or its lack of any discernible identity':[78] once the wreck was identified as being the warship of another sovereign state, its 'jurisdictional mooring line' to the court was severed.[79] Among other things, the case illustrates that an intervention based on sovereign immunity has procedural advantages over one based on ownership alone: in particular, it is a fast-track procedure, which may lead to summary dismissal of the salvor's *in rem* proceedings on the ground that the court is without subject matter jurisdiction. Not only was the salvage claim outwith the jurisdiction of the court, but so also were the claims of Peru and a number of descendants of private cargo owners.[80]

---

[73] Section 1609 of the FSIA states: 'Subject to existing international agreements to which the United States is a party at the time of enactment of this Act the property in the United States of a foreign state shall be immune from attachment arrest and execution except as provided in sections 1610 and 1611'.

[74] 675 F. Supp. 2d 1126, 1130. For a summary of why the exceptions in sections 1610 and 1611 of the FSIA did not apply, see 675 F. Supp. 2d 1126, 1140 n. 17. As in the *Sea Hunt* case, the 1902 Treaty of Friendship and General Relations between Spain and the USA was referred to in support of application of immunity under the FSIA: 675 F. Supp. 2d 1126, 1143.

[75] Spain was not the only party to file a claim against the *res*. The Republic of Peru and twenty-five descendants of passengers transporting goods on the *Mercedes* also did so. The court declined to address these competing claims.

[76] OME Press Release, 23 December 2009.   [77] 657 F.3d 1159.

[78] 675 F. Supp. 2d 1126, 1146.   [79] 675 F. Supp. 2d 1126, 1146.

[80] See Chap. 3, section 4.1.2.

The case of the *Mercedes* gives rise to two specific questions that are of general significance in the context of the immunity of sunken state craft, both of which formed part of the grounds for appeal. First of all, there is the question of whether or not the *Mercedes* was in non-commercial service when she sank. As well as carrying *specie* for the King of Spain, it was also transporting some private commercial cargo in return for payment of freight and some paying passengers. OME therefore contended that the *Mercedes* was in *commercial* service. Spain, however, supported by the submissions of the US, argued that the vessel was providing safe passage to interests and property of Spain, including its subjects, 'in times of war or threatened war',[81] a common function of navies at the time. As such it was performing a public service. The Eleventh Circuit agreed, holding that '[a]lthough the *Mercedes* did transport private cargo of Spanish citizens for a charge, the transport was of a sovereign nature';[82] '[b]ecause Spain was acting like a sovereign, not a private person in the marketplace, we conclude the *Mercedes* was not conducting commercial activity and is immune from arrest under the FSIA'.[83]

Although the focus of attention tends to be on the question of the sovereign immunity of a sunken *vessel*, commercial salvors generally are interested in the cargo, *not* the vessel *per se*. In bringing its salvage action in respect of the *Mercedes*, OME sought to resolve its potential entitlement to the coins on board the vessel. The second question that arose was therefore whether a cargo on a sovereign immune vessel is 'cloaked' by the immunity of the vessel itself. Given the claims put forward by Peru and the descendants of private cargo owners, ownership of the coins on board the *Mercedes* was clearly a matter of some dispute.[84] OME therefore argued that the cargo and vessel should be treated separately: the fact that cargo was carried on a sovereign immune ship should not of itself mean that the cargo is entitled to

---

[81] *Kingdom of Spain's Response to Objections of Odyssey Marine Exploration and Individual Claimants to the Magistrate Judge's June 3, 2009 Report and Recommendation*, 31 August 2009, p. 10.

[82] 657 F.3d 1159, 1177.

[83] 657 F.3d 1159, 1178. In fact, significantly, the Eleventh Circuit concluded that OME's contention that there was a commercial activity exception to section 1609 of the FSIA was unfounded: 657 F.3d 1159, 1176.

[84] According to the Eleventh Circuit, '[w]hile various parties may have cognizable claims against parts of the recovered [property], even by Odyssey's own estimate, approximately 25 per cent of the cargo, measured by value, was Spanish government property': 657 F.3d 1159, 1182.

immunity. However, Magistrate Judge Pizzo refused to treat the cargo separately from the vessel, arguing that they were 'inextricably intertwined'.[85] In his view, to treat them separately would prejudice Spain's sovereign interests and depart from 'traditional admiralty precepts'.[86] The Eleventh Circuit came to the same conclusion, for two reasons. The first was that cargo is treated as part of a shipwreck for the purposes of federal legislation such as the SMCA and the ASA; the second was in the interests of international comity, given that there was an 'undeniable potential for injury to Spain's interest if we separated the *Mercedes* from its cargo and upheld an arrest of the cargo found and salvaged from a warship that is entitled to immunity'.[87] Indeed, even from a purely practical point of view, it is almost inevitable that the recovery of cargo from a sunken vessel will cause disturbance to the vessel itself and also, potentially, any human remains located at the site.[88]

2.4   Assessment of position under customary international law

As seen above, the claim that there should be no interference with sunken state craft without flag state consent is predicated on two assertions: the first is that the title of the flag state persists over time and may be lost only through express relinquishment; the second is that such craft enjoy sovereign immunity. As the landmark decisions in the *Sea Hunt* and *Mercedes* cases show, if a state intervenes in a salvage action brought before the US federal admiralty courts claiming either simply that it is the owner of the wreck and has not expressly authorised salvage or, alternatively, that the wreck is sovereign-owned and subject to sovereign immunity, in both instances the eventual outcome may well be disappointing for the

---

[85] 675 F. Supp. 2d 1126, 1142.   [86] *Ibid.*

[87] 657 F.3d 1159, 1182. The Eleventh Circuit made it clear that it was not holding that the recovered coins were ultimately Spanish property but merely that the sovereign immunity of the shipwreck also applied to any cargo it was carrying. For this reason, Peru and the individual claimants were precluded from pursuing their claims in US courts. See 657 F.3d 1159, 1182.

[88] The site of the *Mercedes* is unusual in that the vessel exploded at the surface and then sank to a depth of 1,100 metres, resulting in a very extensive debris field on the seabed. Little remains of the hull, although copper plates were found at the site which may have been used as hull sheathing. Nonetheless, even if it is conceivable that coins and other valuables could be recovered from a site such as this without disturbing remains of the vessel itself or of human beings, it would still be the case that the sanctity of the site as a gravesite would be disturbed by the intervention.

salvor. Since 2004, the position in this respect has been reinforced by the existence of the SMCA.

The USA and other flag states argue that both of the assertions on which their claims are based reflect rules of international law. However, it is doubtful that this is the case, despite the considerable efforts of the USA in recent years to encourage consistent state practice.[89] The continuing uncertainty on the matter springs not only from questions concerning whether there is sufficiently consistent and widespread state practice, motivated by a sense of legal obligation, to amount to customary law, but more fundamentally from lingering confusion and doubt concerning both the basis for immunity and the respective rights of the flag state and coastal state in respect of warships located in the territorial sea. In their own interests, flag states need more clearly and fully to articulate their position on these matters. However, given the rate at which new wreck sites are being discovered, and the growing willingness of states to act to protect the cultural value of sunken state craft,[90] it seems likely that practice will continue to grow and become more consistent in the future. In time, it is possible that a requirement for the express consent of the flag state to interference with sunken state craft – in whatever waters they are situated – may crystallise into a rule of customary international law.[91]

---

[89] For recent academic opinion on this matter, see Forrest, 'South Africa', pp. 260–1; Garabello, 'Sunken Warships in the Mediterranean', p. 183; O'Keefe, *Shipwrecked Heritage*, p. 52; Strati, 'Protection of the Underwater Cultural Heritage', pp. 48–9 n. 56. Cf. Aznar-Gómez, 'Treasure Hunters, Sunken State Vessels and the 2001 UNESCO Convention on the Protection of Underwater Cultural Heritage', p. 223.

[90] Spain's intervention in the *Sea Hunt* case appears to be the first occasion it asserted its rights in respect of its sunken warships. In noting Spain's previous reluctance to assert its title to colonial period vessels, Varmer suggests that this may have been partly due to Spain's reluctance 'to subject itself to the jurisdiction of a foreign district court sitting in admiralty' and partly to the sensitivity concerning the origins of the treasures on board the galleons: Varmer, 'United States', p. 369. He also suggests that some prompting by the US government may have played a part in Spain's intervention in the *Sea Hunt* case. See also Aznar-Gómez, 'Spain', pp. 272–4.

[91] As will be seen below, this process may be facilitated by practice under the UNESCO Convention 2001. (A caveat may be required with respect to powers of intervention available to coastal states in instances where a wreck poses a hazard, depending on the extent to which these may be applicable to sunken state craft. For a discussion of these powers, see Dromgoole and Forrest, 'The Nairobi Wreck Removal Convention 2007 and Hazardous Historic Shipwrecks'.)

3.   Sunken state craft and the UNESCO Convention 2001

3.1   Background

Given the uncertain status of sunken warships and other state craft under international law, and the political sensitivities surrounding such wrecks, it was inevitable that their treatment would be one of the most challenging issues facing the drafters of the UNESCO Convention. Whether or not international law supports the position of the maritime states with respect to the status of such craft, the staunch defence of this position by these states meant that it needed to be accommodated if there was to be any possibility of creating a treaty text that they would find acceptable. As previously discussed,[92] the 1994 ILA Draft and the 1998 UNESCO Draft opted to deal with the matter by following the approach of many maritime treaties in excluding such craft from their scope of application. However, given that this would have left a significant proportion of UCH outside the treaty's protective framework, it was soon recognised that it would seriously undermine the object of the initiative. Once the provision in those drafts for abandonment to be 'deemed' in certain circumstances was dropped, the opportunity presented itself for state craft to be brought within the Convention's scope.

The ideal outcome from the point of view of the USA and other like-minded flag states would have been for the Convention to 'codify' their stance on express abandonment and immunity by providing that the express consent of the flag state would be required in all cases of proposed interference with sunken state craft.[93] However, it was clear from the start that this was an unrealistic goal and that a compromise would need to be found that would satisfy the interests of other states. In particular, the status of sunken warships is highly sensitive for a number of Latin American and Caribbean states, which refuse to recognise the title of the flag state to colonial-era vessels in their coastal waters.[94] It was also the case that the greater the concession made to flag states on sunken warships, the greater the dissatisfaction would be of those states keen to ensure the Convention provided the coastal state with full and direct jurisdiction over all UCH on the continental shelf and in the EEZ without exception.

---

[92]   See Chap. 3, section 3.2.1.

[93]   See Blumberg, 'International Protection of Underwater Cultural Heritage', p. 496.

[94]   See Garabello, 'Sunken Warships in the Mediterranean', p. 175 n. 14; Aznar-Gómez, 'Treasure Hunters, Sunken State Vessels and the 2001 UNESCO Convention on the Protection of Underwater Cultural Heritage', p. 230 n. 89.

Despite exhaustive efforts to accommodate the interests of the flag states, which continued right into the last hours of the negotiations,[95] the regime for sunken state craft set out in the final text proved to be unacceptable to most of them.[96]

3.2   The Convention's regime for sunken state craft

Article 1(8) of the UNESCO Convention defines 'State vessels and aircraft' to mean:

warships, and other vessels or aircraft that were owned or operated by a State and used, at the time of sinking, only for government non-commercial purposes, that are identified as such and that meet the definition of underwater cultural heritage.

This definition is consistent with those in other treaties, including the LOSC and the Salvage Convention 1989.[97] It excludes state-owned craft that were engaged in trade or other private service, which means that vessels such as the Dutch East Indiamen now in Dutch government ownership[98] are subject to the standard provisions of the Convention, rather than the special regime for state craft. It is also interesting to note that the employment in Article 1(8) of a definition derived from examples that apply to *operational* – rather than sunken – craft leads to the result that vessels and aircraft appear to be covered by the definition even in circumstances where ownership has been lost *after* sinking, through abandonment or otherwise.[99]

It must be kept in mind that, to qualify as a state vessel or aircraft under Article 1(8), a wreck must fall within the scope of the Convention's definition of UCH, which sets a 100-year threshold. This means that while wrecks from the First World War will soon start to fall within the conventional framework, it will be some time before the casualties of the Second World War will do so. As far as pre-twentieth-century wrecks are concerned, O'Keefe has pointed out that the older a wreck the more difficult it will be to establish that it qualifies as a state vessel.[100] As the

---

[95] See O'Keefe, *Shipwrecked Heritage*, pp. 30–1.
[96] For the exceptions, see section 3.3, below.
[97] See LOSC, Art. 32; Salvage Convention 1989, Art. 4(1).
[98] See, further, Chap. 3, section 2.1.
[99] This means that in principle a vessel such as HMS *Birkenhead* would be subject to the treaty's special regime for sunken state craft despite the fact that it appears that the wreck may have been sold by Admiralty agents soon after sinking: see Gribble, 'HMS *Birkenhead* and the British Warship Wrecks in South African Waters', p. 36.
[100] O'Keefe, *Shipwrecked Heritage*, p. 46.

case of the *Mercedes* illustrates, with older wrecks the question of what constitutes public service may well be debatable, and determining that a vessel was engaged *exclusively* on public service is likely to be difficult.[101] Furthermore, the definition set out in Article 1(8) applies only to warships and other state craft that have been 'identified as such'. While it seems only logical that a site must be identified as a state craft before the regime for such craft is applied, as the *Mercedes* case has shown,[102] the positive identification of a wreck can be problematic.[103] It is clear, however, that the onus of proof in respect of this, and the other requirements under Article 1(8), is on the flag state and – where doubt remains – the ordinary conventional regime will apply. Forrest is therefore probably right to suggest that the 'special' regime for sunken state craft is likely to apply only exceptionally, at least in respect of pre-twentieth-century vessels.[104]

The provision that the Convention makes for sunken state craft is essentially a 'package' that comprises a number of specific provisions for such craft according to the maritime space in which they are located and also an important 'saving' provision.

3.2.1   Specific regime for each maritime zone

As discussed above, the position of sunken state craft located in the territorial sea can be a particularly thorny one politically. It was therefore necessary to construct a delicate compromise in respect of this and other maritime spaces under coastal state sovereignty. This compromise is set out in Article 7(3):

Within their archipelagic waters and territorial sea, in the exercise of their sovereignty and in recognition of general practice among States, States Parties, with a view to cooperating on the best methods of protecting State vessels and

---

[101] For example, it is questionable whether privateers, a common participant in naval warfare in previous centuries, would qualify. While authorised by a state – through letters of marque – to attack foreign shipping in times of war, the state would have had no control over the operation of these vessels and therefore it seems unlikely that they would fall within the definition.

[102] See Chap. 3, section 2.2.

[103] The intervention required to identify a wreck would also run counter to the archaeological principle of preservation *in situ* that underpins the Convention's management regime.

[104] Forrest, 'An International Perspective on Sunken State Vessels as Underwater Cultural Heritage', p. 50. Even where that regime does not apply, the flag state will have a verifiable link to the UCH and therefore its interests will still be accorded recognition under the conventional scheme: see Chap. 3, section 4.2.2.

aircraft, *should inform* the flag State Party to this Convention and, if applicable, other States with a verifiable link, especially a cultural, historical or archaeological link, with respect to the discovery of such identifiable State vessels and aircraft.[105]

This provision is one of the most controversial of the entire Convention.[106] The difficulty comes in the words 'should inform', which clearly fall well short of the flag states' ideal outcome. However, although provision merely to 'inform' the flag state patently does not amount to a requirement that there must be flag state *consent* prior to any interference, it appears that a *duty* to inform the flag state – combined with the fact that this would be with 'a view to cooperating' – would have been acceptable to the flag states. However, rather than using the obligatory word 'shall', Article 7(3) uses the hortatory word 'should'. It is this failure to make it a duty to inform the flag state that is the source of the fundamental objection to the provision. A less serious difficulty is that – unlike the other paragraphs of Article 7 – paragraph 3 makes no mention of *internal waters*. In the words of Blumberg, the leader of the US delegation, this omission 'creates a negative implication that flag states have no rights at all over their vessels in these areas'.[107]

At first sight, the provision for sunken state craft in the EEZ and on the continental shelf looks more promising from the point of view of its likely acceptability to the flag states. Article 10(7) provides:

Subject to the provisions of paragraphs 2 and 4 of this Article, no activity directed at State vessels and aircraft shall be conducted without the agreement of the flag State and the collaboration of the Co-ordinating State.

The extent to which this provision accords with the position of flag states is dependent, of course, on the content of the two other paragraphs of Article 10 to which it refers. Again, the central question concerns the degree of control afforded to the coastal state, including in its likely role as co-ordinating state.[108] Article 10(2) gives a state party the right to prohibit or authorise any activity directed at UCH on its continental shelf or in its EEZ in order to prevent interference with its sovereign rights or jurisdiction in these zones. At least to the extent that this provision applies to areas of continental shelf that do not coincide with the EEZ,

---

[105] Emphasis added.
[106] For a discussion of the negotiation process, see Garabello, 'The Negotiating History of the Convention on the Protection of the Underwater Cultural Heritage', pp. 134–6.
[107] Blumberg, 'International Protection of Underwater Cultural Heritage', p. 506 n. 22.
[108] On the concept of coordinating states, see Chap. 1, section 3.2.

it is likely to be regarded as an extension of the rights of the coastal state beyond those provided for in the LOSC.[109] Article 10(4) is also so regarded. Under this paragraph, the co-ordinating state – which in practice may well be the coastal state – is afforded power to take unilateral measures, *prior to consultations*, in order to prevent 'immediate danger' to UCH arising from any cause. Again, this would appear to represent an extension of coastal state rights. A further difficulty with Article 10(7) is that it requires the collaboration of the co-ordinating state prior to the conduct of any activity directed at state craft. This may give an impression that the coastal state or other co-ordinating state could prevent the flag state from determining the fate of its own sunken state craft located in the EEZ or on the continental shelf and to that extent could be regarded as a further extension of coastal state rights regarding UCH beyond the terms of the LOSC.[110]

The final provision of the Convention relating to sunken state craft in specific maritime spaces is Article 12(7). This relates to state craft located on the deep seabed beyond the limits of national jurisdiction:

No State Party shall undertake or authorize activities directed at State vessels and aircraft in the Area without the consent of the flag State.

This provision upholds the flag state position regarding consent and therefore appears to be uncontroversial. Why Article 12(7) adopts the word 'consent' – rather than the word 'agreement' as used in Article 10(7) – is unclear. However, in the context of these articles it is difficult to see how the words can have anything other than identical meanings.

Oddly, while Articles 10(7) and 12(7) appear to require that the flag state, whether or not a party to the Convention, agrees or consents to activity directed at state vessels and aircraft, the provision in Article 7(3) provides that 'the flag *State Party* to this Convention' should be informed of the discovery of such craft.[111] Given particularly that Article 7(3) provides that states 'with a verifiable link', *including* non-states parties,

---

[109] To the extent that the provision relates to the EEZ, it is possible that it would not be regarded as representing any change to the position under general international law. This is by virtue of Art. 58(2) of the LOSC. This makes it clear that 'Articles 88 to 115 and *other pertinent rules of international law*' (emphasis added) apply to the EEZ to the extent that they are not incompatible with the rights and jurisdiction of the coastal state in that zone. (The articles referred to in this provision include Arts. 95 and 96, which provide for the immunity on the high seas of warships and other ships owned or operated by a state and used only on government non-commercial service.)

[110] Blumberg, 'International Protection of Underwater Cultural Heritage', p. 507 n. 22.

[111] Emphasis added.

should also be informed of such discovery, there appears to be no logical reason why Article 7(3) requires the flag state to be party to the Convention before it should be informed of discovery.[112]

3.2.2   Preservation of existing international law

On their face, Articles 7(3) and 10(7) appear to accord coastal states the right to act in respect of sunken state craft without the consent of the flag state, at least in certain circumstances, and thereby undermine the notion that these craft are immune from interference without consent. However, before one can make a full assessment of these provisions, a further significant provision that needs to be taken into account is Article 2(8). This provides:

> Consistent with State practice and international law, including the United Nations Convention on the Law of the Sea, nothing in this Convention shall be interpreted as modifying the rules of international law and State practice pertaining to sovereign immunities, nor any State's rights with respect to its State vessels and aircraft.

What impact does this saving have? The answer to this question depends, of course, on what is being saved.

Oddly, the provision refers not only to 'the rules of international law' but also to 'state practice' pertaining to sunken state craft. As seen above,[113] there is a considerable and growing body of state practice in this regard. However, to be meaningful, it must surely be the case that the state practice referred to in Article 2(8) must amount to customary international law, in other words to 'rules of international law', otherwise it is difficult to see how there is any possibility that it could be 'modified' by the Convention. Therefore, while the express reference to state practice may well have been included to provide comfort for flag states, in substance it appears to add nothing.

Article 2(8) was included in the Convention in order to provide some reassurance for flag states by introducing a degree of flexibility into the interpretation of Articles 7(3) and 10(7). It is difficult to see why it should not succeed in providing that reassurance. Although the rules of international law 'pertaining to sovereign immunities' and to a 'State's rights with respect to its State vessels and aircraft' are uncertain, those flag states that have particular concerns about this question appear firmly to

---

[112] On the status the Convention affords to states with a 'verifiable link', see Chap. 3, section 4.2.2.

[113] Section 2.2.

believe that their policy and practice *is* a reflection of international law. If they are correct (and, indeed, even if they are not), Article 2(8) can be used to reinforce their claim that consent is required in *all* cases.[114]

3.3   Potential for resolving concerns

That there is potential for resolving the concerns of flag states regarding the UNESCO Convention's treatment of sunken warships is demonstrated by the fact that two of the seven states that issued formal statements in 2004 of their position with respect to their sunken state craft[115] – Spain and Japan – voted in favour of the UNESCO Convention in 2001.[116] Although Japan has yet to ratify the Convention,[117] Spain was one of the first states to do so. France too, having originally cited the Convention's treatment of sunken warships as one of its reasons for abstaining from the vote in 2001,[118] now appears poised to deposit its instrument of ratification.[119]

Inevitably, any decision to support and ratify a complex treaty of this kind is based on weighing up the extent to which the benefits that the treaty affords outweigh features that a state may dislike. In this case, technical objections in respect of the Convention's treatment of sunken warships – as well as in respect of jurisdictional issues more generally – need to be weighed against the benefits that its protective regime would afford to UCH, including state craft specifically. Assuming that a state's concern for its sunken warships (at least those that qualify as UCH under the Convention) is motivated by a desire to protect the *cultural* value of these sites (which, it should be noted, *includes* their emblematic status as the gravesites of those lost in public service), the benefits of the Convention for such craft are potentially considerable. The primary objective of

---

[114] Note should also be taken of the general savings for international law, including the LOSC, set out in Art. 3: see, further, Chap. 8, section 2.

[115] See section 2.2, above.

[116] The other states are France, Germany, Russia, the UK and the USA.

[117] In fact, Japan's vote in favour of the Convention is curious. It is not known for having any particular interest in UCH and it is possible that it felt obliged to vote in favour of the treaty in light of the fact that the then UNESCO Director-General was Japanese. It seems unlikely that it will ratify the Convention in the near future. (For Japan's Statement on Vote, see Camarda and Scovazzi, *The Protection of the Underwater Cultural Heritage*, pp. 423–4.)

[118] See the formal Statement on Vote by France, reproduced in Camarda and Scovazzi, *The Protection of the Underwater Cultural Heritage*, p. 427.

[119] In 2009, the French culture ministry announced that France intended to ratify the Convention: Ministry of Culture and Communications, Press Release, Paris, 30 October 2009. See, further, Final reflections, below.

the Convention is to protect sites from unauthorised interference. Under the conventional regime, preservation *in situ* is the preferred management option; any interference that is authorised must be conducted in accordance with the benchmark standards set out in the Annex; application of the laws of salvage and finds is severely restricted;[120] and states parties must ensure that proper respect is given to all human remains.[121] A flag state is likely to find that the general provisions of the Convention conflict with its interests only if it wishes to exploit the potential financial value of a site. Given that most of the flag states with concerns about the Convention's treatment of sunken state craft have made it clear that they strongly support the fundamental principles and objectives of the Convention,[122] it must be assumed that they have accepted that commercial exploitation of all UCH falling within the scope of the Convention is inappropriate.[123]

Although the Convention does not codify the flag states' ideal outcome, it does accord sunken state craft a status distinct from that of other UCH and it makes no attempt to deprive owners of their title.[124] The special regime that the Convention provides for such craft – as set out in Articles 1(8), 2(8), 7(3), 10(7) and 12(7) – must be viewed in the context of the Convention *as a whole*. In particular, it must be taken into account that the cornerstone of the Convention is the principle of cooperation. Article 2(2) provides:

States Parties *shall* cooperate in the protection of underwater cultural heritage.[125]

---

[120] See Art. 4. On this, see, further, Chap. 5, section 4.2.

[121] See Art. 2(9) and Rule 5 of the Annex. On these provisions, see, further, Chap. 9, section 4.4. The UNESCO Convention accords the same treatment to *all* maritime gravesites, whether of servicemen who died in the service of their country or otherwise. It seems that a proposal for specific reference to *military* maritime graves was rejected during the negotiations because of strong opposition from several quarters. For example, Garabello refers to the opposition that it invoked from African states, who argued that all those who died at sea should be treated equally given the large number of slaves that died during transport from Africa to America: Garabello, 'Sunken Warships in the Mediterranean', p. 187. Maarleveld notes the intervention of the Vietnamese delegation, who pointed out that there were many graves of the victims of war that had no military status: Maarleveld, 'International Good Practice or a Few Comments Upon Them', p. 65.

[122] See Chap. 1, section 3.1.2.

[123] Having said that, the case of HMS *Sussex* (see section 2.2, above) demonstrates that some states may be reluctant to give up the option of commercial exploitation. For further details, see Chap. 6, section 2.2.2.

[124] See, further, Chap. 3, section 3.2.   [125] Emphasis added.

This duty applies to everything that states parties do to implement the Convention, *including* in respect of sunken state craft under the controversial provisions in Articles 7(3) and 10(7).

As seen above, the main objection to Article 7(3) is that it provides that the coastal state *should* inform, rather than *shall* inform, the flag state of the discovery of an identifiable state craft within its territorial sea or archipelagic waters. Given that cooperation underpins the entire treaty framework and states parties are under an overarching duty to cooperate with each other under Article 2(2), whatever the precise wording of Article 7(3) it seems inconceivable that a state party would fail to contact another state party where that party was the flag state, 'with a view to cooperating on the best methods of protecting'[126] the site of a sunken state craft. Generally speaking, states already show considerable sensitivity in dealing with the discovery of state craft in waters under their sovereignty[127] and this cooperative spirit is only likely to be enhanced when states are operating under the Convention.[128] It also needs to be noted that, at present, domestic legislation generally does not provide for the notification of the flag state upon the discovery of a warship; however, it could become standard practice for legislation implementing the Convention to make such provision, thereby actually reinforcing the position of flag states. Flag states already recognise that the coastal state has ultimate control and that a cooperative approach is the pragmatic way forward;

---

[126] Art. 7(3).

[127] For examples, see, generally, the papers in University of Wolverhampton/English Heritage, 'Shared Heritage: Joint Responsibilities in the Management of British Warship Wrecks Overseas', International Seminar, 8 July 2008 (available at www.english-heritage.org.uk). The situation in respect of HMS *Swift*, discovered off the coast of Argentina in 1982, provides an interesting example. Despite the fact that Argentina is unlikely to recognise UK title to the vessel, nonetheless its heritage agencies treat the wreck as 'shared heritage' and have consulted with various British authorities over its management: Elkin, 'Case Study: HMS *Swift* – Argentina'. (Elkin notes that the discovery of human remains at the site prompted the first 'joint decision making' with British authorities.)

[128] It is interesting to note that a tentative draft of a proposed regional agreement to protect UCH in the Mediterranean Sea, drawn up in 2003, provides that states parties to that agreement 'shall' inform the flag state (party) of the discovery of identifiable state vessels and aircraft in the territorial sea (and internal waters). It seems that the word 'shall' rather than 'should' was chosen specifically to encourage littoral states in the region to become parties to the agreement even if they were uncomfortable with the provision for state vessels and aircraft in the UNESCO Convention: see Garabello, 'Sunken Warships in the Mediterranean', pp. 197–9. On this regional initiative and its relationship with the UNESCO Convention, see Chap. 10, section 2.

therefore, the fact that the flag state will not have *sole* control over the fate of the site under the treaty merely reflects the present legal and political realities.[129]

Consideration of the objections that flag states have to the UNESCO Convention's treatment of sunken state craft tends to focus on the wording of Article 7(3). This is because the difficulty they perceive with this provision is readily comprehensible. However, technically, Article 10(7) appears to be more prejudicial to their interests. As seen above, it gives coastal states the right to take action prior to consultation in two instances, both of which may represent as an extension of coastal state competence in respect of UCH located on the continental shelf beyond that provided for in the LOSC. However, again it should be borne in mind that any action taken will be for the purpose of protecting the site from unauthorised interference in accordance with the principles of the Convention. It is therefore difficult to see that a flag state party to the Convention would find the action objectionable, or counter to their interests. Here, clearly there is a need to weigh the prejudice that this provision might cause to their overall policy objective regarding consent (and, it should be said, to the more general battle against creeping jurisdiction), with the potential benefits to be derived from the Convention as a whole.

The attention of flag states should also be drawn to the position under the Convention of sunken state craft located in the *contiguous zone*. Article 8 makes provision for this zone, but does not refer specifically to sunken warships. However, Article 8 is '[w]ithout prejudice to and in addition to Articles 9 and 10'. Therefore it must be concluded that Article 10(7) applies to the contiguous zone. This represents a helpful clarification for the flag states. Under the pre-existing position, a coastal state has the right to control removal of UCH in this zone by virtue of Article 303(2) and, as with the territorial sea, there is uncertainty about whether or not it must seek prior flag state consent with respect to sunken state craft.[130] Under Article 10(7), such consent will be required in all but exceptional circumstances.

---

[129] Flag states should also be reminded, perhaps, that they are already under a duty to cooperate in respect of UCH, *wherever located*, by virtue of Art. 303(1) of the LOSC. See, further, Chap. 7, section 3.1.

[130] See, for example, Neyland, who suggests that the position in respect of the contiguous zone would be essentially the same as for the territorial sea: Neyland, 'Sovereign Immunity and the Management of United States Naval Shipwrecks', p. 3.

A further, important, point that appears to be overlooked (or perhaps is simply ignored) by flag states in asserting their rights over a sunken warship or other state craft is that the vessel in question may well have considerable cultural significance for the *coastal state*. Indeed, in some circumstances the cultural significance for the coastal state may be as great as, if not greater than, that for the flag state. A case in point is HMS *Sirius*, flag ship of the First Fleet that left Great Britain in 1787 to establish the penal colony at Botany Bay in Australia. As Staniforth has pointed out, while this wreck is of 'enormous importance to all Australians', it is of only limited interest to Britain.[131] In many circumstances there will be mutual or shared interests on the part of flag and coastal states in ensuring appropriate treatment and management of the site and clearly these are best served by developing a collaborative approach. The cooperative framework established by Articles 7(3) and 10(7) therefore reflects the likely *cultural* realities of the situation. The Convention also explicitly encourages the development of bilateral or other inter-state agreements of the type already frequently resorted to in situations of this kind and, therefore, it can be envisaged that such agreements will continue to be used as a way of resolving particular difficulties.[132] Where they are, they may provide for enhanced levels of protection.[133] The provision made in the Convention for notification and consultation of states with a verifiable link to sites found in the territorial sea,[134] or in the EEZ and on the continental shelf,[135] will also be of direct benefit to flag states in circumstances where questions arise over whether a site falls under the definition of state craft in Article 1(8).

---

[131] Staniforth, 'Australian Approaches to Shared Heritage: Royal Navy Vessels in Australian Waters', p. 22. Staniforth likens the significance of the *Sirius* to Australians to the significance that the remains of the *Mayflower* would have to Americans. Another case that serves to demonstrate the potentially greater significance that a wreck can have for a state other than the flag state is the SS *Mendi*. The *Mendi* was on hire to the British government as a troopship when she was lost in 1917 while carrying members of the South African Native Labour Corps from Cape Town to the Western Front. More than 600 labourers lost their lives. According to Gribble, the wreck is a national symbol to South Africans of the contribution and sacrifice of black South Africans during the First World War: see Gribble, 'HMS *Birkenhead* and the British Warship Wrecks in South African Waters', p. 41. (Unlike a number of other British troopships, the *Mendi* sank off the Isle of Wight, UK, rather than in the coastal waters of South Africa.)

[132] UNESCO Convention, Art. 6. See, further, Chap. 10, section 2.

[133] For example, the attention of flag states should be drawn to the terms of a draft agreement for the Mediterranean in so far as they relate to sunken warships: see Garabello, 'Sunken Warships in the Mediterranean', p. 198. On this agreement, see, further, Chap. 10, section 2.

[134] See Art. 7(3).   [135] See Arts. 9(5) and 10(3).

The presence of the saving in Article 2(8) of the Convention appears to have been a factor assisting Spain to overcome its concerns regarding the treatment of its sunken state craft.[136] As far as France is concerned, its change of heart appears to have been facilitated by the possibility that it could make a formal declaration upon ratification of the Convention, emphasising the significance of Article 2(8), its understanding of 'the rules of international law and State practice' and its interpretation of Article 7(3) in light of this understanding.[137] It may well be the case that the state practice that develops under the conventional regime will reinforce the position of flag states and, over time, enhance the value of Article 2(8).

4.   Concluding remarks

At the time the UNESCO negotiations were taking place, in the late 1990s, the decision to select 100 years as the threshold for application of the Convention meant that casualties of the First and Second World Wars fell quite clearly outside the regime. However, time passes quickly and First World War craft will shortly start to be covered. This may prompt some of the maritime states to review the potential benefits the Convention could provide for the protection of these remains from interference which is otherwise difficult to regulate.[138] Arguably, the legal position of such craft under the treaty is no worse than it is under general international law and potentially it is better.

The fact that the Convention was not designed with twentieth-century wartime remains in mind may help to explain why it does not make any attempt to address the question of the hazards these and other wrecks falling within the scope of the Convention may pose. Although the IMO's Nairobi International Convention on the Removal of Wrecks 2007 is designed specifically to deal with hazardous wrecks, like other maritime treaties it excludes warships from its scope of application and its application to wrecks of any kind that sank before its entry into force is questionable.[139] The treatment of the maritime legacy of the First and

---

[136] See the enlightening discussion of Spain's position in Aznar-Gómez, 'Spain', pp. 286–7.
[137] It seems that the wording of Art. 7(3) was the main French objection: Working Meeting on the 2001 UNESCO Convention on the Protection of the Underwater Cultural Heritage, London, 9 July 2008, Final Report, p. 2. On the French position, see, further, Final reflections.
[138] See, further, Final reflections.
[139] See, further, Dromgoole and Forrest, 'The Nairobi Wreck Removal Convention 2007 and Hazardous Historic Shipwrecks'. The Wreck Removal Convention is not yet in force.

Second World Wars, and of potentially hazardous wrecks dating from earlier times, is a matter that should be addressed by the international community as a matter of urgency. If and when it is, a delicate balance will need to be struck between ensuring that any hazard is appropriately 'removed' or mitigated, while at the same time paying due regard for the preservation of the cultural values that such wrecks may possess. The principles enshrined in the UNESCO Convention should at least provide some valuable guidance for these purposes.

5 Application of salvage law and the law of finds

1. Introduction

It is generally accepted by those involved in UCH protection and management that salvage law is antithetical to cultural heritage protection and its application to UCH should be avoided. At the core of the antithesis is the fact that the law of salvage *encourages* the recovery of material and therefore runs counter to the now firmly established archaeological principle that there should be a presumption in favour of preservation *in situ* until intervention is justified. The law of finds, too, is sometimes applied to UCH and is generally regarded as even less appropriate than the law of salvage because the potential outcome of its application – that the finder becomes 'keeper' – inevitably acts as an incentive for treasure seekers. However, while it is difficult to argue convincingly that either law is suitable for dealing with UCH, attempts to extricate material qualifying as UCH from, in particular, the law of salvage, meet strong resistance. This resistance comes not only from the treasure salvage industry, but also from more traditional sectors of the commercial maritime community.

This chapter begins by providing a general introduction to the laws of salvage and finds, including some consideration of the extent to which these areas of law are regulated by international treaty law. It then goes on to explore the application of these laws in the specific context of UCH, looking at the position under treaty law prior to the UNESCO Convention 2001 and also at the approach taken by some domestic legal systems. Particular attention is devoted to US federal law, as this has been the law of choice for many shipwreck salvors in light of its historically favourable settlements. In the final section, consideration is given to the treatment of the laws of salvage and finds by the UNESCO Convention 2001.

2.   Introduction to salvage law and the law of finds

The law of salvage and the law of finds are essentially matters of private law, in other words law governing relationships between private parties, rather than relating to matters involving the state. They are governed largely by domestic law, although the law of salvage is also subject to regulation by international treaty law. In the context of UCH, the law of finds is seen as an adjunct of the law of salvage, although in fact they are separate areas of law, with quite different antecedents.

2.1   Basic principles of the law of salvage

Salvage law is of ancient origin. Its basis is that for public policy reasons seafarers should be encouraged to rescue the property of others that is in danger at sea.[1] The 'salvor' is regarded as performing a valuable public service and therefore as someone whose actions – which may be time-consuming, costly and hazardous – should be generously rewarded. During the nineteenth and twentieth centuries a professional salvage industry developed, which provides a vital service to vessels in distress. The law of salvage therefore falls within the general domain of commercial maritime law. Internationally, there are sharp differences of view as to whether or not *sunken* property can be salvaged, some states regarding the recovery of sunken ships as something other than salvage. Generally speaking, the law of salvage is applied to *shipwrecks* primarily by admiralty courts in common law jurisdictions and for this reason the following summary is based on common law principles that have their roots in English case law.

Salvage law has a number of fundamental features, including preconditions for its application. Traditionally, it relates to the recovery of 'maritime property', particularly vessels and their cargoes, at sea; the sea, for these purposes, includes all navigable (or, in the case of English common law, tidal) waters.[2] Precisely what constitutes maritime property, and therefore property subject to salvage, varies between jurisdictions, but in many cases definitions have been extended to include aircraft.[3] The maritime property must be rescued from danger and, again, different jurisdictions have different approaches to the concept

---

[1] There is no equivalent of salvage law on land, where rewards for unrequested services generally have never been recognised: see Gaskell, 'Merchant Shipping Act 1995, Schedule 11', p. 21-374.

[2] The material and geographical scope of application of salvage law is wider in circumstances where the Salvage Convention 1989 applies: see section 3.2, below.

[3] For example, see the UK Civil Aviation Act 1982, s. 87(1).

of danger and to what poses a danger. There is a presumption that an owner exists and that the property is being recovered as a service to the owner. Salvage law therefore provides for the payment of a reward by the owner to the salvor. The reward is assessed as a proportion of the commercial value of the salved property and can never exceed that value. For a reward to be payable, the salvage service must be successful, either in whole or in part, and salvage is therefore said to be undertaken on a 'no cure, no pay' basis. A further point to note is that salvage may or may not be undertaken under contract. While it is common for modern ordinary commercial salvage to be undertaken under contract, a salvor – whether a 'contract salvor' or a 'pure salvor' – must be a volunteer. In other words, it must not have been under a *pre-existing* contractual or other legal obligation to perform the service.

In view of the positive light in which salvage services are regarded, salvors are granted extensive legal rights. They benefit from a legal security device known as a 'maritime lien' over the salved property, which means that the property can be arrested by a court, held as security for the salvor's claim and ultimately sold to satisfy that claim.[4] The salvor may also be afforded additional security in the form of rights of possession over the unrecovered property while the salvage operation is underway. Whether such possessory rights can be acquired by the salvor depends on whether or not a vessel is still in the possession and control of its master. In the case of a 'derelict', in other words a vessel where the master is *out* of possession,[5] the salvor who first takes possession will acquire an exclusive right to perform the salvage activity, provided that it appears capable of undertaking salvage successfully. In such circumstances, the salvor is known as the 'salvor-in-possession'.[6]

In cases of shipwreck salvage, where the salvage operations may take months or even years, once the wreck has been located and taken into the salvor's possession, the salvor is likely to wish to secure its interests by applying to an admiralty court to have the wreck arrested. The arrest

---

[4] On maritime liens, see, further, Dromgoole and Gaskell, 'Interests in Wreck', pp. 188–9.

[5] A derelict vessel is one which has been physically abandoned by its master and crew without hope of recovery or intention to return to it: see, further, *ibid.*, p. 189. It is important to distinguish such physical abandonment, where there is an intention only to abandon *possession*, with an intention on the part of an owner to abandon *ownership*. On the abandonment of ownership, see Chap. 3, section 2.3.

[6] The possessory rights of the salvor are a form of property right. The salvor has a possessory title to the property and has an enforceable legal interest. However, it is important to distinguish the possessory title of the salvor from the owner's full title (on which, see Chap. 3, section 2).

marks the start of an action *in rem*, in other words legal proceedings against the property itself (which is known as the *res*).[7] Provided that the salvor is able to demonstrate possession (see the case of the *Tubantia*, below) and shows that it is conducting the salvage operations in a responsible manner, the court may be prepared to declare that the salvor has exclusive rights over the site and to protect those rights by issuing injunctions against competing salvors. Ultimately, when the salvage operations have been successfully completed, the court will determine the salvage reward, taking into account a number of factors. These will include the skill and effort exerted by the salvor, and the risks and costs involved. A liberal award will be made, unless there has been misconduct by the salvor. Generally, the property will be subject to judicial sale, the salvor's award being paid out of the proceeds of sale with the residue held on behalf of the owner.

One of the most famous cases in English salvage law, which involved a sunken ship, illustrates some of the principles of salvage law, as well as the typical judicial attitude to the activities of salvors. The *Tubantia*, a Dutch steamship, believed to have been carrying approximately £2 million of gold, sank in over 100 feet of water in the North Sea in 1916 after being hit by a German torpedo. In 1922, salvors located the wreck and worked on the site whenever the weather and tides permitted during the diving seasons in 1922 and 1923. They marked out the area of the wreck and, by means of buoyed moorings, kept craft in position above the site. In 1923, a rival salvage company arrived at the scene and interfered with the first salvors' operations. The question before the court was whether the first salvors had sufficient possession – or occupation – of the site to afford them exclusive rights. Demonstrating such occupation was difficult, given the depth of the wreck and the fact that the number of hours and days spent working on the site inevitably were limited. Nonetheless, the presiding judge was sympathetic to the first salvors' circumstances:

Must it be said that, because the work of the plaintiffs' divers was that of only one pair at a time, in short spells with long interruptions, and because access to the holds of the *Tubantia* was often prevented altogether by stress of weather, therefore the vessel, and her cargo, were incapable of possession? To my mind this would be an unfortunate conclusion, very discouraging to salvage enterprise at a time when salvage, by means of bold and costly work, is of great public importance. I do not feel bound to come to it.[8]

---

[7] Cf. actions *in personam*, in other words, against a legal person.
[8] *The Tubantia* [1924] P. 78 at 90.

Concluding that the first salvors had demonstrated both *possession in fact* and an *intention to exclude others* from possession, and that there was no manifest incompetence on their part, the judge granted an injunction to restrain the rival salvors from doing acts at or near the *Tubantia* that might hinder the operations of the first salvors.

In the post-war circumstances of this salvage operation there was a need to encourage wreck recovery. However, the favourable light with which the first salvors' activities were regarded is indicative of the approach of the admiralty courts in salvage cases generally. The case also shows the importance of the concept of possession in salvage law and the difficulty of demonstrating possession in the case of deep-water wrecks.[9]

There are also two further points of interest about the case of the *Tubantia* that have contributed to its enduring notoriety. First, there appears to have been an assumption that the wreck of the *Tubantia* was in danger, even though it had been on the seabed for six years. Secondly, the judge did not doubt that the court had jurisdiction over the wreck even though it lay fifty miles from the British coast, in international waters. These two questions are important in the context of UCH and will be returned to later in this chapter.

2.2   Basic principles of the law of finds

While most systems of law have rules to deal with the finding of property, this chapter is concerned primarily with common law principles. Like the principles of salvage law, the common law principles on finds derive from English case law. In contrast to the law of salvage, however, the law of finds is part of general property law, rather than the specialist domain of admiralty law, and the principles derive from cases involving the finding of valuable personal property on land.[10]

---

[9] Clearly, establishing the requisite level of physical possession is likely to be more difficult the greater the depth of the wreck and the question is whether the salvor is able to exercise 'the use and occupation of which the subject matter [is] capable': *The Tubantia* [1924] P. 78 at 90. In the *Columbus-America* case, which involved a wreck at a depth outside the range of divers, a US district court judge concluded that the requisite level of physical possession could be achieved remotely through 'telepossession' or 'telepresence', in other words through real-time imaging of the wreck and the placement, or capability to place, teleoperated or robotic manipulators on or near the wreck: *Columbus-America Discovery Group* v. *Unidentified, Wrecked And Abandoned Sailing Vessel, SS Central America* [1989] AMC 1955, 1958 (ED Va. June 30, 1989).

[10] It should be noted that some systems of law, including English law, developed distinct rules – known as treasure trove – for dealing with finds of precious objects. Under these rules the sovereign acquired title to the find and a reward was paid to the finder. In the

The law of finds may be applied to lost, or abandoned, property. Where property has been merely *lost* by its owner, the finder who first takes possession may acquire a right to the property that is good against all but the true owner. On the other hand, where property has been *abandoned* by its owner, a finder who takes possession may succeed to the position of the true owner. Again, as with the exclusive rights to possession that a salvor may acquire, simply finding property is not enough to acquire possession: there is a need for physical occupancy or control *and* an intention to exclude others. Complications arise where the property is found on land owned or occupied by someone other than the finder; depending on the precise circumstances, the owner or occupier may acquire a better title than the finder. For example, if the property is attached to or embedded in the land, it may be determined that the land owner or occupier has a better right than the finder because possession of the land carries with it possession of things attached to or embedded in the land.

2.3 *International regulation of salvage law*

While the law of finds developed in the context of property found within the territory of a state, salvage law has always had a clear international dimension. Ships of any nationality in all parts of the oceans may be the subject of salvage. Therefore, in the early twentieth century an attempt was made by the Comité Maritime International (CMI) [International Maritime Committee][11] to create uniform rules of law to govern salvage so that the applicable legal regime would be certain and predictable. This resulted in the Brussels Convention of 1910,[12] which was later superseded by the International Salvage Convention 1989. The 1989 Convention was originally drafted by the CMI and then adopted by the International Maritime Organisation (IMO).[13] The 1989 Convention updated the rules to reflect the needs of modern times, in particular to make provision that would encourage salvage operators to prevent or

---

UK (excluding Scotland) treasure trove was abolished by the Treasure Act 1996 and replaced with a new system for dealing with treasure. An object does not constitute treasure under that Act if it qualifies as 'wreck' within the meaning of Part IX of the Merchant Shipping Act 1995 (Treasure Act 1996, s. 3(7)).

[11] The CMI is a non-governmental international organisation which has the objective of contributing to the unification of maritime law.

[12] The full title is Convention for the Unification of Certain Rules of Law respecting Assistance and Salvage at Sea (Brussels, 1910).

[13] The IMO is a specialised agency of the UN. Its main remit is to develop and maintain a comprehensive regulatory regime for international shipping.

minimise damage to the marine environment. Like other maritime treaties, the Salvage Convention 1989 does not apply to warships or other non-commercial state vessels[14] and makes special provision for non-commercial cargoes owned by a state but carried on ordinary commercial vessels.[15]

The Salvage Convention 1989 came into force internationally in 1996 and is now the prevailing international salvage regime. Parties to the Convention include the USA, the UK and many other common law (and other) states.[16]

3. Application of the law of salvage and the law of finds to underwater cultural heritage

With rising awareness of the potential historical and archaeological value of shipwrecks in the 1960s and 1970s, the inappropriateness of salvage law for dealing with maritime property of cultural significance soon became apparent.

An incident that illustrated the degree to which the archaeological integrity of a wreck site can be destroyed in circumstances where access is regulated purely by traditional salvage law involved the British warship, HMS *Association*. In 1707, this flagship of the fleet was returning from battle in the Mediterranean, laden with gold and silver coins, when it ran aground off the Scilly Isles and sank. As a British naval vessel, title was presumed to vest in the Crown and in the early years of scuba-diving the UK's Ministry of Defence (MOD) issued salvage contracts to three competing teams of divers.[17] After the wreck was discovered in 1967, divers from home and abroad fought over the site and thousands of artefacts were later sold at auction (and thereby irretrievably dispersed), to cover the salvage reward. Although the incident led to the introduction of the Protection of Wrecks Act 1973,[18] the damage to the *Association*

---

[14] See Art. 4(1).

[15] See Art. 25. On this provision, see Gaskell, 'Merchant Shipping Act 1995, Schedule 11', p. 21-428–21-429.

[16] As at 31 July 2012, the Salvage Convention had sixty-two states parties. For the full list, see IMO, 'Status of Multilateral Conventions and Instruments in respect of which the International Maritime Organisation or its Secretary-General performs depositary or other functions' (available at www.imo.org/conventions). On the application of the Convention to UCH, see section 3.2, below. On the application of the Convention in US law, see section 3.4.4, below.

[17] For details, see Dromgoole, 'Protection of Historic Wreck', p. 36.

[18] See, further, Chap. 2, section 2.

itself, resulting from crude recovery methods (including the use of explosives), was such that it was not regarded as meriting statutory protection.

In Australia, the discovery in 1963 of the first of four Dutch East Indiamen carrying silver bullion led to litigation in the High Court of Australia.[19] A number of important questions arose in the case concerning the application of salvage law to long-lost vessels: (i) was property that has been on the seabed for decades and even centuries actually in danger?; (ii) does a recovery effort constitute salvage if it is motivated purely by personal gain, rather than undertaken in performance of a service for the owner?; (iii) is it possible to possess a wreck in circumstances where 'time and the seas have left of the ship only scattered remnants which are encrusted with corals and other marine growths, and if not entirely covered by the seabed can hardly be distinguished from it'?[20] The six judges in the case were unable to agree on these issues.[21]

Despite the evident tensions between salvage law and the notion of heritage protection that manifested themselves in these early days, even now a number of jurisdictions still apply salvage law to UCH. Although sometimes it is applied in a modified form to such material, its defining features inevitably remain a source of difficulty. Where a vessel has been lying on the seabed for a period of years, the immediate threat that caused the vessel to sink has clearly passed. From a physical perspective, far from being in danger, it may in fact be in a situation of relative security and the most immediate threat to that security may well be direct human intervention at the site.[22] A traditional mantra of archaeologists is that 'excavation equals destruction': once a site is salvaged or otherwise excavated, it becomes spent as an archaeological resource. It is for this reason that preservation *in situ* has become the preferred management option of archaeologists. The principle of preservation *in situ*

---

[19] *Robinson v. The Western Australian Museum* (1977) 51 ALJR 806.

[20] *Robinson v. The Western Australian Museum* (1977) 51 ALJR 806 per Gibbs J. at 812.

[21] For a discussion of the case, see Prott and O'Keefe, *Law and the Cultural Heritage*, Vol. I, pp. 118–22.

[22] This point has been well made by Varmer: 'As time progresses, the shipwreck becomes part of the marine environment. Once a shipwreck is covered by the seabed, the rate of deterioration becomes very slow due to the lack of oxygen. The shipwreck site is now in a preserved state and is by no means in marine peril. To the contrary, any excavation of the site at this stage will expose the UCH to the water column and oxygen and threaten the stability of the site': Varmer, 'The Case Against the "Salvage" of the Cultural Heritage', pp. 280–1.

does not mean that all archaeological sites *must* be preserved *in situ*; rather it means that there should be a presumption in favour of such preservation until intervention has been justified. This could be because a site is under a threat of some sort, or because intervention will assist in answering immediate scientific questions.[23] Under salvage law, there is no opportunity for such considerations to be taken into account by qualified heritage authorities prior to the commencement of the salvage operation. Once a salvage operation does commence, the fact that a salvage reward is limited to the commercial value of recovered material encourages recovery only of the cargo and other valuables at a site. Those parts of the wreck which tend to be of greatest interest to archaeologists – the hull, fixtures and fittings, for example – may well be damaged or destroyed in the process. Furthermore, salvage operations are expensive and to maximise the profit-element of the reward recovery must be undertaken as quickly and cheaply as possible; by contrast, recovery undertaken in accordance with archaeological methods is a slow and painstaking process, requiring detailed recording of the context in which artefacts are situated and their relationship with one another. The usual outcome of salvage proceedings – judicial sale of recovered items – leads to the irretrievable dispersal of the shipwreck assemblage, an outcome which is contrary to the archaeological principle that artefacts found together should be kept together.

Although less commonly applied than the law of salvage, finds law may be applied to UCH in circumstances where there is patently no known or identifiable owner, or where an identifiable owner is determined to have abandoned ownership. Its application to cultural material leads to outcomes that may be even less appropriate than those arising from the application of salvage law. The law of salvage does at least allow for the possibility of a claim by an owner and, in some systems – through the allied law of wreck or similar laws – material that has been salvaged and is unclaimed by an owner may fall to the Crown. As seen in Chapter 3, an outcome whereby a state becomes owner – either as successor-in-title to the original owner, or by virtue of residual rights to unclaimed material – may be helpful from a cultural heritage perspective. The law of finds, on the other hand, leads to the finder becoming 'keeper' and therefore inevitably promotes treasure-hunting activity.

---

[23] On application of the principle of *in situ* preservation in the context of the UNESCO Convention 2001, see, further, Chap. 9, section 3.2.

3.1   Approach of the Law of the Sea Convention 1982

Once again, it needs to be recalled that the relevant provisions of the LOSC were negotiated in the 1970s and early 1980s, when there was only a primitive understanding of what constitutes UCH and of the appropriate treatment for such material. It is therefore unsurprising that little reason was seen to interfere with the application of well-entrenched principles of private maritime law.

Article 303(3) provides:

Nothing in this article affects the rights of identifiable owners, *the law of salvage or other rules of admiralty*, or laws and practices with respect to cultural exchanges.[24]

As seen earlier,[25] Article 303(3) applies to the first two paragraphs of Article 303 and, by reference, probably also to Article 149. The negotiating history of the LOSC suggests that the reference in Article 303(3) to 'the law of salvage and other rules of admiralty' is to be understood as meaning 'commercial maritime law'.[26] It can be presumed that this includes the law of wreck, as derived from UK merchant shipping legislation, and also the law of finds in so far as this law is applied by commercial maritime law courts such as the US federal admiralty courts.[27]

In attempting to reconcile Article 303(3) with the protective objectives of the other paragraphs of Article 303 and of Article 149, Strati suggested that the reference to 'the law of salvage and other rules of admiralty' in Article 303(3) may have applied only to material that is *less than* 100 years of age; in her view, older material qualified as 'objects of an archaeological and historical nature' and fell outside the salvage law regime.[28] At the time Strati was writing, the age something must be to qualify as an object of an archaeological and historical nature for the purposes of the LOSC provisions was still very debatable. With the development of state practice it has become clear that the term is not limited to very old material, or even that over 100 years of age, but can be interpreted as covering material that is no older than fifty years.[29] The passage of time has also demonstrated that the impact of Article 303(3) is less than some may have anticipated. For the purposes of implementing Article 303, or

---

[24] Emphasis added.   [25] Chap. 3, section 3.1.
[26] See Nordquist, Rosenne and Sohn, *United Nations Convention on the Law of the Sea 1982*, Vol. V, p. 160.
[27] See, further, section 3.4, below.
[28] Strati, *The Protection of the Underwater Cultural Heritage*, p. 173.
[29] See Chap. 2, section 3.1.

indeed Article 149, there is in fact no need for the adoption of a clear-cut (and inevitably arbitrary) dividing line between material subject to salvage law and material of an archaeological and historical nature. The effect of Article 303(3) is simply that the protective provisions in the first two paragraphs of Article 303, and in Article 149, do not *in themselves* interfere with the application of the law of salvage and other rules of admiralty; in other words, there can be no *presumption* that these laws do not apply to objects of an archaeological and historical nature. Instead, the matter is left for national legal systems to determine.[30]

3.2 Approach of the Salvage Convention 1989

The International Salvage Convention 1989 enshrines the fundamental principles of salvage law (in some cases, with minor modifications). Its primary concern is to ensure the payment of an adequate reward to the salvor in the circumstances of modern commercial salvage.[31]

In the context of UCH, there are two questions that need to be asked: (i) to what extent does the Salvage Convention apply to the recovery of material that *may* constitute UCH; and (ii) to what extent does it take account of the fact that material that *does* constitute UCH requires treatment distinctive from ordinary maritime property?

The Salvage Convention defines 'salvage operation' to mean:

any act or activity undertaken to assist *a vessel or any other property in danger* in navigable waters or in any other waters whatsoever.[32]

It goes on to define 'vessel' to mean 'any ship or craft, or any structure capable of navigation', and 'property' to mean 'any property not permanently and intentionally attached to the shore-line', including freight at risk.[33] The concept of danger is not defined.

---

[30] For discussion of how some jurisdictions have dealt with this matter, see section 3.3, below.

[31] There were two reasons why this was felt to be necessary: to prevent a decline in the commercial salvage industry and to incentivise salvors to undertake operations in a way that prevented or minimised damage to the environment: see, further, Gaskell, 'The 1989 Salvage Convention and the Lloyd's Open Form (LOF) Salvage Agreement 1990', pp. 5–7.

[32] Art. 1(a). Emphasis added. In its reference to 'any other waters whatsoever', the Convention defines the nature of the waters in which salvage may be undertaken more broadly than traditionally domestic laws have done. States parties to the Convention may reserve the right not to apply its provisions in inland waters where all vessels involved are of inland navigation or where no vessel is involved (Art. 30(1)(a) and (b)).

[33] See Art. 1(b) and (c). Freight is the money earned for the carriage of goods, usually payable at the port of destination.

Since the definitions of 'vessel' and 'property' (and, indeed, the Convention as a whole) make no specific mention of sunken vessels or other sunken property, the question arises as to whether such property is capable of salvage under the treaty regime. According to Gaskell, an observer at the diplomatic conference leading to the Convention:

Throughout the negotiations there was misunderstanding or disagreement (sometimes both) as to the conceptual nature of services performed to valuable sunken vessels and their cargoes.[34]

In light of varying national approaches to the matter, it seems that some states argued that it was not possible to salve sunken property and others – primarily common law states – argued that it was.[35] After extensive analysis, Gaskell concluded that 'the natural meaning of the English wording, and the understanding of the 1989 diplomatic conference, was that sunken property could be salved'.[36] Nonetheless, he went on to point out that 'it would be a matter for national courts to decide whether the property would be in danger'.[37] It seems that, as a matter of principle, the Convention probably *does* apply to sunken property, but that in their application of the treaty national courts are free to define 'danger' restrictively and in such a way that sunken property, or property that has been on the seabed for some length of time, is excluded. Subject to this possibility, it seems that wrecks of cultural interest fall within the general scope of the Convention. Moreover, the fact that the Convention adopts a very broad definition of 'property' means that it has the potential to apply to a much broader range of UCH than would be the case where the traditional notion of 'maritime property' applies.[38]

The general scheme of the Convention does not make provision to take account of the fact that material falling within its scope may constitute UCH.[39] However, a French proposal that material of cultural interest

---

[34] Gaskell, 'Merchant Shipping Act 1995, Schedule 11', p. 21-376.   [35] *Ibid.*

[36] *Ibid.*, p. 21-377.   [37] *Ibid.*

[38] Under the Convention, the limitations are that it would need to be something that is not 'permanently and intentionally attached to the shoreline' and also something that *does* constitute property. The application of salvage law to very ancient remains, such as a Mesolithic flint axe, would seem inappropriate for all sorts of reasons, but after such material has been recovered from the seabed, questions of entitlement may well arise. Apart from the question of whether a Mesolithic axe constitutes property for the purposes of the Convention, another potential restriction to the application of the Convention in such cases is that it is debatable whether the Convention applies to property of no commercial value (on the theoretical premise that such property cannot be in danger: see *ibid.*, p. 21-410).

[39] Whether this will remain the case is uncertain. See, further, section 4.4, below.

should be explicitly excluded from the scope of the Convention, although rejected, did result in the inclusion of a reservation in respect of 'maritime cultural property'.[40] According to Article 30(1)(d), any state may reserve the right not to apply the provisions of the Convention 'when the property involved is maritime cultural property of prehistoric, archaeological or historic interest and is situated on the sea-bed'.[41] The Convention thereby recognises that states may wish to apply a regime distinct from salvage law to material where it constitutes UCH and it enables them to do so. The fact that a reservation is made under Article 30(1)(d) does not in itself mean that a state has excluded 'maritime cultural property' from the scope of their salvage laws; it simply gives them a *right* to do so.[42] Nevertheless, as O'Keefe has pointed out,[43] the fact that the Salvage Convention includes the reservation in Article 30(1)(d) provides compelling evidence that Article 303(3) of the LOSC does *not* prevent states from taking UCH out of the salvage law regime.

3.3   Domestic law approaches

The negotiation of the Salvage Convention illustrated that there is a fundamental dichotomy of view internationally as to whether or not operations to recover sunken property constitute salvage. It seems to be mainly in common law jurisdictions that the law of salvage is applied to sunken wrecks. It is therefore largely only within such jurisdictions that tensions have arisen between the law of salvage and the public interest in cultural heritage protection. In some cases these tensions have been ameliorated in various ways; in others they have been resolved by taking UCH out of the salvage law regime.

---

[40] Gaskell, 'Merchant Shipping Act 1995, Schedule 11', p. 21-377. According to Gaskell, the notion of a reservation on the matter was 'accepted with very little discussion'.

[41] 'Maritime cultural property' is not further defined by the Convention. Le Gurun points out that the term betrays its French origins: Le Gurun, 'France' (2nd edn), p. 74. At the time of the negotiation of the Salvage Convention, a new French law (now in force) was in the process of adoption which uses the term 'maritime cultural asset'. See, further, Chap. 2, section 2.

[42] Of the sixty-two states currently party to the Convention, twenty-two have entered the reservation. See IMO, 'Status of Multilateral Conventions and Instruments in respect of which the International Maritime Organisation or its Secretary-General performs depositary or other functions, as at 31 July 2012', pp. 443–9 (available at www.imo.org/conventions). A reservation under Art. 30(1)(d) must be entered at the time of signature, ratification, acceptance, approval or accession to the Convention: see Art. 30(1). On this point, see, further, section 4.3, below.

[43] O'Keefe, *Shipwrecked Heritage*, p. 19.

The UK Merchant Shipping Act 1995 enacts the Salvage Convention 1989 into English law. Although the UK exercised a reservation in respect of maritime cultural property when it ratified the Convention, it has yet to exercise its right under that reservation not to apply salvage law to such property. Among other things, this means that the provisions in Part IX of the Act relating to wreck and salvage apply to material of all ages, including that from sites designated for their 'historical, archaeological and artistic importance' under the Protection of Wrecks Act 1973. The provisions in Part IX of the Merchant Shipping Act (which derive from the 1894 statute of the same name) were designed to deal with the safekeeping and disposal of property from vessels in distress or recently wrecked and their original purpose was threefold: to reunite owners with their lost property, to provide a salvage reward for the finder, and to afford an extra source of revenue for the Exchequer by providing the Crown with a right to unclaimed wreck.[44] In the immediate wake of the advent of recreational scuba-diving, the application of these provisions to material of cultural value led to some highly undesirable consequences.[45] However, since the 1990s, holders of the office of Receiver of Wreck have dealt with such material with as much sensitivity as the statutory framework will allow. The Crown now effectively forfeits its financial interest in unclaimed wreck and finders are encouraged to waive their statutory right to salvage in order that finds can be donated to a museum. Nonetheless, the system is such that the private interests of owners and salvors ultimately take precedence over the public interest in culturally significant material.[46]

Outside the UK, a Receiver of Wreck or similar system continues to exist in some form in a number of other jurisdictions, including Australia, Ireland, South Africa and New Zealand. However, the degree to which the system still governs the disposition of cultural material varies. In Ireland and New Zealand the system still has some application,[47] but in Australia and South Africa historic shipwrecks have been removed from the regime.[48]

Removal of a system that financially incentivises the recovery of material almost inevitably gives rise to questions about whether it is

---

[44] See Chap. 3, section 2.1.   [45] See Dromgoole, 'Protection of Historic Wreck', pp. 35–6.
[46] See Dromgoole, 'United Kingdom', pp. 316–20.
[47] See O'Connor, 'Ireland' (2nd edn), pp. 129–34; Davies and Myburgh, 'New Zealand', pp. 199–201.
[48] See Forrest and Gribble, 'Perspectives from the Southern Hemisphere', pp. 30–1.

then necessary to put in place a system to encourage finders to *report* their discoveries. The most developed system of this kind is probably to be found in Australia. In commenting on this system, Forrest and Gribble have stated:

While this is clearly to encourage compliance with the Act [which requires the reporting of UCH], in part [it] was originally designed to compensate a finder for the loss of the ability to salvage the wreck. Such a reward is not 'as of right' and takes into account the heritage value of the finds and not simply its financial value. The reward itself need not therefore be financial, and the Minister may reward the finder by awarding a plaque or medallion commemorating the find, model or replica of the vessel or relic, or an actual award of an historic relic.[49]

The question of whether or not finders should be incentivised, particularly financially, for reporting *discoveries* of UCH is a contentious one and even in Australia the question of rewarding finders is under reconsideration.[50] In South Africa, a finder's reward is not provided for, but the finder may be afforded an incentive to report in the form of an opportunity to participate in any subsequent recovery operation.[51]

Two relatively recent cases, one in Ireland and one in Finland,[52] show courts struggling (but ultimately succeeding) in dealing with the tensions between the law of salvage and heritage objectives. In Ireland, in 1994, a case arose before the High Court concerning three Spanish Armada vessels, *La Lavia*, *Juliana* and *Santa Maria de la Vision*, wrecked off the coast of County Sligo in 1588. In holding that the finders had no rights to the wrecks under the law of salvage, the trial judge stated:

It seems to me that when so much time has elapsed since the original loss of a vessel that the question of ownership, and attendant acolytes such as indemnification, lose their practical significance and merge into history, then the wreck should be regarded as having passed from the commercial realm of maritime salvage law into the domain of archaeological law.[53]

---

[49] *Ibid.*, p. 32 n. 11.
[50] Australian Government, 'Australia's Maritime Heritage', Discussion Paper, June 2009, p. 12.
[51] Forrest and Gribble, 'Perspectives from the Southern Hemisphere', p. 32.
[52] In common with other Nordic countries, Finland's legal system is distinct from both the common law and civil law legal systems.
[53] *King and Chapman* v. *The Owners and all Persons Claiming an Interest in the 'La Lavia', 'Juliana' and 'Santa Maria de la Vision'*, 1986 No. 11076, 11077, 11078 P (Transcript) (Ir. H. Ct. 1994), p. 34.

In this case, the original ownership rights were untraceable.[54] Following an earlier decision of the Irish Supreme Court relating to archaeological finds on land which had no known owner,[55] it was concluded that ownership fell to the state.[56]

Litigation concerning the *Vrouw Maria*, which sank in the south-western archipelago of Finland in 1771, gave rise to some interesting parallels. The wreck, reputedly carrying artworks belonging to Catherine the Great, was discovered in 1999. As a vessel that was over 100 years of age, it qualified for protection under Finnish antiquities legislation and that legislation also provided for state ownership. However, the association of divers that discovered the wreck claimed that they had possession over the site and, in light of this, under maritime legislation were entitled to undertake full salvage for which a salvage reward would be payable. Alternatively, they claimed that, under finds legislation, they were entitled to ownership of the wreck on the basis that the wreck had been abandoned by its original owner.[57] In 2004, the Turku Maritime Court at first instance held that, in the circumstances of the case, the antiquities legislation took precedence over the maritime legislation and had the effect of excluding the provisions on salvage. On appeal from this decision, in 2005, the Turku Court of Appeal concluded that the antiquities legislation did not supersede the maritime legislation and that both pieces of legislation applied to the case. However, it went on to hold that the state had ownership of the site by virtue of the antiquities legislation and, as owner, under the terms of the maritime legislation it was entitled to prohibit salvage on the basis that the vessel was not in 'concrete danger'. Furthermore, since the wreck was protected under the antiquities legislation and could not be interfered with without authorisation, the impact of this was that the finder could not gain

---

[54] It appears that the vessels had been in private ownership and were commandeered by Philip II of Spain: see 1986 No. 11076, 11077, 11078 P (Transcript) (Ir. H. Ct. 1994), p. 3.

[55] *Webb* v. *Ireland* [1988] IR 353. See, further, Chap. 3, section 2.4.

[56] On appeal, these findings were left untouched, although the appeal was allowed on another matter: *In re the Sailing Vessels 'La Lavia', 'Juliana' and 'Santa Maria de la Vision': Alan King and Harry Chapman* v. *Owners and All Persons Claiming an Interest in the Said Sailing Vessels*, [1996] 1 ILRM 194 (Ir. SC). Ireland is a party to the Salvage Convention but did not enter a reservation under Art. 30(1)(d). As Gaskell has pointed out, the approach taken by the Irish court with respect to the Spanish Armada wrecks 'might be another way of saying that there was no danger': Gaskell, 'Merchant Shipping Act 1995, Schedule 11', p. 21-377.

[57] On the question of abandonment in respect of the *Vrouw Maria*, see, further, Chap. 3, section 2.3.

'de facto dominion' and possession over it. Therefore, the association of divers had acquired no rights as finder.[58]

The case of the *Vrouw Maria* also gives rise to another issue relating to conflicts that may arise between rights claimed under salvage or finds laws and the needs of heritage protection. After the Turku Court of Appeal reached its decision in 2005, the finders of the wreck applied to the European Court of Human Rights (ECHR) on the grounds, inter alia, that the state of Finland had interfered with their rights under Article 1 of the First Protocol to the European Convention on Human Rights. Article 1 of the First Protocol reads as follows:

Every natural or legal person is entitled to the peaceful enjoyment of his posses-sions. No one shall be deprived of his possessions except in the public interest and subject to the conditions provided for by law and by the general principles of international law.

The preceding provisions shall not, however, in any way impair the right of a State to enforce such laws as it deems necessary to control the use of property in accordance with the general interest or to secure the payment of taxes or other contributions or penalties.

While the applicants acknowledged that they had not taken possession of the site because the Finnish antiquities legislation prevented such possession from occurring, nonetheless they claimed that, as 'first salvors' (having been 'first on the scene and ready and willing to offer salvage'), they had earned the right to perform salvage and to claim a salvage reward.[59] In light of this, they claimed they had a legitimate expectation of an 'asset' amounting to a proprietary interest protected by Article 1. In a decision handed down in 2010, the ECHR concluded that the applicants had not satisfied the conditions for payment of a reward under Finnish maritime legislation because the state, as owner, in the circumstances of the case had had a right to prohibit salvage.[60]

The ECHR decision is quite particular to the individual circumstances in the *Vrouw Maria* case. However, it draws attention to a more general point. Given the right circumstances, a salvor or finder of a wreck site may gain *possessory* rights over the site. If these rights are later interfered with by the state in order to provide heritage protection, there is a risk of action under Article 1 of the First Protocol (assuming that the state is a party to this Protocol). This is something that is potentially particularly

---

[58] See Matikka, 'Finland', pp. 52–4.
[59] *Koivusaari and others* v. *Finland* (dec.), No. 20690/06, 23 February 2010, p. 10.
[60] *Ibid.*, p. 12.

problematic for jurisdictions such as the UK, where the heritage legislation is based on the designation of individual sites, rather than on
blanket protection.[61] In such cases, sites are designated *after* discovery
and therefore there is clearly a risk that a finder will acquire possessory
rights in the site prior to its designation. The finder might then attempt
to argue that there has been a breach of Article 1 of the First Protocol,
either as a result of the designation itself, or as a result of requirements
imposed after designation.[62] One of the advantages of protective systems
based on blanket protection is that the protection is likely to be in place
before any possessory rights arise.

3.4 US federal admiralty law

'Treasure salvage'[63] as a commercial industry emerged in Florida in the
period after the Second World War. As scuba equipment became increasingly available, the proximity to the Florida coast of the route taken by
fleets of the Spanish Empire between the West Indies and Europe inevitably attracted interest. In the decades that followed, discovery of vessels
from the storm-hit fleets of 1622, 1715 and 1733, along with other
colonial-era shipwrecks, led to the development of a body of admiralty
case law determining the rights of the recoverers. For the most part, the
US federal admiralty courts have regarded the enterprise of the treasure
salvage industry in the same favourable light as the enterprise of salvors
engaged in the more traditional recovery of vessels in distress and
recently wrecked, and this has been reflected in generous rewards. As a
result, the USA – and certain districts and circuits within its federal court
system[64] – has become the jurisdiction of choice for many treasure
salvors, whether or not the salvage activity has taken place off the US
coast, or further afield.

---

[61] See Chap. 2, sections 2 and 4.2.2.
[62] On how such arguments can be dealt with, see Chap. 3, section 2.4. For a specific
instance where this issue arose, see Fletcher-Tomenius and Williams, 'The Protection of
Wrecks Act 1973'.
[63] 'Treasure salvage' or 'historic salvage', as it is sometimes referred to, is a term generally
used to mean the recovery of valuable property from wrecks that have been on the
seabed for some time, under the law of salvage.
[64] Under the federal court system, the court of first instance is the district court, which is
located within a state (some large states having more than one district court). Appeals
from the district courts are heard by the US Court of Appeals, which is organised into
individual circuits. In a few cases, a further appeal may be heard by the final arbiter, the
US Supreme Court.

While the outcome of treasure salvage litigation is not always predict-able, a fairly consistent approach has been taken to certain basic matters. Generally speaking, the federal admiralty courts have regarded sunken vessels, including those that have been long-lost, as capable of being the subject of salvage. Although, as one eminent commentator on US maritime law put it, '[t]he concept of marine peril is stretched to its limit' in cases relating to wrecks on the seabed for hundreds of years,[65] nonetheless the courts have generally looked at the question of peril from an economic rather than heritage perspective: while at the bottom of the sea, the commercial value of a wreck is regarded as lost or immobilised, both to its owner and the world at large; it is therefore a public service to perform a 'rescue' in order that it may be returned to the 'stream of commerce'. The question of motivation and particularly the fact that treasure salvors are likely to be motivated purely by their own self-interests is a matter generally not taken into account. In cases where a wreck is treated not merely as a derelict, but as having been abandoned by its owner, the federal admiralty courts have applied the common law of finds. Indeed, the extent to which the laws of salvage and finds are used and treated as alternatives is such that it has been said that the law of finds has been 'adopted into US admiralty law'.[66] Whether it is the law of salvage or the law of finds that is ultimately determined to apply, the recoverer is likely to be generously rewarded: either with a liberal salvage award (which may amount to 90 or even 100 per cent of the commercial value of the recovered material),[67] or with an award of title as 'finder'.

3.4.1   Early treasure salvage cases

The early years of treasure salvage were characterised by cases in which salvors competed with both the federal government, and state governments, for rights to wrecks. The case that epitomised matters was *Treasure Salvors*,[68] relating to the *Nuestra Señora de Atocha*. This galleon had been part of the Spanish Plate Fleet of 1622 and was discovered approximately four miles off the coast of Florida in 1971.

---

[65] Schoenbaum, *Admiralty and Maritime Law*, pp. 833–4.
[66] McQuown, 'An Archaeological Argument for the Inapplicability of Admiralty Law in the Disposition of Historic Shipwrecks', p. 299.
[67] See section 3.4.3, below.
[68] *Treasure Salvors, Inc. v. Unidentified, Wrecked and Abandoned Sailing Vessel*, 408 F. Supp. 907 (D. Fla. 1976), *aff'd*, 569 F.2d 330 (5th Cir. 1978) (known as Treasure Salvors I).

The case involved competing claims to the wreck and its contents by government authorities and the finder. The latter, Treasure Salvors, Inc., had argued that the wreck and its contents had been abandoned and that it was entitled to the property recovered under the law of finds. A claim by the state of Florida to ownership, on the basis that the *Atocha* was located on the submerged lands of Florida, was refuted when it was determined that the wreck was located on the continental shelf *beyond* those submerged lands.[69] When the federal government intervened to claim ownership, on the ground that it had inherited the English sovereign prerogative over unclaimed wreck on the high seas and brought to shore,[70] its claim was also dismissed in light of insufficient evidence that the US Congress had taken up the prerogative. The Fifth Circuit Court of Appeals concluded that the *Atocha* was indisputably 'an abandoned vessel' and that the district court had correctly applied the law of finds.[71] In commenting on these conclusions, the Fifth Circuit stated:

in extraordinary cases, such as this one, where the property has been lost or abandoned for a very long period … the maritime law of finds supplements the possessory interest normally granted to a salvor and vests title by occupancy in one who discovers such abandoned property and reduces it into possession.[72]

This decision was swiftly followed by that of the district court for the Southern District of Florida in the case of *Cobb Coin*. Again, the claim of the state government to ownership was dismissed and this time the salvor was awarded all the artefacts recovered as 'an award for superlative salvage services'.[73]

---

[69] 569 F.2d 330 at 333. The *Atocha* was located outside state waters and also outside the US territorial sea, which at the time had a breadth of three miles. (The US territorial sea was extended to twelve miles in 1988.)

[70] Interestingly, in 1986 it was determined by an English admiralty court that the English prerogative right to unclaimed wreck did *not* extend to wreck outside the territorial sea: *The Lusitania* [1986] QB 384. Whether the English Crown had ever had such a right is debatable: see Dromgoole and Gaskell, 'Interests in Wreck', pp. 181–2.

[71] 569 F.2d 330 at 336.   [72] 640 F.2d 560, 567 (5th Cir. 1981).

[73] *Cobb Coin Co. v. Unidentified, Wrecked and Abandoned Sailing Vessel*, 549 F. Supp. 540, 561 (SD Fla. 1982). Where, as in this case, the salvor is awarded the property, or part of the property, in lieu of a monetary reward, it is known as an *in specie* award. In this case the district court justified the nature of the award on the ground that 'the property saved is uniquely and intrinsically valuable beyond its monetary value': 549 F. Supp. 540, 560. However, according to a different district court in the later case *Chance*, making a salvage reward *in specie* 'would be violative of underlying salvage law principles since salvage law assumes that title to the personalty remains in the owner': F. Supp. 801, 808 (D. Geo. 1985). (In salvage law generally, *in specie* awards are rare and are usually made only where the value of the award exceeds the value of the property recovered, thereby saving on the costs of sale.) On *in specie* awards, see, further, section 3.4.3, below.

Although at the time the general trend in US case law was that the finder of an ancient wreck became the 'keeper', there were decisions that went in favour of the application of salvage law. In both *Klein*[74] and *Chance*[75] the claims of federal and state governments respectively to ownership were upheld, based on exceptions to the law of finds.[76] Furthermore, claims for a salvage reward were denied on the basis that the wrecks were not in peril. In *Klein*, the Eleventh Circuit reiterated the view of the district court that the 'unscientific removal of the artifacts did more to create a marine peril than to prevent one'.[77] In *Chance*, the district court took cognisance of expert testimony that, after a certain period, a wreck will reach a state of equilibrium and will remain in that state until disturbed. In light of the disturbance caused by removal of artefacts from the site, and the fact that the artefacts so removed were now 'subject to a much greater rate of deterioration than if they had remained on the river bottom', the court concluded that the claim to a salvage reward should be denied.[78]

3.4.2 Introduction of the Abandoned Shipwreck Act

The Abandoned Shipwreck Act of 1987 (ASA) was introduced as a direct consequence of the outcome in the *Treasure Salvors* case and in essence codified the decisions in *Klein* and *Chance*.[79] This federal statute applies to shipwrecks that are both abandoned and also: (i) embedded in the submerged lands of a state, *or* (ii) embedded in coralline formations protected by a state on submerged lands of a state; *or* (iii) resting on submerged lands of a state and included in or determined eligible for inclusion in the National Register of Historic Places.[80] The US federal government asserts title to any shipwreck that satisfies those criteria;

---

[74] *Klein v. Unidentified, Wrecked and Abandoned Sailing Vessel*, 568 F.Supp. 1562 (SD Fla. 1983); *Klein v. Unidentified, Wrecked and Abandoned Sailing Vessel*, 758 F.2d 1511 (11th Cir. 1985).
[75] *Chance v. Certain Artifacts Found and Salvaged from the Nashville*, 606 F.Supp. 801 (D. Geo. 1985).
[76] The two exceptions to the general rule of finds that the finder will be awarded title to an abandoned wreck are: (i) where the wreck is embedded in the submerged lands belonging to a federal or state government, title to the wreck will fall to that government; and (ii) where federal or state government is found to have constructive possession over the wreck, so that the finder is unable to demonstrate the dominion and control required to assert finders' rights. On these exceptions, see McQuown, 'An Archaeological Argument for the Inapplicability of Admiralty Law in the Disposition of Historic Shipwrecks', p. 301.
[77] 758 F.2d 1511, 1515.   [78] 606 F.Supp. 801, 809.
[79] Varmer, 'United States', pp. 355 and 357.   [80] 43 USC sec. 2105(a).

that title is then transferred automatically to the state within whose waters the wreck lies.[81] The ASA disapplies the laws of salvage and finds from those wrecks that fall within its scope.[82] In the legislative history of the ASA, the Congressional House Committee on Merchant Marine and Fisheries made clear that it did not consider that abandoned shipwrecks covered by the Act were 'in marine peril, necessitating their recovery by salvage companies'; further, it did not consider that the laws of salvage and finds 'well serve the protection of our nation's maritime heritage':

This heritage is best protected by States acting through their historic preservation programs consistent with federal guidance.[83]

According to Giesecke, whose expertise in the field was called upon to draft the ASA:

The ASA was meant to be an unambiguous statement that the United States, as the owner of certain abandoned shipwrecks, was placing them beyond the reach of the federal admiralty courts.[84]

While the enactment of the ASA reduced the amount of litigation in this field, it only partially fulfilled its objectives. As Varmer has pointed out, since the Act did not codify the presumption in pre-ASA case law such as *Treasure Salvors* that long-lost shipwrecks had been abandoned through the effluxion of time and the absence of any ownership claim, in ASA cases the judiciary have been 'inclined to presume that there is an owner and require states to prove abandonment as an element of their case'.[85] Therefore, treasure salvors simply altered their tactics. Instead of mounting a strong argument that a wreck had been abandoned in order that finds law would be applied, they argued that the rights of existing owners should not be lightly dismissed in order to ensure that salvage law would be applied and a generous reward would ensue.

The ASA is unusual compared with heritage legislation relating to UCH in many other jurisdictions. This is because it adopts a distinctive multiple-use management regime which *includes* private-sector recovery among the permitted uses. According to Varmer, the Act favours *in situ*

---

[81] 43 USC sec. 2105(a) and (c). The submerged lands of states typically extend to three miles from the coast.
[82] 43 USC sec. 2106(a).   [83] See HR Rep. No. 100-514, Pt. 2, at p. 8 (1988).
[84] Giesecke, 'The Abandoned Shipwreck Act Through the Eyes of its Drafter', p. 171.
[85] Varmer, 'United States', p. 357.

preservation[86] and thus enables sites to be available for a range of purposes including non-intrusive research, education, recreation and tourism.[87] However, in developing their policies for implementation of the Act, among other things states must 'allow for appropriate public and private sector recovery of shipwrecks consistent with the protection of historical values'.[88] Guidelines have been issued under the ASA[89] which acknowledge that recovery activity (be it public or private) has the potential to damage and destroy sites; detailed provision is therefore made for the circumstances in which recovery should be permitted. However, these Guidelines are non-binding on states and consequently are not uniformly followed. Some states continue to allow compensation for private-sector recovery.[90]

3.4.3 Modification of US federal salvage law to accommodate archaeological value

In circumstances that fall outside the scope of the ASA and other federal legislation,[91] shipwreck recovery continues to be governed solely by the federal admiralty courts through their application of the general law on salvage and finds. However, while 'not the norm',[92] there have been efforts by certain elements of the federal judiciary to take into account the historical and archaeological value of some shipwrecks and to modify the traditional precepts of salvage law to accommodate this value. The litigation in respect of the *Central America* and the *Titanic*, both located in deep international waters, serves to illustrate these developments. Both cases fell within the jurisdiction of the US District Court for the Eastern District of Virginia (Norfolk Division) and the Fourth Circuit Court of Appeals.[93]

---

[86] Varmer, 'The Case Against the "Salvage" of the Cultural Heritage', p. 283.
[87] *Ibid.*, p. 288.   [88] 42 USC sec. 2103(a)(2)(C).
[89] Abandoned Shipwreck Act Guidelines, 55 Fed. Reg. 50116 (1990).
[90] For example, the permit issued to Sea Hunt in respect of the *Juno* and *La Galga* under Virginia state law provided for a split of the proceeds of recovery on the basis of 25 per cent to Virginia and 75 per cent to Sea Hunt. See, further, Kang, 'Charting Through Protection for Historic Shipwrecks Found in US Territorial Waters', pp. 106–11. On the *Sea Hunt* case, see, further, section 3.4.4, below.
[91] For details of the relevant legislation, see Varmer, 'United States', pp. 355–74.
[92] Varmer, 'The Case against the "Salvage" of the Cultural Heritage', p. 297.
[93] The circuit system in the US federal courts means that precedents can be created only circuit by circuit. Furthermore, as Varmer has commented, there has been 'no uniform application ... within districts ... much less ... in admiralty courts across the country': *ibid.*, p. 300.

In the case of the *Central America*,[94] the Columbus-America Discovery Group (CADG) spent thirteen years undertaking desk-based research concerning the wreck and its cargo of gold, followed by extensive and expensive efforts physically to locate them. In 1987, it filed a claim with the district court in Norfolk, claiming title as finder, or alternatively a liberal salvage reward. On appeal from a decision of the district court to apply the law of finds, the Fourth Circuit made clear that it favoured the application of salvage law over the law of finds[95] and the call for a liberal reward. It reiterated that a salvage award:

generally far exceeds a mere remuneration *pro opere et labore* – the excess being intended, upon principles of sound public policy, not only as a reward to the particular salvor, but, also, as an inducement to others to render like services.[96]

While it was recognised that the recovery efforts by CADG were motivated by economic self-interest,[97] the efforts were also regarded as representing 'a paradigm of American initiative, ingenuity, and determination'.[98]

Traditionally, US courts take six factors into account in determining the level of a salvage reward. These factors are known as the *Blackwall* factors, after the case in which they were first set out.[99] They are: the labour expended by the salvor; the promptitude, skill and energy displayed; the value of the property employed by the salvor, and the danger to which it is exposed; the risks incurred by the salvor; the value of the property saved; and the degree of danger from which the property was rescued. Referring to the approach in two earlier cases where archaeological considerations had been taken into account,[100] the Fourth Circuit added a seventh factor: 'the degree to which the salvors have worked to

---

[94] *Columbus-America Discovery Group, Inc. v. Unidentified, Wrecked and Abandoned Sailing Vessel*, 742 F. Supp. 1327 (ED Va. Aug. 14, 1990); *reversed by Columbus-America Discovery Group v. Atlantic Mut. Ins. Co.*, 974 F.2d 450 (4th Cir. (Va.) Aug. 26, 1992); *on remand to Columbus-America Discovery Group, Inc. v. Unidentified, Wrecked and Abandoned Sailing Vessel*, 1993 WL 580900 (ED Va. Nov. 18, 1993); *decision rescinded by Columbus-America Discovery Group v. Atlantic Mut. Ins. Co.*, 56 F.3d 556 (4th Cir. (Va.) June 14, 1995). On this case, see, further, Chap. 3, sections 2.2 and 2.3.

[95] 974 F.2d 450, 464.

[96] 974 F.2d 450, 468, citing W. Marvin, *A Treatise on the Law of Wreck and Salvage*, para. 97, at 105 (1858).

[97] 974 F.2d 450, 458.   [98] 56 F.3d 556, 576.

[99] *The Blackwall* 77 US (10. Wall), 1, 13–14 (1869).

[100] *Cobb Coin Co., Inc. v. Unidentified, Wrecked and Abandoned Sailing Vessel*, 525 F. Supp. 186, 208 (SD Fla. 1981); *MDM Salvage, Inc. v. the Unidentified, Wrecked and Abandoned Sailing Vessel*, 631 F. Supp. 308, 310 (SD Fla. 1986).

protect the historical and archeological value of the wreck and items salved'.[101] It concluded that there was no evidence to contradict the district court's finding that 'the efforts to preserve the site and the artifacts have not been equalled in any other case'.[102] The Fourth Circuit also concluded that, while generous, an award of 90 per cent of the value of the recovered gold could not be said to be excessive in the circumstances.[103] It thought it 'proper' that in a case such as this an award be made *in specie*, citing reasoning adopted in an earlier case that when items salvaged are 'uniquely and intrinsically valuable beyond their monetary worth, an award *in specie* is more appropriate'.[104]

The extraordinarily protracted (and, it must be said, also highly untypical) salvage action in respect of the *Titanic* has been referred to as 'the jewel in the crown of U.S. admiralty courts in their attempt to demonstrate concern for, and the ability to protect, the archaeological provenance of historic wrecks'.[105] Indeed, the lengths to which the district court in Norfolk and, in oversight, the Fourth Circuit Court of Appeals have been prepared to go to protect the public interest in this unique wreck are quite remarkable.

Among the unusual features of the case is the fact that, from the very outset, the salvor, RMS *Titanic*, Inc. (RMST), assured the court of its intention not to sell the artefacts it recovered from the site but to keep them together as a collection for exhibition to a paying public. Also, from the outset it was recognised that there was a public interest in maintaining the archaeological integrity of such a unique historical wreck and that such interest was served by ensuring that the artefacts were properly conserved and kept together as a publicly accessible collection.[106]

---

[101] 974 F.2d 450, 468.

[102] 56 F.3d 556, 573. The efforts in this regard appeared to focus on the care taken in handling and preserving the artefacts recovered and public dissemination of information about the project: see 56 F.3d 556, 573.

[103] 56 F.3d 556, 573.

[104] 974 F.2d 450, 469. The earlier case was *Cobb Coin*, 525 F. Supp. 186, 198.

[105] Fletcher-Tomenius, O'Keefe and Williams, 'Salvor in Possession', p. 289. The *in rem* proceedings commenced in 1993 and are still ongoing. The key references for the purposes of the present discussion are: *RMS Titanic, Inc.* v. *Wrecked and Abandoned Vessel*, 924 F. Supp. 714 (ED Va. May 10, 1996); *RMS Titanic, Inc.* v. *Wrecked and Abandoned Vessel*, 9 F. Supp. 2d 624 (ED Va. June 23, 1998); *RMS Titanic, Inc.* v. *Wrecked and Abandoned Vessel*, 286 F.3d 194 (4th Cir. (Va.) Apr. 12, 2002); *RMS Titanic, Inc.* v. *Wrecked and Abandoned Vessel*, 435 F.3d 521 (4th Cir. (Va.) Jan. 31, 2006); *RMS Titanic, Inc.* v. *Wrecked and Abandoned Vessel*, 742 F. Supp. 2d 784 (ED Va. Aug. 12, 2010); *RMS Titanic, Inc.* v. *Wrecked and Abandoned Vessel, Its Engines, Tackle, Apparel, Appurtenances, Cargo, etc.*, 804 F. Supp. 2d 508 (ED Va. Aug. 15, 2011).

[106] See, for example, 924 F. Supp. 714, 722–3 and 9 F. Supp. 2d 624, 639–40.

The fact that RMST manifested an intention not to sell the artefacts raised, but to keep them together as a publicly accessible collection, has been a significant factor taken into account in granting it exclusive rights to the site and in subsequently protecting those rights.[107] Over the years, in order to maintain its status as salvor-in-possession, RMST has mounted regular expeditions to the site and recovered thousands of artefacts. It has been required to submit periodic reports to the court in order to demonstrate that its efforts are ongoing, 'clothed with the prospect of success', and conducted with due diligence. In considering the question of due diligence, the degree to which RMST has worked to preserve the archaeological integrity of the wreck site, as well as the artefacts recovered, has been taken into account.[108] Although in later years RMST has found it difficult to fund the enormous costs of its deepwater salvage work solely by exhibition revenues, it has been precluded by court order from selling individual artefacts (with the exception of pieces of coal)[109] and also from cutting into the hull.[110]

In 2004, RMST requested that the district court award it title to the artefacts so far recovered under the law of finds or, alternatively, an interim salvage award *in specie* (on the ground that the costs of salvage exceeded the value of the artefacts recovered).[111] A preliminary ruling by the district court that the law of finds was inappropriate in the circumstances of the case was affirmed by the Fourth Circuit Court of Appeals in 2006. Niemeyer C.J. confirmed a comment made by the district judge, Beach Smith J., that: 'RMST cannot have its cake and eat it too'.[112] Having accepted the benefits of the role of salvor-in-possession for a period of ten years, under protection of the court, RMST could not then convert its role to finder in order to obtain title to the artefacts while at the same time remaining a salvor-in-possession with exclusive rights to the site. More generally, Niemeyer C.J. noted that 'a free finders-keepers policy is but a short step from active piracy and pillaging' and, because of its 'tendency to encourage acquisitive behaviour', should be 'applied sparingly' and 'only when no private or public interest would be

---

[107] See, for example, 924 F. Supp. 714, 718 and 723.

[108] See, for example, 924 F. Supp. 714, 722–3.

[109] District court prohibitions on the sale of artefacts were affirmed by the Fourth Circuit: 286 F.3d 194.

[110] Order dated 28 July 2000.

[111] 435 F.3d 521, 525. The artefacts referred to exclude 1,800 recovered in an expedition in 1987, which had been subject to separate proceedings in France.

[112] 435 F.3d 521, 530 and 535.

adversely affected'.[113] While concluding that salvage law was preferable to the law of finds in the context of historic wrecks, he acknowledged 'the awkwardness of fit' of salvage law to historic wrecks and dealt with it in the following way:

> Because the traditional law of salvage ... involves the creation of a trust relationship between salvor and the court on behalf of the owner, it is not a major step to apply the same principles to historic wreck, creating a trust relationship between the salvor and the court on behalf of the public interest. ... [A]ny such principles would still yield to one who could establish a right of ownership.[114]

In August 2010, the district judge, Beach Smith J., held that a salvage award in the amount of 100 per cent of the fair market value of the artefacts recovered was appropriate. After considering expert evidence, she found that $110,859,200 was an appropriate approximation of that value.[115] In making her award, the judge took account of the traditional *Blackwall* factors and also the seventh factor recognised by the Fourth Circuit in the *Columbus-America* case. Her overall summation was that the salvage efforts had involved 'unprecedented feats of skill and dedication, both in the salvage of the artifacts and their conservation and exhibition'.[116] However, a decision on the manner in which to pay the award was held over for a further year in order to determine whether an appropriate buyer for the collection might be found, who was capable of maintaining the collection in the public interest.

In the subsequent months, a prospective buyer for the collection could not be identified. Therefore, in August 2011, Judge Beach Smith awarded RMST the collection *in specie*.[117] A notable, and unprecedented, feature of the award was that it was made subject to detailed covenants and conditions.[118] These had been drawn up in extensive consultations between US federal government authorities, the court and RMST, and are designed to ensure that the collection will be maintained intact and managed in accordance with professional standards in perpetuity.[119]

---

[113] 435 F.3d 521, 533.   [114] 435 F.3d 521, 536.

[115] 742 F. Supp. 2d 784, 797. The artefacts referred to, numbering approximately 4,000, were recovered in expeditions in 1993, 1994, 1996, 1998, 2000 and 2004. The court declined to make a deduction from the award for revenues earned from exhibiting the artefacts, accepting RMST's position that the exhibitions had failed to make an operational profit: 742 F. Supp. 2d 784, 807.

[116] 742 F. Supp. 2d 784, 808.   [117] 804 F. Supp. 2d 508.

[118] For a copy of the Covenants and Conditions, see Exhibit A attached to the district court's opinion of 12 August 2010.

[119] At the time of writing, the collection is on the market as one lot through a firm of auctioneers based in New York. The purchase will be subject to the Covenants

3.4.4   Relationship between US federal law and the Salvage Convention 1989

A curious feature of US federal admiralty law is that, despite the fact that the US ratified the Salvage Convention in 1991 and the Convention became part of US law on 14 July 1996 when it came into force internationally, little or no reference appears to have been made to this treaty by the federal admiralty courts. Indeed, remarkably, according to a recent survey, in only one reported case has the Salvage Convention been applied.[120] According to the author of that survey, Davies, the reason that the Convention is to all intents and purposes ignored by the federal judiciary could be that it is a 'self-executing' treaty,[121] in other words there is no need for legislation to make it operative. In consequence, it is not referred to at all in the US Code, the purpose of which is to facilitate the identification of relevant and effective law. In the view of Davies, this means that the fact that the Convention is part of US law may be overlooked.[122] As a result, the federal courts continue to apply the general maritime law of salvage, rather than the terms of the treaty.

In the context of treasure salvage, there are two particular areas where the approaches of the Salvage Convention and the general maritime law of salvage as applied by the US federal admiralty courts merit some comparison.

First of all, Article 19 of the Salvage Convention deals with the prohibition of salvage operations. It provides:

Services rendered notwithstanding the express and reasonable prohibition of the owner or master of the vessel or the owner of any other property in danger which is not and has not been on board the vessel shall not give rise to payment under this Convention.

Under Article 19, a prohibition must be both express *and* reasonable in order to be effective. In US federal jurisprudence, at least in respect of historic wrecks, while the desire of a sovereign owner of a sunken wreck to protect its military gravesites has been looked on with favour, notably in the *Sea Hunt* case,[123] the owner's reasons in this and other cases for prohibiting salvage do not appear to have been subjected to particular scrutiny. Indeed, in *International Aircraft Recovery*, where the Eleventh

---

and Conditions, as well as to the approval of the US District Court for the Eastern District of Virginia.

[120] Davies, 'Whatever Happened to the Salvage Convention 1989?', p. 463. The case did not involve treasure salvage.

[121] *Ibid.*, pp. 503–4.   [122] *Ibid.*   [123] See Chap. 4, section 2.3.2.

Circuit Court of Appeals – like the Fourth Circuit in *Sea Hunt* – emphatically upheld the sovereign owner's right to prohibit salvage, the court could 'find no decision based on the prudence of rejecting salvage services'.[124] Today, cases such as this will be governed by the US Sunken Military Craft Act (SMCA), which makes it clear that the express permission of the sovereign owner is required before salvage rights will accrue.[125] However, in cases falling outside the parameters of the SMCA, the reasonableness of any prohibition is something that, technically, should probably be considered.[126] Would broad cultural reasons alone suffice, such as the desire to protect a gravesite, or to preserve an archaeological site *in situ*, or would the owner be required to show some degree of *misconduct* on the part of the salvor?[127] In light of the fact that Article 19 does not explicitly refer to misconduct, and that the motivation for issuing a prohibition does not appear to be taken into account at all by the US admiralty courts to date, it seems unlikely that they would regard a prohibition with a protective objective in mind as unreasonable.

Where there has been no prohibition, or a prohibition is ineffective, another question that arises is the extent to which it is possible for a salvor of a historic wreck who undertakes poor archaeological work to be penalised by being deprived of a reward, in whole or in part. In US federal treasure salvage jurisprudence, while care taken by salvors to preserve the archaeological integrity of a wreck has been recognised and taken into account in order to *enhance* the payments made,[128] it has been

---

[124] *International Aircraft Recovery, LLC* v. *Unidentified, Wrecked and Abandoned Aircraft*, 218 F.3d 1255, 1261 (11th Cir. 2000). In overturning a district court order upholding the right of the recovery company to complete its salvage efforts, the Eleventh Circuit opined that the district court had 'under-appreciated the authority of a vessel's owner to prevent others from interfering with its property': 218 F.3d 1255, 1261. On the question of what constitutes an effective prohibition, see *International Aircraft Recovery, LLC* v. *Unidentified, Wrecked and Abandoned Aircraft*, 373 F.3d 1147 (11th Cir. 2004).

[125] SMCA, sec. 1406(d). On this statute, see, further, Chap. 4, section 2.2.

[126] This depends on whether Art. 19 applies to *sunken* property. Not only is it debatable whether the Convention as a whole applies to sunken property (see section 3.2, above), but the wording of Art. 19 itself indicates that it was designed very much with floating vessels in mind: see, further, Gaskell, 'Merchant Shipping Act 1995, Schedule 11', p. 21-422.

[127] Under English common law, the question of whether an owner had a right to prohibit salvage of a derelict in the absence of manifest incompetence is a matter of some debate: see Dromgoole and Gaskell, 'Interests in Wreck', p. 190.

[128] While the list of criteria for fixing salvage rewards set out in Art. 13 of the Convention does not refer specifically to the care that a salvor may have taken in preserving archaeological integrity, there seems no reason why criterion (e) – which refers

rare for poor archaeology to be acknowledged and to lead to the *reduction* or *forfeiture* of payment.[129] Would the approach be any different if the Salvage Convention was taken into account? Article 18, which is headed 'The effect of salvor's misconduct', provides:

A salvor may be deprived of the whole or part of the payment due under this Convention to the extent that the salvage operations have become necessary or more difficult because of the fault or neglect on his part or if the salvor has been guilty of fraud or other dishonest conduct.

As can be seen, the word 'misconduct' is used only in the heading of Article 18 and the nature of the behaviour that may lead to deprivation of payment is quite narrowly defined by the terms of the article. Nonetheless, in a treasure salvage context, it is possible to conceive of circumstances that might fall within the provision. In particular, where a salvor has obtained a grant of exclusive salvage rights on the basis that it will adopt archaeologically sensitive recovery methods, or – as in the case of the *Titanic* – will make special provision for the disposition of the artefacts recovered, and it does not then do so, it could be argued that this would amount to 'dishonest conduct' under Article 18. In the *Titanic* case itself, the judge, Beach Smith J., noted that if a salvor did not come to court with 'clean hands, acting "in entire good faith and with honesty of purpose"', its award may be reduced or forfeited entirely.[130] However, she appeared reluctant to entertain the prospect that RMST may have engaged in *disqualifying* misconduct, even though it had made plans to sell artefacts in its care, a course of action in contravention of its own assurances to the court, as well as court orders.[131] Although the judge seemed to regard the plans as amounting to misconduct, a high bar was set for the misconduct required to warrant a reduction in, or forfeiture of, award. Whether a lower bar would be set if heed were paid to Article 18 is doubtful.

Interestingly, the USA made no reservation under Article 30(1)(d) when it ratified the Salvage Convention in 1991. This seems somewhat

to the skill and efforts of the salvor – cannot be interpreted to include archaeological considerations.

[129] For discussion of some examples, see Fletcher-Tomenius, O'Keefe and Williams, 'Salvor in Possession', pp. 286–7.

[130] 742 F. Supp. 2d 784, 803, citing the *Columbus-America* case.

[131] 742 F. Supp. 2d 784, 804. Although the court expressed displeasure to learn that on one expedition 'the damage rate to recovered artifacts was around twenty-one percent', this was treated as a factor weighing *in favour* of an enhanced reward because it emphasised the difficult nature of the task undertaken: 742 F. Supp. 2d 784, 799.

surprising in light of the approach of the ASA, enacted only four years earlier, which – as discussed above – takes shipwrecks falling within its scope out of the salvage regime. Since the ASA pre-dates the Convention, the continuing validity of that statute's exclusion of certain shipwrecks from the salvage law regime does not appear to be seriously questioned.[132] However, the fact that the US has not made this reservation could at least conceivably hamper its ability to ratify international instruments relating to UCH which interfere with the law of salvage.[133]

3.4.5   A void to be filled

As seen in Section 3.4.2 above, the ASA transferred jurisdiction for wrecks to which it applies from the private law domain of the federal admiralty judiciary to public regulatory authorities. However, jurisdiction over wrecks outside the remit of the ASA and other federal legislation continues to be exercised by the federal judiciary. One of the main categories of wrecks for which this is the case is those that lie in international waters.

In respect of these wrecks, one might well ask the question: how is it that the US federal courts can exercise jurisdiction over property that lies *outside* their territorial remit? Clearly they *do* exercise such jurisdiction, as seen from the litigation relating to the *Atocha, Central America* and the *Titanic*, all of which lie (or, at the time jurisdiction was exercised, lay) in international waters.

In exercising extra-territorial jurisdiction over such sites, the federal courts have developed and applied a notional device referred to as 'constructive *in rem* jurisdiction'.[134] In order for a court to invoke ordinary *in rem* jurisdiction, the *res* must be within the territorial remit of the court. The basis of 'constructive *in rem* jurisdiction' is that, by bringing a representative *part* of the property within the geographical jurisdiction of the court, the court gains jurisdiction over the whole of the *res*. For example, in the case of the *Titanic*, a wine decanter was brought within the jurisdiction. By making use of this legal fiction, the courts regard

---

[132] See Nafziger, 'Historic Salvage Law Revisited', p. 94 n. 68.

[133] One such instrument is, of course, the UNESCO Convention 2001. See section 4.3, below.

[134] English courts have not adopted the notion of 'constructive *in rem*' jurisdiction. In *The Tubantia* (see section 2.1 above), the presiding judge cited *Comyn's Digest* and *Blackstone's Commentaries* as authorities for the view that a 'suit in respect of injurious acts done upon the high seas was within the undisputed jurisdiction of the Court of Admiralty': [1924] P. 78 at 86.

themselves as competent to assert control over activities at the site, awarding exclusive salvage rights and issuing injunctions to protect those rights from competing salvors until such time as the salvage operation is successfully completed.[135]

One justification put forward for exercising extra-territorial jurisdiction over shipwrecks in international waters is that the principles applied by the federal admiralty courts are *jus gentium*, in other words, rules of law common to all nations.[136] For example, in the *Mercedes* case, discussed in Chapter 4,[137] while Magistrate Judge Pizzo concluded that the jurisdictional 'mooring line' was severed by the sovereign immunity of the vessel,[138] he explained that both the *jus gentium* and constructive *in rem* jurisdiction 'principles' 'explain[ed] the case's presence' before the court.[139] In attempting to explain why both principles were necessary, he cited a pronouncement of the Fourth Circuit during the *Titanic* litigation:

When nations agree on law to apply on the high seas, they agree to an order even beyond their sovereign boundaries which, while they hope will be honoured on the high seas, can only be enforced completely and effectively when the people or property are brought within a nation's zone of power – its sovereignty.[140]

---

[135] As Nafziger has pointed out, '[a]n admiralty court's subject-matter jurisdiction to adjudicate matters arising anywhere in the world does not imply power to command enforcement of judicial decisions against foreign persons or vessels otherwise beyond its jurisdiction': see Nafziger, 'Historic Salvage Law Revisited', p. 84. It should be noted that in the *Atocha* case, a different jurisdictional mechanism was used, known as '*quasi in rem* jurisdiction'. For an explanation of the distinction between constructive *in rem* jurisdiction and *quasi in rem* jurisdiction, see *Odyssey Marine Exploration, Inc.* v. *Unidentified, Wrecked and Abandoned Sailing Vessel*, 727 F. Supp. 2d 1341, 1346–8 (MD Fla. July 30, 2010).

[136] For an interesting exchange of views on this matter, see Nafziger, 'The Evolving Role of Admiralty Courts in Litigation Related to Historic Wrecks' and Niemeyer, 'Applying *Jus Gentium* to the Salvage of the RMS *Titanic* in International Waters'. It is patently clear from the discussion earlier in this chapter that the laws of salvage and finds as applied by the US admiralty courts are *not* common to all nations. Indeed, in a recent case concerning a French eighteenth-century privateer, *Le Marquis Tournay*, found in the English Channel, it was held that the doctrine of constructive *in rem* jurisdiction did not extend to the law of finds for precisely this reason: see *Odyssey Marine Exploration, Inc.* v. *Unidentified, Wrecked and Abandoned Sailing Vessel*, 727 F. Supp. 2d 1341, 1348 (MD Fla. July 30, 2010).

[137] See Chap. 4, section 2.3.2.

[138] *Odyssey Marine Exploration, Inc.* v. *Unidentified, Shipwrecked Vessel*, 675 F. Supp. 2d 1126, 1146 (MD Fla. Dec. 22, 2009); *aff'd*, 657 F.3d 1159 (11th Cir. (Fla.) Sept. 21, 2011); *cert. denied*, 132 S. Ct. 2379 (US May 14, 2010).

[139] 675 F. Supp. 2d 1126, 1136.   [140] See *RMS Titanic* v. *Haver*, 171 F.3d 943, 966.

Indeed, the Fourth Circuit justified its assertion of extra-territorial jurisdiction over the *Titanic* by referring to the 'state of lawlessness' that
would otherwise exist at the site.[141] This suggests that the assertion of
extra-territorial jurisdiction over wrecks is regarded by the federal
courts as a means of filling a void in public international law.

Since the introduction of the ASA, there has been considerable debate
in the US about whether historic shipwrecks should be governed by
private law administered by the admiralty courts, or be subject to regulation under public law administered, for the most part, by public
heritage authorities. Some commentators favour what is essentially a
free-market approach, advocating the jurisdiction of the admiralty
courts, but suggesting that archaeological values can be safeguarded by
the process of modification of salvage law which has been taking
place.[142] Others counter-argue that public regulation is appropriate
where public interests are at stake.[143]

Aside from any debate about the appropriate roles for public and
private law, from a practical perspective the federal judiciary – no matter
how well-meaning and well-informed it may be (or could become) with
regard to archaeological considerations – is seriously fettered in what it
can do to protect the public interest in historic wrecks. Ultimately, and at
its core, the law of salvage is about financially incentivising *recovery*. Even
in respect of the *Titanic*, a wreck widely regarded as of exceptional

---

[141] 171 F.3d 943, 969. Interestingly, at the time the Fourth Circuit made this
pronouncement, negotiations had commenced in respect of an international agreement
to protect the site of the *Titanic*. However, these were not concluded until 2000. See,
further, Chap. 7, section 4.3.

[142] See, generally, Bederman, 'Historic Salvage and the Law of the Sea' and 'Maritime
Preservation Law'; Alexander, 'Treasure Salvage Beyond the Territorial Sea'; and Dorsey,
'Historic Salvors, Marine Archaeologists, and the UNESCO Draft Convention on the
Underwater Cultural Heritage'.

[143] See, generally, Varmer, 'The Case Against the "Salvage" of the Cultural Heritage';
Nafziger, 'The Evolving Role of Admiralty Courts in Litigation Related to Historic
Wrecks'; and McQuown, 'An Archaeological Argument for the Inapplicability of
Admiralty Law in the Disposition of Historic Shipwrecks'. Interestingly, one district
court judge has recently suggested that where the ownership interests of a foreign state
are potentially involved (which he thought more likely when a wreck was located
outside the territorial waters of the USA), the question of title to the wreck was a matter
for the executive branch of government, rather than the legislative: see *Odyssey Marine
Exploration, Inc.* v. *Unidentified, Wrecked and Abandoned Sailing Vessel*, 727 F. Supp. 2d 1341,
1349 (MD Fla. July 30, 2010). Curiously, his comments were made in the context of
discussing the 'risks' of awarding title to the finder of a *private* sunken vessel and it is
possible that they were influenced by Niemeyer C.J.'s comment in the *Titanic* litigation
that finds law should be 'applied sparingly – only when no private or public interest
would be adversely affected by its application': see section 3.4.3 above.

international cultural significance, the treatment of the artefact collection – not the wreck site – was the primary (and inevitable) focus of attention and RMST's activities were regarded as 'maximizing the wreck's historical value in returning the wreck's artifacts to society for the general use and education of all mankind'.[144] The admiralty courts can oversee recovery, but what they cannot do under salvage and finds laws is address the question of whether recovery should be undertaken at all. The only practical way of doing this is through the institution of a licensing or permit system administered by a competent public agency.[145]

4.   Treatment of the laws of salvage and finds by the UNESCO Convention 2001

The fundamental tensions between the law of salvage and cultural heritage protection lie at the heart of attempts to create an international legal regime for the protection of UCH. In the period leading up to the UNESCO Convention 2001, the US and the UK governments received representations from their powerful maritime industries arguing that any new regime should not upset established maritime law traditions by interfering with the law of salvage. It was therefore inevitable that the question of the treatment of salvage law by the new treaty had the potential to be a 'deal-breaker for the whole negotiations'.[146]

4.1   Background

The first international initiative specifically addressing UCH, Council of Europe Recommendation 848 (1978),[147] took a clear-cut position on the question of salvage law. Member states of the Council of Europe were urged not to apply '[e]xisting salvage and wreck law' to any items subject to the protective regime set out in the Recommendation, in other words objects that had been beneath the water for more than 100 years.[148] In place of such law, they were encouraged to make provision for a 'reward

---

[144] 435 F.3d 521, 536–7.
[145] For details of the Titanic Agreement, an initiative by the US federal government to institute such a system for the site of the *Titanic*, see Chap. 7, section 4.3.
[146] Carducci, 'The Expanding Protection of the Underwater Cultural Heritage', p. 159.
[147] See, further, Chap. 1, section 2.2.1.
[148] It may be worth noting that the possibility of the discretionary inclusion within the protective regime of significant objects of more recent date, as well as the discretionary exclusion of less important objects, was also envisaged.

for honesty' in order to encourage finders to report their discoveries. On the other hand, the 1985 draft European Convention essentially replicated the saving of salvage law and other rules of maritime law, as well as the rights of identifiable owners, enshrined in Article 303(3) of the LOSC.[149]

In fact, in drafting a subject-specific treaty on UCH, one potentially difficult question is the relationship between the LOSC and the new treaty with respect to the law of salvage. Does Article 303(3) of the earlier treaty fetter the approach that the new treaty can take to the question of salvage law? The ILA concluded that it did not: in its 1994 Draft, provision was made that salvage law was not to be applied to UCH to which the Convention applied.[150] After intensive discussion on the issue at the meeting of experts convened by UNESCO in May 1996, this exclusion was dropped and, in the 1998 UNESCO Draft, replaced with the following – rather more ambiguous – provision:

States Parties shall provide for the non-application of any internal law or regulation having the effect of providing commercial incentives for the excavation and removal of underwater cultural heritage.[151]

This provision was buried away in the second paragraph of Article 12 of the draft, which was headed 'Disposition of Underwater Cultural Heritage'. According to the official comment accompanying the 1998 Draft, the paragraph was drafted to avoid what was considered to be the 'principal objection' to the application of salvage law: 'the application of a national law to material brought ashore from outside the national jurisdiction where this would provide monetary incentives to excavate'.[152] While the official comment went on to suggest that 'other provisions of salvage law would need to be examined to ensure that they are not inconsistent with the regime established by the Charter',[153] it is difficult to see what scope there would have been for salvage law to operate given that its whole purpose is provision of a financial incentive to recover.

A number of states, led by Italy and Greece, were dissatisfied with any form of qualified exclusion of salvage law, arguing among other things that the principles of finds and salvage laws had no status in

---

[149] See section 3.1 above.   [150] 1994 ILA Draft, Art. 4. See Chap. 1, section 3.1.1.
[151] 1998 UNESCO Draft, Art. 12(2).
[152] Dromgoole and Gaskell, 'Draft UNESCO Convention on the Protection of the Underwater Cultural Heritage 1998', p. 202.
[153] The reference here to the Charter was a reference to the ICOMOS International Charter on the Protection and Management of Underwater Cultural Heritage, upon which the Rules in the Annex to the UNESCO Convention 2001 are based.

international law. Instead, they wished to see an outright exclusion. At the first session of the Fourth Meeting of the UNESCO negotiations, in March/April 2001, informal discussions between the delegates of these states and those of the USA, UK and Ireland led to a compromise solution, which was adopted by consensus.[154]

4.2 Approach of the UNESCO Convention and its implications

Article 4 of the UNESCO Convention provides:

Any activity relating to underwater cultural heritage to which this Convention applies shall not be subject to the law of salvage or law of finds, unless it:

(a) is authorized by the competent authorities, and
(b) is in full conformity with this Convention, and
(c) ensures that any recovery of the underwater cultural heritage achieves its maximum protection.

When considering this provision, it should be recalled that the final text of the Convention includes within its scope not only abandoned material, as earlier drafts had done, but *all* traces of human existence that have been underwater for at least 100 years. Article 4 therefore applies to any activity relating to such material.[155] Conditions (a), (b) and (c) clearly relate to the circumstances before, during and after recovery respectively. Provided each of the conditions is met, it seems that a salvage reward can be claimed and, in circumstances where it is determined that ownership rights have been abandoned, the finder may be awarded title to the recovered material under the law of finds.

Condition (a) requires that activities be authorised by the competent national authority. The terms of the Convention make it clear that the national authority must consider preservation *in situ* as the first option[156] and may only permit recovery if it is necessary for 'scientific or protective purposes'.[157] Activities 'may be authorised for the purpose of making a significant contribution to protection or knowledge or enhancement' of UCH[158] and there may also be circumstances where excavation or recovery 'is necessary for the purpose of scientific studies

---

[154] See Garabello, 'The Negotiating History of the Convention on the Protection of the Underwater Cultural Heritage', pp. 125–6. See also Carducci, 'The Expanding Protection of the Underwater Cultural Heritage', p. 159; O'Keefe, *Shipwrecked Heritage*, pp. 62–3.

[155] As O'Keefe has pointed out, for some reason Art. 4 refers to any activity 'relating to' UCH, rather than – as one might expect – any activity 'directed at' UCH: O'Keefe, *Shipwrecked Heritage*, p. 63. However, it seems unlikely that the distinction has any practical significance.

[156] Art. 2(5) and Annex, Rule 1.   [157] Preambular clause 13.   [158] Rule 1.

or for the ultimate protection' of UCH.[159] Exactly how these principles are interpreted is a matter that may differ considerably from one national authority to another. Although it is conceivable that the finder of a site could argue that its very discovery has made it vulnerable, and that excavation is the only way to protect it, such an argument would run counter to the entire archaeological ethos of the Convention, which is concerned with limiting direct intervention, and recovery of material, as much as possible.

Assuming that recovery is authorised and condition (a) met, condition (b) then comes into play. This requires that the recovery must be undertaken in full conformity with the Convention. Among other things, this means that it must comply with the Rules laid down in the Annex, which provide for matters such as project funding and design, project team competence, recording of information, conservation of recovered material, site management, the reporting and dissemination of finds and curation of project archives. For the most part these standards are ones that professional treasure salvors could (and perhaps sometimes already do) comply with. However, it must not be forgotten that the Convention's treatment of salvage law is intimately linked with its treatment of commercial exploitation. Where recovery is motivated by economic self-interest, the project may well fall foul of the Rules relating to the sale of recovered material and the funding base for the project. Indeed, generally speaking, unless an adequate funding base is 'assured in advance of any activity', a project will not be authorised in the first place.[160]

The condition that in fact may prove to be the greatest obstacle to the application of salvage and finds laws is condition (c). This provides that any recovery of UCH must achieve its maximum protection. What is 'maximum protection' intended to mean? Article 2, which sets out the objectives and general principles of the Convention, provides that UCH shall be preserved for the 'benefit of humanity',[161] that it 'shall be deposited, conserved and managed in a manner that ensures its long-term preservation'[162] and that it 'shall not be commercially exploited'.[163] As seen earlier, application of salvage law usually leads to a court-ordered sale of the recovered material in order to pay for the salvage reward; in rare cases involving treasure salvage, it has also led to *in specie* rewards, whereby the salvor acquires ownership of the recovered material. Application of the law of finds may well lead to the finder

---

[159] Annex, Rule 4.   [160] For further discussion of these issues, see Chap. 6, section 4.2.
[161] Art. 2(3).   [162] Art. 2(6).   [163] Art. 2(7). See also Rule 2 of the Annex.

becoming the owner. Where the Convention applies, in all these circumstances account would need to be taken of Rule 33 of the Rules which provides that '[t]he project archives, including any underwater cultural heritage removed ... shall, as far as possible, be kept together and intact as a collection in a manner that is available for professional and public access'. Again, compliance with this Rule is likely to pose challenges for courts and commercial operators of a similar nature to those facing the district court and RMST in the case of the *Titanic*.

The conditions set out in Article 4 for the application of the laws of salvage and finds are clearly going to prove highly restrictive. If applied, as O'Keefe points out, there will be 'little left of the original concepts'.[164] The effect of Article 4 is therefore that there is little incentive for the finder of a wreck site to pursue the traditional route through the admiralty courts of common law jurisdictions where those jurisdictions have become party to the Convention.

It is important to note that there is nothing to prevent a state party to the UNESCO Convention going further than the terms of Article 4 and excluding the application of salvage and finds laws from UCH falling within the scope of the Convention. Clearly, those states whose pre-conventional law excluded UCH from the scope of salvage law are likely to continue to maintain this approach. Those states whose pre-conventional law allowed for the application of the law of salvage and finds law to UCH would probably be well-advised to consider the advantages of making a clear and outright exclusion. This would avoid any potential for complex problems to arise regarding the relationship between salvage law and their obligations under the Convention.[165]

4.3   Relationship between the UNESCO Convention and the Salvage Convention 1989

Where a state party to the Salvage Convention has made a reservation under Article 30(1)(d) of that Convention, if it decides to ratify the UNESCO Convention there should be no problem with respect to the

---

[164] O'Keefe, *Shipwrecked Heritage*, p. 64. In the words of Bishop, '[i]n essence Article 4 does away with both areas of law': Bishop, 'The Underwater Cultural Heritage Convention 2001', p. 18. For further discussion of the degree to which the Convention restricts the activities of commercial salvage operators, see Chap. 6, section 4.2.

[165] While there is nothing in the Convention that seems to directly preclude a state party introducing a system of financial or other rewards for *discovery* in order to act as an incentive for finds to be reported, such practices are contentious because they could be seen as incentivising treasure-hunting (thereby undermining the core purpose of the Convention). For this reason they are probably best avoided.

compatibility of the treaties. The question of compatibility arises, however, if the state has not exercised such a reservation. Generally speaking, where two treaties relate to the same subject matter, the earlier treaty prevails over the later treaty as between two states parties to the earlier treaty where only one of them has ratified the later treaty.[166]

In order to comply with the terms of the UNESCO Convention, the state concerned would have two options on salvage law. It could exclude UCH from the scope of this law altogether, or it could adopt the 'halfway house' on salvage law set out in Article 4 of the Convention. If it took the first option, there would certainly appear to be potential for incompatibility: after all, the primary purpose of the Salvage Convention is to ensure the payment of an adequate reward to salvors.[167] If it pursued the second, the particular question it would need to consider is whether a salvage reward could be denied to a national of another state party to the Salvage Convention in circumstances where they did not meet the conditions set out in Article 4 of the UNESCO Convention. Under the Salvage Convention, a salvor is entitled to a reward unless it has acted in a way that amounts to misconduct. As seen earlier,[168] under Article 18 of the Salvage Convention, misconduct is defined restrictively:

A salvor may be deprived of the whole or part of the payment due ... to the extent that the salvage operations have become necessary or more difficult because of fault or neglect on his part or if the salvor has been guilty of fraud or other dishonest conduct.

The references to 'fault' or 'neglect' on the part of the salvor appear to be applicable only where it can be shown that they make the salvage operations necessary, or more difficult. The question therefore seems to be whether activities relating to UCH that are unauthorised by the competent national authority under the UNESCO conventional regime, or that are conducted in a manner that is not in accordance with that regime, would be construed as amounting to 'fraud' or 'dishonest conduct'. Such conduct is usually difficult to prove, although evidence of wilful ignorance of an applicable regulatory regime would probably suffice.

---

[166] Art. 30(4)(b) of the Vienna Convention on the Law of Treaties. If both states have ratified both treaties, the later treaty generally takes precedence in so far as there is any incompatibility: Vienna Convention, Art. 30(4)(a). (On these rules, see General introduction, section 3.2.1, above.)

[167] See section 3.2, above. The introduction of a statutory provision making it clear that material that has been underwater for at least 100 years is not in 'danger' for the purposes of the application of salvage law is one possible way around this.

[168] Section 3.4.4, above.

At the very start of UNESCO's deliberations on a new treaty regime for UCH, an IMO representative indicated that incompatibility between the two treaties would not arise because of 'the private-law, non-mandatory character of the [Salvage] Convention', which meant that 'the right to exclude the application of salvage law existed even without express reservation'.[169] On the other hand, more recently, the CMI expressed the view that if a state party to the Salvage Convention had not entered an Article 30(1)(d) reservation, it would have to denounce the Salvage Convention before adopting the UNESCO Convention.[170] A state in this position should therefore certainly give some consideration to whether it should denounce the Salvage Convention and then (assuming it wished to do so) re-ratify it, at the same time entering the reservation.

The Salvage Convention says nothing about the possessory rights of the salvor; therefore, any question relating to interference with such rights through the implementation of the UNESCO conventional regime would not cause a conflict between the two treaties. Whether such interference would cause problems more generally is another matter,[171] but in any event this issue will only have the potential to cause difficulties where such rights accrued *prior* to the implementation of the conventional regime.[172]

4.4   Response of the international maritime community

Unsurprisingly, the UNESCO Convention 2001 was received with less than enthusiasm by the professional maritime community. In particular, the CMI and the Maritime Law Association of the USA reacted negatively.[173] Although there were several features of the Convention

---

[169] See Report of the Meeting of Experts for the Protection of Underwater Cultural Heritage, UNESCO Headquarters, Paris (22–24 May 1996), UNESCO Doc. CLT-96/ CONF.605/6, p. 12, para. 48. The IMO appeared to change its position on this at the end of the negotiations: see Garabello, 'The Negotiating History of the Convention on the Protection of the Underwater Cultural Heritage', pp. 126–7.

[170] See 'Consideration of the UNESCO Convention on the Protection of Underwater Cultural Heritage: Report of the CMI Working Group' [2002] *CMI Yearbook* 156.

[171] See section 3.3, above.

[172] O'Keefe, *Shipwrecked Heritage*, p. 64. The question of *when* the Convention's regime has been 'implemented' in respect of a particular wreck site lying in international waters may not be a straightforward one, especially if the site is located in the Area.

[173] See 'Consideration of the UNESCO Convention on the Protection of Underwater Cultural Heritage: Report of the CMI Working Group' [2002] *CMI Yearbook* 154–7. See also the report dated 2 August 2001 of Kimball, Chair of the US Maritime Law Association's Study Group on the Draft UNESCO Convention, to that Study Group, para. 24 (available at www.mlaus.org). A number of prominent lawyers engaged in maritime practice in the USA and the UK were also critical of the Convention: see, for example, Bederman,

that caused unease,[174] the primary focus of concern was its potential impact on the law of salvage. While acknowledging the need for special consideration to be accorded to material of historical and archaeological significance, and voicing support for the overall objective of the Convention, it was (and apparently remains) the firm opinion of these organisations that the law of salvage is not incompatible with that objective. Although the original ILA proposal for the exclusion of salvage law was replaced by the provision in Article 4 for conditional application of salvage and finds laws, this is still regarded as an unacceptable encroachment on the traditional domain of maritime salvage law.

In response to the UNESCO initiative, the late Mr Geoffrey Brice QC, a specialist in salvage law at the English Bar, put forward a proposal for a protocol to the Salvage Convention 1989, which in essence would codify the modifications to salvage law already adopted by some US federal courts.[175] A draft text prepared by Brice made provision for damage to the cultural heritage and failure to comply with archaeological standards to qualify as misconduct for the purposes of the Convention and for these matters to be included among the criteria for fixing rewards.[176] In 2001, the CMI expressed support for the adoption of the protocol (which has become known as the Brice Protocol).[177] For some years thereafter, the initiative appeared to be forgotten by the CMI, but more recently it has become the focus of further attention.[178]

'Maritime Preservation Law'; Bishop, 'The Underwater Cultural Heritage Convention 2001'; Brice, 'Salvage and the Underwater Cultural Heritage'; and Dorsey, 'Historic Salvors, Marine Archaeologists, and the UNESCO Draft Convention on the Underwater Cultural Heritage'.

[174] For example, the principle that *in situ* preservation shall be considered as the first option; the provision in Rule 2 of the Annex in respect of sale; the definition of UCH and its lack of reference to significance; and aspects of the Convention that go beyond the LOSC's jurisdictional provisions: see 'Consideration of the UNESCO Convention on the Protection of Underwater Cultural Heritage: Report of the CMI Working Group' [2002] *CMI Yearbook* 154–7. A further concern was the impact of the Convention's provision concerning incidental activities on legitimate commercial activities: Bishop, 'The Underwater Cultural Heritage Convention 2001', p. 20.

[175] Brice, 'Salvage and the Underwater Cultural Heritage', p. 342.

[176] For this text, see [2000] *CMI Yearbook* 412–14.

[177] See 'First Report on UNESCO Draft Convention on the Protection of Underwater Cultural Heritage', CMI 37th Conference, Singapore, 11–17 February 2001 [2001] *CMI Yearbook* 254–8.

[178] Since 2008 there have been moves afoot within the CMI to review various aspects of the Salvage Convention 1989 and the possibility of amendment in line with the Brice Protocol has been under consideration: see 'Report of the International Working Group on Review of the Salvage Convention: For Consideration by Delegates to the CMI Conference: Beijing 2012', 1 May 2012, pp. 18–24 (available at www.comitemaritime.org).

On its own, limited modification of salvage law will not offer UCH protection in line with modern archaeological good practice.[179] Nonetheless, amendment of the Salvage Convention to draw its general scheme into some alignment with the UNESCO Convention and its annexed Rules would be a constructive development. In particular, assuming the USA accepted the amendments *and* the US judiciary took account of them, it would ensure that the modifications to salvage law made by some quarters of the US judiciary were applied consistently across the whole federal court system. While no solution to the fundamental problem, this would be a useful stopgap until such time as the USA ratifies the Convention.

5. Concluding remarks

The issue of salvage law, in the event, did not prove to be a 'deal-breaker' for the UNESCO negotiations. Instead, a compromise was reached that appeared to satisfy at least the government delegations of the common law states with concerns on this issue. The UNESCO Convention 2001 enshrines into international law a notion already accepted by many domestic legal systems: that a cut-off needs to be drawn between the domain of salvage law and the domain of heritage law. In circumstances where the Convention applies, material falling within its scope, in effect, will be treated as 'having passed from the commercial realm of maritime salvage law into the domain of archaeological law'.[180] In light of state practice in recent decades, under which the protection of wreck sites of only fifty years of age is not uncommon,[181] the fact that the negotiators chose to adopt a 100-year threshold means that the overall package on salvage law that the Convention presents could be regarded as a rather

---

[179] As discussed above, salvage law generally only takes effect after some intervention has taken place. However, the following comment is interesting: 'We [the CMI's International Working Group on Salvage] can see no reason in principle why *in situ* preservation could not be the result under the Brice Protocol if widely accepted archaeological practices so dictated and appropriate financial incentives can be devised to reward salvors for locating, protecting and preserving the property *underwater*': 'First Report on UNESCO Draft Convention on the Protection of Underwater Cultural Heritage', CMI 37th Conference, Singapore, 11–17 February 2001 [2001] *CMI Yearbook* 258, para. 19. Emphasis added.

[180] See statement made by the trial judge in the Irish case of *La Lavia, Juliana and Santa Maria de la Vision* quoted in section 3.3, above.

[181] See Chap. 2, section 3.1.

better deal for the international maritime community than might have otherwise emerged from the UNESCO process.

While the US remains outside the Convention's regime, salvors of historic wrecks operating around the world will continue to have the option of landing material in the USA and invoking the application of the laws of salvage and finds as applied by the US federal admiralty courts. However, as far as the law of finds is concerned, it seems likely that its application will become increasingly rare and it does not seem impossible that the US admiralty courts will revert to using it for the purpose for which they used it originally: to determine rights to material found at sea which had previously never been subject to ownership, such as flora and fauna. As far as salvage law is concerned, if the Salvage Convention was subject to appropriate amendment, this could help to ensure that 'the awkwardness of fit' of salvage law to historic wrecks is recognised and, as far as possible, accommodated across the whole of the federal admiralty court system.

6   Commercial exploitation of underwater cultural heritage

1. Introduction

Commercial exploitation of cultural heritage can take many forms. At its widest, the term can encompass any form of money-making enterprise derived from this resource, including the charging of the general public for entry to cultural heritage sites and the selling of related souvenirs, such as guidebooks, DVDs and replicas. More narrowly, but perhaps more commonly, it is a term that carries with it the implication that the *sale* of cultural material is involved. Although all sorts of organisations – public, private and charitable – can undertake commercial exploitation, this chapter is concerned mainly with the activities of entities whose primary (but not necessarily sole) motive is to make a financial profit.

The question of commercial exploitation of cultural heritage is a hugely controversial one, particularly where it involves the irretrievable dispersal of material from a site through the sale of cultural material. Where the circumstances of sale lead to such dispersal, it will breach the fundamental archaeological principle that material recovered from an archaeological site should be kept together as a collection so that it is available for public display and research purposes. The problem is not with sale *per se*, but with the irretrievable dispersal that may result.

The attitude of an individual state to the question of commercial exploitation of cultural heritage is tied in with its political philosophy and approach to the respective roles of government regulation and the free market. It is also influenced by the experiences of the state with respect to cultural heritage matters generally: some states, such as Greece and Italy, have suffered vast depletions of cultural artefacts over the years; others, including the USA, UK and the Netherlands have

210

derived lucrative benefits from commercial exploitation of, and trading in, cultural material. In particular, these states are home to highly active international antiquities markets. Inevitably, so-called 'source' states and 'market' states are likely to have very different, and often opposing, viewpoints on treatment of cultural heritage generally, and on commercial exploitation specifically.

In respect of UCH, while many wreck sites in coastal waters have already been fully excavated or otherwise exploited, there are an unknown number of commercially high-value shipwrecks of cultural interest lying undiscovered in deep waters beyond territorial limits.[1] Traditionally, through the application of the law of salvage, commercial operators have had the opportunity to 'participate' in the recovery of such shipwrecks. As discussed in Chapter 5, salvage law provides an economic incentive to recover UCH and its application usually leads to the sale of recovered material on the open market (and thereby to its dispersal) in order to pay the 'salvor' a reward.

The question of commercial exploitation arouses strong feelings in some sections of the archaeological community. Commercial operators are often regarded with varying degrees of scepticism and suspicion, and occasionally with outright hostility. Given the damage and destruction to underwater archaeological sites that have resulted from the activities of some individuals and companies, particularly those motivated purely by the possibility of financial gain, these feelings are understandable. However, a number of commercial operators claim that they are not interested solely in making a profit, but also in undertaking good archaeology. They argue that it is possible to 'marry good archaeology with [a] business model'[2] and to achieve a compromise between their own interests and those of archaeologists, which will allow for some commercial participation in return for well-funded archaeological research and excavation.

---

[1] UNESCO has cited a figure of 'over three million' for the number of undiscovered shipwrecks globally: UNESCO, 'Protect the Underwater Cultural Heritage', Information Kit (available at www.unesco.org). The number of shipwrecks that are worthy of commercial attention may be relatively small, however, given the vast costs of deepwater search and recovery work, and the risks involved. Stemm, co-founder and Chief Executive Officer of Odyssey Marine Exploration (OME) has indicated that the company has a 'commercial interest in less than 0.03%' of UNESCO's global figure: 'Dave Parham and Greg Stemm Debate Maritime Archaeology Business Models', *Nautical Archaeology Society Newsletter* (summer 2010), p. 5.

[2] 'Is taking treasure from shipwrecks piracy?', *The Times Online*, 21 May 2009.

Whether or not there should be scope for commercial involvement is one of the core issues that needs to be tackled by anyone engaged in drafting an instrument designed to regulate the recovery of UCH. Although the question of commercial exploitation is often discussed in the context of salvage law, it is a distinctly different question from whether or not UCH should be excluded from the scope of salvage law. The approach of the US Abandoned Shipwreck Act (ASA) of 1987 – which excludes the application of salvage law from wrecks to which it applies but allows for some, regulated, private-sector recovery[3] – demonstrates that commercial exploitation is not inextricably linked to salvage law and the statute has been treated as a model whereby commercial participation is regulated by public authorities, rather than by the judiciary through the application of salvage law.

The purpose of the present chapter is to give some consideration to the question of the participation of 'for-profit' organisations in UCH operations and to explore whether the regulatory regime established by the UNESCO Convention 2001 allows for such participation. The chapter is split into three main sections. The first section identifies some models of commercial exploitation that incorporate a level of archaeological ethos; the second considers some of the core arguments against, and in favour of, commercial exploitation; and the third examines the approach of the UNESCO Convention 2001 to commercial exploitation.

2. Commercial exploitation: some models

It should be said at the outset that there are numerous examples of cases where commercial exploitation, undertaken without regard for archaeological and cultural values, has led to the destruction of wreck sites, irretrievable dispersal of material, and loss of most, if not all, of the information contained in these repositories of archaeological information.[4] The purpose here, however, is to give some consideration to models of commercial exploitation that do take some account of archaeological and other cultural values, and do preserve some degree of archaeological information.

---

[3] See, further, Chap. 5, section 3.4.2.
[4] For a summary of specific incidents around the world, see Zamora, 'The Impact of Commercial Exploitation on the Preservation of Underwater Cultural Heritage', pp. 24–7.

2.1 Commercial exploitation excluding sale of artefacts

The approach of the US company RMS *Titanic*, Inc. (RMST) towards the commercial exploitation of the wreck of the *Titanic* is an exceptional one. Since the early 1990s the company has undertaken a series of expeditions to the site to recover artefacts, which it has then exhibited to a paying public around the world. From the start of its operations it manifested an intention not to sell any of the artefacts raised (except for pieces of coal)[5] and instead has attempted to cover the costs of its expeditions to the site – and make a profit – through exhibition revenues, and associated media and merchandising activities.

The *Titanic* is, of course, a unique wreck and its fame means that it inspires an extraordinary level of public interest. However, even given this fact, at times RMST appears to have had difficulty maintaining its business model in light of the huge costs of mounting expeditions to the site and the costs associated with the stabilisation, conservation, recording, storing and exhibiting of thousands of artefacts.[6] Indeed, it seems that RMST suffered a net loss of more than $7 million during the fiscal years 1996–2007.[7] This indicates that a model of commercial exploitation that does *not* involve the sale of at least some artefacts is unlikely to be feasible in respect of lesser-known wrecks located in deep waters.[8]

2.2 Commercial exploitation including sale of artefacts

Another USA-based commercial company that has attempted to incorporate archaeological considerations into its business model is Odyssey Marine Exploration (OME). This company argues that it is possible to combine the highest standards of archaeology with a profit-making objective and advocates that commercial operators and archaeologists should work together to exploit both the commercial and cultural values of UCH. Its model incorporates the sale of some cultural material, as well as broader forms of commercial exploitation.

[5] See, further, Chap. 5, section 3.4.3.
[6] For an outline of the measures taken by RMST with respect to the recovered artefacts, see the judgment of Beach Smith J. in *RMS Titanic, Inc.* v. *Wrecked and Abandoned Vessel*, 742 F. Supp. 2d 784, 801–3 (ED Va. Aug. 12, 2010).
[7] See *RMS Titanic, Inc.* v. *Wrecked and Abandoned Vessel*, 742 F. Supp. 2d 784, 806. This figure relates to artefacts recovered from the site in expeditions between 1993 and 2004. For how the estimate was reached, see the judgment.
[8] There is at least one other commercial project, relating to the pirate ship *Whydah*, that relies upon exhibition revenue rather than artefact sale. However, it does not relate to a deepwater site and therefore does not have to cover the costs of deepwater excavation.

OME's approach is exemplified by its exploitation of the SS *Republic*, a nineteenth-century sidewheel steamer that it discovered in the Atlantic Ocean in 2003. Utilising robotic technology, this deepwater site was extensively excavated and thousands of silver and gold coins and other artefacts recovered. The coins have been made available for purchase by collectors, while the remaining artefacts – including everyday commercial wares – are publicly exhibited and available for study upon request. The project has been extensively marketed and promoted through print and other media, and OME would argue that it has been conducted in accordance with the highest archaeological standards.[9]

2.2.1   ProSEA model

OME is a member of a US professional shipwreck explorers' association, known as ProSEA. This association argues that it is possible for shipwreck exploration and exploitation to be undertaken ethically and has developed a 'Code of Ethics' for its members. This Code requires them to 'establish and maintain the highest professional standards while investigating, excavating, salvaging or otherwise utilizing shipwreck resources'.[10] The Code sets out a number of detailed rules of conduct for its members, which make provision for the employment of a qualified 'Project Archaeologist'; the planning and execution of a project taking account of archaeological values; and provision of funds for conservation, cataloguing and storage of artefacts. The Code also provides:

It is the responsibility of the member who supervises the exploration of any shipwreck to ensure that the activity is undertaken in such a way that as much scientific, historical and archaeological data as practically possible is gleaned from the site. Furthermore, it is their responsibility to ensure that the knowledge is made available publicly in a timely manner through published means.[11]

Self-regulation of this kind, provided it is undertaken in good faith, can have positive benefits. However, the crux of the difficulty with reconciling commercial and archaeological interests is the question of disposal of recovered material. To address this question, the President of ProSEA, Greg Stemm (also Chief Executive Officer of OME), draws a distinction between two types of shipwreck material, which he refers to as 'cultural

---

[9] Some judgment of the standards that were applied may be made by referring to the reports on the work, and recovered artefacts, published in Stemm and Kingsley, *Oceans Odyssey*, chaps. 1–5.
[10] ProSEA Code of Ethics (available at www.prosea.org/about/codeethics.html).
[11] *Ibid.*

artefacts' and 'trade goods'. According to Stemm, 'cultural artefacts' should be retained as part of the project archive; 'trade goods' can be sold. Trade goods comprise cargo and other goods being transported for trade purposes. However, in Stemm's model, not all these items would necessarily comprise trade goods. He argues that three criteria should be used to distinguish trade goods: the number of duplicates on site; the ease of recording or replicating artefacts; and archaeological value versus value of return to the stream of commerce.[12]

Stemm's elucidation of these criteria runs as follows:

1. *Number of duplicates on site:* This is simply an evaluation of the number of artefacts of that particular type available from the site ... I recommend maintaining a minimum five to ten per cent sample of the multiple artefacts in the permanent cultural collection ...

2. *Ease of recording or replicating artefacts:* In the ProSEA Code of Ethics, it states that those artefacts that cannot be 'documented, photographed, moulded or replicated in a manner that allows reasonable future study and analysis' must be kept together. An obvious example is a coin, which can be easily photographed in high resolution, weighed and the dimensions given, thus providing virtually all the data necessary for further study of the coin.

   The one exception would be an analysis of the metal in the coin, but that can be accomplished, for the most part, from the sample collection of similar coins in the permanent collection ...

3. *Archaeological value versus value of return to stream of commerce:* [This] can probably best be illustrated by the following example.

   Consider the case of 1,000 similar gold coins recovered from a ship-wreck from the late 18th Century. In this instance, the market value of those coins could easily reach millions of dollars. In terms of the archaeological value, there are many of the same coins already widely circulated throughout the coin collectors marketplace, so there is very little that can be learned incrementally about 18th Century culture that cannot be learned from records and data which are already in existence. This is especially true when coupled with a representative sample, plus photos and documentation, of the coins that are dispersed.

   In this case, a reasonable conclusion could be drawn that the tiny incremental value of the archaeological knowledge that could be gained from keeping the collection together does not warrant preventing a return of millions of dollars to the stream of commerce.

   On the other hand, a large collection of amphorae from a Mediterra-nean bronze-age site would probably not have a very significant

---

[12] Stemm, 'Differentiation of Shipwreck Artifacts as a Resource Management Tool', pp. 3–4.

intrinsic value. However, so little is known of trade from this era, that minor variations in markings on the amphorae, as well as data that can be gleaned from the remains of their contents, may be data that can be gathered by no other method. In this case a reasonable conclusion could be drawn that the low commercial value would not warrant breaking up this collection.[13]

Archaeologists may well challenge some or all of this reasoning. On the other hand, to a disinterested layperson there may appear to be some sense in the distinctions being drawn and the rationale may seem to have some potential to form a basis for compromise on the question of sale. (Whether such compromise is possible is explored further in section 3.3 below.)

2.2.2 'Partnering agreements'

In 2002, a contract was concluded between OME and the British government for the recovery of coins from HMS *Sussex*, a British warship that sank in deep water off Gibraltar in 1694. The *Sussex* was reputedly carrying gold and/or silver coins valued at £1 million at the time of sinking and, according to some estimates, having a present-day value of up to £2.5 billion.[14] In 2001, after several years of search and survey work, and expenditure estimated at £2 million,[15] a wreck thought to be that of HMS *Sussex* was located by OME. After protracted negotiations with the British government, as owner of the vessel and the coins,[16] an agreement was reached.

The contract was portrayed by its parties as very different in nature to a traditional salvage contract. It was referred to as a 'partnering agreement' and heralded as a public/private partnership to undertake an archaeological exploration of the site. According to a press release issued by the UK's Ministry of Defence, the agreement was:

an important step in the development of a 'partnering' approach to deep sea archaeology whereby any recoveries from the wreck will be conducted under recognised and accepted archaeological methodologies.[17]

---

[13] *Ibid.*   [14] 'Hunt for £2.5bn in gold coins on British wreck', *Sunday Times*, 8 June 2003.
[15] 'Salvagers to keep share of £2.5 bn treasure', *Independent*, 7 October 2002.
[16] It seems that the coins were intended as a bribe to persuade the Duke of Savoy to remain on the side of England and the Grand Alliance in their war with Louis XIV of France.
[17] MOD press release, 7 October 2002.

The press release went on to say:

It is envisaged that the work at the site will eventually provide educational and cultural material aimed at benefiting future generations of researchers, interest groups, and the general public worldwide.

OME, for its part, stated:

This is the first time in history that any government has entered into an agreement with the private sector for the archaeological excavation of a sovereign warship.

And further:

At approximately 3,000 feet below the surface, it will be the deepest extensive archaeological excavation of a shipwreck ever undertaken exclusively by robotic intervention.[18]

Although the precise terms of the agreement remain confidential, a 'Partnering Agreement Memorandum' was published,[19] outlining the principal terms. It is clear from this Memorandum that the basis of the agreement was that OME would explore the shipwreck and recover items from the site in return for a share in the artefacts raised, or in their proceeds of sale. Provision was made for the drawing up of a Project Plan, by agreement between the two parties, detailing equipment, personnel and methodologies to be employed, and making provision in respect of the conservation and documentation of recovered artefacts. There was also provision in respect of the expenses of the project, intellectual property and merchandising rights, and commercial confidentiality.[20]

According to the Memorandum, OME would get 80 per cent of the 'appraised value and/or selling prices of the Artefacts' up to $45 million, 50 per cent from $45 million to $500 million, and 40 per cent above $500 million. Although the Memorandum does not make it clear whether the intention was to sell only coins recovered from the site, or other types of artefact as well, a statement by OME declared that the agreement recognised:

---

[18] OME, 'Sussex Project (formerly known as the Cambridge Project)' (www.shipwreck.net/sussex.html).

[19] See www.shipwreck.net.

[20] For further details and analysis of the agreement, see, generally, Dromgoole, 'Murky Waters for Government Policy'. See also, Garabello, 'Sunken Warships in the Mediterranean', pp. 189 *et seq.*

a distinction between the archaeological significance of different classes of artifacts as a mechanism to allow sale of some artifacts to help fund management of underwater cultural heritage.[21]

This indicated that there may have been an intention to utilise the distinction between cultural artefacts and trade goods articulated by Stemm.

It is certainly not unusual for the governments of states with a maritime tradition, including the UK government, to enter into contracts for the recovery of valuable cargoes from their sunken warships and other state-owned vessels. The motivation of both parties in such cases is usually financial and such contracts commonly provide for a percentage split of the commercial value, or proceeds of sale.[22] What is different about the *Sussex* contract is that it took account of the fact that the wreck was not only a sovereign-owned financial asset, but also an archaeological site. Nonetheless, despite its provision for the preservation of archaeological values, the agreement met with considerable opposition in archaeological quarters.

The grounds for the opposition were essentially summed up in a statement by the Council for British Archaeology:

> Through this deal the British Government are engaged in a joint venture selling antiquities to pay for an investigation of doubtful archaeological feasibility, while also lining its own pockets and those of a foreign company.[23]

The prime concern was the provision in the agreement for the selling of material from the site. However, there were also concerns regarding the appropriateness of robotic techniques for undertaking an archaeological excavation, the arrangements for monitoring of archaeological standards and suspicions that both parties were primarily motivated by profit.

3. Commercial exploitation: the debate

The debate for and against commercial exploitation of shipwrecks, particularly where it involves the sale of artefacts, is a heated one. In the following two subsections, an attempt is made briefly to touch on the

---

[21] See www.shipwreck.net/spa1.html.

[22] A notable example was the contract made by the British government for the recovery of gold bars, worth over £40 million, from HMS *Edinburgh* in 1982. The contract provided for the salvor to receive 45 per cent of the proceeds with the remainder to be split between the USSR and the UK: see Dromgoole and Gaskell, 'Interests in Wreck', p. 195.

[23] Council for British Archaeology, press release, 8 October 2002.

core arguments both against and in favour of commercial exploitation.[24] The arguments are set out neutrally and it should not be assumed that they are supported by the author.

3.1   The case against commercial exploitation

The case *against* commercial exploitation runs along the following lines.

Archaeology is not concerned with the retrieval of objects per se, *but with the retrieval of information. Archaeological sites such as shipwrecks are 'time capsules' of information about the human past. Much of the information is contained in the material that is of least commercial value, such as the hull, fixtures and fittings of the vessel, and the personal effects of passengers and crew. To maximise the information that may be retrieved from a site, excavation must be undertaken using appropriate archaeological skills and techniques. There is a need not only to recover the artefacts with care, but also to record their context and provenance. Artefacts that are recovered from a site need to be appropriately treated and conserved. In the case of material from underwater sites, it may be waterlogged and bulky, and conservation processes may be expensive and lengthy. Proper archaeological work is necessarily painstaking, time-consuming and costly. The excavation must be fully and publicly reported. Work of this kind is fundamentally incompatible with a profit-motive, where maximum returns are required for the minimum of outlay. If undertaken at all, it is not likely to be done properly: corners will be cut.*

Artefacts from a site – a so-called 'assemblage' – must be kept together as a collection so that they are available for public education and for research purposes, both now and in the future. At a minimum, they must be kept in such a way that they can be reassembled if necessary in the future. Any form of sale or disposal that leads to the irretrievable dispersal of the material is inappropriate. For-profit operators will wish to maximise their revenue by selling artefacts at the highest price and this will usually be achieved through sale of individual objects on the open market.

The excavation of sites and the recovery of material should not be treated as the first option. While a shipwreck is lying on or in the seabed, especially in deep water, it is in a relatively safe environment. Much can be learnt from modern non-invasive archaeological techniques, including remote-sensing, to give a good indication of the nature of sites and their degree of preservation, and better tools

---

[24] For more detailed discussion of the issues, see the papers from the Second Newport Symposium on 'Sunken Treasure: Law, Technology and Ethics' (1999) 30 *Journal of Maritime Law and Commerce*, Issue 2. For a more recent 'head-to-head' debate, see 'Dave Parham and Greg Stemm Debate Maritime Archaeology Business Models', *Nautical Archaeology Society Newsletter* (summer 2010), pp. 4–5.

and techniques may be available in the future to undertake invasive work if it is then deemed justified. The excavation of a site is equivalent to the destruction of the site: once excavated, it is no longer of any value as an archaeological resource. Physical intervention should only take place where a site is under threat (from any cause, including human interference or natural processes), or for legitimate research reasons. In the absence of such circumstances, sites should be preserved in situ.

3.2   The case in favour of commercial exploitation

The case *in favour* of commercial exploitation runs along the following lines.

Public funding for archaeology will always be limited. Collaboration with commercial operators can provide a valuable source of funding for cash-strapped archaeological projects. By cooperating together and investing some of the financial profit in good archaeological work, archaeologists and commercial operators can get the best of both worlds. Archaeologists can reap the benefits of well-funded excavation projects and the opportunity to gather new data; their commercial partners can reap the benefits that may be achieved from the enhancement of commercial values that comes from good archaeology. In the words of Bederman, '[i]n short, embracing the values of historic preservation is good for business'.[25] *Conversely, undertaking pure for-profit projects – that is, without taking account of archaeological values – does not make good business sense.*[26]

It is simply unrealistic to save and preserve all the remains to be found at a shipwreck site. There is little to be gained from an archaeological point of view in storing multiple duplicates. Once studied and recorded, a representative sample can be selected for retention and the remaining items can be sold in order to provide funds that can be invested in future projects. Museums often have little interest in acquiring material from marine sites. Some of it is bulky and expensive to conserve and store: ship timbers and multiple duplicates of items such as bottles, amphorae, and porcelain may fall into this category. Commercially valuable items, particularly bullion and coins, raise particular problems because of issues regarding insurance and security. It is preferable to save a carefully selected sample of material and to ensure that it is looked after properly and available for public display than to save everything and to risk it being looked after badly or simply stored away in museum vaults.

Who knows what may happen in the future. It is not a foregone conclusion that economic, technological and other human circumstances will be better in the

---

[25] Bederman, 'Historic Salvage and the Law of the Sea', p. 128.
[26] See Hoagland, 'Managing the Underwater Cultural Resources of the China Seas', p. 272.

future than they are now and therefore it should not be assumed that it will be possible to extract greater information from sites in the future than at present. Furthermore, underwater sites are subject to particular threats compared with sites on land. Therefore, a principle derived from land archaeology – namely, preservation in situ – is not necessarily appropriate for underwater sites. Threats may be posed by nature and by human activities, including activities that incidentally affect wreck sites such as dredging and fishing, and the possibility of intervention by those that are interested only in commercial gain. High-value shipwrecks are particularly vulnerable to treasure hunting now that technology is available systematically to search for them. If no incentive is provided to discover sites, no discoveries will be made and all the values of a site – commercial and archaeological – will be inaccessible to all. Unless discovered and recovered, they 'will be left to rot into nothingness'.[27]

3.3   Room for compromise?

According to Dorsey:

Compromise will not happen unless attitudes on each side change, and the two groups stop regarding each other as the personification of evil on the one hand and intellectual snobs on the other.[28]

Putting to one side the difficult relations that can sometimes exist between archaeologists and those advocating commercial involvement in shipwreck recovery, there appear to be some areas of common ground. In particular, it seems to be generally accepted that sites of archaeological significance must be treated appropriately and that any intervention that does take place must be conducted according to professional archaeological standards. Furthermore, it also seems to be accepted that regulation may be necessary (although there may be differences of opinion about its form), in order to ensure that appropriate standards are maintained.

To a disinterested party, many of the arguments on both sides of the debate are likely to appear reasonable. They may also appear to be not entirely irreconcilable. In broad principle, there seems no reason why collaborative projects that marry good archaeology with a profit-making objective should not be possible, particularly where sites are genuinely under threat. A profit motive is not in itself a bad thing and the fact that

[27] Bryant, 'The Archaeological Duty of Care', p. 136.
[28] Dorsey, 'Historic Salvors, Marine Archaeologists, and the UNESCO Draft Convention on the Underwater Cultural Heritage', p. 47. (At the time this paper was written, Dorsey was President of the US Maritime Law Association.)

the core purpose of a company is to make a profit, and that it owes certain responsibilities to its shareholders and investors in this respect, does not mean that it cannot take into account broader public interests in its business plan. Indeed, that is the basis of the notion of corporate social responsibility. Furthermore, in some jurisdictions – including the UK – well-respected archaeological consultancies operate on a for-profit basis. It is therefore not inevitable that archaeological standards will be compromised by a profit motive. However, there remain a number of specific difficulties.

First of all, it seems to be open to question whether good archaeology, and specifically excavation, can be undertaken at depths outside the range of divers. Although technology is improving all the time, robotic technology is still at a relatively early stage of development.[29] While state-of-the-art robotic manipulators are already remarkably sensitive and agile, and it is conceivable that either now or in the future they may be capable of undertaking a full-scale archaeological excavation meeting professional archaeological standards, their use in such work is still experimental[30] and also enormously costly.

Secondly, and leading on from this latter point, there are questions about whether deep-water shipwreck recovery conforming to professional archaeological standards is economically viable as a business model. The daily hire rates for the sort of specialised equipment that is necessary for such work, particularly submersible vehicles, can run into tens of thousands of dollars and therefore the costs of keeping such equipment in place at a site over the many months required to undertake a thorough archaeological excavation will be immense.[31] Once the excavation itself is done, the costs of conservation, storage and museum premises are likely to run into tens of millions of pounds.[32] The value of

[29] See Webster, 'The Development of Excavation Technology for Remotely Operated Vehicles', pp. 41–64, esp. p. 63.

[30] For details of the techniques used to recover artefacts from the debris field of the *Titanic*, see *RMS Titanic, Inc.* v. *Wrecked and Abandoned Vessel*, 742 F. Supp. 2d 784, 798–9. A 'damage rate' of around 21 per cent was noted with respect to artefacts recovered during the 2004 expedition and 'technical difficulties' operating the ROVs resulted in a failure to recover some artefacts, 'despite serious attempts at their recovery'.

[31] To give some indication of the physical labour and time involved in a major archaeological shipwreck excavation, the excavation of the Tudor warship *Mary Rose* took place over four summer diving seasons and required 27,831 dives to the site, amounting to 11.8 'man-years' on the seabed: see www.maryrose.org.

[32] Again, drawing on the *Mary Rose* project as an example, the projected figure for the cost of creating a major new museum to house approximately 19,000 artefacts recovered

sales and other commercial revenue would need to be extraordinarily high to cover such costs and realise a profit for investors.[33]

The third, and most fundamental, question is whether it is possible for archaeologists to be persuaded to accept a business model based on the sale of artefacts. At first sight, this does not seem likely. However, the question of the *significance* of the artefacts might provide a possible avenue for compromise. In arguing for dialogue between archaeologists and commercial operators, Hutchinson has pointed out that archaeological sites have different levels of significance and that each site should be afforded treatment appropriate to its archaeological and historical value.[34] She has argued:

The concept of appropriateness is central … 'the destination of all material recovered from an underwater site should be appropriate to its archaeological and historical value'.

Commercial operators make money from historic shipwrecks by selling the finds from the sites. For many sites of archaeological value that is unacceptable but for less significant sites there may be little justification for insisting that the assemblage must remain intact.[35]

The 'concept of appropriateness' would appear to provide a potential platform for developing a framework for 'sharing' the total cultural resource based on careful management decisions made *after* a shipwreck has been discovered and its significance evaluated according to factors such as its age, rarity and condition.[36] One difficulty that can be envisaged with it, however, is that something that does not appear significant now may be regarded differently in the future. If sale leads to the irretrievable dispersal of artefacts, the opportunity for making a reassessment will be lost.

---

from the site is £35 million: see www.historicdockyard.co.uk/news/presspacks/maryrosemuseum.

[33] Previous sales of shipwreck material at public auction have raised relatively small sums: US$15 million in respect of ceramics and gold ingots from the *Geldermalsen*; US$7 million for porcelain from the *Vung Tau*; US$3 million for porcelain from the *Diana*; and US$10 million for porcelain from the *Tek Sing*: Flecker, 'The Ethics, Politics, and Realities of Maritime Archaeology in Southeast Asia', p. 12. According to Stemm, the number of potential shipwreck projects that fit the OME model is 'in the low hundreds': personal communication with the author, April 2010.

[34] Hutchinson, 'Threats to Underwater Cultural Heritage', pp. 289–90.

[35] *Ibid.*, p. 289.

[36] An approach of this kind appears to form the basis of the multiple use management programme in operation in the Florida Keys National Marine Sanctuary: see Varmer, 'United States', p. 366.

3.4 Government participation in commercial exploitation

As far as governments are concerned, the question of commercial exploitation is a matter of public policy. Although they will give consideration to the arguments of particular interest groups, ultimately, decisions about whether or not to sanction – or even participate in – commercial exploitation of wreck sites are likely to be made on the basis of what is regarded to be in the best overall public interest.

Some developing states may regard cooperation with commercial operators in the exploitation of colonial-era shipwrecks lying in their coastal waters as a means of acquiring valuable economic benefits. Such shipwrecks are sometimes viewed as of little or no direct relevance to the indigenous cultures and therefore of little or no cultural value from a national point of view.[37] Over the years, there have been many examples of developing states engaging with commercial operators, generally for pure financial gain. In the early 1990s, for example, the government of Uruguay agreed to split the proceeds of sale of gold and other valuables found on the so-called River Plate wrecks on a fifty-fifty basis with a salvor, apparently anticipating that it would be able to pay off a substantial proportion of its foreign debt.[38] Increasingly, there is recognition that economic benefits can arise not simply through a percentage split of the proceeds of sale of artefacts, such as in this case, but also through the potential revenue that may be earned from broader forms of commercial exploitation, including the development of tourism.[39]

The perceived foreignness of the shipwreck resource, as well as financial constraints, may limit the level of interest a developing state may have in trying to exploit the broader cultural and social benefits that may derive from collaborating with commercial operators on shipwreck recovery projects. Nonetheless, some government contracts have

---

[37] See Mohd Nor, 'Protection of Underwater Cultural Heritage in Malaysia', p. 21.

[38] Hoagland, 'Managing the Underwater Cultural Resources of the China Seas', p. 272. According to Hoagland, the government's share of auction proceeds was ultimately less than US$1.5 million, a drop in the ocean compared with its foreign debt at the time of US$3.4 billion. As Hoagland points out, the case demonstrates the 'overblown expectations' that can arise in respect of shipwreck 'treasures'.

[39] The question of the economic benefits that may accrue to a state through contractual collaboration between the state and a commercial operator in respect of shipwreck exploitation has been explored by Vadi, who argues that such benefits constitute an 'investment' for the purposes of international investment law and therefore the 'investor' – the commercial operator – may claim the benefit of certain protections under that law: see, generally, Vadi, 'The Challenge of Reconciling Underwater Cultural Heritage and Foreign Direct Investment'.

attempted to balance the public interest in making money for the Exchequer and its interest in the preservation of features relating directly to the nation's history and culture. The contract made between the Malaysian government and a British company in 1991 for the recovery of items from the 'Country ship' *Diana* appears to be an example. Much of the Chinese blue-and-white porcelain recovered was sold at auction, but some provision was made for artefacts of particular importance to be retained by the state.[40] In some countries, including Malaysia, there also appears to be some interest in investing the financial proceeds from certain underwater projects into others regarded as of more direct national cultural interest.[41]

As the case of HMS *Sussex* illustrates, it is not only developing states that are interested in commercially exploiting shipwrecks. Developed states too may be interested in the potential economic benefits from the recovery of valuable cargoes carried on their sunken warships and other state-owned vessels, and such states may also have the economic capacity to contemplate projects that seek to capture broader cultural and social benefits as well. There is no doubt that shipwreck recovery can excite enormous public interest. This is evidenced by the fact that the raising of the hull of the *Mary Rose* in 1982 was watched live on television by more than 60 million viewers worldwide[42] and the *Vasa* Shipwreck Museum in Sweden attracts 750,000 visitors per year.[43] The recovery of the *Nanhai No. 1*, an 800-year-old trading vessel in Guangdong Province, China, in 2007, and its excavation in full view of the public, is also attracting great interest. Such projects provide both educational and entertainment value. However, the costs of full-scale archaeological excavation are so huge that they are usually beyond the reach of the public purse, which explains their rarity. Collaboration with commercial operators could be viewed by some governments as providing an opportunity that would not otherwise be available.[44]

[40] See Vadi, 'Underwater Cultural Heritage and International Investment Law', p. 35.
[41] See Mohd Nor, 'Protection of Underwater Cultural Heritage in Malaysia', p. 21; see also Flecker, 'The Ethics, Politics, and Realities of Maritime Archaeology in Southeast Asia', p. 19.
[42] 'Mary Rose given £21m cash boost', *BBC Online News*, 25 January 2008.
[43] UNESCO, 'Protect the Underwater Cultural Heritage', Information Kit (available at: www.unesco.org).
[44] An interesting example of public/private collaboration has arisen recently in the case of the *Titanic*. US public agencies, including the National Oceanic and Atmospheric Administration (NOAA), collaborated with the salvor-in-possession, RMST, on a scientific expedition to the site in 2010 for the purpose of comprehensively mapping the entire site

4. Commercial exploitation and the UNESCO Convention 2001

How, then, does the UNESCO Convention deal with the question of commercial exploitation? The following sections consider the background to the Convention's treatment of the issue, including the approach of earlier international initiatives; the provisions of the Convention that relate specifically to commercial exploitation; and the potential implications of the Convention's regime for private-sector involvement in shipwreck projects.

4.1 Background

The first international initiative addressing UCH, Council of Europe Recommendation 848 of 1978,[45] did not refer in its minimum requirements to the matter of commercial exploitation. However, in the report accompanying the Recommendation, the view of the Council's consultant marine archaeologist was fairly unequivocal:

> the motivation of profit must dictate a speed and efficiency in salvage which is inevitably irreconcilable with the painstaking recording and controlled investigation of a site which archaeological standards require. No legislative or administrative framework can be considered satisfactory unless it can eliminate such operations.[46]

The view of the Council's consultant lawyers, Prott and O'Keefe, appeared to be more nuanced. In referring to the difficulty of applying salvage law to shipwrecks of historical value, they commented:

> if the person who has gained possession of the site is interested only in the economic value of the objects recovered there is no guarantee that the site will be correctly treated. Much of the historical and cultural value of the objects may result from their position and relationship to other objects. A salvor will not normally be concerned with this aspect although a good context can increase the commercial value too.[47]

---

to assist in its future management. Among the aims of the expedition was the creation of a three-dimensional visual mosaic using state-of-the-art imaging technology, which would 'virtually raise' the *Titanic* so that it could be better appreciated by the general public. The expedition was funded by RMST. See www.sanctuaries.noaa.gov/maritime/titanic/2010_expedition.html.

[45] See Chap. 1, section 2.2.1.
[46] Parliamentary Assembly of the Council of Europe, 'The Underwater Cultural Heritage: Report of the Committee on Culture and Education (Rapporteur: Mr John Roper)', Document 4200-E, Strasbourg, 1978, p. 39.
[47] *Ibid.*, p. 53.

In recommending that the laws of salvage and wreck should be excluded from applying to objects over 100 years underwater, Prott and O'Keefe made the point that '[i]f a salvor wants to raise such items he must comply with the requirements of the scheme of protection and be satisfied with the reward provisions of that scheme'.[48] These comments suggested that commercially motivated participation, in their view, *might* be acceptable provided it was publicly regulated and in compliance with professional archaeological standards.

Like Recommendation 848, the 1985 draft European Convention also did not refer specifically to the question of commercial exploitation and the question of whether or not there should be any participation by commercial organisations under the conventional regime was left largely for contracting states to determine. Article 5 of the draft Convention provided:

1. Contracting states may provide that authorisations to carry out survey, excavation or recovery operations may be granted to private persons or concerned bodies.
2. Such authorisations may be granted only on the basis of scientific considerations, and may, taking into account special characteristics of certain sites and the facilities and economic resources available to the applicants, specify and require that the applicants possess adequate qualifications and equipment or forbid the use of specific techniques or equipment.[49]

Under this scheme, contracting states were entitled to grant authorisation for operations to private persons or bodies if they so wished. While all remains and objects of at least 100 years of age enjoyed the protection of the Convention, it was recognised that the treatment afforded to each site should be appropriate to its 'special characteristics'. This appeared to reflect Hutchinson's view that, in determining a management plan for a site, 'the concept of appropriateness' is 'central'. Equally, as far as the disposition of artefacts was concerned, the following provision was made:

---

[48] *Ibid.*, p. 70. Recommendation 848 accepted the recommendation that salvage and wreck laws should be excluded and provided for their replacement by a scheme of fixed finder's monetary reward, not necessarily linked to the commercial value of the find. It also provided for the possibility of discretionary exclusion of less important objects or antiquities once properly studied and recorded. See, further, Chap. 5, section 4.1.

[49] DIR/JUR (84) 1, Strasbourg, 22 June 1984. As in earlier chapters, the version of the Draft Convention and Explanatory Report referred to is the declassified version of 1984. (On the issues referred to here, there was no substantive difference between the declassified documents and the final text.)

While respecting ... the archaeological principle of association of finds, each Contracting State shall ... take all appropriate measures in order that recovered underwater cultural property is conserved under conditions facilitating its study by qualified researchers, and that a suitable selection is displayed to the public.[50]

The Explanatory Report accompanying the draft Convention made the following comment on this provision:

The archaeological principle of association of finds implies that information about the find circumstances should be collected and that finds recovered during the same excavation should, *as a general rule*, be kept together so that their mutual relationship and their archaeological context can be interpreted.[51]

The draft Convention as a whole emphasised the importance of recording information and some degree of latitude was built in with respect to the disposition of artefacts, again appearing to permit significance to be taken into account in determining whether or not particular artefacts should be held in perpetuity.

The question of commercial exploitation was dealt with head-on by the Explanatory Report to the Council of Europe's later instrument, the Valletta Convention of 1992.[52] In commenting on Article 3 of that Convention, which requires states parties to have in place a system regulating the conduct of archaeological activities relating to the archaeological heritage (including UCH), the Explanatory Report stated:

Excavations made solely for the purpose of finding precious metals or objects with a market value should never be allowed.[53]

Again, this indicated that involvement by profit-making organisations was permissible, provided that the objective of the excavation was not *solely* the recovery of commercially valuable material.

When the International Law Association (ILA) turned its attention to the question of drafting a treaty on UCH in 1998, it appears to have been quite strongly influenced by the model of the US statute, the ASA, under which multiple interests in UCH are recognised and private-sector recovery permitted, *provided* it is consistent with the protection of 'historical values'.[54] According to O'Keefe and Nafziger (respectively the Chair and Rapporteur of the ILA Committee responsible for preparing a draft treaty):

---

[50] Art. 10(1).   [51] Explanatory Report, para. 35. Emphasis added.
[52] See, further, Chap. 1, section 2.2.3.   [53] Explanatory Report, p. 8.
[54] 42 USC sec. 2103(a)(2)(C). See, further, Chap. 5, section 3.4.2.

it was imperative to identify and take account of all relevant interests to create a conventional regime that would be effective and yet have some chance of gaining the support of the international community.[55]

In its 1994 Draft, the ILA seemed to envisage the possibility of commercial involvement, providing it was appropriately regulated and conducted in accordance with accepted international archaeological standards. Echoing the approach of the ASA, the Draft excluded the application of salvage law to UCH falling within its scope,[56] but in its preamble included 'salvors' in the list of parties whose cooperation was required to protect UCH from 'irresponsible activity'. The preamble recognised that exploration, excavation and protection of UCH necessitated 'the application of special scientific methods and the use of suitable techniques and equipment as well as a high degree of professional specialization' and the Draft provided that states parties were to ensure that activities complied 'at a minimum' with the Charter to be prepared by ICOMOS and annexed to the Convention.[57]

When UNESCO took up interest in the question of UCH protection in the early 1990s, the question of whether a new legal regime should permit some level of commercial participation was not top of the list of the issues that it sought to address. Like the ILA, it saw the major issues that needed to be resolved as the questions of jurisdiction, the role of salvage law and the adoption of appropriate standards for intervention on UCH sites.[58] Although its feasibility study, published in 1995, concluded that the application of salvage law encouraged the removal of artefacts from the seabed for commercial purposes and promoted damage to, and destruction of UCH,[59] the 1998 UNESCO Draft adopted a rather ambivalent position on the question of salvage law and – by implication – the possibility of commercial participation. Following the example of the 1994 ILA Draft, it included salvors in the list of parties whose cooperation was necessary to ensure the protection of UCH and, rather than referring to salvage law specifically, it provided for the 'non-application of any internal law or regulation having the effect of providing commercial incentives for the excavation and removal of

[55] O'Keefe and Nafziger, 'The Draft Convention on the Protection of the Underwater Cultural Heritage', p. 394.
[56] 1994 ILA Draft, Art. 4.   [57] On the Charter, see, further, Chap. 1, section 3.1.3.
[58] UNESCO Secretariat, 'Feasibility Study for the Drafting of a New Instrument for the Protection of the Underwater Cultural Heritage', presented to the 146th Session of the UNESCO Executive Board, Paris, 23 March 1995, Doc. 146 EX/27, para. 22.
[59] *Ibid.*, para. 32.

underwater cultural heritage'.[60] However, although not an explicit exclusion of salvage law, this provision appeared to amount to the same thing in a 'different guise'[61] and its wording suggested that the regime that would ultimately emerge was unlikely to be one encouraging of commercial enterprise.

Inevitably, during the UNESCO negotiations, the attitude of states to the question of commercial exploitation reflected traditional viewpoints, not least on the respective roles of the state versus the private sector. While there was a strong feeling on the part of many delegates that the Convention should adopt a 'no-commercial exploitation' rule as a matter of principle, the USA, in particular – with some support from the UK – was keen to ensure that there was leeway within the conventional scheme for some level of commercial participation. Indeed, it seems to have 'conditioned its support' for the new treaty, in part, on 'the acceptance of some commercial activity so long as it conform[ed] to the scientific standards of the convention'.[62]

It has been pointed out by several commentators that the USA was one of the few states to have representatives of commercial interests on its delegation, including Greg Stemm of OME. However, according to O'Keefe, the historic salvage lobby 'did not exert a significant influence on decisions made by the United States'[63] and certainly it seems likely that the US delegation was at least as influenced by the concerns of its general commercial maritime community,[64] the multiple use management approach of its own domestic legislation[65] and its general political philosophy.

4.2   The Convention's approach to commercial exploitation

The preamble to the final text of the UNESCO Convention provides a first hint to the approach taken by the treaty to the question of commercial participation. Not only has the explicit reference to 'salvors' been

---

[60]   1998 UNESCO Draft, Art. 12(2).
[61]   Dromgoole and Gaskell, 'Draft UNESCO Convention on the Protection of the Underwater Cultural Heritage 1998', p. 188. See, further, Chap. 5, section 4.1.
[62]   Nafziger, 'Historic Salvage Law Revisited', p. 88.
[63]   O'Keefe, *Shipwrecked Heritage*, p. 28.
[64]   See, further, Chap. 5, section 4.4. It is notable that John Kimball, Chair of the US Maritime Law Association's Study Group on the Draft UNESCO Convention was also part of the delegation.
[65]   For example, the USA seems to have had greater concerns about the question of non-intrusive public access to UCH, another crucial feature of its multi-user approach. See O'Keefe, *Shipwrecked Heritage*, p. 28.

omitted from the list of interested parties whose cooperation is deemed essential for the protection of UCH,[66] but also 'the increasing commercial exploitation of underwater cultural heritage, and in particular [. . .] certain activities aimed at the sale, acquisition or barter of underwater cultural heritage' were identified as matters of 'deep concern'.[67] Therefore, even before one looks at the main text of the treaty, it is evident that commercial operators are not regarded as legitimate 'users' of UCH falling within the scope of the Convention.

4.2.1   Basic principle: UCH shall not be commercially exploited

Article 2 sets out the objectives and general principles of the Convention. Paragraph (7) of that article provides as follows:

Underwater cultural heritage shall not be commercially exploited.

The fact that this prohibition is included in the list of general principles and objectives of the treaty shows the strength of feeling at the negotiations against the general concept of commercial exploitation.[68] In itself, however, the statement is rather bald and gives rise to more questions than it answers. What does commercial exploitation mean exactly in the context of the Convention? Does it encompass those forms of commercial exploitation that rely on exhibition revenues, media rights or merchandising? Is sale in any form permissible, for example the sale of multiple duplicates or of an entire collection? More generally, does the prohibition leave any room for the participation of commercial operators in the UCH regime?

In order to answer these questions, it is necessary to look at the Annex to the Convention, which provides some elucidation of what is meant by the reference in Article 2(7) to 'commercial exploitation'. Rule 2 of the Annex provides:

The commercial exploitation of underwater cultural heritage for trade or speculation or its irretrievable dispersal is fundamentally incompatible with the protection and proper management of underwater cultural heritage. *Underwater cultural heritage shall not be traded, sold, bought or bartered as commercial goods.*[69]

Together, the two sentences of this first clause of Rule 2 suggest that commercial exploitation using methods not involving the sale (or other

---

[66] See preambular clause 10.   [67] Preambular clause 8.

[68] O'Keefe, *Shipwrecked Heritage*, p. 50. In fact, Grenier has referred to the principle as 'the cornerstone of the whole Convention': Grenier, 'The Annex', p. 114.

[69] Emphasis added.

exchange) of UCH will not be an infringement of the Convention *unless* they result in the irretrievable dispersal of material.[70] On the other hand, sale of UCH – at least its sale as 'commercial goods' – does appear to be prohibited, and it seems that this is the case even if it would *not* lead to irretrievable dispersal.

What is clear at this stage is that forms of commercial exploitation that do not result in the irretrievable dispersal of material, such as the exhibition of artefacts to a paying public, media exploitation through the making of books, films and DVDs, or the selling of rights to such material, and merchandising of non-artefact souvenirs are all unaffected by the provision. Therefore it seems that these sorts of activities do not fall within the scope of the prohibition on commercial exploitation enshrined in Article 2(7). What is also clear is that Rule 2 sets out a carefully crafted compromise formula which provides some 'wiggle-room' on the question of sale.

Before one can go further in gaining an understanding of the impact of this provision on the possibility of commercial participation in activities directed at UCH under the conventional scheme, especially activities that might entail the sale of recovered material, it is necessary to consider two provisos set out in the *second* clause of Rule 2:

This Rule cannot be interpreted as preventing:

(a)   the provision of professional archaeological services or necessary services incidental thereto whose nature and purpose are in full conformity with this Convention and are subject to the authorization of the competent authorities;

(b)   the deposition of underwater cultural heritage, recovered in the course of a research project in conformity with this Convention, provided such deposition does not prejudice the scientific or cultural interest or integrity of the recovered material or result in its irretrievable dispersal; is in accordance with the provisions of Rules 33 and 34; and is subject to the authorization of the competent authorities.

---

[70] The wording of the provision indicates that irretrievable dispersal in itself, however it arises, is regarded as 'fundamentally incompatible' with the protection of UCH. For example, an arrangement made in the early 1990s between a museum in Sardinia and the Italian national particle physics laboratory for the transfer to the laboratory of part of a cargo of lead ingots from a Roman shipwreck in order that they could be melted down and used as shielding in a scientific experiment would appear to amount to a contravention of Rule 2. (The fact that the physicists provided funding for the archaeological excavation would also probably amount to a trading of the ingots.) See 'Roman ingots to shield particle detector', *Nature News Online*, 15 April 2010.

These provisos were inserted in the text, at least in part, to alleviate the concerns of states – particularly the USA – regarding the extent of the impact of the Convention's non-commercialisation stance.[71] However, what do they actually mean?

4.2.2   Proviso (a): provision of professional archaeological services

It is common practice for professional archaeological services to be commissioned, for payment, to undertake pre-development archaeological assessments, 'rescue' operations and other archaeological services. As mentioned earlier, in some jurisdictions such services are provided by for-profit organisations. Proviso (a) makes it clear that the provision of such services, and services incidental thereto (which would include, for example, the provision of vessels and other equipment), is not affected by the prohibition on commercial exploitation.

From the perspective of commercial operators who wish to be involved in shipwreck recovery work, this proviso appears to provide a window of opportunity. Provided the nature and purpose of the services provided are in full conformity with the Convention and are undertaken with the authorisation of the competent authorities, there is nothing to stop for-profit organisations contracting with governments, private owners and others to undertake archaeological and related services. Such services could include full-scale archaeological excavation, provided it is properly authorised and in full conformity with the Rules in the Annex. The services could be paid for by public or private funding, and/or revenue from methods of commercial exploitation that are permissible under the Convention. However, in making their plans, a commercial operator and the commissioner of their services need to be aware that a project will not be authorised unless they can demonstrate that 'an adequate funding base' for the entire project is in place from the outset.[72] For a full-scale excavation, particularly in deep water, the sums involved will be enormous and it will not be acceptable to rely on the hope or expectation that revenue will be raised from the sale of media

---

[71] See Garabello, 'The Negotiating History of the Convention on the Protection of the Underwater Cultural Heritage', pp. 184–5.

[72] Rule 17 provides: 'Except in cases of emergency to protect underwater cultural heritage, an adequate funding base shall be assured in advance of any activity, sufficient to complete all stages of the project design, including conservation, documentation and curation of recovered artefacts, and report preparation and dissemination.'

rights and merchandise, donations and other forms of income as the project unfolds.[73]

4.2.3   Proviso (b): deposition of UCH

The clarity of the first clause of Rule 2 on the question of sale is tempered by its reference to 'commercial goods' and also by proviso (b) in the second clause. The reference to 'commercial goods' may be designed simply to make it clear that UCH artefacts must not be treated like ordinary products of commerce and, in so far as they are traded, sold, bought or bartered, their special nature must be taken into account. Proviso (b) may therefore be seen as providing some indication as to how such exchange can be done within the terms of the Convention.

'Deposition' is a curious word which is not defined by the Convention. In so far as it has an ordinary meaning in the context of Rule 2 and the treaty as a whole, it would appear to mean the depositing of UCH in a (presumably, safe) place. However, the terms of proviso (b), as well as the negotiating history of the Convention, suggest that in essence it is equivalent to (or at least encompasses) the notion of 'deaccession' used in the context of museum collections management. From time to time, and for a variety of reasons, museums may wish to dispose of objects in their collections. Usually such disposition is strictly regulated. For example, the British Museum's policy on deaccession provides as follows:

The Trustees do not have the power to sell, exchange, give away or otherwise dispose of any object vested in them and comprised in the Collection unless –

(a) the object is a duplicate of another object held in the collection, or
(b) in the opinion of the Trustees the object is unfit to be retained in the Collection and can be disposed of without detriment to the interests of the public or scholars;
(c) it has become useless for the purposes of the Museum by reason of damage, physical deterioration, or infestation of destructive organisms.[74]

Proviso (b) of Rule 2 appears to allow for the management of a UCH project archive in a similar way to a museum collection, enabling the

---

[73] Rule 18 provides: 'The project design shall demonstrate an ability, such as by securing a bond, to fund the project through to completion.' In commenting on this provision, O'Keefe points out that it is not necessary for there to be 'cash in hand' in advance of the project; '[u]ndertakings backed by legal guarantees are sufficient': O'Keefe, *Shipwrecked Heritage*, pp. 171–3.

[74] British Museum Policy on Deaccession of Registered Objects from the Collection, approved by the Trustees of the British Museum on 4 March 2010, para. 3.3.

deaccession of material in certain circumstances.[75] However, it strictly limits the circumstances in which such deaccession, or deposition, may occur. It does not set out permissible reasons for the deaccession of specific objects, as the British Museum's policy does, but rather sets a number of pre-conditions:

(i)   the deposition must not 'prejudice the scientific or cultural interest or integrity of the recovered material';

(ii) the deposition must not result in the irretrievable dispersal of the recovered material;

(iii) the deposition must be in accordance with the provisions of Rules 33 and 34,[76] which relate to the curation of the project archives (the most prescriptive element in the present context appearing to be that 'as far as possible' the project archive must be 'kept together and intact as a collection in a manner that is available for professional and public access'); and

(iv) the deposition must be subject to the authorisation of the competent national authority.

One of the main difficulties for commercial operators seeking to acquire revenue from sale of UCH would appear to be pre-condition (ii). For example, although Stemm's business model of selling only 'trade goods' potentially might fit with some museums' deaccession policies (for example, the British Museum's policy allowing for the sale of duplicates),[77] the sale of such material on the open market in a way

---

[75] In fact, it is possible the provision was inspired by the practice under the Florida Keys National Marine Sanctuary programme of permitting authorised users of the UCH resource to apply for a 'special use' permit (which, it seems, is also referred to as a 'deaccession/transfer permit') to have transferred to their custody objects which the permitting authority no longer consider of archaeological significance: see Varmer, 'United States', p. 366. According to Varmer, objects eligible for transfer include duplicates. Deaccession therefore could be regarded as a potential mechanism for implementing Hutchinson's 'appropriateness' concept.

[76] Rule 33 provides, inter alia: 'The project archives, including any underwater cultural heritage removed and a copy of all supporting documentation shall, as far as possible be kept together and intact as a collection in a manner that is available for professional and public access as well as for the curation of the archives.' Rule 34 provides: 'The project archives shall be managed according to international professional standards, and subject to the authorisation of the competent authorities.'

[77] It should be noted, however, that the British Museum's deaccession policy also provides: '[d]ecisions to dispose of objects comprised within the Collection cannot be made with the principal aim of generating funds though any eventual proceeds from such disposal must be used to add to the Collection': British Museum Policy on Deaccession of Registered Objects from the Collection, approved by the Trustees of the British Museum on 4 March 2010, para. 3.3.

that dispersed it to different buyers would appear to be a method of deposition that would not meet the terms of proviso (b). However, the sale, exchange, giving away, or other disposal of parts – or the whole – of a collection of UCH material might be acceptable if it was done in such a way that all parts were traceable and could be reassembled if necessary. Given that such disposition would need to be *authorised* by the competent national authority, it seems likely that that authority would require that any sale also be conditioned upon provision for study and public access.[78] Furthermore, in light of some national attitudes to the treatment of cultural heritage generally, some competent authorities may regard any form of sale as a breach of the fundamental principle in Article 2(7), especially if it entails a disposition into private hands.[79]

Attempts may be made by commercial operators to find a means of meeting the conditions set out in proviso (b) that enables profit to be made through the sale of material.[80] However, to do so is likely to entail highly complex procedures, the acceptability of which will be judged by the relevant competent national authority in each case. Outcomes will therefore be unpredictable, and unpredictability does not afford the best basis for a business plan.

4.3   Implications of the Convention's regime

The provisions in Article 2(7) and Rule 2 are not the only obstacles the Convention places in the way of commercial operators wishing to participate in shipwreck recovery work. The absence of a significance criterion in the definition of UCH in Article 1(1)(a) of the Convention effectively means that no shipwrecks over 100 years underwater fall

---

[78] Whether such provision could be provided through 'virtual' access online, rather than through direct physical access, is an interesting question. Different competent authorities are likely to take different views on this.

[79] See the discussion of Rule 2 in the UNESCO Manual for Activities Directed at UCH, which emphasises that UCH should remain in the public domain. On this Manual, see Chap. 9, section 3.1.

[80] See, for example, a proposal for a system of 'private curatorship': Stemm and Bederman, 'Virtual Collections and Private Curators: A Model for the Museum of the Future'. The difficulties faced by those responsible for drafting the covenants and conditions in respect of the *Titanic* artefact collection illustrate the complexities that are likely to be involved. In this case, in order to ensure that the collection is kept together in perpetuity, appropriately cared for and managed, and publicly available, it has been considered necessary to make detailed provision for trustee obligations, a reserve fund, trustee default procedures, collection management, deaccession, bankruptcy procedures and independent oversight: see *RMS Titanic, Inc.* v. *Wrecked and Abandoned Vessel*, 742 F. Supp. 2d 784, Exhibit A (ED Va. Aug. 12, 2010).

outside the treaty's regime.[81] Therefore, there is little opportunity for archaeologists and commercial operators to share the UCH resource over that age on the basis of significance (at least at the level of an entire site).[82] As a result, if the Convention becomes widely accepted in the future, those commercial operators whose business models are substantially reliant on the sale of material may orient their activities to sites that have been underwater for *less* than 100 years.[83] Although the conventional regime provides some room for commercial operators to participate in activities directed at sites *more* than 100 years underwater, through the offering of archaeological or other services under the terms of proviso (a) to Rule 2, the terms of such engagements will be limited by the tightly defined proviso with respect to sale in Rule 2(b) and the rules on advance provision for funding, as well as by the emphasis the Convention places on the principle of preservation *in situ*. In light of this principle, and the rules underpinning this principle, the circumstances in which full excavation is likely to be authorised are limited and within the discretion of the competent national authority.[84] Overall, therefore, there is little scope for commercial operators whose business plans rely on sale of material to engage in shipwreck recovery work within the Convention's regime. Among other things, it is already clear that archaeological projects which rely for their funding on the sale of 'deaccessioned' artefacts are unlikely to be regarded as acceptable.[85]

Merryman has referred to the 'anti-market bias' of the UNESCO Convention and suggested that the initial slow rate of take-up of the

[81] See, further, Chap. 2, section 4.2.2.
[82] Proviso (b) to Rule 2 could be regarded as providing some scope for the 'sharing' of *artefacts* on the basis of significance, but in practice is unlikely to be treated in this way: see section 4.2.3, above.
[83] There may be many twentieth-century deep-water wrecks with valuable cargoes that are only now becoming viable salvage propositions. For example, in 2010 and 2011 the UK government entered into salvage contracts with OME for the recovery of consignments of silver, owned by the government, on board two deep-water merchant casualties from the First and Second World Wars, the *Gairsoppa* and the *Mantola*. In 2012, OME recovered more than 1,000 silver bars from the *Gairsoppa*, reportedly worth approximately £24 million: '£24m haul of silver recovered from sunken merchant ship off Irish coast': *Guardian*, 18 July 2012. The wreck lies at a depth of approximately three miles. (For a discussion of the circumstances of these wrecks from an Irish perspective, see, generally, Symmons, 'Recent Off-Shore Treasure-Seeking Incidents Relating to Wrecks in Irish Waters'.)
[84] For details of the authorisation scheme under the Convention, see Chap. 9, section 3.
[85] See Recommendation 5 of the Scientific and Technical Advisory Body to the Meeting of States Parties, made at the Third Meeting of the Advisory Body in April 2012 (UCH/12/3. STAB/220/9 REV, 20 April 2012, p. 9).

Convention might be due, at least in part, to 'a reaction to the severity of the Convention's prohibition of commercial exploitation'.[86] However, while undoubtedly the approach of the Convention to commercial exploitation is more heavily weighted towards that of 'source' states than 'market' states, there is no evidence that this has had any significant impact on decision-making by traditional market states with respect to the Convention. Statements made by the USA outlining its objections to the Convention do not refer to the question of commercial exploitation[87] and therefore it must be assumed that the formula set out in Rule 2 satisfied its original concerns. Statements made by the Netherlands and the UK explaining their abstentions also made no mention of commercial exploitation.[88]

Despite the fact that no state appears to have voiced concerns on this matter, there is nonetheless a possibility that the reticence of some states to ratify the Convention may be due, at least in part, to its impact on their ability to engage in commercial exploitation of state-owned shipwrecks. It is notable that the UK negotiated its 'partnering agreement' with OME in respect of HMS *Sussex* at the very same time that it was involved in negotiating the UNESCO Convention. Despite its stated support for the principles of the Convention and the Rules in the Annex,[89] it entered the agreement apparently without full consideration of whether it was in compliance with the letter (or spirit) of the Convention, or the Annex.[90] The furore caused by this agreement meant that the discovery by OME in 2008 of another of the UK's sunken historic warships, HMS *Victory*,[91] also potentially carrying a large consignment of

---

[86] Merryman, 'Thinking about the Elgin Marbles', pp. 130–1.
[87] See the statement of the USA reproduced in Camarda and Scovazzi, *The Protection of the Underwater Cultural Heritage*, pp. 433–4. See also the more-detailed statement by Blumberg, Head of the US delegation, published on the US State Department website (www.state.gov/documents/organization/16676.pdf).
[88] For the statements, see Camarda and Scovazzi, *The Protection of the Underwater Cultural Heritage*, pp. 424–5 and 432–3.
[89] In its Statement on Vote, the UK declared that it could 'support most of the articles in [the Convention], particularly the provisions of the Annex'.
[90] The UK government went on formally to recognise the Annex as best practice for maritime archaeology in 2005: Hansard, HC, col. 46W (written answers for 24 January 2005).
[91] This *Victory* was the direct predecessor of Admiral Nelson's flagship preserved at Portsmouth. It was a 100-gun 'first rate' ship of the line and the flagship of Admiral Sir John Balchin. It sank in a storm in 1744 in international waters in the western English Channel with the loss of all hands (over 1,000 men). As well as being a major gravesite, remains of 'first rate' British warships from this period are rare and the wreck has been referred to by the British government as a 'once in a generation find'. The vessel was reputed to have been carrying valuable cargo from vessels captured as prize, as well as

coins, posed a quandary for the government. Initially it appears to have again toyed with the possibility of engaging in a *Sussex*-type agreement with OME. However, after cross-government discussions, along with independent advice that bullion and other assets of monetary value – with the exception of cannon – were unlikely to exist at the site, it embarked on a public consultation exercise concerning the future management of the wreck.[92] The consultation document sought views on three options: management *in situ*, recovery of artefacts visible on the seabed (including forty-one cannon) and more extensive excavation. In response to the consultation, the government announced that it intended to take a 'phased' approach to the management of the wreck.[93] In line with the UNESCO Annex, *in situ* management would be adopted 'as an initial approach, pending further study of the site, before deciding on any further physical intervention'. At the same time, it announced that it supported a proposal put forward to establish a charitable trust to manage the site, 'subject to appropriate archaeological safeguards'.[94]

5. Concluding remarks

The central aim of the Convention is to preserve UCH 'for the benefit of humanity'.[95] The recovery of UCH which is 'intended to profit few at the expense of many'[96] is clearly incompatible with this aim and therefore

---

private cargo of bullion. The bronze cannon carried by the vessel are also of significant commercial value, illustrated by the fact that a salvage reward paid to OME by the government for two cannon recovered from the site in the period after its discovery was reported to be US$160,000: *CBA Conservation*, Latest News, October 2009 (available at www.archaeologyuk.org/conservation/marine).

[92] Department for Culture, Media and Sport and Ministry of Defence, 'HMS *Victory* 1744: Options for the Management of the Wreck Site', 2010 (available at www.culture.gov.uk/consultations/6773.aspx).

[93] Ministry of Defence and Department for Culture, Media and Sport, 'Public Consultation on Options for the Management or the Wreck Site of HMS *Victory* (1744): Report', p. 2 (www.culture.gov.uk/consultations/6773.aspx).

[94] In 2012, the government transferred title to the wreck, and responsibility for its day-to-day management, to the Maritime Heritage Foundation: see www.gov.uk/government/news/hms-victory-1744-a-rare-gift-to-foundation. Shortly after the transfer, OME announced that it had entered into an agreement with the Trust for archaeological excavation of the wreck: see 'Odyssey Marine Exploration Executes Agreement with Maritime Heritage Foundation for Admiral Balchin's HMS *Victory* Shipwreck', OME press release, 2 February 2012.

[95] Art. 2(3).

[96] ICOMOS International Charter on the Protection and Management of Underwater Cultural Heritage 1996, Introduction (http://international.icomos.org/18thapril/18april2003e-charte.htm).

unacceptable under the Convention. While the treaty regime permits recovery of UCH where it is regarded by a competent national authority as of benefit to humanity (judged by conformity with the treaty's provisions) and the participation of for-profit organisations in recovery operations in such circumstances is not prohibited,[97] the scheme of the Convention is such that (assuming it is properly interpreted) organisations seeking anything other than a very modest profit are unlikely to find the engagement worthwhile. In particular, the 'wiggle-room' for sale of artefacts seems to be tiny.

The huge costs involved in major shipwreck excavation projects, such as those involving the *Vasa*, the *Mary Rose* and the *Nanhai No. 1*, mean that they will always be few and far between. While the restrictions imposed by the Convention with respect to the means by which such projects can be funded must be interpreted carefully and in good faith, it is to be hoped that it will be possible to find ways of harnessing funding – be it public or private, or a combination of both – to enable such projects to take place from time to time in the future. Whatever the possibilities for utilising digital technology 'virtually to raise' a wreck in order to provide the public with an impression of what is lying on the seabed, the opportunity to see the 'real thing' has the power to excite the public interest to a far greater extent and can provide enormous benefits to humanity.

---

[97] Among other things, the organisation would need to show that the individuals involved in any activities directed at UCH had the competence and qualifications appropriate for the project: see, further, Chap. 9, section 4.2.

7   Rights, jurisdiction and duties under general international law

1. Introduction

To exercise control over activities that might adversely impact upon UCH located in the marine environment, a state must have the requisite authority under international law. There are some general principles of international law that may be helpful in this respect and there is also a specific international legal framework for the seas set out in the LOSC. This framework establishes the rights and jurisdiction of states in respect of marine spaces and the activities that take place within them. As will be clear from earlier chapters, the LOSC includes only limited provision relating specifically to UCH.

The fact that a state may have the legal authority, or competence, to take action in respect of treasure hunting and other activities that interfere with UCH does not mean that it will necessarily *use* that competence. In practice, states may make use of the authority available to them where their own national interests are clearly at stake, but may need encouragement to use it to protect the interests of the international community more generally. This encouragement may come in the form of duties imposed by international law.

This chapter examines the authority available to states to take action to protect UCH, as well as the duties imposed upon them, under general international law.[1] The primary focus is on the mechanisms that are available to regulate the activities of commercial salvors and others who have the intention of interfering with shipwrecks and other UCH and who have the capacity to undertake activities on deepwater sites beyond

---

[1] The expression 'general international law' as used here means the international legal framework outside the UNESCO conventional regime. The jurisdictional framework established by the UNESCO Convention 2001 is considered in Chap. 8.

coastal areas. However, brief consideration is also given to the question of regulation of commercial activities that may *inadvertently* interfere with UCH, such as trawling, dredging and the construction of renewal energy installations. The chapter is split into three sections. The first identifies two general principles of international jurisdiction which afford states some means whereby they can control, or at least have some indirect influence upon, activities beyond their territorial limits. The second discusses the rights, jurisdiction and duties of states with respect to each of the internationally recognised maritime zones under the regime set out in the LOSC. The final section explores how the jurisdictional mechanisms identified and discussed in the first two sections could be utilised to their full potential in order to afford protection to UCH located in extra-territorial waters.

Some readers, especially non-lawyers, may find it helpful to review parts of the General introduction before reading this chapter. In particular, Section 2.2 provides an introduction to the law of the sea and outlines the recognised maritime zones and their interrelationship with one another. Section 3.1 may also be useful: it provides a brief introduction to the concepts of sovereignty and jurisdiction.

2.   Use of general principles of international jurisdiction in the context of underwater cultural heritage

A number of general principles of international jurisdiction are recognised whereby a state can exercise control over individuals and legal entities in respect of both civil and criminal matters.[2] While some of these principles are controversial, the two that are relevant in the present context are well-established rules of customary international law. These principles will simply be noted at this stage, before attention is turned to the principles relating specifically to maritime jurisdiction. However, they will be returned to later in the chapter.

2.1   *Territorial principle*

Under the territorial principle of jurisdiction, as a matter of general principle a state has legislative and enforcement jurisdiction over all matters arising in its territory. Generally speaking, it can therefore prohibit or restrict activities in its territory and can do so whether those

---

[2] For a general outline of all the principles, see Brownlie, *Principles of Public International Law*, chap. 15.

activities are undertaken by its own nationals, or the nationals of other states. The territory of the state includes its ports, internal waters and territorial sea. As will be discussed further in section 3.2 below, subject to certain exceptions the state can regulate the activities not only of the nationals of other states that come within its territory, but also of their flag vessels.

By making judicious use of the territorial principle, it is possible for a state to counter interference with wreck sites lying *beyond* its territorial limits. For example, by restricting or prohibiting use of its ports, or by making their use dependent on prior consent, it could use the principle to hamper the activities of foreign vessels operating in international waters by restricting their lines of supply.[3] It could also require that material found outside territorial limits, but then brought within those limits, be reported, as well as restrict or ban the importation of material raised from particular sites.

UK legislation provides some relevant examples. One is the well-known provision in the Merchant Shipping Act 1995 requiring that any person finding or taking possession of any wreck outside UK territorial waters, and bringing it within those waters, must report it to the Receiver of Wreck.[4] Another UK statute that is less well known in the UCH context but which illustrates the potential of the territorial principle to assist in deterring inappropriate activities on extra-territorial wreck sites is the Dealing in Cultural Objects (Offences) Act 2003.[5] This Act creates an offence of 'dealing with tainted cultural objects'.[6] While the 'dealing' must take place in the UK (for example, the acquisition of an object, or its disposal), the 'tainting' of an object can take place anywhere. Among other things, an object will be 'tainted' if it is removed from a wreck site of historical or archaeological interest, wherever that wreck site may be, provided that the removal constitutes an offence under UK law, or the law of any other country.[7] The constituent elements of the offence are complex, but its scope is remarkably broad. To take just one example, it could encompass the situation where

[3] Any restrictions of this sort would need to comply with international law rules on access to ports, including those relating to ships in distress: see, further, Churchill and Lowe, *The Law of the Sea*, pp. 61–5.

[4] Merchant Shipping Act 1995, s. 236(1).

[5] This statute was enacted to reinforce the UK's implementation of the 1970 UNESCO Convention on Illicit Trade in Cultural Property. (The UK acceded to the 1970 Convention, somewhat belatedly, in 2002.)

[6] Dealing in Cultural Objects (Offences) Act 2003, s. 1.

[7] Dealing in Cultural Objects (Offences) Act 2003, s. 2.

either a British or foreign national, without authorisation, acquires, disposes of, imports or exports an item removed from the wrecks of HMS *Prince of Wales* or HMS *Repulse*, situated off Malaysia, since access to these wreck sites is restricted under the UK Protection of Military Remains Act 1986.[8]

Carefully crafted domestic legislation utilising the territorial principle of jurisdiction can provide a means whereby a state can indirectly – but potentially quite effectively – influence activities undertaken at UCH sites in international waters.

2.2 Nationality principle

The utilisation of another established basis for jurisdiction – the nationality principle – can also be helpful in protecting extra-territorial sites. Under this principle, a state has the power to exercise legislative and, in some cases, enforcement jurisdiction over the activities of its own nationals when they are outside its territory.[9] The nationality principle extends not only to the nationals of the state, but also to vessels registered with the state, since the authorisation to fly the flag of the state effectively confers the nationality of the state on the vessel. A state can therefore legislate to regulate the activities of its flag vessels and of anyone on board those vessels, including non-nationals.

Although, generally speaking, the nationality principle is reserved for dealing with serious criminal offences committed abroad, such as treason and murder, it can also be used to control other activities which the state would like to see regulated and clearly it has some potential for providing states with control over extra-territorial activities affecting UCH. Again, it is possible to find examples of legislation that does this. Two statutes previously discussed,[10] the UK Protection of Military Remains Act 1986 and the US Sunken Military Craft Act of 2004, make use of the nationality principle in order to afford protection to sunken military vessels and aircraft lying beyond the territorial sea. The UK statute creates offences applicable to certain military wrecks in international waters, making it clear that those offences can be committed only by someone on board a British-controlled ship, or by a British

---

[8] On this statute, see, further, Chap. 4, section 2.2. Whether the offence *would* encompass such a situation depends on whether the removal did in fact constitute an offence under the 1986 Act (see the terms of ss. 2 and 3).

[9] Generally speaking, the legislation of one state cannot be *enforced* in another state: see Aust, *Handbook of International Law*, p. 44.

[10] See Chap. 4, section 2.2.

national.[11] The US statute enacts various prohibitions that are not subject to any geographical limit, but again makes it clear that the application of those prohibitions to non-nationals is limited.[12]

'Long-arm' provisions of this kind are undoubtedly useful, although they have the obvious limitation that they cannot be used to regulate the activities of *foreign* flagged vessels and nationals.[13]

3. Rights, jurisdiction and duties under the Law of the Sea Convention

Aside from general principles of international jurisdiction, there are also specialist rules set out in the LOSC relating to the rights and jurisdiction of states over maritime areas.

As discussed in Chapter 1, in light of concerns about the lack of legal protection for UCH in the Mediterranean Sea, proposals were put forward at UNCLOS III that would have given coastal states direct jurisdiction over UCH located on the continental shelf. This would have meant that the coastal state would have been able to regulate activities related to UCH conducted in this area not just by its own nationals and flag vessels, but by those of other states as well. However, these proposals were rejected by some maritime states (most notably, the USA, the UK and the Netherlands). These states were of the view that a departure from the pre-existing position – that coastal state rights and jurisdiction on the continental shelf should be tied to natural resources – would lead to creeping jurisdiction and, ultimately, to claims of full coastal state sovereignty over these areas.[14] As a result, the LOSC contains only limited provision with respect to UCH, making available to coastal states a special jurisdictional tool in respect of the maritime zone immediately contiguous to the territorial sea and making some provision for UCH located on the deep seabed beyond areas of national jurisdiction.

It is usually the case that rights are accompanied by responsibilities and the LOSC makes provision for both. The following discussion starts by looking at the duties the Convention imposes upon states with respect to UCH. It then goes on to consider the rights and jurisdiction afforded to

[11] Protection of Military Remains Act 1986, s. 3(1).

[12] Sunken Military Craft Act of 2004, sec. 1402.

[13] Aside from limitations with regard to enforceability *in law* against foreign vessels and nationals, there may also be difficulties in enforcing the provisions *in practice* where activities take place in waters far from the state's territorial boundaries.

[14] See Chap. 1, section 2.1.2.

states in each of the maritime zones and the implications these have for UCH protection.

3.1   Duties under Article 303(1)

Article 303(1) of the LOSC provides:

States have the duty to protect objects of an archaeological and historical nature found at sea and shall cooperate for this purpose.[15]

There are several points to note about this provision. First, the duty is twofold, comprising two related duties: (i) a duty to protect *and* (ii) a duty to cooperate. Secondly, the provision refers to UCH (or, more specifically, 'objects of an archaeological and historical nature')[16] found *at sea*. In light of the fact that Article 303 is located in Part XVI of the Convention, which is headed 'General Provisions', it is generally accepted that the duties set out in paragraph 1 apply to *all* sea areas. Thirdly, and importantly, the provision is 'internationalist' in nature, in other words it requires states to act to protect UCH no matter what its origins may be: the fact that a state has no direct *national* interest in the UCH concerned is irrelevant. Finally, the second limb of the duty, which requires that states *cooperate* for the purpose of protecting UCH, represents – in the specific context of UCH – a more general duty that exists under international law requiring states to cooperate with one another for the good of all.[17] In the marine zone, the necessity for cooperation to ensure the effective regulation of activities is self-evident. Furthermore, given the international nature of shipping and trade, and the resultant international significance of much UCH, cooperative action is clearly appropriate in determining how such UCH should be protected.

When the LOSC was still in draft form, Caflisch argued that the duties under Article 303(1) 'appear far too general and vague to have any significant normative content'.[18] More recently, Blumberg argued that Article 303(1) is hortatory only, on the basis that it '[could not] be construed to provide specific regulatory competence over UCH located

---

[15] For the historical development of this provision, see Chap. 1, section 2.1.2.

[16] The meaning of the phrase 'objects of an archaeological and historical nature' is discussed in Chap. 2, section 3.1. As that discussion shows, modern state practice generally treats the expression expansively so as to include even relatively recent material. In light of this, and for the sake of simplicity, this chapter for the most part employs the term UCH and treats it as synonymous with the phrase used by the LOSC.

[17] See, further, Lowe, *International Law*, pp. 110–13.

[18] Caflisch, 'Submarine Antiquities and the International Law of the Sea', p. 20. See, further, Chap. 1, section 2.1.3.

in any geographic zone of a coastal state's jurisdiction'.[19] It is certainly true that the provision is general and vague, providing no guidance as to what the duties comprise, or how they should be fulfilled.[20] It is also true, as Blumberg pointed out, that Article 303(1) does not in itself create specific regulatory competence. Nonetheless, as the discussion below will show, there are ways that states can use competences otherwise available to them in order to protect UCH in all sea areas. Arguably, what Article 303(1) does do is to oblige states to be *active* in seeking ways to use the methods open to them under international law to protect UCH, wherever it might be located, both on an individual basis and collaboratively.[21]

Article 303(1) refers to states, rather than states parties. The extent to which this provision can be said to be representative of customary international law and, as such, binding on non-states parties to the LOSC is impossible to answer given that its normative content is uncertain. It is clear that many states do now take action of one form or another to

---

[19] Blumberg, 'International Protection of Underwater Cultural Heritage', p. 493.

[20] A comparison can be drawn between the general obligation to protect UCH in Art. 303(1) and a similar general obligation to protect and preserve the marine environment set out in Art. 192. Art. 192 is accompanied by a substantial number of detailed provisions (together with Art. 192, making up Part XII of the Convention) that provide flesh to the duty and clarification as to how it should be fulfilled. The Convention provides no such guidance with respect to Art. 303(1).

[21] The precise content and extent of the duty, and the degree to which it is enforceable in international law, are highly debatable. Scovazzi has suggested that '[a] State which knowingly destroyed or allowed the destruction of elements of the underwater cultural heritage would be responsible for a breach of the obligation to protect it': Scovazzi, 'The Protection of Underwater Cultural Heritage', p. 121. However, even the imputation of a duty as basic as this would require some qualification to take account of circumstances where other interests may take precedence. For example, it may be necessary for a state to take action to deal with a serious hazard posed by a historic shipwreck and, in the course of doing so, to damage or possibly even destroy the wreck. Implementation of the duty in these circumstances might entail ensuring that any damage to the wreck is minimised, or undertaking rescue archaeology in advance of destruction. Interestingly, the question of breach of the duty in Art. 303(1) has recently arisen before an international tribunal. In the M/V *Louisa* case, before the International Tribunal for the Law of the Sea (ITLOS), Saint Vincent and the Grenadines intitially claimed that the Kingdom of Spain had been excessive in its actions to protect UCH when it detained a vessel flying the flag of Saint Vincent and the Grenadines, operating in Spanish inshore waters under a permit to undertake marine scientific research, on the basis that the recovery of 'several cannon balls, some pieces of pottery, and a stone with a hole in it' (in the words of the applicant) was a violation of Spanish heritage legislation: see M/V *Louisa*, ITLOS Case No. 18 (quotations from the Request for the Prescription of Provisional Measures of 23 November 2010, pp. 20–1). Later, the applicant asserted that it was not in fact 'claiming a substantive right under Art. 303' and that the previous reference to Art. 303 had been a 'typographical error'. See, further, Chap. 10, section 4.

protect UCH, including that located extra-territorially, but the extent to which they do so because they believe they are under a *legal obligation* to do so is debatable.[22] Having said that, there is little doubt that one of the major non-parties to the LOSC – the USA – regards Article 303(1) as a significant obligation.[23]

3.2   Maritime spaces subject to coastal state sovereignty

According to Article 2(1) of the LOSC:

> The sovereignty of a coastal State extends, beyond its land territory and internal waters and, in the case of an archipelagic State, its archipelagic waters, to an adjacent belt of sea, described as the territorial sea.

Sovereignty over the territorial sea is exercised subject to the provisions of the LOSC and to other rules of international law.[24] In particular, it is subject to the right of innocent passage that the ships of all states enjoy through the territorial sea.[25] The LOSC establishes the maximum breadth of the territorial sea as twelve miles from baselines.[26]

Landward of its territorial sea limits the coastal state enjoys exclusive jurisdiction over all matters, subject to the restrictions on sovereignty referred to above. This means that, subject to those restrictions, it is free to legislate in any way it sees fit to protect UCH.[27] Inshore areas are likely

---

[22] In other words, one of the two requisite elements for the creation of customary international law, *opinio juris*, may not be present: see General introduction, section 3.2.2, above. The participation of as many as ninety states at the UNESCO negotiations is perhaps the best evidence of widespread recognition that protection of UCH is a matter of both individual and collective state responsibility and it is possible that the very existence of the UNESCO Convention 2001, and the enhanced profile it gives to the question of UCH protection, will foster in all states an increasing sense of legal obligation with respect to UCH protection.

[23] The USA was in fact responsible for the proposal for a general duty to protect UCH to be included in the LOSC: see Chap. 1, section 2.1.2. As will be seen below, the USA has made considerable efforts to protect UCH, including that lying beyond its territorial limits, and has sought to act cooperatively with other states in this regard. When it intervened on behalf of Spain in the *Mercedes* case (see Chap. 4, section 2.3.2), it referred to its 'duty [under international law] to protect cultural resources found at sea and to cooperate with other nations in safeguarding them': 'Statement of Interest and Brief of the United States as *Amicus Curiae* in Support of the Kingdom of Spain', 27 August 2009.

[24] LOSC, Art. 2(3).

[25] LOSC, Art. 17. For the rules on innocent passage, see LOSC, Part II, section 3.

[26] LOSC, Art. 3.

[27] Caflisch has pointed out that the right of innocent passage has 'no direct bearing' on the matter of UCH: Caflisch, 'Submarine Antiquities and the International Law of the Sea', pp. 10–11. However, another restriction that has more bearing is that relating to sovereign immunity: see Chap. 4, sections 2.1 and 2.2.

to be particularly rich in UCH of all types and therefore it is clearly important that this material is afforded appropriate protection. As previously discussed,[28] many states have exercised jurisdiction in this regard and it can be argued that – by virtue of Article 303(1) – they are under a duty to do so.

States that are entitled to draw up 'archipelagic baselines' under Part IV of the LOSC,[29] such as Indonesia and the Philippines, have sovereignty over their archipelagic waters, as well as the territorial sea and internal waters.[30] In the context of UCH protection, the legal status of archipelagic waters is significant because they can be very extensive areas, crisscrossed by important historical trading routes.

3.3   The contiguous zone

The contiguous zone is a twelve-mile strip of water lying immediately adjacent to the territorial sea. In the general scheme of ocean space, it represents a relatively small geographical area, but in the context of UCH it is important because the *only* UCH-specific jurisdictional tool afforded to coastal states by the LOSC applies to this zone.

Article 303(2) of the LOSC provides:

In order to control traffic [in objects of an archaeological and historical nature], the coastal State may, in applying article 33, presume that their removal from the seabed in the zone referred to in that article without its approval would result in an infringement within its territory or territorial sea of the laws and regulations referred to in that article.[31]

To understand the meaning of this provision, one needs to consider it alongside the provision to which it refers, Article 33. This provides:

1. In a zone contiguous to its territorial sea, described as the contiguous zone, the coastal State may exercise the control necessary to:
   (a) prevent infringement of its customs, fiscal, immigration or sanitary laws and regulations within its territory or territorial sea;
   (b) punish infringement of the above laws and regulations committed within its territory or territorial sea.

---

[28] See, in particular, General introduction, section 1.3 and Chap. 2, section 2.

[29] See General introduction, section 2.2.2, above.

[30] See LOSC, Art. 49. The sovereignty of an archipelagic state over its archipelagic waters is exercised subject to Part IV of the treaty, which accords foreign vessels the right of innocent passage and a right of archipelagic sea lanes passage. Caflisch has pointed out that neither of these rights has a 'direct bearing' on the matter of UCH: Caflisch, 'Submarine Antiquities and the International Law of the Sea', pp. 10–11.

[31] For the historical development of this provision, see Chap. 1, section 2.1.2.

2. The contiguous zone may not extend beyond 24 nautical miles from the baselines from which the breadth of the territorial sea is measured.[32]

So, what does Article 303(2) permit the coastal state to do? This is a question that has been the subject of much academic reflection. Uncertainty about the matter arises not simply from the fact that the wording of the provision itself, and of the provision to which it refers, is somewhat tortuous. It also arises because the question is politically controversial. It is clear that the jurisdiction afforded to coastal states over the contiguous zone by virtue of Article 33 was intended to be tightly limited. It covers only the four functions specifically referred to in the article: matters relating to customs, taxation, immigration and sanitation. It also provides *enforcement* jurisdiction only. On the other hand, the provision in Article 303(2) represented a concession to states which had called for full coastal state jurisdiction over UCH on the continental shelf and therefore it was clearly intended to provide at least some degree of coastal state control over activities taking place in the more limited area of the contiguous zone.

Under Article 33, a state may, within its contiguous zone, enforce the customs, fiscal, immigration and sanitary laws that are applicable to its territory and territorial sea. In other words, the state is given the power to take action in the contiguous zone which will prevent the infringement *within its territory or territorial sea* of the laws referred to; it may also take action in the contiguous zone to punish those that commit such infringements. What the coastal state cannot do under Article 33 is to create laws and regulations applicable to the contiguous zone itself. In other words, Article 33 accords it no *legislative* jurisdiction within the zone. This means that it cannot legislate to regulate or prohibit activities (relating to the four matters referred to in the article) taking place in the zone itself.

While Article 303(2) is tied in with Article 33, it is a rather different creature. At least in part, this is because it is based on a 'legal fiction'.[33] Under the provision, the coastal state is allowed to presume that the removal of UCH from the seabed in the contiguous zone without its approval *would* amount to a breach of the laws and regulations applicable in its territory and territorial sea relating to customs, fiscal, immigration

---

[32] Art. 33 of the LOSC is based on Art. 24 of the 1958 Geneva Convention on the Territorial Sea and the Contiguous Zone, although under the 1958 Convention the maximum extent of the contiguous zone was twelve miles from baselines.

[33] For the meaning of a legal fiction, see Chap. 1, section 2.1.2.

and sanitary matters. The fiction itself is actually twofold: first of all, an offence that is committed in the contiguous zone may be treated *as if* it took place in the territorial sea; secondly, although there is little likelihood that removal of UCH from the seabed (even if took place *within* the territorial sea) would amount to a breach of the laws referred to, nonetheless it can be treated *as though* it was such a breach.[34] It was for the sake of political expediency that Article 303(2) was annexed to the provision in Article 33.[35] However, an unfortunate consequence of this annexation is that it has created uncertainty about exactly what Article 303(2) permits a state to do. The core uncertainty is whether Article 303(2) – like Article 33 – affords only enforcement jurisdiction, or whether it goes further and affords legislative jurisdiction.

One view, which will be referred to here as the restrictive view, is that Article 303(2) allows a state to treat removal of UCH from the seabed in the contiguous zone as though it was an infringement of its customs, fiscal, immigration and sanitary laws applicable to its territory, including its territorial sea. Article 303(2) refers specifically to the 'removal' of objects from the seabed 'in the zone referred to' and there seems little doubt that it provides a mechanism for the coastal state to control such removal (with the object of controlling 'traffic' in such objects).[36] However, under the restrictive viewpoint, such control should be treated as the *enforcement* of laws applicable to its territory and should not be exercised by means of legislation in respect of the contiguous zone itself.[37] Even under this restrictive view, a subtle but crucial distinction between Article 303(2) and Article 33 needs to be noted: while Article 33 only permits the coastal state to prevent or punish infringements taking place within the twelve-mile territorial sea, Article 303(2) permits a

---

[34] The protection of heritage *in situ* is a matter very largely unrelated to customs, fiscal, immigration and sanitary laws. Once heritage items are *removed* from their location and attempts are made to import them into, or export them from, a state, customs or fiscal regulations may become relevant.

[35] See Oxman, 'Marine Archaeology and the International Law of the Sea', p. 363.

[36] Aust, for example, states: 'a wreck in the contiguous zone is assimilated to one found in the territorial sea, and the coastal state can require its approval to remove the wreck': Aust, *Handbook of International Law*, p. 300.

[37] According to Oxman, the whole aim of the fiction in Art. 303(2) was to avoid 'converting the contiguous zone from an area where the coastal State has limited enforcement competence to one where it has legislative competence': Oxman, 'The Third United Nations Conference on the Law of the Sea', p. 240. The view that Art. 303(2) provides only enforcement jurisdiction is supported by some academic commentators: see, for example, Brown, 'Protection of the Underwater Cultural Heritage', pp. 329–30 and Long, *Marine Resources Law*, p. 533.

coastal state to take action to regulate certain activities taking place in the contiguous zone itself.[38]

Where some commentators take a more liberal view is on the question of whether or not Article 303(2) affords states *legislative* competence in respect of UCH in the contiguous zone – in other words, whether they can apply their heritage laws directly to this area. Strati, for example, has suggested that it is the combination of the jurisdictional mechanism in Article 303(2) *and* the duty to protect in Article 303(1) that together 'in substance' provide the authorisation for a state to extend its heritage laws to the contiguous zone.[39] She argues that this enables them to establish a twenty-four-mile 'archaeological zone' distinct from the general contiguous zone.[40]

In fact the two viewpoints are merely a reflection of a constructive ambiguity in the provision, designed to accommodate different viewpoints.[41] Nonetheless, if one accepts that Article 303(2) permits a coastal state to control activities taking place in the contiguous zone itself – which the wording of the provision surely obliges one to do – it is difficult to see how this can be implemented in practice without reference to an appropriate legislative framework. Legislation relating to customs, fiscal, immigration and sanitary matters is self-evidently inappropriate. Reference to heritage laws applicable in the territorial sea would be more appropriate, but it must be borne in mind that the jurisdiction afforded by Article 303(2) is limited: the state is permitted to take action only in so far as it relates to controlling *removal* of objects from the seabed and the *trafficking* of objects. Institution of a permit system in respect of archaeological excavation or other recovery activities would appear to be permissible, but other measures found in heritage legislation designed to protect UCH in the territorial sea may be more questionable.[42]

[38] For the nature of measures that could be taken, see Brown, *The International Law of the Sea*, Vol. I, p. 135.

[39] Strati, *The Protection of the Underwater Cultural Heritage*, p. 168.

[40] *Ibid.* Strati also argues that there is no need for the declaration of a general contiguous zone before the application of Art. 303(2), arguing that Art. 303(2) has 'an independent character that enables its autonomous declaration': *ibid.*, pp. 168–9.

[41] See Chap. 1, section 2.1.2.

[42] For example, Le Gurun has pointed out that the French provision for the contiguous zone refrains from providing for state ownership of maritime cultural assets (something provided for in the French territorial sea) because this would be 'viewed as exceeding the opportunity offered by article 303(2)': Le Gurun, 'France' (2nd edn), pp. 75–7. This view is probably correct because provision for state ownership is not a measure directly connected to the *removal* of UCH (although it seems that some states, for example

To what degree is the more liberal viewpoint supported by state practice? Contiguous zones do not exist automatically but need to be claimed by the coastal state.[43] The latest table of claims to maritime jurisdiction published by the UN suggests that more than eighty states have exercised this right,[44] but there is no official collation of details of the usage to which the zone is put. However, it seems that in recent years a growing number of states are establishing a contiguous zone with UCH specifically in mind.[45]

Within Europe, Denmark may have been the first state to make use of Article 303(2) when it introduced legislative provision in 1984 to the effect that underwater monuments, including shipwrecks over 100 years old, located within twenty-four miles, could not be damaged or removed without authority.[46] France also implemented Article 303(2) at a relatively early stage, in its Law of 1989.[47] In 1992, Spain proclaimed a

Denmark and South Africa, do claim ownership of UCH in the contiguous zone: see, further, below). Many other typical heritage protection measures can be justified on the basis that they relate in one way or another to preventing unauthorised removal of, or trafficking in, objects. For instance, Le Gurun has pointed out that a reporting duty can be justified on the basis that it is easier to control traffic in UCH if its existence is known: ibid., p. 76. (It has sometimes been argued that provisions that are designed merely to protect UCH from inadvertent damage or interference would be inappropriate. However, bearing in mind that the contiguous zone will fall under the continental shelf and EEZ regimes, such provisions may be justifiable under those regimes, rather than under Art. 303(2). See, further, section 4, below.)

[43] See General introduction, section 2.2.2, above. Various commentators, including Strati, argue that a state does not need to declare a contiguous zone for the purposes of Art. 33 prior to exercising jurisdiction over UCH under Art. 303(2). See Strati, *The Protection of the Underwater Cultural Heritage*, pp. 168–9. However, as far as it is possible to tell, it seems that the majority of states do declare a contiguous zone before exercising jurisdiction under Art. 303(2).

[44] DOALOS, Table of Claims to Maritime Jurisdiction as at 15 July 2011 (available at www.un.org/Depts/los/LEGISLATIONANDTREATIES/claims.htm).

[45] At the time of writing, the UK has not declared a contiguous zone. However, there appears to be an intention to do so when a suitable legislative opportunity arises. (It is interesting to note that a draft Heritage Protection Bill of 2008 (yet to be enacted) made provision enabling the future amendment of the definition of UK waters in the Act to include the contiguous zone. See s. 226(4) of the draft Bill.)

[46] The Danish Museum Act of 2001 (as amended) goes further and makes provision for reporting of finds and state ownership of everything reported. Denmark did not formally declare a contiguous zone until 2005. Despite some question regarding the impact of the 2005 Law on the Contiguous Zone on the formerly established 'heritage protection zone' (see Strati, 'Protection of the Underwater Cultural Heritage', p. 30, including nn. 24 and 25), it seems that the official Danish text of the Law makes it 'crystal clear' that the Law simply formalises the 'heritage protection zone' and does not alter or abolish it: personal communication with Thijs Maarleveld, 17 March 2010.

[47] Law No. 89-874, now consolidated in the 2004 Code for Heritage. As Le Gurun points out, France implemented Art. 303(2) prior to its ratification of the LOSC in 1996: Le Gurun, 'France' (2nd edn), p. 77.

contiguous zone and its heritage laws apply by implication to the twelve- to twenty-four-mile area.[48] In 2004, Norway made a similar proclamation and announced a prohibition on the destruction or removal of material in the contiguous zone that would be subject to protection by the heritage legislation applicable to its territorial sea.[49] In the same year, without formally declaring a contiguous zone, Italy introduced a legislative measure providing that archaeological objects in the twelve- to twenty-four-mile zone are to be treated in accordance with internationally accepted archaeological standards.[50] In 2005, the Netherlands established a contiguous zone and, in 2007, extended its monuments legislation to apply – at least in part – to the zone.[51]

With the exception of Norway, the states referred to above assert legislative competence of one sort or another over UCH in the contiguous zone. Outside of Europe, there are also examples of states that have taken action in fairly recent years and again these show that a legislative approach is favoured. For example, since 1994, South Africa has exercised legislative competence over a 'maritime cultural zone' co-extensive with its contiguous zone and expressly exerts 'the same rights and powers' in this zone as it does in respect of UCH in its territorial sea.[52] Most interesting of all is the position of the USA. In 1999, President Clinton proclaimed a contiguous zone, stating that the extension was 'an important step in preventing the removal of cultural heritage found

---

[48] See Aznar-Gómez, 'Spain', pp. 277 and 284. As we will see below (section 4.1), Spanish heritage legislation expressly applies to the continental shelf and, therefore, by implication to the contiguous zone. Legislation making specific provision for the recovery of archaeological objects in the contiguous zone has been under consideration in the Spanish Parliament: personal communication with Mariano Aznar-Gómez, 23 March 2010.

[49] See Kvalø and Marstrander, 'Norway', pp. 221, 223 and 225.

[50] The legislation refers specifically to the Rules in the Annex to the UNESCO Convention 2001: Article 94 of the Italian Cultural Code (Legislative Decree 42/2004). Personal communication with Nicola Ferri, 10 March 2010.

[51] The Act on Archaeological Heritage Management, published on 6 February 2007, amends the Dutch Monuments Act 1988. The amendments require reporting and permits for archaeological excavation in the twelve- to twenty-four-mile zone. Personal communication with Thijs Maarleveld, 17 March 2010. See also Maarleveld, 'The Netherlands', p. 172.

[52] Maritime Zones Act No. 15 of 1994, s. 6. See Forrest, 'South Africa', p. 256. This includes blanket protection for all wrecks over sixty years of age, the assertion of state ownership of all such material, and the institution of a permit system for all activities that might disturb, damage or destroy such material. For details, see *ibid.*, pp. 267 *et seq.*

within 24 nautical miles of the baseline'.[53] In light of the fact that the USA already had legislation in place affording protection to cultural resources out to 200 miles, which provides for a permit system in respect of the removal of, or injury to, such resources,[54] it regarded the proclamation as an aid to enforcement of that pre-existing legislation against foreign flag vessels and nationals in the twelve- to twenty-four-mile zone.[55] It therefore also exercises *legislative* jurisdiction in this zone under the authority of Article 303(2).

From the limited information available, it seems that an increasing number of states are turning to the Article 303(2) mechanism to afford some level of protection to UCH in their coastal waters and also it seems that, generally speaking, they are asserting both legislative and enforcement competence. It is interesting to note that their actions do not appear to have given rise to protest. Furthermore, among the states concerned are France, the Netherlands and the USA, all of which are vocal opponents of creeping jurisdiction. Certainly there appears to be no evidence that the usage is leading to the legislative approach being extended to the matters referred to in Article 33 and, for those concerned about jurisdictional 'creep', that should be reassuring.[56] However, it seems that Caflisch may have been prescient when, in 1982, he commented that the 'practical effect' of Article 303(2) 'will be to extend coastal state legislative competence to the 24-mile limit as far as submarine antiquities are concerned'.[57]

Given the permissive nature of Article 303(2), it is difficult to argue that states are under a *duty* to utilise the jurisdiction it affords them in light of their general duty under Article 303(1). Nevertheless, states

---

[53] Presidential Proclamation 7219 of August 2, 1999: The Contiguous Zone of the United States, 64 Fed. Reg. 48,701 (September 9, 1999).

[54] Title III of the Marine, Protection, Research and Sanctuaries Act of 1972, 16 USC s. 1431 *et seq.* See, further, sections 4.2.1 and 4.2.2, below.

[55] Personal communication with Ole Varmer, US National Oceanic and Atmospheric Administration, 9 March 2010. For further details, see Varmer, 'United States', pp. 363 and 382–3. As Varmer points out, the USS *Monitor* is located approximately seventeen miles offshore and is therefore a direct beneficiary of the contiguous zone proclamation.

[56] In fact, in relation to the contiguous zone the main concern is any sign of functional creep to the matter of security, rather than usage of the zone under Art. 303(2): see Roach, *United States Responses to Excessive Maritime Claims*, p. 166.

[57] Caflisch, 'Submarine Antiquities and the International Law of the Sea', p. 24. Churchill and Lowe also make the point that, under the LOSC, the contiguous zone is part of the EEZ (assuming the coastal state claims an EEZ) and therefore no longer part of the high seas. Therefore the former presumption against coastal state jurisdiction in the zone is removed, making it easier to defend claims to both enforcement and legislative jurisdiction. Churchill and Lowe, *The Law of the Sea*, p. 139.

should consider the benefits of using this jurisdictional tool: even taking the simple step of making a statement such as that by President Clinton in 1999 sends a clear signal that the state is committed to protecting UCH and will make full use of the authority available to it under international law to do so.

3.4   The continental shelf and the exclusive economic zone

One of the fundamental elements of the overall package deal established in the LOSC was that coastal states were afforded the right to claim an exclusive economic zone (EEZ) of 200 miles, to complement already firmly established rights in respect of the continental shelf. In both these maritime zones the coastal state is afforded sovereign rights[58] and juris-diction relating to natural resources. The two zones taken together represent a significant ocean space, a proportion approaching 50 per cent of the entire oceans.[59]

Part V of the LOSC sets out the regime for the EEZ and Part VI that for the continental shelf. As discussed earlier,[60] the continental shelf and EEZ regimes are closely intertwined, as are Parts V and VI. However, where states claim an EEZ, the two regimes will apply in tandem to the area out to 200 miles from baselines.[61] In the case of broad-margin states, Part VI makes provision for the outer continental shelf (OCS) – in other words, the physical continental margin beyond 200 miles.[62] (As many states do claim an EEZ,[63] unless otherwise indicated the following discussion assumes that the two regimes apply in tandem.)

---

[58] It is important to distinguish the 'sovereign rights' attributed to the coastal state in respect of its continental shelf and EEZ from the full sovereignty that a coastal state has over its internal waters, territorial sea and archipelagic waters. In contrast with the full or 'plenary' jurisdiction which comes with sovereignty, the sovereign rights of a coastal state in the EEZ and on the continental shelf are limited *functionally*, to the specific purposes provided for in the relevant parts of the LOSC (Parts V and VI).

[59] This very rough estimate is based on figures cited by Prescott and Schofield that suggest that the Area (in other words the seabed and its subsoil beyond national jurisdiction) accounts for approximately 50.5 per cent of the oceans and that the total ocean surface covered by territorial sea (which is not part of the EEZ or continental shelf) is perhaps less than 1 per cent: see Prescott and Schofield, *Maritime Political Boundaries of the World*, pp. 30 and 33.

[60] See General introduction, section 2.2.2, above.   [61] See LOSC, Art. 56(3).

[62] For the definition of the juridical continental shelf and an explanation of the term 'broad-margin States', see General introduction, section 2.2.2, above.

[63] See DOALOS, Table of Claims to Maritime Jurisdiction as at 15 July 2011 (available at www.un.org/Depts/los/LEGISLATIONANDTREATIES/claims.htm). The table illustrates that it is not just states parties to the LOSC that claim an EEZ. Both the USA and Turkey, for example, do so.

Article 56 of Part V sets out the rights, jurisdiction and duties of the coastal state in its EEZ. The key paragraph of Article 56 is paragraph 1, which provides:

In the exclusive economic zone, the coastal State has:

(a) sovereign rights for the purpose of exploring and exploiting, conserving and managing the natural resources, whether living or non-living, of the waters superjacent to the seabed and of the seabed and its subsoil, and with regard to other activities for the economic exploitation and exploration of the zone, such as the production of energy from the water, currents and winds;

(b) jurisdiction as provided for in the relevant provisions of this Convention with regard to:

   (i) the establishment and use of artificial islands, installations and structures;

   (ii) marine scientific research;

   (iii) the protection and preservation of the marine environment;

(c) other rights and duties provided for in this Convention.

As far as the OCS is concerned, the rights of the coastal state are set out in Article 77 of Part VI, which makes provision in respect of the continental shelf simpliciter (in other words, where it does not coexist with an EEZ).[64] Article 77(1) provides:

The coastal State exercises over the continental shelf sovereign rights for the purpose of exploring and exploiting its natural resources.

The natural resources referred to in Article 77 are natural resources relating to the seabed and its subsoil, namely mineral and other non-living resources, together with sedentary species, such as corals, sponges, oysters and clams.[65]

The rights and jurisdiction of the coastal state under Articles 56 and 77 will be considered in more detail below.[66] For the moment, it is suffice to note that – within 200 miles – a coastal state that has declared an EEZ is afforded rights and jurisdiction in respect of natural resources, specifically rights in relation to the exploration, exploitation, conservation and

---

[64] Art. 77 therefore applies within 200 miles in cases where the coastal state does not claim an EEZ.

[65] See LOSC, Art. 77(4). Exactly what counts as a sedentary species, in other words, 'organisms which, at the harvestable stage, either are immobile on or under the seabed or are unable to move except in constant physical contact with the seabed or the subsoil' is a matter of some debate: see, for example, Churchill and Lowe, *The Law of the Sea*, pp. 151–2 and 156, including n. 36.

[66] See section 4.2.

management of such resources and with regard to other activities for the economic exploitation and exploration of such resources,[67] as well as jurisdiction over several matters relating thereto, namely the establishment and use of artificial islands, installations and structures; marine scientific research; and the protection and preservation of the marine environment.[68] In 1956, the International Law Commission (ILC) made clear its view that shipwrecks were not natural resources and that view has been generally accepted ever since.[69]

The LOSC makes no specific provision for UCH located on the continental shelf or in the EEZ beyond twenty-four miles. As noted above, proposals to give coastal states such rights were explicitly rejected. The basic international legal regime governing the search for, and recovery of, shipwrecks and other UCH beyond twenty-four miles is therefore dependent on the fundamental juridical (in other words, legal) nature of these zones. As far as the continental shelf simpliciter is concerned, the juridical status of the zone is high seas.[70] As a result, there is a presumption in favour of the exercise of high seas freedoms and the search for, and recovery of, UCH are regarded as within these freedoms.[71] There is, however, a significant difference with respect to the situation in the EEZ. Here the juridical status of the zone is *sui generis*: it is neither high seas nor is it an area over which the coastal state has

---

[67] While Art. 56(1) does not explicitly state that the rights 'with regard to other activities for the economic exploitation and exploration of the zone' are limited to natural resources and other natural features of the zone, this is widely accepted to be the case in light of the negotiating history of the Convention. In the words of Oxman, '[the phrase] is qualified by the words "such as", which introduce the reference to the production of energy from the water, currents and winds. ... It would not be reasonable to construe these words as embracing wrecked ships or marine archaeology': Oxman, 'Marine Archaeology and the International Law of the Sea', p. 366. See also Strati, *The Protection of the Underwater Cultural Heritage*, p. 264.

[68] It should be noted that the reference in Art. 56(1)(c) to 'other rights and duties provided for in this Convention' appears to be a reference mainly to the provisions in the LOSC relating to the contiguous zone and to the right of hot pursuit: see Churchill and Lowe, *The Law of the Sea*, p. 169.

[69] See Chap. 1, section 2.1. The ILC's pronouncement on this matter will be returned to again at the end of this book: see Final reflections.

[70] The continental shelf comprises the seabed and subsoil, not the water column above, which constitutes high seas and, as such, is governed by the high seas regime set out in Part VII: see Art. 86.

[71] Part VII of the LOSC sets out the regime for the high seas. Art. 87 of that Part provides that '[t]he high seas are open to all States' and then goes on to set out a list of freedoms which do not relate to the search for, and recovery of, UCH. However, the list is non-exhaustive and the freedoms cover any legitimate uses of the seas not otherwise provided for. See, further, Churchill and Lowe, *The Law of the Sea*, pp. 205–6. The freedoms must be exercised with 'due regard' for the interests of other states: Art. 87(2).

sovereignty (which would give rise to a presumption in favour of coastal state jurisdiction). Instead, the relative rights of the coastal state and the international community as a whole are governed by the specific provisions of Part V of the treaty, which sets out the regime for the EEZ. Since Part V does not attribute the right to search for and recover UCH to either the coastal state or to other states, it is regarded as an 'unattributed' right.[72] As such, any dispute relating to these activities must be resolved under an 'elusive' formula set out in Article 59 of Part V.[73]

Under the Article 59 formula:

[conflicts] should be resolved on the basis of equity and in the light of all the relevant circumstances, taking into account the respective importance of the interests involved to the parties as well as to the international community as a whole.[74]

This means that when a conflict arises between two states with respect to activities in the EEZ, all the relevant factors need to be weighed up on a case-by-case basis. On matters relating to access to UCH sites, Strati has suggested that the following factors are relevant:

(a) the existence of a cultural link between the cultural property in question and one of the parties of the dispute; (b) in case of relatively recent wrecks, the qualification of one of the parties as the flag State of the sunken vessel; (c) the accommodation of the interests of the international community in the protection and preservation of the underwater cultural property; (d) interference with the exercise of the rights of the coastal or flag States.[75]

Another commentator has suggested that where a dispute relates to the exploration and exploitation of natural resources, it should probably be resolved in favour of the coastal state; where, on the other hand, it relates to other matters, then the interests of other states – or of the international community as a whole – would be favoured.[76] If this is the case, in circumstances where activities targeting UCH are the cause of concern to the coastal state, if it can be shown that they represent a potential threat to its legitimate economic interests in the zone, for example if the party undertaking the activities is engaged in gathering significant quantities of survey data about the seabed and subsoil of the

---

[72] Churchill and Lowe, *The Law of the Sea*, p. 175.   [73] *Ibid.*, p. 461.
[74] LOSC, Art. 59. Arguably, in areas of the EEZ within the twenty-four-mile limit, Art. 59 would not apply with respect to disputes involving activities targeting UCH because – by virtue of Art. 303(2) – the coastal state is attributed the right to control recovery activity: see section 3.3, above.
[75] Strati, *The Protection of the Underwater Cultural Heritage*, p. 266. For an interesting and detailed discussion of Art. 59 in the context of UCH, see *ibid.*, pp. 265–6 and 268–9.
[76] Nordquist *et al.*, *United Nations Convention on the Law of the Sea 1982*, Vol. II, p. 569.

EEZ,[77] this would seem to be a strong factor weighing in favour of the coastal state's interests taking priority. Even if the activities pose no such threat, in light of the duty in Article 303(1) on states to protect UCH in all sea areas, the interests of the coastal state and those of the international community as a whole may well be seen to coincide. Again this would suggest a resolution of the dispute in favour of the coastal state.

It is clear that the LOSC makes no direct provision for coastal state jurisdiction over UCH in the EEZ and on the continental shelf beyond twenty-four miles. However, the extent to which states have unilaterally exercised such jurisdiction is a matter that will be considered later in this chapter.[78]

3.5   Beyond the limits of national jurisdiction

As previously noted,[79] one of the primary purposes of the LOSC was to establish an international regime for the mineral resources of the deep seabed in order to ensure that they were exploited equitably and in the interests of all mankind. The Convention therefore established an entirely new maritime zone, the 'Area', which it defines as 'the seabed and ocean floor and subsoil thereof, beyond the limits of national jurisdiction'.[80] It also established an international authority, the International Seabed Authority (ISA), to administer the Area and its resources on behalf of states parties.

Detailed provision for the Area is made in Part XI of the LOSC.[81] As with the continental shelf simpliciter, it needs to be borne in mind that the Area is the seabed itself and its subsoil, and the concept does not apply to the water column above. The superjacent waters retain their status as high seas and fall under the high seas regime set out in Part VII of the Convention.[82] This regime is therefore operative subject to the specific regime in Part XI governing the exploration and exploitation of the mineral resources of the zone.

Article 149 of Part XI makes specific provision for UCH in the Area:

All objects of an archaeological and historical nature found in the Area shall be preserved or disposed of for the benefit of mankind as a whole, particular regard

---

[77] On this matter, see, further, section 4.2.2, below.
[78] See section 4.2, below.   [79] See General introduction, section 2.2.1, above.
[80] LOSC, Art. 1(1)(1). '[B]eyond the limits of national jurisdiction' means beyond the limits of the juridical continental shelf as defined by Art. 76(1) of the LOSC.
[81] It should be noted that Part XI is implemented as modified by the 1994 Agreement relating to the implementation of Part XI of the United Nations Convention on the Law of the Sea of 10 December 1982.
[82] See LOSC, Arts. 86 and 135.

being paid to the preferential rights of the State or country of origin, or the State of cultural origin, or the State of historical and archaeological origin.

Several aspects of this article have been discussed in previous chapters.[83] Here the concern is with the question of the rights, jurisdiction and duties of states, as well as the ISA, in respect of UCH located beyond the limits of national jurisdiction. Again, the proportion of ocean space under discussion is substantial: roughly 50.5 per cent.[84]

Article 149 has been much criticised over the years and deservedly so. The most significant criticism is that it provides that things must be done without providing for *who* should do them, or *how* they should be done. By definition, the Area is 'beyond the limits of national jurisdiction'. There is nothing in Article 149 that accords any form of jurisdiction to individual states, or to states acting in concert, or that requires them to make use of general principles of international jurisdiction, in order to further the objectives of the article. The obvious candidate to be charged with responsibility for ensuring that Article 149 is implemented – the ISA – is not referred to by Article 149 and it is clear from the provisions of Part XI that its role is limited to controlling activities related to the exploration and exploitation of the mineral resources of the zone.[85] Proposals to extend its role to UCH were not taken up.[86] In consequence, Article 149 is essentially an empty shell.

---

[83] For discussion of the meaning of 'objects of an archaeological and historical nature', see Chap. 2, section 3.1; for discussion of the nature of the interests of 'mankind as a whole' and the 'preferential rights' referred to in Art. 149, see Chap. 3, section 4.1; for an outline of the historical development of the article, see Chap. 1, section 2.1.1.

[84] See Prescott and Schofield, *Maritime Political Boundaries of the World*, p. 30. Oxman suggested that at the time of UNCLOS III there was 'relatively slight concern' that much UCH would be found in this area: Oxman, 'The Third United Nations Conference on the Law of the Sea', p. 240. However, while the density of shipwrecks on the deep seabed might be less than in other maritime areas, it has been argued that those that do exist 'may be in an excellent state of preservation': O'Keefe, *Shipwrecked Heritage*, p. 95. Other forms of UCH that are likely to be found in the Area are aircraft wrecks and space debris.

[85] The ISA's functions are limited to controlling and organising 'activities' in the Area (Art. 157(1)), which are defined as 'activities of exploration for, and exploitation of, the resources of the Area' (Art. 1(1)(3)). The resources of the Area are defined to include only mineral resources (Art. 133(a)). It should be noted that as well as having the powers and functions expressly conferred upon it by the LOSC the ISA also has 'such incidental powers, consistent with [the LOSC], as are implicit in and necessary for the exercise of those powers and functions': Art. 157(2). Among other things, it has responsibilities with respect to the protection of the marine environment: see Art. 145.

[86] For details, see Hayashi, 'Archaeological and Historical Objects under the United Nations Convention on the Law of the Sea', pp. 292–3.

What, then, is the position as far as shipwrecks and other UCH located in the Area are concerned? As with the continental shelf simpliciter, there is a presumption in favour of the exercise of high seas freedoms, including the freedom to search for, and recover, UCH. However, it should be borne in mind that the general duty imposed on states by Article 303(1) to protect UCH and to cooperate for this purpose applies to the area beyond national jurisdiction, as it does to all other sea areas, and Article 149 provides a degree of flesh to this duty by providing that UCH found in the Area must be preserved or disposed of for the benefit of mankind and with regard to the preferential rights of states of origin. Therefore, in so far as states may have legitimate jurisdictional or other mechanisms available to them to take action in respect of UCH found in this zone, they must take cognisance of Article 149.[87] To date, circumstances do not appear to have arisen in which a shipwreck located in the Area has given rise to questions concerning the practical application of this provision.[88]

An activity in the Area that is potentially as significant – if not more significant – than unregulated activities targeting UCH, in terms of the likely damage or destruction to UCH that may arise, is deep seabed

---

[87] Mechanisms they may consider using are the nationality and territorial principles of jurisdiction and also, where applicable, the assertion of sovereign immunity and ownership rights. Indeed, the potential application of these measures to afford protection to UCH located in the Area gives rise to some interesting scenarios. For example, take the discovery of a shipwreck lying in the Area in which a state has ownership rights. One might argue that, by virtue of Art. 303(1), the state would have a duty to assert its rights before, say, a US federal admiralty court in the event of the initiation of an *in rem* salvage action with respect to the wreck. Assuming that the state was awarded the recovered material (a reasonable assumption given the landmark judgment in the *Juno* and *La Galga*, discussed in Chap. 4, section 2.3.1), the provisions of Art. 149 indicate that it must then ensure that the material is 'preserved or disposed of' for the benefit of mankind as a whole. In so far as one or more other states might come forward to claim some form of preferential rights, particular regard would need to be paid to these rights.

[88] It was by an accident of fate that the *Titanic* came to rest on the outer continental shelf of Canada, rather than the deep seabed. If it was located in the Area, the implications of Art. 149 may well have been explored more thoroughly by now. (Interestingly, the provisions of Art. 149 have been called in aid of a shipwreck that was *not* located in the Area: the *Mercedes* (see Chap. 4, section 2.3.2).) Given that the Area is, by definition, beyond the jurisdiction of any state, domestic heritage legislation generally does not refer to this zone. However, Chinese legislation is a notable exception. China claims to have an exclusive right to regulate UCH in the Area that originated from China. In commenting on this legislation, Fu concludes that China's position in this respect is justifiable under Art. 149, given that particular regard must be given to the preferential rights of states of origin: Fu, 'China (including Taiwan)', p. 35.

mining, along with operations associated with such mining. It is here that, in practice, the ISA is in a position to play a useful role. In implementing the regulatory framework for mineral exploration and exploitation set out in Part XI, the ISA can ensure that contractors take appropriate account of UCH in the course of their work. While commercial exploitation of the mineral resources of the Area probably remains unlikely for some time to come, a number of exploration licences have been issued and the ISA is developing a Mining Code to govern activities in respect of the mineral resources of the zone. In 2000, it adopted Regulations on Prospecting and Exploration for Polymetallic Nodules in the Area, which require that contractors notify the ISA of archaeological finds and take all reasonable measures to avoid disturbing such objects.[89] More recently it has developed sets of regulations relating to two other mineral resources, polymetallic sulphides and cobalt-rich crusts, and these include enhanced provisions in respect of UCH finds.[90]

4. Plugging the gap(s)

As pointed out in Chapter 1,[91] a geographical 'gap' in the specific provision the LOSC affords to UCH is frequently noted and that gap relates to the area between twenty-four miles and the outer extent of the juridical continental shelf (which forms the boundary with the Area). In this marine area (which, at a minimum, will be 176 miles in breadth and may be much more extensive)[92] deliberate interference with UCH is

---

[89] See Regulations on Prospecting and Exploration for Polymetallic Nodules in the Area, Reg. 34 (available at www.isa.org.jm). See also Reg. 8, which provides that those merely prospecting for nodules in the Area must also notify the ISA of archaeological finds.

[90] See Regulations on Prospecting and Exploration for Polymetallic Sulphides in the Area, adopted in 2010, and Regulations on Prospecting and Exploration for Cobalt-Rich Ferromanganese Crusts in the Area, adopted in 2012, Regs. 8 and 37 in both (available at www.isa.org.jm). It is significant that in all three sets of Regulations, the second of the two provisions relating to archaeological objects is located in Part V headed 'Protection and Preservation of the Marine Environment'. This suggests that the ISA may regard UCH as so intimately associated with the natural marine environment that it falls under its mandate to protect the marine environment under Art. 145. (As the ISA acts on behalf of states parties to the LOSC, one could also argue that this is an example of the implementation of Art. 303(1).) On the close physical link between the cultural and natural environment, see, further, section 4.2.1, below. On the relationship between the Mining Code and the UNESCO Convention 2001, see Chap. 10, section 3.2.

[91] See Chap. 1, section 2.1.3.

[92] By virtue of the definition of the juridical continental shelf set out in Art. 76 (see General introduction, section 2.2.2, above), the 'gap' will be at least 176 miles in breadth. In the case of broad margin states, it may be up to (and even beyond) 326 miles. (The rules for

subject to the general rules of the LOSC outlined above and neither Article 303(2) nor Article 149 will apply. Furthermore, given the absence of any means within the Convention for implementing the protective objectives set out in Article 149, in practice the actual jurisdictional gap can be regarded as *all* waters beyond twenty-four miles.

The question that arises is: how can states implement their duty under Article 303(1) to protect UCH and to cooperate for this purpose in the substantial proportion of the oceans that falls into the gap? This question is becoming of critical significance. Not only is the technology now available to search for, and locate, shipwrecks in deep waters, but in various parts of the world systematic search operations are already taking place over extensive areas of the continental shelf and there seems little doubt that these will extend to the deep seabed in the foreseeable future.[93]

4.1 Unilateral extensions

In a detailed survey of creeping jurisdiction published in 1991, Kwiatkowska reported that a number of states – among them, Australia, Cape Verde, Cyprus, Ireland, Morocco, Spain and the Seychelles – required prior consent for the removal of UCH on the continental shelf beyond twenty-four miles.[94] Generally, these unilateral extensions of jurisdiction preceded the adoption of the LOSC.[95] In noting the extensions, Kwiatkowska commented:

the delimitation of the outer limit of the continental shelf in cases where the outer edge of the continental margin extends beyond 200 miles from baselines are complex: see Art. 76(3)–(7).)

[93] The activities of OME illustrate current capabilities. In recent years, the company has conducted systematic search operations over thousands of square miles of seabed around the coasts of Europe. Apparently targeted discoveries include the eighteenth-century British warship HMS *Victory* (depth: 80 metres), the seventeenth-century British warship HMS *Sussex* (depth: 1,000 metres) and the Spanish colonial-era warship the *Mercedes* (depth: 1,100 metres). In 2010, the company announced that it had technology 'on the drawing board' that would extend its capabilities to 6,000 metres' depth: 'Odyssey Marine Exploration Announces 2009 Financial Results', OME press release, 10 March 2010 (available at www.shipwreck.net). It should be noted, too, that a wreck such as HMS *Victory* is well within the range of divers using specialised equipment (see General introduction, section 1.3, above).

[94] Kwiatkowska, 'Creeping Jurisdiction Beyond 200 Miles in the Light of the 1982 Law of the Sea Convention and State Practice', p. 163; see also Churchill and Lowe, *The Law of the Sea*, p. 175 n. 52.

[95] For details of some of the legislation, see Prott and O'Keefe, *Law and the Cultural Heritage*, Vol. I, pp. 95–7, 99, 107.

It thus cannot be excluded that the concept of an 'offshore cultural protection zone', coextensive even with the continental shelf or a 200-mile zone or both, will gain further support in the future.[96]

In fact, there have been few further extensions of this kind in recent years[97] and therefore the prospect that they would lead to the emergence in customary international law of a 'cultural protection zone' coextensive with the EEZ or continental shelf has not materialised. Nonetheless, most if not all of these states continue to have legislation on the statute book asserting control of UCH beyond twenty-four miles. For example, the Australian Historic Shipwrecks Act 1976 applies to 'waters adjacent to the coast of a state', which are defined by the Petroleum (Submerged Lands) Act 1967 to include waters out to a set of co-ordinates corresponding to the outer edge of the continental shelf.[98] In Ireland, Section 3 of the National Monuments (Amendment) Act 1987, which makes provision for the protection of wrecks and archaeological objects, applies to areas 'on, in or under the seabed to which section 2(1) of the Continental Shelf Act 1968 applies'.[99] The Spanish Law 16/1985 of 25 June 1985 requires authorisation for any activity directed at UCH on the continental shelf.[100] However, interestingly, there appear to be no examples of attempts by these states to

---

[96] Kwiatkowska, 'Creeping Jurisdiction Beyond 200 Miles in the Light of the 1982 Law of the Sea Convention and State Practice', p. 164.

[97] One exception is the Dominican Republic. It introduced legislation in 2007 which provides, among other things, that 'salvage operations with respect to treasures from ancient sunken vessels within the exclusive economic zone which constitute part of the National Cultural Heritage' ... 'shall be a national priority': for an interesting discussion of this provision, see Kopela, '2007 Archipelagic Legislation of the Dominican Republic', pp. 524–32. While it seems that earlier extensions were not subject to protest, Kopela notes that the provision in the Dominican Republic's 2007 Act was protested by the USA and the UK: *ibid.*, p. 524.

[98] Jeffery, 'Australia' (2nd edn), p. 3. Section 28 of the 1976 Act provides: 'Subject to the obligations of Australia under international law ... this Act extends according to its tenor to foreigners and to foreign ships'. It might therefore be argued that the Act only purports to apply to foreign flag vessels and nationals to the extent permitted by international law.

[99] See, further, O'Connor, 'Ireland' (2nd edn), p. 131; Long, *Marine Resources Law*, p. 547; Symmons, *Ireland and the Law of the Sea* (2nd edn), pp. 128–35. For an interesting discussion of the Irish government's decision not to make use of its legislation to place an underwater heritage order on the *Carpathia*, which is located on the Irish continental shelf beyond twenty-four miles, see O'Connor, 'Ireland' (2nd edn), pp. 142–3.

[100] See Espósito and Fraile, 'The UNESCO Convention on Underwater Cultural Heritage', p. 206 n. 22. See also Aznar-Gómez, 'Spain', p. 277 *et seq.*

enforce this legislation against foreign flag vessels and nationals operating beyond twenty-four miles.[101]

These unilateral extensions of jurisdiction are distinguishable from the more limited controls exercised by some states in the course of licensing natural resource exploration and exploitation activities in the EEZ and on the continental shelf. These controls are in fact more analogous to those exercised by the ISA in respect of mineral operations on the deep seabed. Greece and Norway were among the first states to include provision for the reporting, and subsequent treatment, of UCH discovered incidentally during offshore operations, and other states have followed.[102] Imposition of such permit conditions, together with pre-consent processes that take account of archaeological considerations, provide states with effective means to prevent or mitigate inadvertent damage and destruction by development activities in their offshore waters.[103] However, the question arises as to the lawfulness of these controls in so far as a state might seek to enforce them against foreign

[101] It is possible that the attempt of the Spanish authorities to apply Spain's heritage legislation to the proposed activities with respect to HMS *Sussex* (see Chap. 4, section 2.2) may be a case in point, although the precise location of the site has not been disclosed and it may be located within twenty-four miles of baselines.

[102] The Greek and Norwegian provision, dating back to the 1970s, relates to hydrocarbon exploration and exploitation: see Strati, *The Protection of the Underwater Cultural Heritage*, p. 261; see also Strati, 'Greece' (1st edn), p. 74; and Kvalø and Marstrander, 'Norway', pp. 223–4. It is interesting to note that the European Communities Hydrocarbon Licensing Directive 94/22 ([1994] OJ L164/3) provides that 'Member States may, to the extent justified by national security, public safety, public health, security of transport, protection of the environment, protection of biological resources and of *national treasures possessing artistic, historic or archaeological value* ... impose conditions and requirements on the exercise of' activities of prospecting, exploration and exploitation of hydrocarbons (Art. 6(2), emphasis added). (On this Directive, see, further, Long, *Marine Resources Law*, pp. 350 *et seq.*) In light of this, archaeological conditions on hydrocarbon licences – at least within Europe – may be more common than is generally supposed. It is certainly the case that Ireland and the Netherlands impose such conditions. Indeed, the reporting requirements in the Netherlands extend quite broadly across marine sectors, for example to include general geophysical survey and dredging: personal communication with Thijs Maarleveld, 26 April 2010. This type of provision should be distinguished from the voluntary reporting schemes adopted in some other states, for example the Joint Nautical Archaeology Policy Committee (JNAPC) Code of Practice for Seabed Development in the UK (available at www.jnapc.org.uk).

[103] The ratification and implementation by many European States of the Valletta Convention 1992, along with several European Union Directives relating to environmental impact assessment and strategic environmental assessment, has been instrumental in triggering government reviews of the relationship between archaeology and the development control process, including in respect of marine areas 'within the jurisdiction' of the state concerned (Valletta Convention, Art. 1(2)(iii)). On the Valletta Convention more generally, see Chap. 1, section 2.2.3.

operators. It might be argued that if the coastal state has the right to explore and exploit the natural resources of these zones, it can determine how these activities are carried out. However, the matter may not be quite as straightforward as this because, in both zones, due regard must be paid to the interests of other states.[104] Nonetheless, justification for the imposition of reasonable conditions designed to protect UCH may come in the form of the duty on states under Article 303(1) to afford protection to UCH: given the rate of commercial development of the offshore marine environment, it is vital that states are able to offer UCH protection of this nature.

4.2   Making full use of the Law of the Sea Convention provisions

In light of advances in technology over recent decades, the maritime area that is at most immediate risk of unregulated UCH recovery is the geological continental shelf.[105] Graduating to a depth of approximately 140 metres, this area is well within the reach of divers utilising sophisticated diving equipment, as well as commercial salvors utilising submersibles. For this reason, attention has been turning increasingly to the question of whether the rights and jurisdiction afforded to states with respect to the natural resources of their offshore areas could be utilised to better effect in the interests of UCH protection.

4.2.1   Protection of sovereign rights

As noted above, by virtue of Articles 56 and 77 respectively, a state has sovereign rights over the natural resources of its EEZ and continental shelf and is entitled to act, where necessary, to protect those rights (provided it does so with due regard to the interests of other states). In the course of so acting, it may also be able to afford some level of protection to UCH. Although wreck sites are not a natural resource in themselves, they are very often inextricably connected with such resources, especially with the passage of time. In some cases they may be partially or totally embedded in seabed deposits, such as sand and gravel. In many cases they act as magnets for living natural resources: fish congregate in and around wreck sites and various species of animals and plants attach themselves to wreck surfaces. Wrecks may therefore form artificial reefs, providing an attractive habitat for both fauna and

---

[104] See Arts. 56(2), 78(2) and 87(2).
[105] For the relationship between the geological continental shelf and the juridical continental shelf, see General introduction, section 2.2.2, above, including n. 41.

flora. In recent years research has shown that there is a strong relationship between wreck sites and marine life, and that such sites can be of considerable ecological value.[106] Interference with, or recovery of material from, a wreck will almost inevitably disturb or damage the living resources of both the water column and the seabed to some degree.[107] Certain shipwreck recovery methods also have the potential to damage mineral resources, for example the use of prop-wash deflectors[108] or explosives. Physical intervention on wreck sites may therefore interfere with the sovereign rights of the coastal state.[109]

Utilising the close relationship between wrecks and living resources to afford indirect protection to UCH beyond twenty-four miles is not a new idea. In 1984, O'Connell stated:

> Legislators have … a simple weapon to control the activities of marine archaeologists on the continental shelf, and that is to regulate the disturbance of the seabed. So a wreck site embedded in coral could be immunized by the expedient of forbidding interference with the coral, which is a 'natural resource' of the continental shelf.[110]

Interestingly, this idea is supported by one of the firmest adherents to the LOSC regime: the fact that it is a control mechanism tied firmly to the natural resources of the EEZ and continental shelf means that it has been positively promoted by the US State Department.[111] Probably the best example of state practice in this regard is the US National Marine Sanctuaries Act of 1972 (NMSA).[112] This statute provides for the

---

[106] See the reports on wrecks and ecology produced by Wessex Archaeology (available at www.wessexarch.co.uk/tags/coastal-and-marine).

[107] Within the EEZ, a coastal state has sovereign rights over all living resources. On the continental shelf simpliciter, interference would need to take place with sedentary species. For the meaning of sedentary species, see n. 65 above.

[108] According to Varmer, '[p]rop-wash deflectors (or 'mailboxes') can punch a hole in the seabed 30 feet across and several feet deep in hard packed sediment in fifteen seconds': Varmer, 'United States', p. 361.

[109] Questions arise, of course, regarding the degree of interference with living resources required. In some cases there may be a demonstrable adverse impact (see Blumberg, 'International Protection of Underwater Cultural Heritage', p. 495); in others the impact may be notional. However, as O'Keefe has argued, it is unlikely that any state would challenge action taken by another state to protect its sovereign rights: O'Keefe, *Shipwrecked Heritage*, p. 90.

[110] O'Connell, *The International Law of the Sea*, Vol. II, p. 918.

[111] See, for example, Blumberg, 'International Protection of Underwater Cultural Heritage', p. 495. Blumberg led the US delegation to the UNESCO negotiations.

[112] Title III of the Marine, Protection, Research and Sanctuaries Act of 1972, 16 USC sec. 1431 *et seq.* (as amended by Public Law 106-513, November 2000).

designation of areas of the marine environment as 'national marine sanctuaries' to 200 miles offshore.[113] Activities in each sanctuary are governed by a tailor-made set of regulations which are designed to protect the sanctuary's particular 'resources', among which may be 'historical', 'cultural' and 'archeological' resources.[114] According to Varmer,[115] the two activities prohibited by all the sanctuary regulations that assist particularly in the protection of UCH are the removal of, or injury to, sanctuary resources and any alteration of the seabed.[116]

4.2.2   Utilisation of jurisdictional rights

As well as providing the coastal state with sovereign rights over natural resources on the continental shelf and in the EEZ, the LOSC also provides it with jurisdiction for specific purposes related to these resources. To what extent can these jurisdictional rights be called in aid of UCH?

Two particular potential mechanisms for controlling activities directed at UCH have been identified.[117] First of all, Article 81 provides:

The coastal State shall have the exclusive right to authorize and regulate drilling on the continental shelf for *all purposes*.[118]

The term 'drilling' is not defined by the Convention and the extent to which it might cover excavation and other activities directed at UCH is unclear.[119] However, broadly interpreted, it could encompass any activities that probe or otherwise disturb the seabed, including digging or blowing, use of prop-wash deflectors and other similar devices, and perhaps even the use of explosives.

[113] Areas of the marine environment 'possess[ing] conservation, recreational, ecological, *historical*, scientific, educational, *cultural*, *archeological*, or esthetic qualities which give them special national, and in some cases international, significance' may be designated: 16 USC sec. 1431(a)(2), emphasis added. There are currently thirteen designated sanctuaries, the largest of which is almost 138,000 square miles. For details, see www.sanctuaries.noaa.gov.
[114] 16 USC sec. 1432(8). The extent to which shipwrecks and other UCH are regarded as integral and important sanctuary resources is apparent upon visiting the official sanctuaries website: www.sanctuaries.noaa.gov.
[115] See Varmer, 'United States', p. 363.
[116] For a detailed discussion of the operation of the NMSA in the context of UCH, including the question of enforcement of regulations against foreign flag vessels and nationals, see Varmer, 'United States', pp. 359–66.
[117] See, for example, Oxman, 'Marine Archaeology and the International Law of the Sea', pp. 369–70; Blumberg, 'International Protection of Underwater Cultural Heritage', pp. 495–6; Varmer, 'A Perspective from Across the Atlantic', p. 25.
[118] Emphasis added.
[119] Blumberg, 'International Protection of Underwater Cultural Heritage', p. 496.

Secondly, by virtue of Article 60(1):

In the exclusive economic zone, the coastal State shall have the exclusive right to construct and to authorize and regulate the construction, operation and use of:

(a) artificial islands;
(b) installations and structures for the purposes provided for in article 56 and other economic purposes;
(c) installations and structures which may interfere with the exercise of the rights of the coastal State in the zone.

By virtue of Article 80, this provision also applies *mutatis mutandis* to artificial islands, installations and structures on the continental shelf. Where those targeting UCH make use of equipment constituting an 'installation' or 'structure',[120] either for economic purposes or in such a way as interferes with the exercise by the coastal state of its rights in the EEZ or on the continental shelf, again it would seem to fall within the coastal state's regulatory competence.[121]

Oxman has suggested that, at least in some cases, the impact of these mechanisms, taken together, 'may be so substantial that the coastal state will be in an effective position to determine whether, and if so under what conditions, marine archaeology may occur'.[122] In fact, to date it seems that the USA may be the state that has taken fullest advantage of these options by employing them to afford protection to historical, cultural and archaeological resources under its National Marine Sanctuaries programme. According to Varmer, any activities involving altering the seabed, the placing of structures on the seabed, drilling or digging, would be regarded as a breach of NMSA regulations enforceable against foreign salvors.[123]

---

[120] Again, these terms are undefined by the Convention. However, it has been argued that they include both mobile and fixed equipment, which may be manned or unmanned: Wegelein, *Marine Scientific Research*, pp. 135 *et seq*. The main distinction to draw is with ships, which are capable of navigation. 'The question may arise whether a permanently moored ship ceases to be a ship and becomes an installation. The answer would depend on the ship's capacity to navigate despite the mooring, i.e., if the mooring can be removed without imminent loss of the vessel, the ship will remain a ship even without actually navigating': *ibid.*, p. 140.

[121] It is doubtful that the reference to 'other economic purposes' in Art. 60(1)(b) includes the recovery of UCH for commercial gain: see Strati, *The Protection of the Underwater Cultural Heritage*, p. 267.

[122] 'Marine Archaeology and the International Law of the Sea', p. 369.

[123] Varmer, 'United States', p. 363. In Varmer's view, *any* salvage activity is likely to involve one of these offences: *ibid*. In the UK, activities of a similar nature on the continental shelf may require a licence under the Marine and Coastal Access Act 2009. The degree to which activities commonly undertaken by archaeologists and others involved in the

As the US experience has shown, utilisation of Articles 60, 80 and 81 of the LOSC undoubtedly can be helpful to afford protection to UCH, but these mechanisms do have drawbacks. For example, they can be used only in specific circumstances, require close investigation of the nature of ongoing activities, and can be utilised only after a salvage operator has started to make an expensive investment in respect of a particular site.

Another potential – but rather more controversial – control mechanism which would avoid these drawbacks is to treat at least certain activities undertaken by such operators and others targeting UCH as *marine scientific research*. This activity is subject to direct coastal state control in the EEZ and on the continental shelf.[124] As is the case with the terms 'drilling', 'installation' and 'structure', 'marine scientific research' is a term left undefined by the LOSC. However, what is clear is that it encompasses scientific research directed *at* the natural marine environment, rather than merely undertaken *in* the marine environment.[125] The generally accepted position is that archaeological excavation or other types of direct and deliberate intervention on UCH sites do *not* qualify as marine scientific research on the basis that such work – while in many instances making use of scientific methodology – is directed at the human, rather than the natural, environment.[126] However, it is arguable that an increasingly common precursor to direct intervention – remote-surveying of the seabed and subsoil using side-scan sonar, bathymetric and related technologies – may, at least in certain circumstances, qualify as marine scientific research. Such survey operations are directed at the seabed and subsoil, components of the natural marine environment. Importantly, in circumstances where they are undertaken systematically and over wide areas, the data gathered could be of direct significance for the exploration and exploitation of natural resources. As such, the sovereign rights and jurisdiction of the

---

investigation or excavation of UCH sites may be licensable under this relatively new statute – and the extent to which offences may be enforceable against foreign flag vessels and nationals – is a matter still under consideration by the Marine Management Organisation, the public body set up to administer the licensing regime.

[124] See LOSC, Art. 56(1)(b)(ii) and, more particularly, Art. 246.

[125] See Dromgoole, 'Revisiting the Relationship between Marine Scientific Research and the Underwater Cultural Heritage', p. 43. Relevant activities would include physical and chemical oceanography, marine biology, and marine geology and geophysics: Soons, *Marine Scientific Research and the Law of the Sea*, pp. 6, 124.

[126] While this may have been true in the past, increasingly archaeological research is directed to an understanding of the environment in which material remains of the human past may be found. It is therefore becoming difficult to draw tenable distinctions between the disciplines of archaeology and those of the physical sciences.

coastal state over such resources could be prejudiced unless it has a right to control the activity.[127]

The question of whether or not survey operations of *any* kind constitute marine scientific research is itself controversial and this may be the biggest barrier to broad acceptance of the argument set out.[128] However, the considerable advantage it has over the other options outlined is that it would enable the coastal state to take regulatory measures *prior* to any intervention taking place, thereby avoiding potential destabilisation of sites, the evidentiary problems of other regulatory methods and the possible vigorous defence of its legal position by any salvor that has expended considerable time and resources on a particular operation.

A final question that is occasionally asked is: could the jurisdiction provided to coastal states in respect of the protection and preservation of the marine environment of the EEZ be of indirect benefit to UCH? Although the Convention does not define 'marine environment', again there seems little doubt that it means the *natural* marine environment.[129] Nonetheless, as discussed above, in practice there is a close relationship between the natural and human (or 'historic') environments and protective measures aimed at one are likely to benefit the other. Having said that, it needs to be borne in mind that the jurisdiction provided to coastal states by Article 56(1) in respect of the protection and preservation of the marine environment is not general in nature, but is that 'provided for in the relevant provisions of [the] Convention', namely those in Part XII.[130] These provisions are designed to address the very specific threat of *pollution*. Nonetheless, UCH may derive some indirect benefit from action taken under these provisions.[131]

---

[127] For a detailed analysis of this argument, see, generally, Dromgoole, 'Revisiting the Relationship between Marine Scientific Research and the Underwater Cultural Heritage'. Some of the more sophisticated ocean exploration companies involved in shipwreck recovery may have a direct interest in natural resource exploration. Even where this is not the case, survey information is a marketable commodity.

[128] Having said that, according to Long: 'State practice . . . appears to support the view that hydrographic surveying within the EEZ is within the jurisdiction of the coastal State and that the consent of the coastal State must be obtained prior to the commencement of survey activities': Long, *Marine Resources Law*, pp. 695–6. The strongest opposition to the notion that survey operations constitute MSR comes from the USA: see, for example, Roach and Smith, *United States Responses to Excessive Maritime Claims*, pp. 446–9.

[129] See, for example, Nordquist *et al.*, *United Nations Convention on the Law of the Sea 1982*, Vol. IV, pp. 42–3.

[130] Churchill and Lowe, *The Law of the Sea*, p. 169.

[131] Interestingly, the impact on UCH of action taken under these provisions may be wider than the potential benefits of being protected indirectly from damage from polluting substances. The activities of archaeologists and others involved in physical intervention

4.3   Making full use of the territorial and nationality principles of international jurisdiction

The discussion set out above relates to the jurisdiction afforded to coastal states with respect to their offshore waters. Therefore, the potential means of providing benefits to UCH identified above can apply no further seaward than the outer limit of the juridical continental shelf, which marks the limit of their national jurisdiction. However, it will be recalled that there are some general principles of international jurisdiction which can be useful in the context of UCH protection. As pointed out in section 2, above, these principles can be used by states acting individually to impact upon activities in international waters generally, *including* the Area. In practice, however, the most effective way of utilising these principles is if two or more states *coordinate* their use of them.

A good example of the coordinated application of these principles is the international agreement concluded in 2000 for the protection of RMS *Titanic*.[132] The discovery of the *Titanic* in 1985 lying on the outer edge of Canada's continental shelf posed a challenge to the international community: how could legal protection be afforded to the world's most famous shipwreck? After considerable efforts on the part of the US government,[133] in 1997, formal negotiations commenced between a number of states closely connected (historically or geographically) to the wreck: the USA, the UK, France and Canada. The outcome of these negotiations was a text for an agreement, finalised in 2000.[134] The

at UCH sites may pollute the marine environment and therefore be subject to regulation. For example, if a large amount of sediment is removed from a site and deposited elsewhere on the seabed, it may constitute dumping. According to Art. 210 of the LOSC, '[dumping] within the territorial sea and the exclusive economic zone or onto the continental shelf shall not be carried out without the express prior approval of the coastal State'. Parties contemplating activities that will deposit material on the seabed may require a licence under domestic legislation such as the UK Marine and Coastal Access Act 2009.

[132] For a detailed discussion of the agreement, see Dromgoole, 'The International Agreement for the Protection of the *Titanic*: Problems and Prospects'.

[133] In the wake of the discovery of the *Titanic* in 1985, the US Congress passed the RMS Titanic Maritime Memorial Act of 1986 (Pub. L. No. 99-513, 100 Stat. 2048 (1986)). This Act included direction to US authorities to enter into negotiations with other interested nations to establish an international agreement providing for the designation of the wreck as an international maritime memorial. Initial attempts by the US State Department to follow this direction by engaging the UK, France and Canada in discussions met with little interest: see, further, Dromgoole, 'The International Agreement for the Protection of the *Titanic*: Problems and Prospects', pp. 3–5.

[134] The Agreement was signed by the UK in 2003 and the USA in 2004, but has yet to be signed by Canada or France. It will come into force after implementing legislation has

regulatory framework which the Agreement sets out (which, it may just be noted here, adopts standards closely based on the Annex to the UNESCO Convention 2001)[135] relies upon the full and effective exercise of the nationality and territorial principles by the states parties to the Agreement. It provides that each party 'shall take the necessary measures, in respect of its nationals and vessels flying its flag' to regulate their activities at the site through a system of project authorisations[136] and each party 'shall [also] take appropriate actions to prohibit activities in its territory including its maritime ports, territorial sea, and offshore terminals, that are inconsistent with [the] Agreement'.[137] If (as appears to be the eventual intention) all those states in the general geographical vicinity of the wreck, together with all those states with the technology to access the wreck, become parties to the Agreement, the jurisdictional mechanisms it employs could be very effective in regulating future activities at the site.[138]

It is noteworthy that the preamble to the Titanic Agreement refers specifically to the relevance of Article 303 of the LOSC. Inter-state agreements of this kind, utilising the nationality and territorial principles of jurisdiction to afford protection to UCH, provide a potentially helpful means whereby states can act in accordance with their twofold duty under Article 303(1). They have the potential to be used not just to protect one particular site, such as the *Titanic*, but to protect a number of related sites (for example, a battlefield such as Jutland or Trafalgar), or to afford protection to UCH generally within an enclosed or semi-enclosed sea.[139] However, 'mini-treaties' are only ever likely to be used in exceptional circumstances to protect sites in the open oceans.[140] This is because – to be effective in respect of such sites – they require multiple parties. As the Titanic Agreement has demonstrated, it can be difficult to engage sufficient political interest and will to bring them to fruition. It is striking that, to date, there appears to be only one such agreement in

---

been enacted by the US Congress. Such legislation has been drawn up and is currently under consideration: see RMS Titanic Maritime Memorial Preservation Act of 2012 (available at www.gc.noaa/gov/gcil_titanic-legislation.html).

[135] On this aspect of the Titanic Agreement, see, further, Chap. 10, section 2.

[136] Art. 4(1).   [137] Art. 4(5).

[138] Some might argue that the horse has already bolted in light of the extensive salvage activities that have taken place at the site in the years since its discovery: see, further, Chap. 5, section 3.4.3.

[139] For further discussion of inter-state agreements, see Chap. 10, section 2.

[140] Cf. bilateral treaties to protect sites in the territorial sea, which are relatively common: see Chap. 4, section 2.2.

force protecting a wreck site in international waters: that relating to the passenger ferry M/S *Estonia*, which sank on the Finnish continental shelf in 1994.[141]

5. Concluding remarks

It is clear that the state that has been most active in exploring and utilising the authority available to it under general international law in order to protect UCH located in extra-territorial waters is the USA. This may strike some as ironic in light of the fact that the USA was one of the states that blocked attempts at UNCLOS III to provide coastal states with direct jurisdiction over UCH on the continental shelf. However, the USA has taken the duty under Article 303(1) seriously and utilised the authority available to it under general international law to the fullest extent possible in order to implement the duty. It seems likely that other states that remain non-parties to the UNESCO Convention 2001 will increasingly follow its lead.[142] However, the jurisdictional mechanisms available to them are makeshift and, in some cases, controversial. Given their piecemeal nature, they rely on considerable political will to be employed effectively. What is really required to deal with the step-change in marine technology that took place in the period immediately following the adoption of the LOSC is a clear and comprehensive treaty framework that builds on what is already in place in order to plug the obvious gaps. The purpose of the UNESCO Convention 2001 is, of course, to provide that framework.

---

[141] This Agreement, which seeks to criminalise activities disturbing the peace of the resting place of more than 800 victims of the disaster, was originally made in 1995 between Estonia, Finland and Sweden, but was later amended to allow for accession by other states. Denmark, Latvia and the UK became parties in 1999, Poland and Russia in 2000 and Lithuania in 2002: for the Agreement and accession details, see (1995) *Finnish Treaty Series* 49. (The Agreement is reprinted in (1996) 31 *UN Law of the Sea Bulletin* 62.) For further discussion of this agreement, see Chap. 9, section 4.4.

[142] The Statements on Vote by the major maritime powers made in 2001 at the end of the UNESCO negotiations indicated a general commitment to the strengthening of efforts to protect UCH, individually and collaboratively, based on action taken in conformity with the LOSC but with reference to the UNESCO Annex as the relevant standard for the conduct of activities. For the Statements, see Garabello and Scovazzi, *The Protection of the Underwater Cultural Heritage*, pp. 243 *et seq.*

8   UNESCO Convention 2001: jurisdictional mechanisms

1. Introduction

As discussed in Chapter 7, the jurisdictional mechanisms available under general international law to control activities affecting, and more particularly, targeting, UCH are limited. Articles 149 and 303 of the LOSC make only limited provision for UCH beyond areas under coastal state sovereignty and no specific provision at all for UCH in the EEZ and on the continental shelf beyond twenty-four miles. The fundamental purpose of the initiative taken up by UNESCO in 1993 was to provide jurisdictional mechanisms to enable states effectively to regulate the activities of anyone intent on interfering with UCH located in maritime areas beyond the territorial sea and thereby to ensure that any interference with such sites is undertaken in accordance with internationally accepted archaeological standards. As noted in Chapter 1, the question of how to afford states such jurisdiction thwarted earlier efforts to create a UCH-specific treaty and it was clear from the outset of the UNESCO negotiations that it would be the most challenging of the issues to be addressed. The reason it was so challenging was that the new jurisdictional framework would need to be one that could reconcile two diametrically opposing viewpoints that existed within the international community: the view that '[i]t would be meaningless to simply repeat the provisions of the [LOSC] ... without bringing any improvements'[1] and the view that there should be no extension of coastal state jurisdiction beyond the position enshrined in the LOSC. In attempting to reconcile those viewpoints, the UNESCO negotiators resorted to devising a highly complex jurisdictional

---

[1] A view expressed by Italy during the initial ILA meetings: see O'Keefe, 'The Buenos Aires Draft Convention on the Protection of the Underwater Cultural Heritage Prepared by the International Law Association', p. 99.

framework in respect of the continental shelf and EEZ, which incorporates a number of constructive ambiguities. A similarly complex, if less contentious, framework was also devised for the Area.

This chapter examines the jurisdictional regime established by the UNESCO Convention 2001. First of all, consideration is given to the question of the formal relationship between the UNESCO Convention and the LOSC. Secondly, the control mechanisms employed by the new Convention are outlined and some consideration given to the concerns that have been expressed about those mechanisms and the degree to which they may or may not be in conformity with the LOSC. The chapter then concludes with a brief evaluation of the potential effectiveness of the regime.

2. Relationship with the Law of the Sea Convention

The LOSC appears to anticipate the development of a subject-specific treaty relating to UCH protection that would build on its own scant provision in this regard. The second of its two articles on the subject, Article 303, states:

This article is without prejudice to other international agreements and rules of international law regarding the protection of objects of an archaeological and historical nature.[2]

It is widely assumed that the reference in this provision to 'other international agreements and rules of international law' includes instruments and rules made subsequent to, as well as antecedent to, the LOSC and, therefore, that any new treaty is not fettered by the provisions of Article 303 (and perhaps, by reference, Article 149).[3] Furthermore, O'Keefe has pointed out:

Paragraph 4 says nothing about the general relationship between such agreements and [the LOSC]. It relates solely to the effect of Article 303 itself.[4]

As was made clear in Chapter 7, Articles 303 and 149 provide no specific regulatory competence with respect to UCH with the exception of the control mechanism in Article 303(2) relating to the removal of UCH in the contiguous zone. Instead, the jurisdictional framework governing activities affecting UCH for the most part is set out in other articles of the LOSC

---

[2] LOSC, Art. 303(4). [3] See, further, Chap. 1, sections 2.1.2 and 2.1.3.
[4] O'Keefe, *Shipwrecked Heritage*, p. 19. But see n. 10, below.

278 UNESCO CONVENTION 2001: JURISDICTIONAL MECHANISMS

of general application. A question on which opinion is divided is whether a new treaty dealing with UCH is able to derogate from this framework.

At the UNESCO negotiations, some states – among them the G-77 – were of the view that the new treaty should not be 'subordinated' to the LOSC.[5] To support this view, reference is sometimes made to the general rule of treaty law regarding successive treaties on the same subject matter: that as between parties to both treaties, the rules of the subsequent treaty prevail.[6] On the other hand, many other states, including the major maritime states, regard the LOSC as having an enhanced status more akin to a constitution than to an ordinary treaty.[7] Like other constitutions, it is considered to have greater weight than ordinary rules of law and, in consequence, as being more difficult to overturn or amend. The justification for the special status of the LOSC is that it enshrines a delicately crafted 'package deal', which balances the respective rights of flag states and coastal states. It therefore represents an integral and indivisible treaty regime which is not open to contracting out on specific issues. To counter the suggestion that the new treaty could go beyond the terms of the LOSC on the question of jurisdiction, it is sometimes pointed out that the general rule on priority as between successive treaties is residual in nature and is subject to any specific provision made in the treaties themselves.[8]

Article 311 of the LOSC sets out the relationship between the LOSC and other international agreements. Paragraph 3 of that article limits the right of states parties to derogate from the LOSC in later agreements they might enter into. Its precise terms are as follows:

Two or more States Parties may conclude agreements modifying or suspending the operation of provisions of this Convention, applicable solely to the relations between them, *provided* that such agreements do not relate to a provision

[5] See Aznar-Gómez, 'Treasure Hunters, Sunken State Vessels and the 2001 UNESCO Convention on the Protection of the Underwater Cultural Heritage', p. 231. See also Blumberg, 'International Protection of Underwater Cultural Heritage', p. 496.
[6] See the terms of the Vienna Convention, Art. 30, set out in the General introduction, section 3.2.1, above.
[7] This view was reinforced by the UN General Assembly, which repeatedly called for 'full conformity' between the new treaty and the relevant provisions of the LOSC: see the annual UN General Assembly Resolutions on Oceans and the Law of the Sea, UN Doc. A/RES/53/32, 6 January 1999, para. 20; UN Doc. A/RES/54/31, 18 January 2000, para. 30; UN Doc. A/RES/55/7 of 2 May 2001, para. 36. The discomfort of DOALOS and the awkwardness of its position during the UNESCO negotiations have been noted by various commentators: see, for example, Blumberg, 'International Protection of Underwater Cultural Heritage', p. 502 n. 11; O'Keefe, *Shipwrecked Heritage*, p. 29.
[8] See, for example, Aust, *Modern Treaty Law and Practice*, p. 227.

derogation from which is incompatible with the effective execution of the object and purpose of this Convention, and *provided further* that such agreements shall not affect the application of the basic principles embodied herein, and that the provisions of such agreements do not affect the enjoyment by other States Parties of their rights or the performance of their obligations under this Convention.[9]

This provision makes it clear that two or more states parties to the LOSC may conclude a subsequent agreement that modifies the operation of the provisions of the LOSC, *provided*:

(i)   it is compatible with the effective execution of the object and purpose of the LOSC;
(ii) it does not affect the application of the basic principles of the LOSC; and
(iii) it does not impinge on the rights of states parties to the LOSC who do not become parties to the subsequent agreement.

Although the outcome of the UNESCO initiative could be regarded as an 'effective execution' of one of the objects and purposes of the LOSC (to encourage states to protect UCH in all sea areas and to cooperate for that purpose), assuming Article 311(3) applies,[10] the provisions of the new treaty must not affect the application of the basic principles of the LOSC. There can be little doubt that these principles include those relating to the delicate jurisdictional allocation which is core to the 1982 treaty. Further, the provisions of the new treaty must not interfere with the rights of *non*-states parties to the new treaty.

---

[9] Emphasis added. The LOSC contains a number of other provisions that are designed to preclude States Parties from contracting-out of the 'package' it sets out. These include a prohibition on reservations, unless expressly permitted (Art. 309); a tough procedure for amendment of the Convention (Arts. 312–13); and compulsory dispute settlement machinery in Part XV. (For further reference to the dispute settlement machinery, see Chap. 10, section 4.)

[10] By virtue of Art. 311(4), 'States Parties intending to conclude an agreement referred to in paragraph 3 shall notify the other States Parties through the depositary' of the LOSC of their intention to do so. This does not appear to have happened with respect to the UNESCO Convention. It is possible that the reason for this is that the majority of states may not have regarded the Convention as constituting an agreement falling within the purview of Art. 311(3). Art. 311(5) makes it clear that Art. 311 as a whole 'does not affect international agreements expressly permitted or preserved by other articles of' the LOSC and some suggest that Art. 303 of the LOSC is an example of such an article by virtue of paragraph 4, sometimes citing statements to this effect by Nordquist: see Nordquist, Rosenne and Sohn, *United Nations Convention on the Law of the Sea 1982*, Vol. V, pp. 161, 240, 243. See, for example, Strati, 'Protection of the Underwater Cultural Heritage', p. 35, including n. 36.

The UNESCO Convention 2001 contains an equivalent provision setting out its relationship with the LOSC. Article 3 of the UNESCO Convention provides:

Nothing in this Convention shall prejudice the rights, jurisdiction and duties of States under international law, including the United Nations Convention on the Law of the Sea.

This Convention shall be interpreted and applied in the context of and in a manner consistent with international law, including the United Nations Convention on the Law of the Sea.

On its face, Article 3 seems to acknowledge that – in the event of any incompatibility between the two treaties – the LOSC will prevail. However, Article 3 contains a constructive ambiguity designed to accommodate the sharp division of viewpoints on the status of the new treaty vis-à-vis the LOSC. The ambiguity comes in the wording 'international law, including', which appears in each sentence of the article.[11] This wording provides states parties with a degree of latitude in their interpretation of the terms of the UNESCO Convention because it allows for an assumption to be made that the rules set out in the LOSC are not 'set in stone', but instead are part of an ongoing and evolutionary process of development of international law.[12] It suggests two things: (i) that the interpretation of the LOSC can change over time with the development of state practice and (ii) that new rules of customary international law could emerge to displace those enshrined in the LOSC. In the context of any law-making treaty, both of these propositions would be controversial; they are all the more so when raised in the context of the LOSC.[13]

Le Gurun has observed that Article 3, along with a number of other references to the LOSC in the text of the new Convention, while 'aimed at calming down the concerns of the most reluctant states', 'may have paradoxically confirmed and strengthened their fear'.[14] Whatever the

---

[11] It is instructive to compare the wording of Art. 3 with the equivalent provision in the UN Straddling Stocks Agreement of 1995. Art. 4 of the 1995 Agreement provides: 'Nothing in this Agreement shall prejudice the rights, jurisdiction and duties of States under the [LOSC]. This Agreement shall be interpreted and applied in the context of and in a manner consistent with the [LOSC].'

[12] See O'Keefe, *Shipwrecked Heritage*, p. 58.

[13] On the question of the evolutionary interpretation of treaties in the context of the LOSC, see Boyle, 'Further Development of the Law of the Sea Convention', pp. 567 *et seq.* On the question of new rules of customary law emerging to supplant the rules of a law-making treaty, see Aust, *Modern Treaty Law and Practice*, pp. 13–14.

[14] Le Gurun, 'France' (2nd edn), p. 78.

intention behind the article, it is clear that it failed to provide the sought-after reassurance on the question of jurisdictional compliance.[15]

3. Control mechanisms

The overall aim of those responsible for drafting the UNESCO Convention was to ensure that activities 'directed at' UCH[16] in all sea areas are governed by the Rules set out in the Convention's Annex. As discussed in Chapter 1, these Rules, which form an integral part of the Convention, are based on the 1996 ICOMOS International Charter on the Protection and Management of Underwater Cultural Heritage and are widely regarded as representing international good practice with respect to the intentional disturbance of UCH sites. At their heart, they enshrine the fundamental archaeological principle that preservation *in situ* should be the first management option for any site and that activities should be authorised only when scientifically justified.[17] It was a comparatively straightforward exercise to put in place provisions to ensure that the annexed standards were applied to activities taking place in the maritime zones out to twenty-four miles, but the challenge was to create a jurisdictional basis for regulation of activities in accordance with these standards in the maritime areas beyond this limit.

The focus of the UNESCO initiative, first and foremost, was on plugging the gap in respect of the continental shelf, since this is the area most immediately at risk from unregulated activities. Echoing the debate that had taken place at UNCLOS III two decades previously,[18] some states, including Greece, called for a 'cultural heritage zone' co-extensive with the continental shelf, providing full coastal state jurisdiction over UCH; others, including the USA, wanted an outcome that ensured the elimination of any notion of direct coastal state regulatory

---

[15] See, further, section 3.6, below.

[16] The Convention distinguishes between activities 'directed at' UCH and activities 'incidentally affecting' UCH. This chapter focuses on the regulation of activities directed at UCH, which are defined to mean 'activities having underwater cultural heritage as their primary object and which may, directly or indirectly, physically disturb or otherwise damage underwater cultural heritage': Art. 1(6). For a discussion of the impact of the Convention on activities 'incidentally affecting' UCH – defined as activities that may physically disturb or otherwise damage UCH, but which do not have UCH as their primary object or one of their objects (which would include activities such as fishing, dredging and marine construction) – see Chap. 10, section 3.

[17] For details of the authorisation scheme envisaged by the Convention, see Chapter 9, section 3.

[18] See Chap. 1, section 2.1.2.

competence over UCH in this area.[19] One significant change that had taken place, however, was that there was now general acceptance of the need for action to protect UCH located in waters far from shore. The USA and other like-minded states were therefore supportive of the general objective of the initiative, but called for controls that utilised existing jurisdictional principles, including the nationality and territorial principles, and coastal state jurisdiction linked to natural resources.[20]

The 1994 ILA Draft included a provision enabling states parties to establish a 'cultural heritage zone' over an area extending beyond the territorial sea up to the outer limit of the continental shelf, within which the coastal state would have jurisdiction over activities affecting UCH.[21] Inevitably, the proposal proved unacceptable to some states and was dropped. The equivalent article in the 1998 UNESCO Draft permitted states parties to regulate and authorise activities affecting UCH in the EEZ and on the continental shelf, 'in accordance with [other provisions of the draft] and other rules of international law'; it also obliged coastal states parties to require the notification of any discovery relating to UCH occurring in these zones.[22] Again, this article proved unacceptable: the first part, because it incorporated an ambiguity not dissimilar to that in Article 3 of the final text of the Convention; the second, because it was regarded as overstepping the jurisdictional bounds of the LOSC to give coastal states a right to be informed of finds. The difficulty the negotiators had in finding an acceptable compromise on this issue is evidenced by the fact that a working text produced a year later resorted to setting out for consideration *three* alternative options in respect of jurisdiction.[23]

The final text of the Convention incorporates a set of control mechanisms for the continental shelf and EEZ based on combining use of the nationality and territorial principles, existing coastal state jurisdiction under the LOSC *and* a novel concept: that of a 'coordinating' state. The general idea is that this state acts on behalf of all states which have

---

[19] Among other things, it was hoped that the Convention would lead to the reining-in of a number of unilateral claims to such competence. On these claims, see Chap. 7, section 4.1.

[20] See Blumberg, 'International Protection of Underwater Cultural Heritage', pp. 494–6. In other words, they called for controls along the lines of those outlined in Chap. 7, sections 4.2 and 4.3.

[21] 1994 ILA Draft, Arts. 1(3) and 5. See, further, Chap. 1, section 3.1.1.

[22] 1998 UNESCO Draft, Art. 5.

[23] UNESCO Doc. CLT-96/CONF.202/5 Rev. 2. For a good synthesis of the complex negotiating history with respect to this issue, see Garabello, 'The Negotiating History of the Convention on the Protection of the Underwater Cultural Heritage', pp. 138–51.

declared an interest in the UCH in question on the basis of their having a 'verifiable link'.[24] In practice, the coordinating state is likely to be the coastal state, although this is not automatically the case. The notion of a coordinating state acting not on its own behalf but on behalf of all interested states was designed to provide reassurance that the balance between coastal and flag state rights on the continental shelf and in the EEZ was not being disturbed by the introduction of new responsibilities for coastal states which could be viewed as new rights.[25] To provide further reassurance on this matter, nowhere in the provisions for the continental shelf and EEZ, or indeed in the Convention as a whole, is there any reference to the term 'coastal state'. A control scheme mirroring that for the EEZ and continental shelf is also extended to the Area and the control mechanisms in respect of these, and other, zones are supplemented by a set of general provisions requiring states parties to utilise the nationality and territorial principles to regulate and deter activities that are not in conformity with the Convention.

In the following sections, the control mechanisms established by the Convention are outlined, starting with the general provisions (set out in Articles 14 to 16) and moving on to the specific provision for each maritime zone (set out in Articles 7 to 12). Consideration is then given to the aspects of the scheme which have been the primary causes of concern and to the question of the compliance of the provisions with the LOSC.

3.1 General mechanisms

As discussed in Chapter 7, the nationality and territorial principles are well-established principles of international law and, as such, their utilisation by the UNESCO Convention was not a matter of controversy. Although these principles are available to states under general international law, the fact that there is no *obligation* on states to use them to protect UCH means that few have sought to do so. Their use by states on a unilateral and uncoordinated basis is also of only very limited effectiveness. By incorporating them into a conventional regime, not only can states parties be placed under a *duty* to make use of the principles to assist in controlling activities directed at UCH, but their full

---

[24] For discussion of the notion of a 'verifiable link', see Chap. 3, section 4.2.2.

[25] The Convention provides explicitly that any action taken by the coordinating state shall not 'constitute a basis for the assertion of any preferential right or jurisdictional rights not provided for in international law, including the [LOSC]': Art. 10(6). Note the wording, which adopts the same contentious formula as Art. 3.

potential can be harnessed because the regime can facilitate coordinated action. This fact was recognised by the ILA during the course of its work on drafting a new treaty. Its 1994 Draft sought to utilise these principles to hamper activities taking place in extra-territorial waters inconsistent with the Charter[26] and the model established by that Draft was built upon in Articles 14, 15 and 16 of the UNESCO Convention.

Article 14 requires states parties to:

> take measures to prevent the entry into their territory, the dealing in, or the possession of, UCH illicitly exported and/or recovered, where recovery was contrary to [the] Convention.

This article has potentially wide ramifications which are considered more fully in Chapter 9.[27] However, the general point to be noted now is that by making it difficult to deal with material that has been recovered contrary to the Convention, Article 14 acts as a deterrent to such recovery. The precise nature of the measures that may be taken is left to the discretion of individual states parties. However, it could include the introduction of legislation of a similar nature to the UK Dealing in Cultural Objects (Offences) Act 2003,[28] as well as measures to enforce the legislation such as customs checks and provision for the seizure of material.[29]

Article 15 again requires states parties to 'take measures', this time to prohibit the use of their territory, including their ports, as well as artificial islands, installations and structures under their exclusive jurisdiction or control, in support of activities directed at UCH which do not conform to the Convention. Deep-water recovery operations can take many months and if lines of supply of food, fuel, equipment and personnel are uncertain this may act as a deterrent to those seeking to operate outside the conventional framework. Again, the precise measures to be taken are left to individual states to determine. However, to be effective, action under Article 15 will need to be coordinated on a *regional* basis, ensuring participation by all the bordering states.

The third and final general jurisdictional provision, Article 16, requires states parties to take 'all practicable measures' to ensure that their nationals and vessels flying their flag do not engage in activities

---

[26] See 1994 ILA Draft, Arts. 7 and 8. On the Charter, see Chap. 1, section 3.1.3.
[27] See Chap. 9, section 5.2.   [28] See Chap. 7, section 2.1.
[29] In fact, states parties are required to take measures providing for the seizure of UCH brought within their territory that has been recovered in a manner not in conformity with the Convention: see, further, Chap. 9, section 5.1.

that do not conform to the Convention. While capable of operating as a freestanding obligation, this provision is designed, in part, to reinforce obligations the Convention imposes in respect of the continental shelf and EEZ, and the Area.[30] Correlation with the wording of these other obligations probably explains the reference in Article 16 to states taking 'all practical measures', rather than simply 'measures', as provided for in Articles 14 and 15.

Articles 14, 15 and 16 provide states with means to control (or at least deter) activities that do not conform to the Convention, wherever those activities take place. They therefore supplement and reinforce the specific control regimes established for each maritime zone, which are addressed below.

3.2 Maritime spaces subject to coastal state sovereignty

Although the primary focus of the UNESCO initiative was on the regulation of activities in extra-territorial waters, in order to ensure uniformity of standards across all waters of a maritime character provision is also made for the territorial sea and other waters subject to coastal state sovereignty.[31] This provision is found in Article 7.

Article 7(1) provides:

States Parties, in the exercise of their sovereignty, have the exclusive right to regulate and authorize activities directed at underwater cultural heritage in their internal waters, archipelagic waters and territorial sea.

As discussed in Chapter 7,[32] in the exercise of its sovereignty, a coastal state has the right to regulate and authorise activities in their internal waters, archipelagic waters and territorial sea, subject to the provisions of the LOSC and other rules of international law. Many states have utilised this right by putting in place domestic legislation regulating activities affecting UCH. Article 7(2) adds to the existing international legal regime by *obliging* states parties to the UNESCO Convention to ensure that the Rules in the Annex are applied to activities directed at UCH in these waters.[33]

[30] See sections 3.4 and 3.5, below.
[31] Art. 28 of the Convention permits a state to declare that the Rules shall apply to inland waters not of a maritime character, upon ratification, acceptance, approval or accession to the Convention, or at any time thereafter.
[32] See Chap. 7, section 3.2.
[33] The provision for application of the Rules in Art. 7(2) is without prejudice to 'other international agreements and rules of international law' relating to the protection of UCH. In so far as there are such other agreements and rules, and they are inconsistent

Article 7 has two controversial features. The first is paragraph 3 of the article, which makes specific provision relating to the discovery of identifiable sunken state vessels and aircraft in the territorial sea or archipelagic waters. This provision is discussed in Chapter 4.[34] The second, which interrelates with the first, is the use of the word 'exclusive' in Article 7(1), giving the impression that the right of the coastal state to regulate and authorise activities in the territorial sea and archipelagic waters is unconditional. This runs counter to Articles 2(3) and 49(3) of the LOSC, which make it clear that the sovereignty of a coastal state in these areas is exercised subject to rights accorded to other states by other provisions of the LOSC, or by other rules of international law. While the rights of innocent passage and archipelagic sea lanes passage generally have no particular bearing on the matter of UCH protection,[35] the rules of international law relating to sovereign immunity certainly do have such bearing. The inclusion of the word 'exclusive' in Article 7(1) is therefore particularly contentious because it contributes to the concerns of maritime states about the status of their sunken warships located in the coastal waters of other states under the conventional regime.

States minded to ratify the UNESCO Convention will need to scrutinise their domestic heritage legislation carefully to ensure that it meets the terms of Article 7(2). Not only will they need to ensure that provision is in place for the Rules to be applied, but also that the scope of this provision accords with the Convention's broad definition of UCH:[36] as seen in Chapter 2, domestic heritage legislation has very different approaches to the question of subject matter and in some cases it still only extends to shipwrecks.[37] Some domestic laws may also include provisions that do not accord with the Rules in the Annex, in particular Rule 2 regarding commercial exploitation.[38] In some states, especially

with the Rules in the UNESCO Annex, the former will prevail. A relevant agreement is the Council of Europe's Valletta Convention (see Chap. 1, section 2.2.3), but it seems unlikely that there is any significant inconsistency between the two treaties.

[34] See Chap. 4, section 3.2.1.

[35] See Caflisch, 'Submarine Antiquities and the International Law of the Sea', pp. 10–11. For an example of circumstances where the right of innocent passage does relate directly to the question of UCH protection, see O'Keefe, *Shipwrecked Heritage*, p. 57.

[36] See Art. 1(1)(a). See, further, Chap. 2, section 4.

[37] See Chap. 2, section 2.

[38] Jeffery has pointed out that Australian federal and state legislation may potentially conflict with Rule 2: see Jeffery, 'Australia' (2nd edn), p. 11. A conflict of this sort would certainly arise with respect to the UK Merchant Shipping Act 1995 in view of its provision for the sale of unclaimed wreck and for a salvage reward to be paid from the proceeds (see ss. 240 and 243).

federal states, there is a complex web of relevant legislation and the question of its review and amendment may give rise to sensitive internal politics.[39] The work involved in ensuring conformity for those states that already have in place a well-developed scheme of protection for UCH may deter them from ratifying the Convention; on the other hand, where states are starting with a 'blank slate', the Convention may be seen as providing a valuable source of guidance.

3.3   *The contiguous zone*

Provision is made for the contiguous zone in Article 8. This states:

> Without prejudice to and in addition to Articles 9 and 10, and in accordance with Article 303, paragraph 2, of the United Nations Convention on the Law of the Sea, States Parties may regulate and authorize activities directed at underwater cultural heritage within their contiguous zone. In so doing, they shall require that the Rules be applied.

Like Article 303(2) of the LOSC, Article 8 is permissive, rather than mandatory, in nature.[40] However, in so far as a state party to the UNESCO Convention does choose to act under the authority of Article 8, it will be under a duty to apply the Rules in the Annex.

Article 8 reaffirms and amplifies the basis for action provided by Article 303(2) of the LOSC. As seen in Chapter 7,[41] under Article 303(2) a coastal state is allowed to presume that the removal of objects from its contiguous zone without its approval would amount to an infringement within its territory or territorial sea of customs, fiscal, immigration or sanitary regulations. The coastal state may therefore exercise the control necessary to prevent and punish such infringement. To date, only a small number of states have taken up the option of using this provision and

[39] During the UNESCO negotiations, the US delegation referred to there being more than a dozen relevant federal laws and more than fifty-six relevant state and federal territorial laws in the USA: Garabello, 'The Negotiating History of the Convention on the Protection of the Underwater Cultural Heritage', p. 134 n. 73. Article 29 of the Convention provides federal states and others with self-governing territories with some leeway in this respect, permitting them to make a declaration upon ratification that the Convention will not apply to specific parts of their territory, internal waters, archipelagic waters or territorial sea until the appropriate conditions are in place: see, further, Chap. 10, section 7. See also O'Keefe, *Shipwrecked Heritage*, pp. 145–6.

[40] Interestingly, although Strati argues that a coastal state does not need formally to declare a contiguous zone prior to exercising the authority under Art. 303(2) of the LOSC, she suggests that there is an implication within the wording of Art. 8 of the UNESCO Convention that such a zone must be declared as a precursor to the exercise of authority under the article: see Strati, 'Greece' (2nd edn), p. 121.

[41] See Chap. 7, section 3.3.

this may be, at least in part, because of uncertainty as to precisely what it permits a coastal state to do.

Article 8 of the UNESCO Convention goes further than simply requiring states making use of the jurisdictional device in Article 303(2) to ensure that any removal of UCH is conducted in accordance with the annexed Rules. Rather than referring to the 'removal' of objects from the seabed, it refers to 'activities directed at UCH'. It also refers to the 'regulation' and 'authorisation' of these activities and makes no reference to the basis for action being the making of certain presumptions. On the other hand, it categorically states that its application must be 'in accordance with' Article 303(2) and does not adopt the ambiguous formula, 'international law, including', used in other provisions. It therefore makes clear beyond doubt that Article 8 must be interpreted in a way that does not go beyond the authority provided by Article 303(2).

Le Gurun has suggested that the 'elaboration' of Article 303(2) by Article 8 has strengthened the provision and ended its 'somewhat clandestine existence'.[42] The differences of wording provide some helpful clarity on matters that, in practice, have proved to be uncontroversial[43] but do not affect the inbuilt ambiguity in Article 303(2) relating to whether or not legislative jurisdiction is afforded.

The phrase '[w]ithout prejudice to and in addition to Articles 9 and 10', at the beginning of Article 8, acts as a reminder that the contiguous zone is part of the continental shelf and the EEZ, the zones to which these articles apply. However, the wording 'without prejudice to' is controversial because it could give the impression that the coastal state may, in at least some instances, need to consult with other interested states before acting under Article 8.[44]

3.4   The continental shelf and the exclusive economic zone

The regime for the continental shelf and the EEZ, found in Articles 9 and 10, lies at the core of the entire treaty framework.[45] The length and complexity of these articles are a testament to the difficulty faced in

---

[42] Le Gurun, 'France' (2nd edn), p. 77.   [43] See, further, Chap. 7, section 3.3.

[44] This matter was cited by Greece as one of the reasons why it abstained from voting in favour of the Convention: see Strati, 'Greece' (2nd edn), pp. 119–21. In Strati's words, Art. 8 'superimposes the system of consultations envisaged for the continental shelf/EEZ on the contiguous zone': ibid., p. 121. On the position of Greece with respect to the Convention more generally see, further, section 3.6, below.

[45] Given the fact that the continental shelf is at least as extensive as the EEZ, and given that UCH is generally found on the seabed rather than floating in water, one might question why the regime set out in Arts. 9 and 10 explicitly refers to the EEZ as well as the

creating mechanisms to control activities directed at UCH in these zones. Article 9 makes provision for reporting and notification; Article 10 for consultation and protection.

Article 9(1) provides:

All States Parties have a responsibility to protect underwater cultural heritage in the exclusive economic zone and on the continental shelf in conformity with this Convention.

This provision reflects the general duty enshrined in Article 303(1) of the LOSC to protect UCH in all sea areas and echoes the internationalist approach of that article by making it clear that each state party has a responsibility to protect UCH found not only in its *own* offshore waters, but also in those of other states around the world. Consistent with the basic objective of the Convention, it also makes it clear that the duty must be fulfilled in a manner that is in conformity with the UNESCO Convention which, by definition, includes the annexed Rules.

The subsequent paragraphs of Article 9 begin to elaborate the means by which the duty must be put into effect. They set out a system for reporting and notification of any discovery of UCH, and of any intention to engage in activities directed at UCH, on the continental shelf or in the EEZ. The starting point for the system is that a state party is obliged to require its national,[46] or the master of a vessel flying its flag, to report any discovery of UCH or any intention to engage in activities directed at UCH, either in its own EEZ or on its continental shelf, *or* in the EEZ or on the continental shelf of another state party.[47] (The question of to whom such reports should be made and, indeed, of exactly who is entitled to *require* a report, is one of the most controversial aspects of the Convention and is discussed separately below.)[48] All reports must be passed on, or 'notified', to the Director-General of UNESCO, who shall promptly

continental shelf. The answer appears to be that it is conceivable that UCH could be found floating in water. During the UNESCO negotiations, it seems that an example of a message in a bottle associated with the Italian national hero, Mr Giuseppe Garibaldi, was cited: Scovazzi, 'The Protection of Underwater Cultural Heritage', p. 124 n. 13. While such a notion may appear fanciful, it was recently reported that a Scottish fisherman had found what was thought to be the oldest known example of a message in a bottle (at sea). The bottle, which was released in 1914 along with others as part of an oceanography experiment, had apparently been adrift for 97 years and 309 days: see www.news.discovery.com/history/oldest-message-in-bottle-120906.html.

[46] According to O'Keefe, there was general agreement among negotiators that references to 'national' should be regarded as references to the *leader* of the operation: see O'Keefe, *Shipwrecked Heritage*, p. 84.
[47] See Art. 9(1)(a) and (b).   [48] See section 3.6.

make the information available to all states parties.[49] Any state party may declare an interest in being consulted on how to ensure effective protection of the UCH in question, based on it having a 'verifiable link' to that UCH.[50]

Once information is available that UCH has been discovered, or that someone is planning to engage in activities directed at UCH, mechanisms are clearly then required to enable any such activities to be regulated. Article 10 is designed to provide those mechanisms.

A key provision is Article 10(2). This states:

A State Party in whose exclusive economic zone or on whose continental shelf underwater cultural heritage is located has the right to prohibit or authorize any activity directed at such heritage to prevent interference with its sovereign rights or jurisdiction as provided for by international law including the United Nations Convention on the Law of the Sea.

This paragraph gives a state party the basis to act to prohibit or authorise activities directed at UCH in its EEZ or on its continental shelf. It is able to so act, provided that its 'sovereign rights or jurisdiction' under international law, including the LOSC, are threatened. In respect of both the EEZ and the continental shelf, the LOSC affords the coastal state rights over natural resources, living and non-living; in the EEZ it also affords the coastal state rights or jurisdiction in respect of economic exploration and exploitation, installations and structures, marine scientific research, and preservation of the marine environment.[51] Article 10(2) of the UNESCO Convention makes it clear that where a threat is posed to any of these sovereign rights or jurisdiction by activities directed at UCH, the coastal state can act to prohibit or authorise the activity.

Article 10(2) is a potentially powerful provision. It explicitly acknowledges the link – increasingly recognised and scientifically understood – between UCH and natural resources and it provides states parties with a concrete basis for taking action to prevent activities directed at UCH from damaging natural resources. By providing that the coastal state 'has the right to prohibit or authorize' activities, it makes it clear that the coastal state has the right not simply to ensure that activities are conducted according to acceptable standards, but to implement the *in situ* preservation principle by precluding activities altogether unless they are fully justified. If a state becomes aware that there is the possibility of interference, either through the notification procedures in Article 9 or in

---

[49] Art. 9(3) and (4).   [50] Art. 9(5).   [51] See Chap. 7, section 3.4.

another way, it has a basis for preventing that interference until the competent authorities determine whether or not it is justified. If it is, the coastal state can ensure it is conducted in accordance with the Rules in the Annex. Bearing in mind that UCH is defined, for the purposes of the Convention, as material that has been underwater for at least 100 years, in many cases it *will* have become an integral part of the marine environment and, therefore, any interference with the UCH *is* likely to have some impact upon natural resources.[52] Even where there is no demonstrable adverse impact, it seems unlikely – as O'Keefe has suggested[53] – that any state would challenge the action taken by another to protect its sovereign rights.

In circumstances where Article 10(2) cannot be applied, or a state does not seek to use it, paragraphs 3 to 6 of Article 10 provide an alternative scheme for controlling activities directed at UCH. The scheme is based on consultation between the coastal state and states parties that have declared a verifiable link to the UCH with a view to identifying and agreeing on the best means of affording protection. Provision is made for the appointment of the coastal state, or another state, as the 'Coordinating State'.[54] Among other things, this state may be required to implement any protective measures that are agreed and to issue all necessary authorisations for such agreed measures.[55] It may also conduct any necessary preliminary research and must issue all necessary authorisations for such work.[56] The results of such research must be transmitted to the Director-General of UNESCO, who must make the information 'promptly' available to other states parties.[57] In all its actions under Article 10, the coordinating state must act on behalf of the 'States Parties as a whole and not in its own interest'.[58]

One of the most controversial features of Article 10 is that in circumstances where UCH is threatened by an 'immediate danger', the coordinating state may take measures *prior* to consultation with other interested

---

[52] See, further, Chap. 7, section 4.2.1.   [53] O'Keefe, *Shipwrecked Heritage*, p. 90.

[54] The coastal state will be the coordinating state unless it declares a wish not to be: Art. 10(3)(b). It may declare such a wish if, for example, it has concerns about the expenditure the role might entail, especially if it has no direct connection with the UCH in question. Although the Convention does not say so explicitly, if the coastal state is not appointed as the coordinating state, any state (even, it seems, a non-state party) could be appointed to the role. However, in practice it is likely to be one of the states that has declared an interest.

[55] Art. 10(5)(a) and (b). The coordinating state shall implement the agreed measures unless it is agreed that another state party shall implement those measures: Art. 10(5)(a).

[56] Art. 10(5)(c).   [57] Art. 10(5)(c).   [58] Art. 10(6).

states.[59] The threat may arise 'from human activities or any other cause, including looting'. Therefore, as well as encompassing activities *directed at* UCH, such as looting, it could also include threats arising from other causes, including natural causes and activities *incidentally affecting* UCH, such as dredging and fishing.[60] The measures that may be taken are 'all practicable measures' and/or the issuing of any necessary authorisation in conformity with the Convention to prevent the danger. As with all action taken by a coordinating state under Article 10, any action it does take must be on behalf of the states parties as a whole and – by virtue of Article 3 – must be consistent with 'international law, including' the LOSC. Measures that could be taken which would be consistent with general international law, and uncontroversial, would be action in accordance with Articles 14, 15 and 16.[61]

Article 10 fails to provide any guidance on the relationship between Article 10(2) and Article 10, paragraphs 3–6. A particular question that arises is whether a coastal state acting under Article 10(2) to prohibit or authorise activities that threaten its sovereign rights and jurisdiction has to consult other states parties who may have declared an interest and to follow the other procedures set out in paragraphs 3 to 6. On their face, paragraphs 3–6 apply to all circumstances where there has been the discovery of UCH, or where there is an intention that activity shall be directed at UCH, in a state party's EEZ or on its continental shelf. However, the consultative procedures set out in these paragraphs could clearly conflict with the coastal state's right to act to prevent interference with its sovereign rights and jurisdiction, a right implicitly enshrined in the LOSC, as well as in Article 10(2) of the UNESCO Convention. It surely cannot have been envisaged that in such circumstances the coastal state should have to consult with other interested states and implement only *agreed* measures of protection. For this reason, it must be presumed that Article 10(2) is intended as a stand-alone provision. Nevertheless, given that the whole scheme of the Convention is based on the principle of cooperation between states parties, the coastal state may feel at least morally obliged to consult with other interested states, in so far as any come forward, before taking action under Article 10(2).

---

[59] Art. 10(4). The controversial nature of this provision is discussed further at section 3.6, below.

[60] For a discussion of the implications of the regime set out in Arts. 9 and 10 on activities incidentally affecting UCH, see Chap. 10, section 3.1.

[61] All other states parties would also be under a duty to protect UCH in such circumstances 'by way of all practicable measures': see Art. 10(4). See also Art. 2(4).

In the past, a number of states have made controversial unilateral assertions of jurisdiction over UCH on the continental shelf and in the EEZ.[62] The very fact that they did this indicates that they are concerned that UCH is adequately protected. Therefore, it can be assumed that these states will have some interest in ratifying the UNESCO Convention. Spain, for example, has already done so, and Australia and Ireland may do so in the future.[63] Some debate has therefore arisen about whether such ratification would require a 'reining in' of the extended jurisdiction.[64]

These states might point to the wording of the Convention to argue that it would not. By providing that nothing in the Convention 'shall prejudice the rights, jurisdiction and duties of States under international law, including' the LOSC, Article 3 provides room for these states to argue that their claims are in accordance with customary international law. Article 10(2) also assists in this respect. It refers to the sovereign rights or jurisdiction of coastal states in these areas as being those 'provided for by international law, including' the LOSC, opening up the possibility that the sovereign rights and jurisdiction of states on the continental shelf and in the EEZ could extend to matters other than those provided for in the LOSC.

Whether or not one regards the extensions as lawful or unlawful under international law,[65] the potential for a conflict with the UNESCO Convention relates mainly to the question of consultation with other states parties that have declared an interest. Given that a core principle of the Convention is that states parties must cooperate with one another,[66] whether or not states such as Australia, Ireland and Spain decide formally to amend their legislation in this respect if they ratify

---

[62] See Chap. 7, section 4.1. Although there have been few extensions of this kind in recent years, one notable exception is with respect to the Dominican Republic. See, further, Chap. 7, n. 97.

[63] Both states voted in favour of the Convention in 2001. In 2009, the Australian government announced that it was considering ratification: Australian Government, 'Australia's Maritime Heritage', Discussion Paper, June 2009. In Ireland it appears that ratification is being held back simply because the requisite legislative changes have a low political priority: Kirwan and Moore, 'Update on Ireland and the UNESCO Convention on the Protection of Underwater Cultural Heritage', pp. 51–2.

[64] For example, see Aznar-Gómez, who is of the view that Spanish legislation on this point conflicts with the UNESCO Convention but that it is unlikely to be amended: Aznar-Gómez, 'Spain', p. 291. See also Jeffery, 'Australia' (2nd edn), p. 12; O'Connor, 'Ireland' (2nd edn), p. 141; Kirwan, 'Ireland and the UNESCO Convention on the Protection of the Underwater Cultural Heritage', pp. 109–10. See also O'Keefe, *Shipwrecked Heritage*, p. 59.

[65] See Chap. 7, section 4.1.   [66] Art. 2(2).

the Convention, in practice they will surely find it difficult not to consult with other states parties who declare an interest, in just the same way as coastal states generally – when seeking to act under the authority of Article 10(2) – will do so.[67]

Finally, before moving away from the regime for the continental shelf and the EEZ, note should be made of Article 10(7). This makes provision in respect of sunken state vessels and aircraft in these areas. Like the equivalent provision in respect of such craft in the territorial sea, Article 10(7) is controversial. Like that provision, it is discussed in detail in Chapter 4.[68]

3.5   The Area

The potential importance of the Area (in other words, 'the seabed and ocean floor and subsoil thereof, beyond the limits of national jurisdiction')[69] from an archaeological perspective was acknowledged by UNESCO in its feasibility study for the drafting of an instrument on UCH, published in 1995.[70] Although specific provision was made for the Area in Article 149 of the LOSC, that provision was clearly inadequate in light of the fact that it gave no indication as to *who* would be responsible for implementing its protective objectives, or *how* they should go about doing so.[71] The UNESCO Convention seeks to make provision for the 'who' and the 'how'. The regime it sets out for the Area – in Articles 11 and 12 – reflects the form, if not the entire substance, of the regime for the EEZ and continental shelf set out in Articles 9 and 10.

Article 11(1) provides that states parties have a responsibility to protect UCH in the Area, in conformity with the terms of the Convention

---

[67] O'Connor 'consider[s] it unlikely that Ireland would take unilateral action on the further reaches of the continental shelf without consultation with relevant States Parties and only in circumstances where either the extent of adversarial impact or the importance of the given UCH merited it': O'Connor, 'Ireland' (2nd edn), p. 141. Jeffery suggests that the provision in the UNESCO Convention for interested states to be involved in decision-making in respect of UCH on the continental shelf 'would not seem to be a problem for Australia', pointing to its successful collaboration with the Netherlands in respect of the Dutch East Indiamen located off the Australian coast: Jeffery, 'Australia' (2nd edn), p. 12. Australia has been in the process of reviewing its legislation, including its provision for the continental shelf: see Australian Government, 'Australia's Maritime Heritage', Discussion Paper, June 2009.

[68] See Chap. 4, section 3.2.1.   [69] LOSC, Art. 1(1)(1).

[70] UNESCO Secretariat, 'Feasibility Study for the Drafting of a New Instrument for the Protection of the Underwater Cultural Heritage', presented to the 146th Session of the UNESCO Executive Board, Paris, 23 March 1995, Doc. 146 EX/27, para. 10.

[71] See Chap. 7, section 3.5.

and with Article 149 of the LOSC. As previously discussed,[72] in referring to the 'preservation' or 'disposal' of 'objects', Article 149 gives the impression that it envisages a scenario in which objects must be found, and possibly even recovered, before the duty it enshrines takes effect. While this is probably a reflection of the undeveloped state of underwater archaeological theory and practice at the time of UNCLOS III, it does not sit comfortably with modern archaeological principles. The duty established in Article 11(1), on the other hand, reflects the general aim of the UNESCO Convention: that the first option should be preservation *in situ*.

Echoing the provisions of Article 9, Article 11 establishes a system for the reporting and notification of discoveries of UCH, or of the intention to engage in activities directed at UCH, in the Area. A state party is obliged to require its national, or the master of a vessel flying its flag, to report to it any discovery of UCH or any intention to engage in activities directed at UCH in the Area.[73] The state must then relay such reports to the Director-General of UNESCO and also to the Secretary General of the ISA.[74] The Director-General of UNESCO is then required to make such reports promptly available to all states parties.[75] Those with a verifiable link may then declare an interest in being consulted on the means to ensure effective protection.[76]

Article 12 establishes a similar consultation and protection scheme to that set out in Article 10, paragraphs 3–6. However, in respect of the Area, the Director-General of UNESCO must invite states parties that have declared an interest to consult together on the best means of protection and to appoint a coordinating state to implement agreed protective measures.[77] The ISA must also be invited to participate in the consultations. As there will be no coastal state to act as coordinating state, it seems likely that the coordinating state will be either the state to whom the report was made or a state that has declared a verifiable link (although there is no requirement that this is so). As in respect of the continental shelf and EEZ, the coordinating state must implement agreed measures of protection and issue all necessary authorisations for such agreed measures, in conformity with the Convention.[78] It may also conduct any necessary preliminary research and must issue

---

[72] See Chap. 2, section 3.1.   [73] Art. 11(1).

[74] Art. 11(2). On the ISA and its functions, see Chap. 7, section 3.5.

[75] Art. 11(3).   [76] Art. 11(4).   [77] Art. 12(2)–(5).

[78] Art. 12(4)(a) and (b). The consulting states may agree that another state party implement the agreed measures and issue those authorisations.

authorisations in that regard.[79] Under Article 12(3), *all* states parties (not just the coordinating state, or those states with a verifiable link), may take all practicable measures, if necessary prior to consultations, where UCH is threatened by immediate danger 'from human activity or any other cause including looting'.[80] In contrast to Article 10(4), Article 12(3) does not state in terms that the measures taken must be in accordance with international law. However, given the overarching nature of Article 3, it is clear that this is the case. In practice, this means that the action that can be taken under Article 12(3) is essentially that specified in Articles 14, 15 and 16.

The regime set out in Articles 11 and 12 is clearly designed to dovetail with Article 149 of the LOSC. Aside from the fact that Article 11(1) specifies that any action taken by states parties under Articles 11 and 12 must be in conformity with Article 149, Article 12(6) makes it clear that, in taking action, the coordinating state must act '*for the benefit of humanity as a whole*, on behalf of all States Parties'.[81] The general notion that coordinating states do not act on their own behalf is thereby upheld, but at the same time there is an explicit tie-in with the principle enshrined in Article 149 that mankind as a whole should benefit from UCH located in the Area. The preferential rights referred to in Article 149 are also explicitly acknowledged.[82] In establishing that a state party has a verifiable link and thereby qualifies as a party that will be invited to participate in the consultation process set out in Article 12, 'particular regard [shall be] paid to the preferential rights of States of cultural, historical or archaeological origin'.[83] Further, in taking action, the coordinating state must pay '[p]articular regard' to such rights.[84] It is clear from these provisions that although a *non*-state party to the UNESCO Convention entitled to preferential rights under Article 149, by virtue of being a qualifying state of origin, will not be accorded the opportunity to participate directly in the consultation process,

---

[79] Art. 12(5). Again provision is made that the Director-General will be notified of the results and that information will be made available to other states parties.

[80] For a discussion of the impact of the regime set out in Arts. 11 and 12 on activities *incidentally affecting* UCH, see Chap. 10, section 3.2.

[81] Emphasis added. Cf. Art. 10(6).   [82] On these rights, see Chap. 3, section 4.1.2.

[83] Art. 11(4). Rather than repeating the rather clumsy formulation used in Art. 149 (which refers to the preferential rights of 'the State or country of origin, or the State of cultural origin, or the State of historical and archaeological origin'), the UNESCO Convention uses the neater formulation: preferential rights of 'States of cultural, historical or archaeological origin'. This should not make a difference in practice.

[84] Art. 12(6).

nevertheless, when action is taken by the coordinating state the rights of such a state must be taken into account. To the extent that the 'right' of such states – as recognised in Article 149 – affords *priority* over other interests,[85] there is nothing in Articles 11 and 12 to suggest that it should not be afforded the same level of priority here. However, there is clearly potential for conflict to arise where such a state wished to see action taken with respect to the site that is not in accordance with the principles of the Convention, for example, commercial exploitation or simply the recovery of material in circumstances where it is not regarded as justified by the competent national authority.[86]

The scheme for the Area set out in Articles 11 and 12 places considerable reliance upon the office of the Director-General of UNESCO. It must act as a conduit for all reports and must also coordinate declarations of interest by states with a verifiable interest. It will also need to liaise with the ISA. As previously discussed,[87] the role of the ISA under the LOSC is to control activities connected with the exploration and exploitation of the mineral resources of the Area; proposals at UNCLOS III that it should have a direct role with respect to UCH were not accepted. The UNESCO Convention does not envisage that the ISA should have responsibility for regulating activities directed at UCH in the Area, but simply that it should be notified of finds and involved in consultations concerning how best to protect them. Given that those making discoveries of UCH in the Area may well be organisations contracted with the ISA to undertake mineral exploration and exploitation, and given also that the activities of these contractors have the potential to endanger UCH (and, conversely, measures to protect UCH may impact upon such activities), the involvement of the ISA in practice could be quite significant.[88]

Finally, brief note should be made of Article 12(7). According to this provision, no state party shall undertake or authorise activities directed

[85] See Chap. 3, section 4.1.2.
[86] The coordinating state might counter such proposals by arguing that the state with preferential rights must take cognizance of the duty in Art. 303(1) of the LOSC to protect UCH and to cooperate for that purpose, and of Art. 149 of the LOSC which makes it clear that UCH found in the Area must be 'preserved or disposed of for the benefit of mankind as a whole'. It might also argue that the Rules set out in the UNESCO Annex represent widely accepted standards and, as such, are the relevant benchmark for action under Art. 303(1).
[87] See Chap. 7, section 3.5.
[88] For more detailed consideration of the relationship between the regulation of deep-seabed mining activities by the ISA under the regime set out in Part XI of the LOSC and the provision made for the Area in the UNESCO Convention, see Chap. 10, section 3.2.

at state vessels and aircraft in the Area without the consent of the flag state. In contrast to the provision in respect of state vessels and aircraft located in other maritime zones, Article 12(7) is uncontroversial.[89]

3.6   Compliance with the Law of the Sea Convention: a matter of interpretation

At the end of the UNESCO negotiations, a number of maritime states – France, Germany, the Netherlands, Norway, Russia, the UK and the USA – made it clear that they had serious reservations about the Convention's jurisdictional provisions. Some of the statements made by their official delegations in 2001 to explain their objections pinpointed the fundamental concern they all held in common:

> The text purports to *alter* the fine balance between the equal, but conflicting rights of Coastal and Flag States, carefully negotiated in [the LOSC], in a way that is unacceptable to the United Kingdom.[90]

> For [the Netherlands], it is extremely important that the careful balance between rights and obligations of Coastal States and Flag States, as foreseen in [the LOSC], will not be disturbed or infringed upon by other international instruments on specific issues, like underwater cultural heritage. Unfortunately, there is some *strain* between the text we have at hand and [the LOSC], especially with regard to the provisions on jurisdiction.[91]

> [T]he Convention ... includes parts, which *jeopardise* the fine balance of jurisdiction achieved through the carefully drafted UN Convention on the Law of the Sea (UNCLOS).[92]

Notably, the UN General Assembly also failed to endorse the final text. Instead, its annual Resolutions on Oceans and the Law of the Sea from 2004 onwards urged 'all states to cooperate, directly or through competent international bodies, in taking measures to protect and preserve objects of an archaeological and historical nature found at sea, *in conformity with* [the LOSC]'.[93]

---

[89] See, further, Chap. 4, section 3.2.1.

[90] See UK Statement on Vote reproduced in Camarda and Scovazzi, *The Protection of the Underwater Cultural Heritage*, pp. 432–3. Emphasis added.

[91] See Statement on Vote by the Netherlands, reproduced in Camarda and Scovazzi, *The Protection of the Underwater Cultural Heritage*, pp. 424–5. Emphasis added.

[92] See Statement on Vote by Norway, reproduced in Camarda and Scovazzi, *The Protection of the Underwater Cultural Heritage*, pp. 429–39. Emphasis added.

[93] See para. 7 of UN General Assembly Resolutions on Oceans and the Law of the Sea from A/RES/59/24 of 4 February 2005 until A/RES/65/37 of 17 March 2011. Emphasis added. (A notable change of tack took place in 2011: see Final reflections.)

In what ways, then, might the UNESCO Convention be seen to 'alter', or at least to 'strain' or 'jeopardise', the fine balance of rights enshrined in the LOSC? Some examples have already been referred to relating to the conventional regimes for the territorial sea and the contiguous zone. However, the aspects of the Convention that were and remain of most concern relate – inevitably – to the regime for the continental shelf and EEZ.

First of all, as indicated earlier, there are particular problems with the reporting provisions in Article 9(1). The concerns relate to Article 9(1)(b), which provides for the reporting by the nationals or flag vessels of one state party in respect of discoveries or activities in the EEZ or on the continental shelf of another state party. The fact that this matter is one of particular sensitivity is illustrated by the fact that Article 9(1)(b) sets out two alternative processes for such reporting:

in the exclusive economic zone or on the continental shelf of another State Party:

(i)   States Parties shall require the national or the master of the vessel to report such discovery or activity to them and *to that other State Party*;

(ii) alternatively, a State Party shall require the national or master of the vessel to report such discovery or activity *to it* and shall ensure the rapid and effective transmission of such reports to all other States Parties.[94]

These alternatives are both problematic because the wording in each case is ambiguous. A straightforward reading of paragraph (i), taken with the precursory sentence, suggests that it obliges states parties whose nationals or flag vessels have discovered UCH, or are intent on engaging in activities directed at UCH, to report that discovery or intent to them and also to the coastal state. Under this reading, the coastal state may be regarded merely as a recipient of the report and not as having a right to demand the report.[95] However, paragraph (i) could be read so that the reference to 'States Parties' *includes* the coastal state, in which case the coastal state will be not merely a recipient of the report, but will have a right to demand the report. This is seen as giving the coastal state

---

[94] Art. 9(1)(b). Emphasis added. By virtue of Art. 9(2), on deposit of its instrument of accession, a state party must declare the manner in which reports will be transmitted under Art. 9(1)(b). To date, only a small minority of states parties appears to have made such a declaration. Generally, they have opted for the procedure under Art. 9(1)(b)(ii).

[95] See O'Keefe, *Shipwrecked Heritage*, p. 82. This interpretation itself is controversial. For some, any form of direct notification of the coastal state amounts to the creation of a new coastal state right: see Blumberg, 'International Protection of Underwater Cultural Heritage', pp. 504–5.

a new jurisdictional right over foreign flag vessels and nationals on its continental shelf and in its EEZ. The formulation of the alternative reporting process, set out in paragraph (ii), is also ambiguous and for similar reasons. Again, a straightforward reading of the provision would suggest that it means simply that states parties are obliged to require *their own* nationals and flag vessels to report to them; on the other hand, the reference to 'a State Party' could be read to *include* the coastal state, in which case again it is seen as giving the coastal state a right to demand a report and thereby a new jurisdictional right. Proposals to amend the provision in order to remove the ambiguities were rejected,[96] indicating that the majority of the negotiators wished to see the possibility of alternative interpretations left open.

A second area of concern is in respect of the competences afforded to the coordinating state. As mentioned above, the Convention does not use the term 'coastal state'. However, in creating the role of coordinating state, it gives the coastal state a potentially prominent role in respect of UCH in the EEZ and on the continental shelf (assuming that the coastal state wishes to take on that role). Despite the efforts taken to provide reassurance on the role of the coastal state, considerable unease remains in respect of the rights afforded to the coastal state, as coordinating state, under Article 10, paragraphs 3 to 6. It may be recalled that these rights, unlike the right referred to in Article 10(2), are unlinked to any interference with the sovereign rights and jurisdiction of the coastal state in these zones. Of particular concern is the right of the coordinating state, under Article 10(4), to take 'all practical measures' – if necessary prior to consultations – to prevent 'immediate danger' to UCH. From a jurisdictional point of view, there are two problems with this: first, the measures can be undertaken *prior* to consultations, thereby undermining the notion of a 'coordinating state' implementing *agreed* measures; and, secondly, the measures that can be taken are undefined and potentially unlimited.[97] Depending on precisely what is meant by 'may take all

---

[96] See Garabello, 'The Negotiating History of the Convention on the Protection of the Underwater Cultural Heritage', p. 145, including n. 92. See also, O'Keefe, *Shipwrecked Heritage*, pp. 82–3.

[97] There is a third problem too, though it is a wider one, and that is the wording of the provision appears to permit measures to be taken in respect of all types of human activities, *including* those incidentally affecting UCH, apparently undermining an understanding reached at an early stage of the negotiations that the scope of the Convention was generally to be limited to regulating activities *directed at* UCH. On the potential impact of the Convention on activities incidentally affecting UCH, see, further, Chap. 10, section 3.

practicable measures, and/or issue any necessary authorizations', Article 10(4) could be regarded as an expansion of coastal state jurisdiction.

The wording of the provision in Article 10(2) in respect of the protection of sovereign rights and jurisdiction is also problematic. Although on the face of it, it may appear to be a simple restatement of existing rights, the formulation of the provision – especially its reference to 'sovereign rights or jurisdiction as provided for by international law including [the LOSC]' – is a cause of concern. In adopting the same contentious formula as Article 3, it suggests that states may have sovereign rights and jurisdiction that go beyond what is provided for in the LOSC. Furthermore, the fact that Article 10(2) gives coastal states the right to act in order to 'prevent interference' with its sovereign rights and jurisdiction indicates that coastal states can control activities that only *may* interfere with, as well as that *do* interfere with, such rights and jurisdiction.[98]

As discussed above, the maritime states argue that the UNESCO Convention is an *inter-se* agreement falling within the scope of Article 311(3) of the LOSC. As such, it must not affect the application of the basic principles of the LOSC, nor impinge on the rights of non-states parties to the new treaty. As well as potentially affecting the application of the basic jurisdictional principles of the LOSC in the ways set out above, the wording of some of the provisions of the UNESCO Convention could also be read as impacting on the rights of *non*-states parties. In particular, a number of the provisions in Article 10, and indeed in Article 12, could be read to permit the regulation of activities of nationals and flag vessels of non-states parties.[99]

It has been argued that the regime set out in Articles 9 and 10 creates a cultural heritage zone coexistent with the continental shelf and EEZ, 'although by means calculated to obscure [such an] intent'.[100] On the

---

[98] See Garabello, 'The Negotiating History of the Convention on the Protection of the Underwater Cultural Heritage', p. 148.
[99] See Blumberg, 'International Protection of Underwater Cultural Heritage', p. 506. One other provision that is also a cause of concern is Art. 2(11). This provides that: '[n]o act or activity undertaken on the basis of this Convention shall constitute grounds for claiming, contending or disputing any claim to national sovereignty or jurisdiction'. There are concerns that this could be read to preclude challenges to excessive claims based on provisions of the Convention. Others argue that the provision was intended to refer to maritime territorial disputes only and 'should be interpreted in this limited fashion': see Garabello, 'The Negotiating History of the Convention on the Protection of the Underwater Cultural Heritage', p. 115; see also O'Keefe, *Shipwrecked Heritage*, p. 56.
[100] Bederman, 'Maritime Preservation Law', p. 201.

other hand, the reaction to these provisions of Greece, a state which has argued for decades in favour of such a zone, might indicate otherwise. Greece felt compelled to reject the final terms of the Convention, in part, because of what it regarded as the *limited* role afforded to the coastal state in these zones. In the opinion of the Greek delegation:

This system [in Articles 9 and 10] leaves to the coastal state *only* a 'coordinating role' on its own continental shelf and does not ensure its right to be notified of discoveries of UCH or intended activities directed at UCH found in the area (see in particular article 9(1)(b)(ii)).[101]

The reality is that the regime the Convention sets out is a half-way house that attempts to accommodate the interests of those espousing the view that there was no point in simply repeating the provisions of the LOSC without bringing about improvements and those arguing that there should be no extension of coastal state jurisdiction beyond the position enshrined in the LOSC. In order to accommodate the two sets of interests, Articles 9 and 10 deploy the device of constructive ambiguity (in just the same way as Article 303(2) of the LOSC had done previously). A number of other articles in the UNESCO Convention do likewise, including Article 3.

In discussing the relationship between the two treaties, as far as the EEZ is concerned, reference is sometimes made to Article 59 of the LOSC. As pointed out in Chapter 7,[102] Article 59 provides a basis for the resolution of disputes arising between the interests of the coastal state and any other state or states in respect of matters over which the LOSC does not attribute rights or jurisdiction to either the coastal state or to other states. The right to search for and recover UCH appears to be such an 'unattributed' right. Therefore, any dispute relating to such activities must be resolved:

on the basis of equity and in the light of all the relevant circumstances, taking into account the respective importance of the interests involved to the parties as well as to the international community as a whole.[103]

---

[101] Emphasis added. For the full Statement on Vote by Greece and related discussion, see Strati, 'Greece' (2nd edn), pp. 118–21. One problematic provision for Greece is Art. 13. This provides an exemption (with certain provisos) for warships and other vessels operating for non-commercial purposes from the reporting obligations under Arts. 9–12: *ibid.*, p. 119. Art. 13 represents an important concession to maritime states. On this provision, see, further, O'Keefe, *Shipwrecked Heritage*, pp. 101–2.

[102] Chap. 7, section 3.4.

[103] Art. 59. On the application of this formula, see, further, Chap. 7, section 3.4.

It is arguable that this provision in the LOSC may help to bolster the legitimacy of the role afforded by the UNESCO Convention to the coastal state as coordinating state, at least as far as the EEZ is concerned. The UNESCO Convention is, after all, a concrete manifestation of the interest of the international community as a whole in ensuring that all activities directed at UCH are undertaken in accordance with benchmark archaeological standards; the fact that the coastal state – when fulfilling the role of a coordinating state – *acts on behalf of interested states*, strengthens the argument that the interests of the coastal state and those of the international community are fundamentally one and the same.[104]

4. Potential effectiveness of the regime

The regime adopted by the UNESCO Convention for the continental shelf and EEZ, and the Area, incorporates a complex array of reporting, notification, consultation and protection mechanisms. Complexity tends to give rise to problems and it is possible to foresee a myriad of problematic issues arising in the course of the implementation of these mechanisms.[105] It will therefore require a considerable degree of commitment on the part of states parties, at both a political level and at the level of their competent agencies (along with robust support from the UNESCO Secretariat), to ensure that the problems do not threaten the entire system. However, leaving the technical day-to-day implementation of the regulatory regime to one side, a more fundamental question is: to what extent does the Convention have the potential to fulfil its fundamental objective – to plug the gaps in the LOSC's provision for UCH in order to ensure that activities directed at UCH in international waters are regulated in accordance with accepted archaeological standards? Given that these standards are based on the notion that preservation *in situ* should be the starting point in determining the future management of a UCH site, clearly the system set up by the Convention must be capable of ensuring that activities are subject to regulation by competent authorities *prior* to any physical intervention taking place. To what extent does it do so?

One particular difficulty that can be envisaged relates to the focus placed by Articles 9–12 on the *identification* of a UCH site. Where the UCH involved is a shipwreck (as will often be the case in offshore waters),

---

[104] By virtue of the duty to protect set out in Art. 303(1) of the LOSC. See Chap. 7, section 3.4.

[105] For some examples, see O'Keefe's commentary on the relevant articles: O'Keefe, *Shipwrecked Heritage*, pp. 80–100.

it may take many months of investigation, much of it invasive, to determine with reasonable certainty the identity of the wreck.[106] Therefore, in many circumstances protective measures will need to be in place long before one or more states are able to establish a verifiable link to the site. For this reason, in practice it seems likely that only one or, possibly, two states will be involved in the early stages when many of the crucial decisions need to be made: the coastal state (assuming the UCH is located on the continental shelf or in the EEZ), and the flag state of the reporting vessel (assuming the flag state is a party to the Convention).

As far as the continental shelf and EEZ are concerned, despite the emphasis in Articles 9 and 10 on the notion of the coastal state acting as a coordinating state and on there being a group of states consulting together to decide on protection measures, in practice it seems quite likely that in many circumstances the coastal state may have to make decisions alone during the crucial early stages, simply because there are no other states directly involved. Nonetheless, Article 10(2) provides it with a clear basis for acting independently and permits it to prohibit or authorise activities directed at UCH. Therefore, whether or not it would *prefer* to act within a consultative framework, it seems likely that – when faced with the prospect of unregulated interference – it will take action under the authority of Article 10(2), rather than under the more contentious route provided by Article 10(4). For this reason, if for no other, it seems likely that Article 10(2) will become the primary mechanism for protecting UCH in these areas. This is not to say that consultation will not take place, but it is possible that it will take place only months or even years after the original discovery, and long after the 'immediate threat' has been dealt with. Assuming that the coastal state has the means to monitor activities taking place on its continental shelf and in its EEZ (and this is a big assumption),[107] it should be possible to ensure that regulation generally takes effect *before* activities

---

[106] The difficulties that can arise in the identification of wreck sites is discussed, in the context of the establishment of ownership claims, in Chap. 3, section 2.2.

[107] The question of capacity is an important one more generally. Many states have little experience or established capacity in the field of UCH protection, as well as limited resources more generally. Therefore, there are likely to be particular challenges in implementing the conventional regime in some regions. According to Art. 2(4), in taking the necessary measures to protect UCH, states parties must use 'the best practicable means at their disposal and *in accordance with their capabilities*'. Emphasis added. Some states will need considerable support from others in the early years. Specific provision is made for cooperation in respect of training in archaeological and conservation techniques, and in the transfer of relevant technology: see Art. 21. See, further, Chap. 9, section 2.

directed at UCH are conducted. Provided most, if not all, of the coastal states in a particular region are parties to the Convention, this system – supplemented by coordinated use of Article 15 to cut off lines of supply – could effectively put an end to unregulated interference with UCH in enclosed or semi-enclosed sea areas.

The regulation of activities in the Area is likely to be more problematic, however. Unless the identity of a site is obvious, the operation of the system in Articles 11 and 12 will be reliant on the flag state (or perhaps the state of the expedition leader)[108] being a party to the Convention. If that is not the case, the system these provisions establish will not be triggered at all. In such circumstances, if it becomes known that a vessel is undertaking UCH search operations in the Area, or is engaged in investigating a site, there appears to be little states parties can do to *stop* intervention taking place. The prohibition of the use of their ports and other facilities under Article 15 may have some effect, but where activities are taking place in the open oceans it is only likely to do so if the Convention is widely ratified. Article 14 relates to controls in respect of *recovered* artefacts and is therefore only relevant *after* intervention has taken place. In circumstances where it becomes operative, other mechanisms in the Convention to all intents and purposes will have failed.

Article 16 is pivotal to the scheme the Convention establishes, not just for the Area, but also (given the contentiousness of the issue of direct reporting to the coastal state) for the continental shelf and EEZ as well. The reliance the Convention places on the nationality principle of jurisdiction, and more specifically flag state jurisdiction, means that the support of flag states, particularly the handful that have deepwater technological capability, is absolutely crucial if the Convention is to succeed in fulfilling its primary objective. Those states include the USA, the UK, Germany, France, Norway and Russia, all of whom expressed reservations about the Convention in 2001. Until the Convention has their support, its protective framework cannot be fully functional and can only have piecemeal effect.

5. Concluding remarks

After the UNESCO negotiations, Blumberg, Head of the US delegation, noted that the leaders of the Group of 77 at the negotiations were 'primarily the same Latin American countries that had advocated, but

---

[108] See n. 46 above.

failed to achieve, general regulatory authority over all activities within 200 miles during the UNCLOS negotiations'. In light of this, he questioned whether the efforts these states were making during the negotiations to extend jurisdiction over UCH were in fact a political attempt to have 'another bite at the "jurisdictional apple"', rather than a necessary practical tool to protect UCH.[109] It seems likely that suspicions of this kind about the motives of coastal states lie at the root of flag state concerns on the matter of jurisdiction: as was the case at UNCLOS III, the concern is not so much with the exercise of jurisdiction over UCH *per se*, but with where it might lead.[110]

---

[109] Blumberg, 'International Protection of Underwater Cultural Heritage', p. 499.
[110] For further discussion of this point, see Final reflections.

9 UNESCO Convention 2001: implementation issues

1. Introduction

In practical terms the primary aim of the UNESCO Convention 2001 is to ensure that all activities directed at UCH are governed by the principles of the Convention and, more particularly, by the Rules set out in its Annex. These Rules, which form an integral part of the Convention,[1] embody internationally accepted standards for the conduct of underwater archaeological activities. Chapter 8 explored the jurisdictional framework set in place by the Convention to enable states parties, working individually and jointly, to regulate activities across all maritime zones; the present chapter considers what each state party will need to do on a more practical, day-to-day, basis to implement the Convention and ensure the management of UCH according to its terms.

The management ethos of the Convention is reflected in a number of the objectives and general principles enshrined in Article 2, which are reiterated and amplified in Part I of the Annex. The overall management objective is the preservation of UCH for the 'benefit of humanity'.[2] With this in mind, there are three core management principles: (i) preservation *in situ* shall be considered as the first option;[3] (ii) in so far as recovery is permitted, material shall be deposited, conserved and managed in a manner that ensures its long-term preservation;[4] and (iii) responsible non-intrusive public access shall be encouraged.[5] The entire scheme of the Convention, including the Rules in the Annex, is framed to ensure that this ethos is applied – as far as possible – to all UCH as defined by the Convention.

---

[1] Art. 33. [2] Art. 2(3). [3] Art. 2(5). See also Rule 1.
[4] Art. 2(6). [5] Art. 2(10). See also Rule 7.

What, then, are the practical measures that states must take to ensure that UCH is managed in accordance with these principles and what impact are these measures likely to have on legitimate 'users' of the resource, such as recreational divers, amateur archaeologists and the public at large? What sanctions does the Convention require states to impose for violations of the measures taken and what further action are they required to take to discourage such violations from taking place? This chapter considers, in turn, the role of competent national authorities; the authorisation process (with particular focus on the application of the preservation *in situ* principle); the question of who has *access* to UCH (*in situ* and *ex situ*) and on what basis; and, finally, the important question of sanctions and related deterrents. Through its exploration of these matters, the chapter draws attention to some of the defining characteristics of the Convention.

2.   The role of competent national authorities

According to Article 22(1):

In order to ensure the proper implementation of this Convention, States Parties shall establish competent authorities or reinforce the existing ones where appropriate, with the aim of providing for the establishment, maintenance and updating of an inventory of underwater cultural heritage, the effective protection, conservation, presentation and management of underwater cultural heritage, as well as research and education.

By virtue of Article 22(2):

States Parties shall communicate to the Director-General [of UNESCO] the names and addresses of their competent authorities relating to underwater cultural heritage.

It is interesting to note there is nothing in Article 22, or elsewhere in the Convention, to suggest that each state party must nominate only one competent authority. Indeed, Article 22(1) gives the distinct impression that the possibility that states may nominate more than one competent authority has been deliberately left open. For many states, especially federal states, this will be politically convenient. However, in light of the reliance the Convention's regulatory regime places on swift exchanges of information and prompt collaborative action, the nomination of one national contact point undoubtedly would be desirable from an administrative perspective where this is possible.

Many states already have public authorities with responsibility for the management of UCH. In many cases, these authorities are departments or agencies with a heritage remit: sometimes discrete units with UCH responsibility and sometimes units that combine marine and terrestrial heritage responsibilities. Sometimes the responsible government unit will be based in a department or agency that has a maritime, rather than heritage, focus. Where there are existing authorities, they may need to be reinforced in order to meet the demands of the Convention, for example by building up their archaeological expertise; where there are no existing authorities, they will need to be established.

Article 22(1) envisages a broad remit for competent national authorities. The aim is that they will provide for the effective protection, conservation, presentation and management of UCH, as well as for research and education in the field. In its outline of the role of the authorities, by referring first to the establishment, maintenance and updating of national inventories, the article emphasises that an inventory is a core tool in heritage management. In order to manage any resource effectively, there needs to be an awareness of the composition and extent of the resource so that priorities can be determined and management decisions made which are based on an informed assessment of the resource as a whole. Many states have already begun to compile such inventories for their coastal waters: these may be based on a combination of historical records of losses, reports of finds and systematic surveys. The geographical remit of the inventories to be maintained under the Convention is not defined but – given the extra-territorial nature of the Convention's framework and objectives – presumably it is envisaged that the inventories will not, at least ultimately, be confined to UCH located within territorial limits. Indeed, to fulfil the duties on states parties under Articles 9 and 10,[6] the development of national inventories for their offshore areas will be a crucial tool; as discoveries are gradually reported under the terms of these articles, they will clearly feed into the process of inventory development. In states with a naval tradition, the inclusion of historical records of national losses, wherever they have taken place, will also clearly contribute to the effective management of the global UCH resource.

The broad role envisaged for the competent national authorities reflects the breadth of the duties that the Convention imposes upon states parties. Although the focus of the treaty is on protecting UCH by

---

[6] See Chap. 8, section 3.4.

regulating activities that target it directly, the obligations on states parties extend far more widely. Article 2(4) makes it clear that states parties are required to take active steps to afford protection, in general terms, to UCH:

States Parties shall, individually or jointly as appropriate, take all appropriate measures in conformity with this Convention and with international law that are necessary to protect underwater cultural heritage, using for this purpose the best practicable means at their disposal and in accordance with their capabilities.

Among other things, this means that they are required to take action to protect UCH from *all* types of threat. In this respect, the duty is exemplified by Article 10(4), which calls for action by all states parties in respect of UCH that is in 'immediate danger ... whether arising from human activities or any other cause, including looting' on the continental shelf and in the EEZ,[7] and also by Article 5, which provides that states parties 'shall use the best practicable means at [their] disposal to prevent or mitigate any adverse effects that might arise from activities under [their] jurisdiction incidentally affecting UCH'.[8]

Aside from countering direct threats to UCH, the Convention imposes upon states parties a range of other duties and expectations that will enhance the general well-being of UCH. These include expectations in respect of the investigation, excavation, documentation, conservation, study and presentation of UCH,[9] and duties in respect of the raising of public awareness[10] and training.[11] However, the Convention also recognises that states do not have unlimited resources at their disposal for heritage management and that some states have more limited means and capabilities than others. Article 2(4) makes it clear that while states must take 'all appropriate measures' 'that are necessary' they need only use 'the best practicable means at their disposal' and that are 'in accordance with their capabilities'. For some states, capabilities may be very limited at the start, but with the support and assistance of other states parties it is envisaged that over time their capabilities will grow and the measures they take will strengthen.

---

[7] On this provision, see Chap. 8, section 3.4. The equivalent provision in respect of the Area, Art. 12(3), should also be noted (see Chap. 8, section 3.5). However, Art. 12(3) is framed permissively and does not *oblige* states parties to take action in circumstances where an immediate danger arises from human activity or any other cause.

[8] On this provision, see Chap. 10, section 3.   [9] See Art. 19(1).

[10] See Art. 20.   [11] See Art. 21.

In providing that states parties shall take measures 'individually or jointly as appropriate', Article 2(4) represents a specific application of Article 2(2). As previously noted, this sets out one of the fundamental principles and objectives of the Convention:

> States Parties shall cooperate in the protection of underwater cultural heritage.

As discussed in Chapter 8, cooperation underpins the jurisdictional schemes for the continental shelf and EEZ, and the Area, but it is clear from Article 2(4) that the Convention envisages the development of a broad protective framework for UCH in which collaborative effort will form a key part. Article 19(1) makes it clear that cooperation is expected across all relevant areas:

> States Parties shall cooperate and assist each other in the protection and management of underwater cultural heritage under this Convention, including where practicable, collaborating in the investigation, excavation, documentation, conservation, study and presentation of such heritage.

Article 19 includes three further paragraphs that relate specifically to the sharing of information between states parties and with the UNESCO Secretariat. Sharing of information obviously facilitates general cooperation and assistance; however, it is also crucial to many of the regulatory mechanisms outlined in Chapter 8 and is therefore a core component of the regime as a whole.[12]

In some parts of the world, national heritage authorities already cooperate with one another at a regional level, for example through the European Archaeological Council[13] or Baltic Sea Heritage Cooperation.[14] Such cooperation can lead not only to improvements with respect to the day-to-day practicalities of management of UCH within the region, but also – through the sharing of ideas, experiences and best practice – with respect to the general management techniques employed. Similarly, but with the added benefits that are likely to come from collaboration on a global scale, states parties to the Convention will benefit not only from direct cooperation and assistance, but also from the sharing of best practice and leadership by example. In the shorter

---

[12] Art. 19(3) recognises the need for care to be taken regarding the dissemination of information about the discovery or location of UCH in circumstances where disclosure might put such UCH at risk. In such circumstances, it provides that such information must be 'kept confidential and reserved to competent authorities of States Parties', at least 'to the extent compatible with their national legislation'.

[13] Maarleveld, 'The Netherlands', p. 182.   [14] Adlercreutz, 'Sweden', p. 311.

term, it is envisaged that the limited capabilities recognised by Article 2(4) will be made up for by direct assistance from other states parties: for example, the Convention provides that states parties 'shall' cooperate in the provision of training in underwater archaeology, in techniques for conservation of UCH and, 'on agreed terms', in the transfer of technology.[15] In the longer term, it is envisaged that the cooperation fostered by the Convention will lead to an improvement in the effectiveness of measures at national, regional and international levels for the preservation and management of UCH.[16]

3. Authorisation of activities directed at underwater cultural heritage

Nowhere in the main body of the Convention does it clearly and explicitly state that activities directed at UCH must be authorised by a competent authority *in all cases*, before they are capable of complying with the Rules in the Annex and are thereby compliant with the Convention. However, if this was not the case, it would open up the prospect of an individual or group undertaking activities directed at UCH without authorisation and then arguing that the activities were conducted in accordance with the archaeological standards in the Annex and – in its judgment – were justified in the circumstances. Clearly this would be absurd and the whole structure of the Convention's regulatory framework indicates that the intention was that activities can be compliant only if authorised by a competent authority. In fact, confirmation of this can be found in the Rules themselves, most specifically in Rule 9. This provides:

> Prior to any activity directed at underwater cultural heritage, a project design for the activity shall be developed and submitted to the competent authorities for authorization and appropriate peer review.

This makes it clear beyond doubt that there must be authorisation in advance in all cases and that authorisation must come from a competent authority.

---

[15] Art. 21. The inclusion of the wording 'on agreed terms' is in recognition of the fact that the issue of technology transfer is a sensitive and complex one: see Garabello, 'The Negotiating History of the Convention on the Protection of the Underwater Cultural Heritage', p. 168.

[16] See preambular clause 13.

3.1   Authorisation scheme

Again, while the final text of the Convention does not explicitly refer to the notion of a 'permit' or 'licence', it is difficult to envisage an authorisation scheme that does not involve some form of permit or licensing scheme.[17] As previously noted, activities 'directed at' UCH are defined to mean:

> activities having underwater cultural heritage as their primary object and which may, directly or indirectly, physically disturb or otherwise damage underwater cultural heritage.[18]

Many forms of human activity in the marine environment 'may, directly or indirectly, physically disturb or otherwise damage' UCH, but the key to the scope of these activities is the reference to their having UCH 'as their primary object'. While it does not say so in terms, this appears to mean that the activities must be undertaken with the deliberate intention of *interfering* with UCH.[19] The definition therefore includes activities such as treasure and souvenir hunting, archaeological investigations involving the physical disturbance of the site and physical intervention by way of 'rescue' activities in the course of development work. It does *not* include non-intrusive diving on a site, or non-intrusive archaeological survey work. Moreover, it does *not* include activities that only 'incidentally affect' UCH, in other words activities that do not have UCH as their primary object, but which nonetheless cause physical disturbance.[20] While the latter activities may be affected in various ways by the Convention,[21] they are not subject to the authorisation scheme, nor to the Rules in the Annex. As the heading of the Annex makes clear, the Rules only concern activities *directed at* UCH.

---

[17] By this is meant a scheme that provides a documented record of the authorisation which can be used as evidence that the activities were in fact authorised. As Forrest has pointed out, states commonly make use of permits (or 'licences') – either pre-intervention permits, or import permits – and earlier drafts of the UNESCO Convention provided for the issuance of import permits (in other words, permits issued by a state allowing entry of UCH into its territory): see Forrest, 'A New International Regime for the Protection of Underwater Cultural Heritage', pp. 546–7. In practice, it seems likely that permits will be used under the conventional regime and some standardisation of practice in this respect will clearly be important. Among other things, the system needs to dovetail with other international treaty regimes, particularly that under the 1970 UNESCO Convention on Illicit Trade in Cultural Property. On this Convention, see, further, section 5.2, below.

[18] Art. 1(6).   [19] See O'Keefe, *Shipwrecked Heritage*, p. 45.

[20] See Art. 1(7).   [21] See, further, Chap. 10, section 3.

In 2011, UNESCO published a Manual, authored by eminent archaeologists from around the world, which is designed to assist competent authorities in their application of the annexed Rules.[22]

3.2   *Preservation* in situ

Central to the Convention's ethos for the management of UCH is the notion of preservation *in situ*. This notion derives from terrestrial archaeology and appears to have been formally adopted for the first time in respect of UCH specifically in the Council of Europe's draft European Convention of 1985.[23] The adoption of this principle as one of the central tenets of the UNESCO Convention is a well-known feature of its regime but its implications may not always be fully understood.

Article 2(5) provides:

The preservation *in situ* of underwater cultural heritage shall be considered as the first option before allowing or engaging in any activities directed at this heritage.

It is clear from this statement, which is reiterated in Rule 1, that the Convention does not require that UCH be preserved *in situ* as a matter of course, but that preservation *in situ* be considered as the *first* management option. The words 'first option', rather than 'preferred option', were deliberately chosen because the latter might give a misleading impression.[24] In each individual case, preservation *in situ may* be the preferred option; however, it depends on the precise circumstances. It is certainly not the only option and it is not the inevitable outcome of application of the Convention.

In essence, the approach taken by the Convention is a precautionary one. When a site is discovered, rather than making an immediate assumption that it should be excavated, or in any other way physically disturbed, the full circumstances must first be assessed so that an informed decision can be made on the best course of action. While

---

[22] See UNESCO Manual for Activities Directed at Underwater Cultural Heritage, 2011 (available at www.unesco.org/new/en/culture/themes/underwater-cultural-heritage/ unesco-manual). The Manual was written as a source of informed discussion of issues relating to the practical application of the Rules, rather than as an authoritative interpretation of the Rules. However, its status has the potential to be contentious: see, further, Chap. 10, n. 96.

[23] See Chap. 1, section 2.2.2.

[24] At the negotiations, the US delegation sought an amendment to ensure that *in situ* preservation 'would merely be a first option to be considered, but not the presumed choice': see Dorsey, 'Historic Salvors, Marine Archaeologists, and the UNESCO Draft Convention on the Underwater Cultural Heritage', p. 30.

preservation *in situ* is the first option to be considered, the Convention clearly anticipates that physical intervention – including excavation and recovery – will take place in some circumstances: the very fact that detailed Rules have been drawn up to regulate such activities indicates that this is the case. Clause 13 of the preamble to the Convention gives some indication of when those circumstances will be, referring to the 'careful recovery' of UCH 'if necessary for scientific or protective purposes'. The Annex elucidates on those purposes. Rule 1 provides that activities 'may be authorised for the purpose of making a significant contribution to protection or knowledge or enhancement' of UCH and Rule 4 refers to circumstances where excavation or recovery is 'necessary for the purpose of scientific studies or for the ultimate protection' of UCH. These guidelines are quite 'loose' and competent national authorities are therefore left with some latitude to determine when intervention is justified in individual cases. However, Rule 1 makes it clear that in all cases the benefit to be derived from any intervention must be 'significant'.

There is an implicit assumption within the preservation *in situ* concept that archaeological deposits *may* be 'safest' left in the natural environment in which they are found. A point that is frequently made in the UCH context is that once a shipwreck has been lying on the seabed for some time, it will stabilise within its natural environment and the rate of its physical deterioration will slow down to a considerable extent.[25] However, it will not stop altogether.[26] Furthermore, the marine environment is more dynamic than the terrestrial environment,[27] and certain marine areas – such as the Wadden Sea in Northern Europe and the Goodwin Sands off the English coast – are particularly so.[28] Therefore, in some cases sites may be threatened by the natural environment, rather than protected by it. Human activities may clearly also pose a threat. As well as the risks posed by commercial infrastructure projects, such as the installation of wind-turbines and pipelines, day-to-day activities such as dredging and trawling can cause extensive damage. Also, once a UCH site is discovered, if it is suspected to contain items of commercial value, it

---

[25] See, further, Chap. 5 section 3, especially n. 22 and associated text.

[26] This is illustrated by the case of the *Titanic*. There are concerns that the wreck is rapidly deteriorating in condition, at least in part because of bacterial activity: see 'The 2010 Scientific Expedition to *Titanic*' (available at www.sanctuaries.noaa.gov/maritime/titanic/2010_expedition.html).

[27] Panter, '*In Situ* Preservation Versus Active Conservation', p. 59.

[28] Manders, '*In Situ* Preservation', p. 34.

may be at risk from (to use the Convention's terminology) 'looting'. Therefore, as sites are discovered, a risk assessment needs to be done on a case-by-case basis to determine if some form of intervention is justifiable for protective purposes. This intervention could range from simply taking measures physically to protect the site *in situ*, for example with sandbags and polypropylene nets,[29] to recovering artefacts that lie vulnerable on the surface of the site, or undertaking a more extensive excavation. Intervention may also be justifiable for 'scientific' purposes, for example physically to monitor the condition of a site, or to add to the body of human knowledge about the past. However, the conventional requirement that the benefits must be 'significant' indicates that in all cases the benefits must clearly outweigh any detriment arising as a result of the intervention.

To get some sense of how these principles may work in practice, it is instructive to take a look at national policy statements that apply these principles. In light of Spain's ratification of the UNESCO Convention in 2005, a National Plan for the Protection of Underwater Cultural Heritage has been drawn up, which is partly designed to align Spanish practice with the Convention in respect of archaeological interventions. In a section relating to prerequisites for all archaeological projects, the Spanish National Plan provides:

Intrusive projects should be kept to an absolute minimum while prioritising conservation *in situ* and authorisation should not be given for any project unless the latter's focus on the cataloguing of the heritage, the benefits for scientific research and protection against clear risk of damage to the heritage are *clearly proven*.[30]

The (roughly) equivalent policy statement made by English Heritage, which relates primarily to 'research excavation' and applies to the historic environment generally, provides:

Intervention in significant places primarily to increase knowledge of the past involving material loss of evidential values, should normally be acceptable if:

---

[29] Manders has pointed out that taking protective measures *in situ* may slow down the process of degradation but that it is impossible to halt the process altogether. However, he also points out that the same is the case for objects that are recovered and preserved *ex situ*: Manders, *ibid.*, p. 32.

[30] Green Paper: Spanish National Plan for the Protection of Underwater Cultural Heritage, 2009, p. 70 (available at http://museoarqua.mcu.es/web/uploads/ficheros/verde_ingles.pdf). Emphasis added.

(a) preservation *in situ* is not reasonably practicable; or
(b) it is demonstrated that the potential increase in knowledge
  • cannot be achieved using non-destructive techniques; and
  • is unlikely to be achieved at another place whose destruction is inevitable; and
  • is predicted *decisively to outweigh* the loss of the primary resource.[31]

While there might be a slight difference of emphasis, the two statements do not seem to differ in essence, despite the fact that the UK does not currently anticipate ratifying the Convention. This might suggest that the position on *in situ* preservation under the UNESCO Convention reflects (as it is intended to do) standard modern heritage practice. The English guidance also highlights a further implication of the adoption by the Convention of the *in situ* preservation principle. When consideration is given to an application to undertake activities in the pursuit of knowledge of the past, a factor that should be weighed in the balance is whether or not the knowledge sought is unlikely to be gained from another site where intervention may be necessary in any event for protective purposes, or where damage or destruction is inevitable as a result of natural causes or activities incidental to UCH.[32]

The Rules in the Annex to the Convention make it clear that where activities *are* permitted they must not 'adversely affect the underwater cultural heritage more than is necessary for the objectives of the project';[33] 'must use non-destructive techniques and survey methods in preference to the recovery of objects';[34] must avoid the 'unnecessary disturbance of human remains or venerated sites';[35] and must be 'strictly regulated to ensure proper recording of cultural, historical and archaeological information'.[36] In all cases, a project design, subject to peer review, must be submitted providing details of, among other things, the project objectives; proposed methodology and techniques; provision for project funding and duration; the composition, qualifications and

---

[31] English Heritage, Conservation Principles, Policies and Guidance: Sustainable Management of the Historic Environment, April 2008, Principle 12 (available at www.english-heritage.org.uk). Emphasis added.

[32] In its guidance on Rule 1, the UNESCO Manual for Activities Directed at Underwater Cultural Heritage explains that excavation 'destroys the coherence and context of a site' from an archaeological perspective and 'also compromises to a greater or lesser extent the site's authenticity, the quality that is most respected in experiencing and enjoying a place, in identifying with it, or in terms of commemoration'.

[33] Rule 3.   [34] Rule 4.   [35] Rule 5. See, further, section 4.4, below.   [36] Rule 6.

experience of the project team; conservation and site management programmes; arrangements for documentation and dissemination of the
project results; and arrangements for deposition of the project archives,
including recovered material.[37] The project design must be approved by
the competent authority in advance of *any* activity.[38] One of the justifications for adoption of the *in situ* preservation principle is that resources
for archaeological intervention are inevitably limited. Past experiences at
national level have shown the risks of embarking on intervention before
the resources are in place to see the project through to completion.
Therefore, the Convention seeks to ensure that the full implications of
the project have been properly thought through and that adequate
financial and other resources will be in place as required to prosecute
every stage of the project.[39]

Before leaving the matter of *in situ* preservation, one interesting question that arises relating to the conventional regime is: what is the procedure envisaged for when *isolated objects* are discovered? On the face of it, the
conventional scheme would appear to require that even the recovery of
one isolated object lying on the seabed will require authorisation from a
competent national authority and the submission of a project design for
approval and peer review, in accordance with the requirements set out
above. However, Rule 13 appears to cover this situation. It states:

In cases of urgency or *chance discoveries*, activities directed at the underwater
cultural heritage, including conservation measures or activities for a period of
short duration, in particular site stabilization, may be authorized in the absence
of a project design in order to protect the underwater cultural heritage.[40]

This provision allows the recovery of a chance discovery in order to
ensure its protection without the need for the preparation of a detailed
project design, although authorisation will still need to be sought *in
advance* of the recovery. However, in many cases modern communications should allow for the discovery to be reported, and authorisation to
recover the object sought, while a vessel is still stationed in the proximity
of the object, thereby minimising the risk that it will not be possible to
find the object at a later stage.

---

[37] See Parts II to XIV of the Rules.   [38] Rule 9.
[39] For example, and as previously discussed (see Chap. 6, section 4.2.2), an adequate
funding base must be assured in advance of any activity, sufficient to complete all stages
of the project design including conservation, documentation and curation of recovered
artefacts, and report preparation and dissemination: see Rule 17.
[40] Emphasis added.

3.3   Treatment of recovered artefacts

In the case of archaeological sites underwater, the availability of resources for conserving, and ultimately housing, recovered material is a factor that is of particular significance. The conservation process for waterlogged material is highly specialised and expensive, requiring specially trained and experienced conservators and specialised laboratories.[41] Material from shipwreck sites, such as wooden timbers, can be bulky and may require the maintenance of special environmental conditions over an extended period.[42] This can mean that it is especially hard to find temporary or permanent homes for material from UCH sites in museums or other suitable institutions. For these reasons, the Convention insists that arrangements for the curation of the project archives, which include any recovered UCH, must be agreed before any activity commences,[43] and the funding base for the project must be sufficient to include conservation, documentation and curation of recovered artefacts.[44]

In so far as activities directed at UCH are permitted, and recovery of objects is deemed to be justifiable and adequately resourced, Article 2(6) of the Convention provides that the recovered objects:

shall be deposited, conserved and managed in a manner that ensures [their] long-term preservation.

Rule 33 elaborates on what this means in practice by providing that the project archives, including any UCH removed and all supporting documentation:

shall, as far as possible, be kept together and intact as a collection in a manner that is available for professional and public access.

The wording of Rule 33 suggests that the 'preferred option' is for all recovered UCH to be kept together as a collection in a manner that ensures access for both the general public and for research purposes.

---

[41] See, generally, Panter, 'In Situ Preservation versus Active Conservation', pp. 59–62.

[42] For example, in the case of the Mary Rose, immediately after the wreck was recovered in 1982 and brought to shore in Portsmouth it needed to be wrapped in protective foam and polythene, and constantly sprayed with water. In 1994, the water spray was replaced with a polyethylene glycol spray, marking the start of the active conservation process. After seventeen years, this spray was turned off, but the conservation process will not be fully complete until 2016 when the vessel can finally emerge from its protective encasement. Even thereafter, the temperature, light and humidity of the building in which it is kept will need to be carefully controlled in perpetuity. (See www.maryrose.org.)

[43] Rule 32.   [44] Rule 17.

However, the reference to 'as far as possible' indicates that there is recognition that pragmatic considerations may mean that it is not always possible to keep an entire assemblage together or intact. For example, as previously discussed,[45] the conventional regime recognises that some states will have a particular interest in UCH and provides that the interests of states with a 'verifiable link' must be taken into account in certain specified circumstances. It is conceivable that an assemblage may be split to take account of such interests or, in the case of material recovered in the Area, to take account of the preferential rights of states of cultural, historical or archaeological origin.[46] Furthermore, the practice of 'deaccession', which leads to the disposal of certain items from museum collections,[47] is permissible with respect to project archives under the Convention provided – among other things – it 'does not prejudice the scientific or cultural interest or integrity of the recovered material or result in its irretrievable dispersal'.[48]

Finally, Rule 34 makes it clear that the project archives must be managed according to international professional standards.

4. Access

In order to fulfil the general objective of the Convention – the preservation of UCH for the benefit of humanity – there need to be means for humanity to gain awareness, understanding, appreciation and enjoyment of the UCH resource. The most effective way this can be done is

[45] See Chap. 3, section 4.2.2 and Chap. 8, sections 3.4 and 3.5.
[46] The best-known example internationally of an assemblage of UCH material kept in different places to accommodate the interests of different states was the arrangement made between Australia and the Netherlands for the sharing of artefacts from the Dutch East Indiamen lying off the coast of Australia. The arrangement – which provided for the equitable sharing of artefacts between the governments of Australia and the Netherlands and the state of Western Australia – was made under the Agreement between the Netherlands and Australia Concerning Old Dutch Shipwrecks of 1972. (On the background to the Agreement, see Chap. 3, section 2.3.) However, it is notable that the Netherlands returned its share of the artefacts to Australia in 2010. Although both states emphasised at this time that the artefacts remained 'shared heritage', it seems that it was also recognised that the material was best 'kept as one collection, as close as possible to [its] original resting place' with 'virtual' access to the entire collection available to all via an online database: 'Australia Receives Important Dutch Maritime Collection', press release, Parliamentary Secretary for Sustainability and Urban Water, Australia, 9 November 2010 (www.environment.gov.au/minister/farrell/2010/pubs/mr20101109.pdf). It is conceivable that this will become the model for the international 'sharing' of assemblages between interested states under the Convention.
[47] See, further, Chap. 6, section 4.2.3.   [48] See Rule 2(b).

through *direct access* to the resource. In circumstances where activities directed at UCH are permitted under the regime, as seen above, Rule 33 makes it clear that the public will have access to the project archive, which will include recovered objects. Nonetheless, under the Convention the first option to be considered in the management of a UCH site is preservation *in situ* and – even where activities are permitted – 'excavation or recovery' will be limited to what is necessary 'for the purpose of scientific studies or for the ultimate protection of' UCH.[49] On the face of it, these principles seem to run counter to the notion of public access: how is the public to benefit from UCH if it is left at the bottom of the sea?

In fact, the Convention reconciles the principles of preservation *in situ* and of public benefit, in part, by emphasising the benefits that can come from access to UCH *in situ*. Article 2(10) sets out one of the key principles and, indeed, hallmarks of the Convention:

Responsible non-intrusive access to observe or document *in situ* underwater cultural heritage shall be encouraged to create public awareness, appreciation, and protection of the heritage except where such access is incompatible with its protection and management.

The elevation of the enjoyment of the educational and recreational benefits of access to UCH *in situ* to a notional 'right' by the preamble to the Convention[50] makes it clear that UCH lying *in situ* is not solely the preserve of professional archaeologists. It also indicates a belief that even greater benefit can be derived from public access to UCH *in situ*, than *ex situ*. Therefore, one of the justifications for the *in situ* preservation principle is the benefit the public can reap from access *in situ*.

Questions arise about the impact of Article 2(10), and the Convention more generally, on a number of important interest groups: recreational divers, avocational archaeologists and the public at large.

4.1   Impact on recreational divers

In some parts of the world recreational diving has been a thriving activity for many years; in others, its popularity is growing. In some cases, income from diver tourism is an important contributor to the local, regional or even national economy.[51] The interests of recreational divers in wrecks and other UCH sites are various, but the primary

---

[49] Rule 4.   [50] See preambular clause 5.
[51] See, for example, Jeffery, 'Federated States of Micronesia', pp. 145–59.

motivation for many is the desire for exploration and excitement. The fundamental requirement of recreational divers is access. 'Responsible non-intrusive access' to observe and explore a UCH site is unlikely to cause damage unless a site is particularly sensitive; indeed, access by recreational divers to the majority of UCH sites on a 'look but don't touch' basis is widely recognised by marine archaeologists to be compatible with the protection of heritage values. It is also recognised that responsible diver access can have positive benefits for the protection of the UCH resource: divers can act as 'eyes and ears' for public heritage agencies by reporting any changes or damage to sites, or behaviour that breaches the 'look but don't touch' code. The Convention recognises that the cooperation of divers is essential for the protection of UCH (thereby acknowledging that divers are a legitimate 'user')[52] and encourages access by sport divers, *provided* it is 'responsible' and 'non-intrusive'.[53]

The conventional scheme is such that authorisation is only required for 'activities directed at' UCH. To constitute such activities, not only must there be a risk that the activities 'may, directly or indirectly, physically disturb or otherwise damage' UCH, but also the activities must have UCH as their primary object, meaning that there must be an intention physically to disturb UCH.[54] Therefore, provided the intention of divers is to approach a site on a 'look but don't touch' basis, there is no requirement under the Convention that their activities must be authorised. On the other hand, Article 2(10) recognises that some sites may be so fragile or otherwise sensitive that public access may need to be restricted, or even prohibited, because it is incompatible with the protection and management of the site and therefore incompatible with the broader public interest. Nevertheless, it is clear that the restriction of access is to be exceptional.

Different states have different attitudes to recreational diving, reflecting their national experiences. In the USA, diver access is an important aspect of the multiple-use management approach now firmly enshrined in its relevant federal legislation.[55] In some states the activity is positively promoted in light of the revenue it generates: in such cases, diving may be restricted only on certain designated archaeological sites, or in environmentally sensitive areas. Other states, at least traditionally, have regarded diving in a less favourable light. For example, in some states

---

[52] Preambular clause 10.   [53] Art. 2(10).   [54] See section 3.1 above.
[55] See Varmer, 'United States', p. 377. In fact, during the UNESCO negotiations the USA was a strong advocate of the principle of non-intrusive public access: see O'Keefe, *Shipwrecked Heritage*, p. 28.

bordering the Mediterranean Sea, recreational diving was – and may still be – prohibited except in a limited number of areas. In Eastern Europe too, until relatively recently diving was strictly regulated. In states and regions where recreational diving is a well-established and well-organised activity, the 'look but don't touch' code is widely promoted and followed; in others, it may need to be inculcated through an ongoing, active, process of education.

The importance of education as a means of protecting UCH is recognised by the Convention. Article 20 provides:

> Each State Party shall take all practicable measures to raise public awareness regarding the value and significance of underwater cultural heritage and the importance of protecting it under this Convention.[56]

As seen above, competent national authorities are charged with responsibility for education and 'presentation'.[57] Many national heritage authorities already see these matters as important aspects of their work: where this is the case, there may already be close liaison between these authorities and diver organisations in order to promote respectful treatment of UCH and there are likely to be 'outreach' initiatives which are designed with both education and presentation in mind. Through the cooperative framework established by the Convention, experiences and best practice in this regard can be widely shared.

4.2   Impact on avocational archaeologists

Some recreational divers wish to have access to UCH sites not merely to 'observe' and 'document' (for example, by taking photographs), but also actively to participate in archaeological fieldwork. As with recreational diving, attitudes to avocational archaeology vary between jurisdictions. In some parts of the world, including the Mediterranean region, archaeology both on land and at sea traditionally has been the preserve of professionals. In others the engagement of amateurs is welcomed and, indeed, may be a mainstay of fieldwork activity. Inevitably, given the differences of practice on this matter internationally, the prospect of an international treaty on UCH raised some concerns among avocational archaeologists that they might be precluded from participating in archaeological activities on sites falling within the scope of the Convention.

---

[56] See also preambular clause 4. To reinforce the Convention, UNESCO has produced a Code of Ethics for Diving on Submerged Archaeological Sites (www.unesco.org/new/en/culture/themes/underwater-cultural-heritage/divers/code-of-ethics/).
[57] Art. 22(1).

As discussed above, the Convention's regime encourages access to observe or document sites and institutes a permit system only for activities that will physically interfere with UCH. Much archaeological investigation is now done using non-intrusive survey techniques and, to the extent that fieldwork involves non-intrusive methods, under the conventional scheme it may be undertaken freely by anyone, whatever their qualifications or experience. However, to what extent can avocational archaeologists participate in activities 'directed at' UCH, in other words those that involve physical disturbance?

Section VII of the Annex, entitled 'Competence and qualifications', contains two Rules:

Rule 22. Activities directed at underwater cultural heritage shall only be undertaken under the direction and control of, and in the regular presence of, a qualified underwater archaeologist with scientific competence appropriate to the project.
Rule 23. All persons on the project team shall be qualified and have demonstrated competence appropriate to their roles in the project.

Domestic laws and practice commonly require that archaeological activities on protected sites are undertaken under the direction and control of an appropriately qualified professional archaeologist. On UCH sites, that party is also generally required to be a diver and to be present on site sufficiently regularly to provide direct 'hands-on' supervision. Rule 22 reflects this practice. Although the wording 'qualified underwater archaeologist' is somewhat vague, the implication is that it means a professional underwater archaeologist with an appropriate educational qualification.[58] On the other hand, Rule 23 – in referring to qualified 'persons' – suggests that the *project team* may include avocationals, provided they are appropriately qualified and have competence to the level required for their respective roles in the project.[59] This allows for on-site training, the acquisition of new competences, and skills progression.

---

[58] In its guidance on competence and qualifications, the UNESCO Manual for Activities Directed at Underwater Cultural Heritage states: 'It should ... be a qualified and competent professional who sets the research agenda and controls and directs any project'; '[t]o be deemed qualified and competent an archaeologist must ... possess a university degree in archaeology' (www.unesco.org/new/en/culture/themes/underwater-cultural-heritage/unesco-manual-for-activities-directed-at-underwater-cultural-heritage/unesco-manual/).

[59] In its guidance on competence and qualifications, the UNESCO Manual for Activities Directed at Underwater Cultural Heritage emphasises that qualification may be based on 'a formal training process with a measurable outcome' and refers to the well-established

4.3   Impact on the general public

Not everyone can, or would want to, dive. In light of this, how can the non-diving public community gain access to UCH under a conventional regime which has adopted preservation *in situ* as its core management principle?

In fact, modern technology is now facilitating many forms of 'virtual' access. Some of the most cutting-edge developments in this regard are illustrated by the work of the US National Oceanographic and Atmospheric Administration (NOAA) Office of Ocean Exploration.[60] Through the use of satellite-aided live-streaming of video images to the Internet, it is possible to 'bring the public onboard the [research] ships to share new discoveries as they happen'[61] and to give them 'telepresence' at the bottom of the ocean. The projects undertaken by the Office of Ocean Exploration involve a broad range of complementary activities that include daily Internet-based broadcasts and the opportunity for school children and the wider public to interview researchers live online. An innovative project using imaging technology and sonar devices to create a three-dimensional map of the *Titanic* has also been undertaken with the intention 'virtually to raise the *Titanic*' so that it can be better appreciated by the general public.[62]

While public outreach programmes on this scale are prohibitively expensive in all but exceptional cases, they give some sense of the possibilities that modern technology open up for engaging the general public with UCH and maritime archaeology in an exciting and imaginative way. It falls to individual competent authorities to consider how best to 'present' UCH and raise public awareness regarding its value and significance, and the importance of protecting it, within the means available to them. While the Convention provides for public access to project archives (and modern technology can open up such archives to an international audience),[63] under its terms the notion of public access is to be regarded much more broadly than simply access to these archives.

---

training scheme run by the Nautical Archaeology Society. Interestingly, it also suggests that training 'may take place as part of the project'.

[60] See, generally, Weirich, 'Connecting with the Past'.   [61] *Ibid.*, p. 79.

[62] See Chap. 6, n. 44. Well-heeled members of the general public can also gain direct physical access to the site by means of a tour conducted in a submersible. In 2012, the centenary of the sinking of the wreck, these tours were priced at approximately $60,000.

[63] See, for example, the recently revised arrangements for the collection of artefacts from the Dutch East Indiamen off the coast of Australia: see n. 46, above.

Access of one form or another is important in order for the general public to benefit from UCH. However, the principle of preservation *in situ* affords broader public benefits, some more tangible than others. Varmer has pointed out that a wide variety of specific interest groups, such as fishermen, dive-boat operators, tour guides, restaurants and hotels may gain direct financial benefits from *in situ* preservation.[64] Less tangibly, but no less importantly, humankind benefits when UCH is left *in situ* as an untouched archaeological repository for future generations to enjoy and investigate, or to serve as an artificial reef providing habitat for flora and fauna. In these or other circumstances (see below), on exceptional occasions direct public access may need to be restricted, or even prohibited altogether, in the broader public interest.

4.4   Maritime memorials

Inevitably, when a ship or other type of craft sinks at sea, there may be loss of human life. In some cases, for example where a fishing boat sinks, there may be the loss of several crew members. In other cases, hundreds, or even thousands, of people may have lost their lives and the wreck will represent a major gravesite. The Royal Mail ships, *Titanic* and *Lusitania*, are frequently cited examples, but there are many others, civilian and military, lost in times of conflict and in times of peace. Kowalski has drawn attention to the *Wilhelm Gustloff* and a number of other vessels that sank off the Polish coast at the end of the Second World War while evacuating many thousands of refugees from East Prussia:[65] the sinking of these vessels is believed to represent the greatest loss of life in maritime history.[66] While it will be some time before they fall within the scope of the Convention, the *Titanic* already does so and the *Lusitania* will do so in 2015. Other wrecks that featured in earlier chapters and fall well within the Convention's 100-year threshold are also associated with great loss of life: when HMS *Victory* sank in 1744, there were more than 1,000 fatalities; in the case of HMS *Sussex* (1694), *Juno* (1802), *Mercedes* (1804) and *Central America* (1857) the number of crew and passengers lost with the vessels ran into several hundreds.

What approach does the Convention take to gravesites and to human remains more generally? By virtue of Article 2(9):

---

[64] Varmer, 'The Case Against the "Salvage" of the Cultural Heritage', p. 291.

[65] Kowalski, 'Poland', pp. 235–6.

[66] The precise number of refugees on board the *Wilhelm Gustloff* and the other vessels was not recorded, but conservative estimates have suggested that 7,000 people may have been on board the *Wilhelm Gustloff*, 6,000 on the *Goya* and 3,000 on the *General von Steuben*.

States Parties shall ensure that proper respect is given to all human remains located in maritime waters.

Rule 5 of the Annex goes on to provide:

Activities directed at underwater cultural heritage shall avoid the unnecessary disturbance of human remains or venerated sites.

Whether or not human remains exist at a wreck site depends on many factors, including the environmental conditions at the site. Human remains can be found at sites that are several hundred years old;[67] on the other hand, it seems that none has yet been found at the site of the *Titanic*, despite its comparatively recent loss.[68] In any event, the question of the treatment of human remains is a matter that the archaeological profession is well used to dealing with and it has developed codes of practice to ensure that such remains are accorded appropriate respect.[69] However, whether or not human remains are present at a site, there is a broader question about the approach that should be taken to a site where it represents a grave, particularly one where many lives were lost. It may seem odd, perhaps, that the Convention does not say more about this issue, but the explanation may be that it proved to be a politically sensitive one during the negotiations: the maritime states argued for a special status to be afforded to military graves; others argued that civil gravesites merited equal respect.[70] As a result, the matter is dealt with by Rule 5, which makes reference to 'venerated sites' and requires that activities directed at UCH must be regulated in such a way that they 'avoid *unnecessary* disturbance' of these sites.[71] The fact that a site is a substantial gravesite will therefore be an important factor to be weighed in the balance in determining its management.

[67] For example, human remains have been found at the site of HMS *Victory*: see Department for Culture, Media and Sport and Ministry of Defence, 'HMS *Victory* 1744: Options for the Management of the Wreck Site', 2010 (available at www.culture.gov.uk/consultations/6773.aspx).
[68] So far, only items of clothing positioned in a way that suggests they were being worn at the time of loss have been found: see 'The 2010 Scientific Expedition to *Titanic*' (available at www.sanctuaries.noaa.gov/maritime/titanic/2010_expedition.html).
[69] For example, the Vermillion Accord on Human Remains, adopted at the World Archaeological Congress 1989 Inter-Congress, South Dakota, USA.
[70] See Chap. 4, n. 121.
[71] Emphasis added. The guidance on Rule 5 in the UNESCO Manual for Activities Directed at Underwater Cultural Heritage points out that the notion of a venerated site includes not only gravesites, but also sites such as 'prehistoric or historic offering places, sunken temples and the abodes of sacred animals'. On this point, see also O'Keefe, *Shipwrecked Heritage*, p. 162.

The treatment of human remains as objects of study by archaeologists is a highly sensitive matter, but there is no doubt that human remains such as bones, hair and other tissue can yield important insights into past human life, for example concerning the diet and working conditions of sailors. The reference to 'unnecessary disturbance' in Rule 5 might suggest that any human remains falling within the scope of the Convention should not be disturbed for the purpose of archaeological study as, strictly speaking, such disturbance is 'unnecessary'. However, surely it cannot have been the intention to exclude archaeologists from access for study purposes to *all* such remains? Dunkley, a marine archaeologist, has questioned why it seems 'acceptable ... to recover and study human remains from the *London* [lost in 1665] yet morally wrong to do the same for the *Storaa* [lost in 1943]';[72] he concludes that the objection in the case of the *Storaa* arises from the fact that there are living descendants who *knew* the victims. In light of this, he suggests that 'at least four generations' should pass before human remains are treated as archaeological samples. This would indicate that in his view some – but by no means all – human remains to which the Convention applies should be out of bounds for the purpose of archaeological study and it seems quite possible that competent authorities will also take this view. In light of this, the notion of 'unnecessary disturbance' may in practice be deemed to equate to the notion of 'proper respect' in Article 2(9). What amounts to treatment according 'proper respect' is likely to depend on the circumstances, including the age of the remains. If there are interested parties, their feelings are an important factor that needs to be taken into account.[73]

It may be that in some instances a maritime gravesite will be regarded as falling within the proviso to the general principle in Article 2(10) that responsible non-intrusive access to observe or document *in situ* UCH

---

[72] Dunkley, 'Catastrophic Burials', p. 22. The *London* was a 'second rate' warship that blew up in the Thames Estuary with the loss of more than 300 individuals. The wreck is designated under the UK Protection of Wrecks Act 1973. The SS *Storaa*, an armed merchantman carrying war supplies in convoy, sank off the south coast of England after being hit by an E-boat torpedo. Twenty-two lives were lost and the wreck is protected by the UK Protection of Military Remains Act 1986.

[73] The guidance on Rule 5 in the UNESCO Manual for Activities Directed at Underwater Cultural Heritage places particular emphasis on the need for respect for people's feelings and suggests that, where such feelings are involved, the '[i]nterested parties should not only be informed but involved' in the planning or authorising of activities directed at the site. It also states that '[t]he preference for *in situ* preservation as the first option presents itself strongly in this case'. If a site represents an *intentional* burial there may be relevant domestic laws that will need to be taken into consideration.

must be encouraged *except* where 'incompatible with its protection and management'. Although obviously a relatively recent wreck, in the case of the passenger ferry *Estonia*, which sank in 1994 with the loss of more than 800 lives, a decision was taken at international level soon after the disaster that it was in the best public interest to prohibit access altogether.[74] In the case of the *Titanic*, while the debris field has been much explored over the years since its discovery, attempts have been made to regulate access to the hull sections where many people were trapped at the time of the sinking.[75] While it does not say so in terms, the UNESCO conventional regime provides room for a competent authority to conclude that a particular site should be treated as a maritime memorial and preserved *in situ*, with access (either for recreational diving or for archaeological research) strictly limited or even prohibited. In such circumstances, the broad public interest in treating a site as a maritime memorial may be regarded as outweighing the loss arising from not permitting these activities.[76]

5.   Sanctions and deterrents

Article 17 of the Convention requires each state party to impose sanctions for violation of measures it has taken to implement the Convention,[77] as well as to cooperate with other states parties to ensure

---

[74] See Chap. 7, section 4.3. At the time, the decision was criticised by relatives who wished to see the bodies, or the wreck itself, recovered. More recently, relatives' associations have pressed for an amendment of the international agreement protecting the site to enable divers to investigate the wreck to acquire evidence about the circumstances of its loss. See Klabbers, 'On Maritime Cemeteries and Objective Regimes', p. 2. See, more generally, Jacobsson and Klabbers, 'Rest in Peace?'

[75] The Titanic Agreement (see Chap. 7, section 4.3) requires states parties to regulate entry into the hull sections of the wreck 'so that they, other artifacts and any human remains are not disturbed': Titanic Agreement, Art. 4(1). Art. 4 as a whole makes it clear that while states parties will be able to authorise non-intrusive access to the hull, they will not be able to authorise activities that cause any disturbance: see Dromgoole, 'The International Agreement for the Protection of the *Titanic*', p. 6.

[76] If the site lies outside the territorial limit of the competent authority's state, questions will arise concerning the international legal authority of the state to prohibit diving by foreign nationals on a 'look but don't touch' basis. For example, if the site is on the continental shelf or EEZ of that state, the legal basis for the jurisdictional provision in Art. 10(2) will not be relevant: see Chap. 8, section 3.4. Where the international legal authority is questionable, a specific inter-state agreement to protect the site may be the most appropriate way forward. Art. 6 of the Convention encourages such agreements: see Chap. 10, section 2.

[77] Art. 17(1).

enforcement of sanctions imposed under the article.[78] The sanctions taken shall be:

adequate in severity to be effective in securing compliance with [the] Convention and to discourage violations wherever they occur and *shall deprive offenders of the benefit deriving from their illegal activities.*[79]

Standard sanctions, such as civil fines, or fines and imprisonment following criminal prosecution, are important measures but will not have the effect of depriving offenders of the benefit derived from their activities. Therefore, it is clear that the Convention envisages the use of other sorts of sanctions alongside more traditional penalties. In fact, the Convention requires states parties to adopt a specific sanction of an administrative nature specifically aimed at depriving offenders of the benefit of their activities. The provision is found in Article 18 and the sanction is the seizure of UCH.

5.1   Seizure

Under Article 18(1):

Each State Party shall take measures providing for the seizure of underwater cultural heritage in its territory[80] that has been recovered in a manner not in conformity with this Convention.

This obligation is broad-ranging. The measures that must be taken relate not only to UCH that is recovered within the territory of the state, but also to that brought within the territory at any time.[81] Moreover, the seizure may be from *anyone*, not simply a party involved in the recovery of the material.

Once UCH has been seized under Article 18(1), a state party is required to 'record, protect and take all reasonable measures to stabilise'[82] the material seized and to give notification of the seizure to the

---

[78] Art. 17(3).   [79] Art. 17(2). Emphasis added.

[80] For the purposes of this provision, it seems that 'territory' can be interpreted as including the contiguous zone in light of the fact that seizure of UCH in the circumstances set out in Art. 18(1) will amount to a measure relating to the trafficking in UCH for the purposes of Art. 303(2) of the LOSC.

[81] The UNESCO Convention 2001 does not make any provision with respect to retroactivity. When implementing Art. 14, states parties will therefore need to have cognizance of Art. 28 of the Vienna Convention on the Law of Treaties. This provides: 'Unless a different intention appears from the treaty or is otherwise established, its provisions do not bind a party in relation to any act or fact which took place or any situation which ceased to exist before the date of the entry into force of the treaty with respect to that party.'

[82] Art. 18(2).

Director-General of UNESCO and to any other state (whether a state party or not) with a verifiable link to the UCH concerned.[83] It is also required to ensure that the disposition of the material is for 'the public benefit' and in doing so must take account of the need for conservation and research; for reassembly of a dispersed collection; for public access, exhibition and education; and also of the interests of any state with a verifiable link.[84] These measures are potentially onerous and costly, and it must be assumed that responsibility for their implementation, in the first instance, falls within the broad 'protection, conservation, presentation and management'[85] remit of the competent national authorities.

Undoubtedly, the cooperation and assistance of other states parties will be required for a state to be able to fulfil all the requirements of Article 18. Such cooperation and assistance will be particularly important in eliciting information about the provenance of material recovered outside the territory of the seizing state and the circumstances of its recovery. Curiously, perhaps, Article 18 does not itself refer to the matter of cooperation; however, its provisions can be seen as a specific application of the duty in Article 17 to impose sanctions depriving offenders of the benefit of their activities; therefore, the duty to cooperate to enforce such sanctions – imposed by Article 17(3) – applies. Furthermore, the detailed provision made in Article 19 for cooperation and information-sharing between states parties in relation to the protection and management of UCH is clearly pertinent in respect of the implementation of seizure measures.

The provisions in Article 18 in respect of seizure give rise to a host of questions about the respective rights of the seizing state, states with a verifiable link, and private individuals and entities with a proprietary interest in the seized material. The Convention provides little, if any, guidance on these matters and they will therefore need to be dealt with on a case-by-case basis. Nonetheless, a few general observations can be made.

When a notification of seizure is received by the UNESCO Secretariat, it will presumably take steps to disseminate details of the seized material to all states parties. However, there is no suggestion in Article 18 that a state with a verifiable link must declare an interest in seized material in order to have its interests taken into account; further, as noted above, the references in Article 18 to states with a verifiable link – unlike some of the references to such states in other parts of the treaty[86] – do not

---

[83] Art. 18(3).   [84] Art. 18(4).   [85] Art. 22(1).   [86] See Chap. 3, section 4.2.2.

refer specifically to *states parties*. Bearing in mind that the seizing state is placed under a duty to notify states with a verifiable link and to take account of their interests, it may well have to take the initiative in investigating the identity and provenance of the seized material in order to ascertain potential links. In practice, some national authorities may already undertake this sort of task from time to time;[87] others may lack the wherewithal to pursue such investigations and may require considerable assistance.

There is nothing in the Convention to suggest that it is envisaged that seized material will necessarily remain in the seizing state. It is quite possible that the seizing state will have little or no cultural connection with the material, not the least in circumstances where it has been imported into the state some time after its original recovery. The crucial requirement is that its disposition must be for the 'public benefit' and decisions in this regard must be made 'taking into account' a number of specific factors, including the 'interests' of any state with a verifiable link.[88] During the UNESCO negotiations there was some concern on the part of Italy, a traditional 'source' state, that the seizure provisions could be open to abuse by a seizing state if they were interpreted as meaning that any state party – having seized UCH 'for its simple presence on its territory' – can then keep it even if that state has no cultural link to the UCH in question.[89] In fact, while this concern is understandable, there seems some likelihood that a seizing state might welcome an expression of interest by another state in providing a suitable home for the material since it would relieve it of the potentially onerous and costly responsibility of having to care for the material itself.

Where interest in providing a home for the material comes from another *state party*, the seizing state will have reason to feel confident that – in handing over the material to that state – it will have fulfilled its

---

[87] For example, the UK's Receiver of Wreck sometimes goes to considerable lengths to investigate the provenance of wreck reported under the Merchant Shipping Act 1995 in order that contact can be made with potential owners and the final disposition of the material determined: see Dromgoole, 'United Kingdom', pp. 315–20.

[88] See Art. 18(4).

[89] See Carducci, 'The Expanding Protection of Underwater Cultural Heritage', pp. 180–4. Indeed, it was pointed out that retention of material by a seizing state in certain circumstances could amount to a breach of the 1970 UNESCO Convention on Illicit Trade in Cultural Property: see Garabello, 'The Negotiating History of the Convention on the Protection of the Underwater Cultural Heritage', p. 164. On the 1970 Convention, see section 5.2, below.

duty to ensure disposition for the public benefit.[90] However, it may not necessarily have that confidence where a *non*-state party with a verifiable link requests the handing over of the material. Clearly such a state will not be bound by the terms of the Convention and therefore may not be prepared to agree to arrangements for disposition of the material in accordance with the Convention. Where such a claimant is able to establish *ownership* of the material, the seizing state could find itself in the difficult position of having to choose between refusing to hand over the material – which could amount to a breach of general international law – and breaching its conventional duty to ensure disposition for the public benefit.[91] In the case of seized material recovered from the Area, there will also be questions regarding the account to be taken of the 'preferential rights' of states of origin under Article 149 of the LOSC. While Articles 11 and 12 of the UNESCO Convention establish a control scheme for the Area which acknowledges that 'particular regard' must be paid to these rights,[92] there is no mention of them in Article 18. Nonetheless, it is implicit from the scheme of the Convention that particular regard must be paid to these rights when material is subject to seizure.[93]

As previously discussed,[94] generally speaking, it will only be states – rather than private individuals and entities – that are likely to be able to establish ownership to UCH via succession-in-title from the original owner, especially to material pre-dating the mid nineteenth century. Nevertheless, it is conceivable that occasionally private claimants may come forward. In so far as such claims are made and established, exactly how they should be dealt with is a matter left to each individual state to determine, in accordance with its domestic property laws and general international law. While there is nothing in the Convention to preclude the disposition of material into private hands, according to O'Keefe:

---

[90] Where more than one state has a verifiable link to the material, the seizing state and those states with a verifiable link will need to cooperate to determine the best means of ensuring that the disposition of the material is for the public benefit. The provision in Art. 18(4) that account must be taken of 'the need for reassembly of a dispersed collection' suggests that it would be acceptable for an assemblage to be split after seizure, provided it was possible to reassemble it at a later date.

[91] In such circumstances both states may need to be reminded of the duty under Art. 303(1) of the LOSC to protect UCH and to cooperate for that purpose.

[92] See Chap. 8, section 3.5.

[93] However, non-states parties to the UNESCO Convention will need to take cognizance of Art. 149 of the LOSC, which makes it clear that UCH found in the Area must be 'preserved or disposed of for the benefit of mankind as a whole'.

[94] Chap. 3, section 2.2.

The true nature of seizure as being both an aspect of punishment for wrongdoing and as furthering the public interest by reclaiming material for the public domain must be emphasized.[95]

In many circumstances it seems likely that the conclusion will be reached that the public interest will be best served by a disposition in the public, rather than private, domain. In such cases provision may need to be made for the payment of compensation.[96] The fact that material must be seized whenever it has been recovered in a manner not in conformity with the Convention, no matter in whose hands it may be, also raises questions regarding the interference this might cause to the rights of *bona fide* third-party purchasers. The original recoverer may well have sold or otherwise disposed of the material and it may have been the subject of several transactions. Traditionally, common law and civil law jurisdictions have taken different approaches to the question of good faith acquisition and each state party will need to consider the circumstances in the light of its own domestic law, as well as its obligations under general international law.

Finally, a state party will need to address the question of the ownership of material it has seized in circumstances where, ultimately, it remains in its own hands. Unless some sort of accommodation is made with another interested party over ownership, the most obvious approach would be for the property rights to be deemed to be abandoned and the material taken into state ownership.

5.2   Related deterrents

The provision the Convention makes for seizure acts not only as a sanction for, but also as a deterrent to, the recovery of material in a manner not in conformity with its regime. Related measures that will also act as deterrents to such behaviour are provided for in Article 14. This states:

States Parties shall take measures to prevent the entry into their territory,[97] the dealing in, or the possession of, underwater cultural heritage illicitly exported and/or recovered, where recovery was contrary to this Convention.

---

[95]   O'Keefe, *Shipwrecked Heritage*, p. 114.   [96]   See Chap. 3, section 2.4.
[97]   As with Art. 18(1), it seems that 'territory' for the purposes of Art. 14 can be interpreted to include the contiguous zone in light of the fact that the measures outlined in the article amount to measures to combat trafficking in UCH and therefore fall within Art. 303(2) of the LOSC.

This article, previously referred to in Chapter 8,[98] requires that states parties take measures in respect of UCH material in three situations:

(i) where it has been recovered contrary to the Convention;
(ii) where it has been illicitly exported;
(iii) where it has been recovered contrary to the Convention *and* illicitly exported.

It is therefore designed to tackle not only the specific matter of recovery in contravention of the Convention, but also the more general problem of illicit trade in UCH material.

There is clearly a close relationship between Article 14 and the seizure provisions in Article 18. The seizure of material is an obvious measure that may be taken in fulfilment of Article 14 and – in light of Article 18 – a state party is *obliged* to take this particular measure in respect of UCH located in its territory in situations (i) and (iii) above, in other words where recovery was contrary to the Convention. Seizure is a measure that could also be applied in respect of illicitly exported material more generally, although a state party is under no obligation to use it in that respect.

Like Article 18, Article 14 is broadly framed. In the case of UCH recovered contrary to the Convention, measures must be taken in respect of material recovered anywhere and at any time.[99] In respect of illicit export, Article 14 is not restricted to illicit export from states parties to the Convention, but extends to illicit export from *any* state. In all cases, the identity of the party bringing the material into the territory, dealing in it or possessing it is irrelevant: it could be a party who was involved in the recovery; on the other hand, it could be someone who has no knowledge of the fact that it was recovered in contravention of the rules of the UNESCO Convention, or illicitly exported. This means that not only will measures taken under Article 14 impede the disposal of material by someone involved in its recovery, but they should also deter potential third-party purchasers and thereby assist more generally by dampening the market for such material. Curiously, perhaps, there is no requirement that states make it illegal to *export* material that is recovered contrary to the Convention; nor, indeed, is there an obligation to require a permit for the export of material falling within the Convention's definition of UCH. Nonetheless, implementation of such measures

---

[98] See Chap. 8, section 3.1.

[99] As noted in n. 81 above, states parties will need to take account of Art. 28 of the Vienna Convention on the Law of Treaties on the question of retroactivity.

would clearly be helpful in supporting the general objectives of the Convention.

The UNESCO Convention 2001 is designed, in part, to complement international instruments relating specifically to trade in movable cultural heritage, particularly the 1970 UNESCO Convention on Illicit Trade in Cultural Property.[100] In many cases, measures that states are already taking to fulfil commitments under the 1970 Convention – and other international instruments in the field[101] – are likely to go some way to fulfilling the obligation under Article 14, or those under Articles 17 and 18.[102] For example, in 2001, Australian federal agencies seized more than 70,000 pieces of porcelain from the trading vessel *Tek Sing*, which had been recovered from Indonesian waters and illegally exported to Australia, using powers made available in legislation giving effect to the 1970 Convention.[103] In part as a result of steadily growing support for the 1970 UNESCO Convention (especially from 'market' states),[104] there has been a general improvement in recent years in respect of the regulation of illicit trade in cultural artefacts generally. However, the problem of illicit trade is far from solved[105] and implementation of the provisions

[100] The 1970 Convention came into force on 24 April 1972. As at 31 July 2012, it had 122 states parties.

[101] The most notable of these instruments is the UNIDROIT Convention on Stolen or Illegally Exported Cultural Objects 1995, which came into force on 1 July 1998. As at 31 July 2012, it had thirty-three contracting states (see www.unidroit.org). There are a number of relevant regional instruments, including – in respect of the European Union – the European Council Regulation No. 3911/92 on the export of cultural goods to third countries, [1992] OJ L395/1 and Council Directive 93/7/EEC on the return of unlawfully removed cultural objects, [1993] OJ L74/74.

[102] Equally, implementation of the 2001 UNESCO Convention will go some way towards fulfilling duties under the 1970 Convention. For example, see Art. 5(d) of the 1970 Convention, which provides for the setting up of national services for the purpose of 'organizing the supervision of archaeological excavations, ensuring the preservation "*in situ*" of certain cultural property, and protecting certain areas reserved for future archaeological research'.

[103] See Jeffery, 'Australia' (2nd edn), p. 9. The Australian agencies acted in response to a request by the Indonesian government and the material seized was returned to Indonesia. The powers – made available under the Australia (Commonwealth) Protection of Movable Cultural Heritage Act 1986 – are designed to implement Article 7(b)(2) of the 1970 Convention. In the UK, the Dealing in Cultural Objects (Offences) Act 2003 (previously referred to in Chap. 7, section 2.1), which was enacted to reinforce the UK's implementation of the 1970 Convention, would also assist in implementing Art. 14 of the 2001 Convention.

[104] Despite initial reticence, many traditional 'market' states are now parties, including Australia, Belgium, Canada, France, the Netherlands, the USA and the UK.

[105] See European University Institute Working Paper, 'The Illicit Traffic of Cultural Objects in the Mediterranean'.

of the 2001 UNESCO Convention should strengthen the overall international law regime in this field.

6. Concluding remarks

While the primary aim of the UNESCO Convention 2001 is to set in place a regulatory framework for all activities directed at UCH in order to ensure that they are governed by the standards of the Convention, the discussion in this chapter shows that the Convention's scope is considerably broader than that. There are plenty of aspects of the Convention that feed into the general objective set out in Article 2(1) – to 'ensure and strengthen' the protection of UCH – and that make it clear that this objective is to be seen in broad terms, rather than as simply about regulating activities directed at UCH *in situ*. Ultimately, as the Convention's preamble points out,[106] effective implementation of the Convention's regime as a whole is dependent upon active cooperation, not just among states parties, but among states more generally and also 'international organizations, scientific institutions, professional organizations, archaeologists, divers, other interested parties and the public at large'. All 'users' of the resource, and interested states, will need to play their part.

---

[106] Preambular clause 10.

10 UNESCO Convention 2001: further matters

1. Introduction

Before this book concludes, there are several further aspects of the 2001 UNESCO Convention that merit some attention. The first two are of a substantive nature and the remaining matters are procedural and/or institutional.

2. Inter-state agreements furthering the Convention's objectives

In the preceding chapters, reference has been made to various agreements that have been concluded between states relating to specific shipwrecks.[1] Some of these agreements take account of historical and archaeological values; others do not.

The majority of these agreements are of a bilateral nature and relate to the sunken warship(s) of one state located in the territorial sea of another state. A number of these agreements were referred to in Chapter 4.[2] As explained there, their principal purpose is to deal with the sensitive question of the relative rights of the coastal state and the flag state, particularly with respect to the right to control access.[3] Another bilateral agreement previously referred to is the Agreement between Australia

---

[1] Some, but not necessarily all, of these agreements are treaties legally binding on the parties. Whether or not they have this status can be a difficult question to determine, especially if they are embodied in an Exchange of Notes or Memorandum of Understanding. In such circumstances, the instrument may need to be closely scrutinised to determine the intention of the parties: see Aust, *Modern Treaty Law and Practice*, chaps. 2 and 3, especially pp. 25–6.

[2] See Chap. 4, section 2.2.

[3] As explained in Chap. 4, there is a tension between the sovereignty of a coastal state over its territorial sea and claims by flag states that their sunken warships are sovereign immune and, as such, subject to their exclusive jurisdiction.

338

and the Netherlands Concerning Old Dutch Shipwrecks of 1972. This, too, was initiated to resolve the question of respective legal rights, in this case relating to ownership of several Dutch East Indiamen discovered off the coast of Australia.[4] It is rare for agreements relating to wreck sites to involve more than two states and there appear to be only two examples, both designed to protect civil wrecks as maritime memorials: the first is the agreement of 1995 for the protection of the passenger ferry M/S *Estonia* and the second is the agreement (not yet in force) negotiated by the USA, France, Canada and the UK in the late 1990s for the protection of RMS *Titanic*.[5] Both of these wrecks lie in international waters and the agreements are designed to make use of the nationality and/or territorial principles of jurisdiction to regulate (directly or indirectly) activities at these sites.

Article 6 of the UNESCO Convention seeks to build on the potential that agreements such as these have to complement and enhance the protection afforded by the Convention. Article 6(1) provides:

States Parties are encouraged to enter into bilateral, regional or other multilateral agreements or develop existing agreements, for the preservation of underwater cultural heritage. All such agreements shall be in full conformity with the provisions of this Convention and shall not dilute its universal character. States may, in such agreements, adopt rules and regulations which would ensure better protection of underwater cultural heritage than those adopted in this Convention.

Harnessing the benefits of inter-state cooperation is a strategy that lies at the heart of the Convention: a logical extension of that strategy is to offer positive encouragement to states parties to utilise inter-state agreements in order to supplement the protection provided by the Convention. Article 6 reflects two facts about the Convention: first, that it is intended as a *minimum* standards regime; and, secondly, that in itself it is limited in the protection it can afford. Alongside the encouragement that Article 6(1) provides, there is also a clear and explicit duty. While any supplementary agreements that are made may ensure 'better' protection than the Convention itself and, indeed, that may well be their objective,

---

[4] See Chap. 3, section 2.3. The Netherlands claimed ownership of the wrecks on the basis that it was the successor-in-title to the original owner; Australia, on the other hand, was of the view that the wrecks had been abandoned.

[5] See Chap. 7, section 4.3 and Chap. 9, section 4.4. The parties to the Estonia Agreement are Denmark, Estonia, Finland, Latvia, Lithuania, Poland, Russia, Sweden and the UK. The Titanic Agreement has been signed by the UK and the USA. It will come into force after implementing legislation has been enacted by the US Senate.

nonetheless they must be in 'full conformity' with the Convention and must not 'dilute', in other words weaken, its 'universal character'.

The duty in Article 6(1) applies not only to new agreements that may be entered into, but also to circumstances where one or more states parties to the Convention become involved in developing an existing agreement.[6] In such circumstances the original terms of the agreement may need to be scrutinised quite closely to determine whether or not they are in full conformity with the Convention. To the extent that they are not, the agreement would need to be revised to deal with the non-conformity. Some existing agreements are clearly in conflict with the principles of the Convention. For example, the agreements negotiated by the UK government in 1989 and 1997 relating to its sunken warships, HMS *Birkenhead*, and HMS *Erebus* and HMS *Terror*, are manifestly out of line with the whole ethos of the Convention because they provide for the recovery and sharing of gold (treating it as a financial, rather than cultural, asset) between the governments involved. On the other hand, the reciprocal agreements of 1989 and 2003 between the USA and France relating to their warships, the *Alabama* and *La Belle*, explicitly acknowledge the historical and archaeological importance of these sites and establish management regimes that appear to be broadly compliant with the Convention. Despite its early origins, the Agreement between Australia and the Netherlands Concerning Old Dutch Shipwrecks established a regime for cooperation and management which has proved to be remarkably resilient and successful: recent changes made with respect to the practical arrangements for the deposition of the artefacts ensure that they are in line with modern heritage practice and, as such, in line with the rules of the Convention on the treatment of project archives.[7]

The relationship between the Titanic Agreement and the UNESCO Convention is of particular interest in the context of Article 6. The Titanic Agreement was drafted at the same time that the UNESCO negotiations were in progress and was heavily influenced by the UNESCO

---

[6] Art. 6(3) makes it clear that the Convention does not 'alter the rights and obligations of States Parties regarding the protection of sunken vessels, arising from other bilateral, regional or other multilateral agreements concluded *before*' the adoption of the Convention. Emphasis added. This provision, with its reference to the protection of 'sunken vessels', was included as a result of the intervention of certain Scandinavian states, with the agreement for the protection of the *Estonia* in mind: see Garabello, 'The Negotiating History of the Convention on the Protection of the Underwater Cultural Heritage', p. 132. Having sunk in 1994, the *Estonia* is too recent a wreck to qualify as UCH under the Convention, but will do so in the (somewhat distant) future.

[7] See Chap. 9, n. 46.

initiative.[8] Although tailored to the special circumstances of the *Titanic*, the objectives and general principles of the Agreement are essentially the same as those of the Convention. The Agreement seeks to ensure the protection of the wreck and its associated artefacts 'for the benefit of present and future generations'.[9] It enshrines the fundamental archaeological principle of preservation *in situ* and permits the recovery of artefacts only where scientifically justified.[10] Rules annexed to the Agreement (which are designed to govern activities 'aimed at' the site) follow the same model as the Annex to the Convention.[11] Of the original negotiating parties, it seems unlikely that the USA or the UK will ratify the UNESCO Convention in the near future, but it is possible that France and Canada may do so.[12] It is therefore conceivable that the Agreement will eventually come to represent an interesting model of cooperation between states parties to the UNESCO Convention and non-states parties, based on the principles of the Convention and assisting in the fulfilment of its objectives.[13]

Of some debate during the UNESCO negotiations was the question of exactly who could participate in *future* agreements relating to the preservation of UCH negotiated by states parties to the Convention.[14] In

---

[8] For a detailed discussion of the Agreement, see, generally, Dromgoole, 'The International Agreement for the Protection of the *Titanic*'.

[9] Titanic Agreement, preambular clause 7.

[10] See preambular clause 8 and Art. 4(2) of the Agreement. Art. 4(2) states that protection *in situ* is the 'preferred management technique'.

[11] Both sets of rules were based on the ICOMOS Charter on the Protection and Management of Underwater Cultural Heritage 1996. The similarity of approach between the UNESCO Convention and the Titanic Agreement is such that some concern was expressed within the US commercial maritime community that the implementing legislation for the Titanic Agreement might be a 'stalking horse' for the UNESCO Convention: see 'Formal Report of the Committee on Salvage', US Maritime Law Association, 5 January 2000 (available at www.mlaus.org).

[12] Canada voted in favour of the Convention. France abstained from the vote; however, in 2009, its culture ministry announced that it intended to ratify the Convention: Ministry of Culture and Communications, press release, Paris, 30 October 2009. Although both states were involved in the negotiation of the Titanic Agreement, neither has yet signed it.

[13] It needs to be borne in mind that the Titanic Agreement is not yet in force, nor has it been signed by France or Canada. In principle, questions could arise about whether the Agreement qualified as an 'existing' agreement for the purposes of Art. 6(1) of the Convention, and about whether the saving provision in Art. 6(3) applied (which would depend on when the Agreement was deemed to have been 'concluded'). However, in practice, nothing much would appear to turn on these matters because the Agreement is broadly compatible with the Convention in any event.

[14] See Garabello, 'The Negotiating History of the Convention on the Protection of the Underwater Cultural Heritage', pp. 128–32.

particular, could *non*-states parties participate and, if so, in what circumstances? Article 6(2) provides:

The parties to such bilateral, regional or other multilateral agreements may invite States with a verifiable link, especially a cultural, historical or archaeological link, to the underwater cultural heritage concerned to join such agreements.

By providing that states with a 'verifiable link' (whether or not states parties to the Convention) may be invited to participate in such agreements, Article 6(2) reinforces the recognition that the Convention accords to states that have a particular connection with UCH.[15] However, there appears to be nothing in this provision, or elsewhere in the Convention, to preclude the possibility of *any* state joining an agreement, whether or not it has a verifiable link, provided that the agreement is 'in full conformity with' the Convention and does not 'dilute its universal character'. Indeed, if a restriction on the states that could participate existed, it could well thwart the purpose of certain agreements. For example, if a verifiable link was essential, it might be difficult to construct an agreement making fully effective use of the territorial and nationality principles of jurisdiction: geographical proximity alone is unlikely to provide a sufficient 'link'[16] and simply possessing the technological capacity to access a site amounts to no link at all.[17] In any event, it would seem to further the objectives of the Convention to encourage *all* states, whether or not party to the Convention, to participate in such agreements: clearly it is a means of achieving *better* protection than can be achieved by states parties acting under the conventional regime alone.

There seems little doubt that inter-state agreements will continue to be used – by non-states parties to the Convention and by states parties – in the type of circumstances in which they have been used in the past. No doubt they will continue to be used for dealing with sensitivities concerning matters of ownership and jurisdiction and, in the manner of the

---

[15] See, further, Chap. 3, section 4.2.2.

[16] The Convention refers consistently to states with a 'verifiable link, especially a cultural, historical or archaeological link'. For a discussion of the meaning of this phrase, see Chap. 3, section 4.2.2.

[17] For example, an intention behind the Titanic Agreement appeared to be that all those states in the general geographical vicinity of the wreck, along with all those states with the technology to access the wreck, would eventually be encouraged to become parties to the Agreement, thereby ensuring that the jurisdictional principles on which it is based are utilised to best effect: see Chap. 7, section 4.3.

agreements with respect to the *Titanic* and *Estonia*, they may occasionally be employed to reinforce protection for particularly significant or vulnerable wrecks. It also seems likely that experience gained in the environmental arena of employing regional agreements in respect of enclosed or semi-enclosed seas[18] will be drawn on to develop UCH-focused regional agreements: indeed, discussions have already taken place concerning a potential regional agreement to protect UCH of all kinds in the Mediterranean Sea.[19] As well as following the example of previous agreements, there are many other possibilities for the utilisation of inter-state agreements to pursue the objectives of the Convention. For example, 'shared heritage' agreements to diffuse tensions between states such as Spain and the Netherlands and their former colonies over their respective interests in colonial-era wreck sites have already been mooted.[20] Since the Convention is a minimum standards regime, the engagement of states parties to the Convention in agreements that protect sites that do not yet fall within the Convention's scope would appear to be an obvious way of furthering its general objectives. For example, bilateral or multilateral agreements could be used to deal with the sensitive and often complex circumstances relating to casualties of the First and Second World Wars: the *Wilhelm Gustloff* and other refugee vessels that sank off Gdansk, Poland in 1945,[21] the remains of the Japanese Second World War vessels and aircraft located in Chuuk Lagoon[22] and the First

---

[18] See Birnie and Boyle, *International Law and the Environment*, pp. 390–8.

[19] See Garabello, 'Sunken Warships in the Mediterranean', pp. 197–9. Note should also be made of the Barcelona Protocol concerning Specially Protected Areas and Biological Diversity in the Mediterranean 1995. This instrument, which came into force on 12 December 1999, is concerned with protecting the marine environment generally rather than UCH specifically, but it does include provision for the establishment of specially protected areas, among other things, on the ground of their cultural interest.

[20] See Aznar-Gómez, 'Spain', pp. 293–4; Maarleveld, 'The Netherlands', pp. 182–3.

[21] See Chap. 9, section 4.4.

[22] For details, see, generally, Jeffery, 'Federated States of Micronesia'. Interestingly, Jeffery also gives some consideration to whether the Chuuk Lagoon wrecks might qualify for protection under the 1972 World Heritage Convention (WHC): 'Federated States of Micronesia', p. 157. To qualify for inscription on the World Heritage List, a site must be regarded as of 'outstanding universal value'. Although the WHC does not say so in terms, it has been generally assumed that, to qualify, a site must be located within the territory of states parties and must also constitute immovable property (see, for example, the Operational Guidelines for the WHC (2012 version), paras. 134 and 48). Shipwrecks are seen as problematic because, as noted in Chap. 2 (section 3.1), some jurisdictions treat them as movable and others as immovable. Having said that, an important feature of the 'Bikini Atoll Nuclear Test Site', inscribed on the World Heritage List in 2010 (list ref. 1339), is the so-called 'nuclear fleet' which sank as a result of Operation Crossroads in 1946.

World War maritime battlefield of Jutland come to mind. It is also important to note that the agreements envisaged by Article 6 are not limited to ones relating to the protection of sites *in situ*: there is no reason why agreements could not be trade-related, or provide for other forms of cooperation.[23]

It is possible to envisage the development – over the course of time – of a range of agreements that promote the principles and standards of the Convention and reinforce its protective framework. It is quite conceivable that some of these agreements will *not* involve states parties to the Convention. Many states have made it clear that they support the general principles and objectives of the Convention, including the Rules in the Annex, even where they have objections to some of the technical provisions of the Convention. It is therefore possible that the very existence of the Convention will encourage non-states parties to implement their duty under Article 303(1) of the LOSC to protect UCH (and to cooperate for that purpose) by developing agreements that incorporate the conventional standards and perhaps even directly reference the Annex to the Convention.

3.   Impact of the Convention on activities 'incidentally affecting' underwater cultural heritage

There is no doubt that serious damage and destruction can be caused to UCH, quite inadvertently, by many forms of human activity that take place at sea. Some types of fishing, particularly bottom trawling, as well as dredging, dumping, pipeline- and cable-laying, hydrocarbon development and renewable energy generation can all have a negative impact, as can even the simple activity of anchor dropping. The closer to shore, the greater the general impact of human activities is likely to be, owing to the intensity of activities and shallowness of water. However, increasing pressures on the marine environment, as well as advances in

---

[23] Formal cooperative arrangements may take place at the sub-state level, for example between government departments or agencies in different states. In 2010, the US National Oceanic and Atmospheric Administration (NOAA) entered into a Memorandum of Understanding (MOU) with the Ministry of Culture in Spain setting out 'a framework to jointly identify, protect, manage and preserve underwater cultural resources of mutual interest within their respective areas of responsibility': NOAA press release, 1 December 2010 (www.noaanews.noaa.gov/stories2010/20101201_spain.html). The arrangement between these two states is particularly interesting given the fact that Spain is a party to the UNESCO Convention 2001, but the USA is not.

technological capabilities, mean that UCH in every maritime zone may be inadvertently affected by human activities of one sort or another.

From the very beginning of the process of creating a treaty on UCH, the primary threat that the initiative sought to address was that posed by deliberate interference with UCH. Nonetheless, during the course of the UNESCO negotiations, the extent to which other types of human activity that have the potential to impact upon UCH should be covered by the Convention became the subject of some debate. While the threat posed by such activities is manifest, the importance to national economies of commercial activities in the marine environment is such that any potential interference with them is a matter that is highly politically sensitive.[24] Moreover, the negotiators recognised that attempting to regulate the multitude of activities that take place in the marine zone would be a complex and ambitious task, and one well beyond the remit of a UNESCO-sponsored treaty.[25] It was as a result of a Canadian proposal that the distinction between activities 'directed at' UCH and activities 'incidentally affecting' UCH was adopted and a decision taken to focus on activities that had UCH as their primary object.[26] Nevertheless, as touched on in earlier chapters, the Convention does not ignore the impact of activities that may inadvertently disturb, or otherwise damage, UCH.

The wording of preambular clause 7 serves to demonstrate the delicate touch that the drafters felt obliged to use to deal with the question of general marine activities:

Conscious of the need to respond appropriately to the possible negative impact on underwater cultural heritage of legitimate activities that may incidentally affect it, . . .[27]

---

[24] The potential conflict between cultural and economic interests is exemplified by the situation in the Niger Delta. Revenue from the export of crude oil is vital to Nigeria's economy but the effects of oil exploitation, including oil spillage, threaten important UCH related to the slave trade in the delta region: see Final Report of the Second Meeting of the Scientific and Technical Advisory Body established under the Convention, Doc. UCH/11/2.STAB/220/7, 8 May 2011, p. 4. (Nigeria ratified the Convention in 2005.)

[25] Garabello, 'Negotiating the Convention on Underwater Cultural Heritage', p. 109.

[26] The 1994 ILA Draft and the 1998 UNESCO Draft both referred to 'activities affecting' UCH. The Canadian proposal, in 1999, led to the definitions of activities 'directed at' and 'incidentally affecting' UCH in Art. (1)(6) and (7) and to the insertion of a specific provision relating to the latter form of activities, which became Art. 5 (see below).

[27] Cf. preambular clause 6, which provides: 'Aware of the fact that underwater cultural heritage is threatened by unauthorized activities directed at it, and of the need for stronger measures to prevent such activities'.

The clause avoids using words such as 'threat', 'damage' or 'destruction'; indeed, it does not even acknowledge the certainty that harm is done by such activities. Instead, it refers only to the *'possible* negative impact'.[28] It also explicitly makes clear that such activities are 'legitimate' under the conventional regime.

The Convention includes one article devoted to activities incidentally affecting UCH. Article 5 places states parties under a specific duty with respect to such activities:

> Each State Party shall use the best practicable means at its disposal to prevent or mitigate any adverse effects that might arise from activities under its jurisdiction incidentally affecting underwater cultural heritage.

To avoid reference to specific maritime zones, the article applies to activities 'under [the] jurisdiction' of states parties.[29] All that a state party must do is use the 'best practicable means at its disposal'. This is a relatively 'soft' obligation, which mirrors the more general obligation in Article 2(4) for states to protect UCH using 'the best practicable means at their disposal and in accordance with their capabilities'.[30] As O'Keefe has succinctly put it, 'states cannot sit back and do nothing';[31] on the other hand, Article 5 recognises and takes account of the fact that different states have different means at their disposal.

Clearly, an appropriate balance needs to be found between fulfilling the Convention's aim of protecting UCH, while at the same time not unduly interfering with 'legitimate' activities. This is reflected in the fact that Article 5 does not call on states parties necessarily to *prevent* adverse effects and instead recognises that *mitigation* may be all that can be done. Although the principle of preservation *in situ* is one of the keystones of the Convention, it is recognised that in some circumstances preservation *in situ* simply may not be practicable. In the case of a major infrastructure project, such as the dredging of a navigation channel or the construction of a transnational oil or gas pipeline, the mitigation of adverse effects may be all that is possible: mitigation might be effected by

---

[28] Emphasis added.
[29] This was at the suggestion of the UK: Garabello, 'Negotiating the Convention on Underwater Cultural Heritage', p. 128. Art. 5 extends to activities within the jurisdiction of the coastal state in the EEZ or on the continental shelf (on which, see, further, Chap. 7, section 3.4), as well as to activities engaged in by flag vessels and nationals of states parties, including in the Area (on which, see, further, section 3.2, below).
[30] See Chap. 9, section 2.   [31] O'Keefe, *Shipwrecked Heritage*, p. 65.

undertaking 'rescue' archaeology prior to the destruction of a site;[32] more rarely, it might involve moving a wreck.[33] In the case of day-to-day activities such as fishing, dumping and aggregate dredging, it may be possible to prevent adverse effects altogether, without unduly prejudicing the activities, simply by ensuring that they do not take place where there are known UCH sites, or areas of particular archaeological sensitivity.[34] However, in order to ensure that negative impact can be prevented or mitigated, there need to be systems of marine development control in place that take account of archaeological and other cultural considerations. Furthermore, when deliberate interference with UCH is found to be necessary in order to mitigate negative impact, states parties will need to ensure that it is authorised in accordance with the Convention and conducted in accordance with the Rules in the Annex.[35]

According to Bederman, Article 5 'could give license to a vast regulatory scheme for offshore activities'.[36] However, this is not what is envisaged. Article 5 does not require the establishment of new, or additional, regulatory frameworks; it simply requires states parties to make use of,

---

[32] One of a number of Swedish wooden warships scuttled in 1715 in the Bay of Greifswald in Germany was excavated in 2009 to make way for the Nord Stream gas pipeline under construction between Russia and Germany: Nord Stream press release, 15 July 2009 (available at www.nord-stream.com). Pipelines and cables have a special status under the LOSC. Among other things, by virtue of Art. 79(1) of that treaty, all states are entitled to lay cables and pipelines on the continental shelf, but must do so in accordance with the other provisions of that article. These provide, inter alia, that the delineation of the course of such pipelines is subject to the consent of the coastal state: see Art. 79(3).

[33] In 2008, the wreck of a First World War German U-boat, *UB38*, was lifted and transported to a new underwater location by British maritime authorities in light of the fact that it had become a hazard to shipping in the Dover Strait (one of the busiest navigation routes in the world): Trinity House, *Horizon*, 11 (winter 2008), pp. 6–9. The fact that wrecks and other forms of UCH may pose a hazard to activities in the marine environment, as well as being endangered by those activities, is a matter that the UNESCO Convention fails to address. See Chap. 4, Concluding remarks.

[34] In the case of fishing, there may be some coincidence between the presence of fish stocks and UCH but, on the other hand, fishermen will be keen to avoid areas of the seabed which include features – so called 'fasteners' – that can snag their nets.

[35] Possibly the first example of the Rules in the Annex being applied in such circumstances arose in Norway (which may seem surprising in light of the fact that Norway was one of the four states that voted against the UNESCO Convention in 2001). In 2005, when the Norwegian oil company Statoil reported its discovery of a late nineteenth-century German cargo ship *Luise Horn* while surveying for a pipeline on the Norwegian continental shelf, the Norwegian Directorate for Cultural Heritage responded by saying that any permission granted to interfere with the wreck would be conditional on the Rules in the Annex to the UNESCO Convention being met: Kvalø and Marstrander, 'Norway', pp. 223–4.

[36] Bederman, 'Maritime Preservation Law: Old Challenges, New Trends', p. 196.

and to develop, the regulatory frameworks already in place governing activities in the marine zone; in other words, to 'use the best practicable means' at their disposal. In some parts of the world, such frameworks may be virtually non-existent, or else of a rudimentary nature; in others they may be fragmented along sectoral lines. However, certainly in developed regions, increasingly marine control procedures are holistic in approach and employ sophisticated management tools, including spatial planning and environmental impact assessment. Furthermore, as part of the trend towards full inclusiveness, archaeological considerations are increasingly taken into account in both pre- and post-consent phases.[37]

Although Article 5 is the only article of the Convention devoted to activities incidentally affecting UCH, consideration of this article alone is insufficient to appreciate the extent of the potential impact of the Convention on activities incidentally affecting UCH. The Convention's specific regulatory schemes in respect of the continental shelf and EEZ, and the Area, must also be taken into account.

3.1   The continental shelf and the exclusive economic zone

Although primarily designed to deal with activities directed at UCH, the conventional regime in respect of the continental shelf and EEZ set out in Articles 9 and 10 will also have an impact on activities incidentally affecting UCH. This fact is somewhat 'hidden' in light of the complexity of these articles.[38]

A close reading of the reporting provision set out in Article 9(1) will show that it extends to the reporting of discoveries by *anyone* undertaking activities on the continental shelf and in the EEZ, not just by those who intend to engage in activities directed at UCH. As a means of achieving the general objective of the Convention – to protect UCH – this is a valuable feature of the regime. As mentioned in Chapter 9,[39] an inventory is the core tool in heritage management and the reporting of finds allows for the gathering of information about the presence of UCH that can feed into inventories and, from there, into development plans. Although industries working in these sectors are unlikely to be enthusiastic about the imposition of a general duty to report, it is undoubtedly

---

[37]   In Europe, the ratification and implementation of the Valletta Convention 1992 has been instrumental in improving the degree to which archaeological considerations are taken into account in both the terrestrial and marine contexts: see, further, Chap. 1, section 2.2.3.

[38]   See Chap. 8, section 3.4.   [39]   See Chap. 9, section 2.

the case that much of what is currently known about the UCH resource has come from reports by these industries.[40] To that extent, they may need to do little more to fulfil a reporting obligation than they already do in practice. Of more concern to them will be the potential consequences of making a report. Under the conventional scheme, any report of a discovery will trigger the procedures set out in Articles 9 and 10 relating to notification and protection; this will prompt the attention of the coastal state, generally in its role as coordinating state, and possibly one or more other states with a verifiable link to the UCH. In fact, it is quite possible that the activities in question will be regarded as posing an 'immediate danger' to the UCH. As pointed out in Chapter 8,[41] the provision in Article 10(4) in respect of measures that may be taken by the coordinating state in the event of 'immediate danger' to UCH located on the continental shelf and in the EEZ explicitly extends not only to dangers presented by activities directed at UCH, or by natural causes, but also from human activities *of any kind*, including those arising from activities incidentally affecting UCH. Article 10(4) specifies that the coordinating state 'may take all practicable measures, and/or issue any necessary authorizations in conformity with this Convention and, if necessary prior to consultations'.[42]

As previously discussed,[43] the regime for the continental shelf and EEZ set out in Articles 9 and 10 is deeply controversial from a jurisdictional point of view and that controversy extends to its impact on activities incidentally affecting UCH. The full implications of the scheme for such activities are many and complex, not least because they vary depending on the precise nature of the activities. However, several general observations can be made. First of all, in so far as measures taken by states parties under Articles 9 and 10 relate to activities incidentally affecting UCH, they must be seen as implementation of the general duty with respect to such activities set out in Article 5. That duty relates to activities 'under [the] jurisdiction' of states parties. It therefore reinforces the fact that states parties may only act to the extent that it is within their

---

[40] Several significant shipwrecks have been located in deep water in the Gulf of Mexico as a result of survey work by the oil industry: 'Sinking oil threatens historic Gulf shipwrecks', *Associated Press*, 4 July 2010. In many cases reports will be made on a voluntary basis or out of necessity in cases where UCH poses a major obstacle. They may also be made as a result of contractual obligations to report: see, further, below.

[41] Chap. 8, section 3.4.

[42] Art. 10(4) will apply in *any* circumstances in which UCH is endangered, not only in circumstances where the discovery of UCH has been reported under Art. 9(1).

[43] See Chap. 8, section 3.4.

jurisdiction to do so. Secondly, as far as coastal state jurisdiction is concerned, it was pointed out in Chapter 7 that some states already require that contractors engaged in natural resource exploration and exploitation on the continental shelf and in the EEZ report UCH finds made in the course of their work and ensure their appropriate treatment.[44] Arguably, such requirements are justifiable in international law (when applied to foreign contractors) in light of the duty in Article 303(1) of the LOSC to protect UCH in all sea areas. What the Convention appears to be doing, in effect, is simply encouraging states parties to adopt this practice. It is worth recalling that the 1985 draft European Convention included a provision that would have had much the same effect and, although never adopted, the draft was approved by states such as France, Germany, the Netherlands and the UK.[45] Finally, provision for reporting and 'rescue' archaeology is commonplace and well-accepted in respect of development control in the terrestrial environment. The provisions in the UNESCO Convention do no more than harmonise protection for UCH with that for archaeological remains on land and, therefore, require no more of marine developers than is already required of their land-based counterparts.

3.2   The Area

Given that the conventional regime for the Area mirrors that for the continental shelf and EEZ, it is not surprising to find that Articles 11 and 12 of the Convention, relating to the Area, have the potential to impact on general activities in a manner not dissimilar to Articles 9 and 10.[46] Under Article 11(1) a state party is obliged to require its nationals, or the master of vessels flying its flag, to report discoveries of UCH, whether or not they intend to engage in activities directed at UCH. Again, a report will trigger the procedures set out in Articles 11 and 12 in respect of notification and protection. These include provision that '[a]ll States Parties may take all practicable measures in conformity with [the] Convention, if necessary prior to consultations, to prevent any immediate danger' to UCH from human activity.[47]

Given the depth of waters beyond the continental margin, the primary activity that is likely 'incidentally [to] affect' and endanger UCH is deep

---

[44] See Chap. 7, section 4.1. As noted there, this practice may be more widespread than commonly supposed.
[45] See Chap. 1, section 2.2.2.
[46] For details of the regime for the Area set out in Arts. 11 and 12, see Chap. 8, section 3.5.
[47] Art. 12(3). Emphasis added.

seabed mining. As previously discussed,[48] the International Seabed Authority (ISA) has responsibility for controlling activities connected with the exploration and exploitation of the mineral resources of the Area. The regime set out in Articles 11 and 12 therefore provides for the Secretary-General of the ISA to be notified by states parties to the UNESCO Convention of any reports of discoveries[49] and to be invited to participate in consultations on how best to protect the UCH discovered.[50]

As noted in Chapter 7,[51] as part of its functions under the LOSC, the ISA is developing a Mining Code to regulate activities in respect of the mineral resources of the Area. As part of this process, in 2000, it adopted Regulations on Prospecting and Exploration for Polymetallic Nodules in the Area. These require that a mining contractor notify the ISA of an archaeological find, that the Secretary-General of the ISA transmit such information to the Director-General of UNESCO, and that the contractor take all reasonable measures to avoid disturbing the find.[52] More recently, the ISA adopted further sets of regulations, this time relating to prospecting and exploration for two other mineral resources, polymetallic sulphides and cobalt-rich ferromanganese crusts.[53] These regulations are more developed with respect to archaeological discoveries and provide for the cessation of activities 'within a reasonable radius' of finds 'until such time as the [ISA] Council decides otherwise after taking account of the views of the Director-General of [UNESCO] or any other competent international organization'.[54]

Exactly how the mineral exploration regime established under the LOSC and the regime for protection of UCH in the Area under the UNESCO Convention will interact is an interesting question.[55] Some

---

[48] See Chap. 7, section 3.5 and Chap. 8, section 3.5.   [49] Art. 11(2).
[50] Art. 12(2).   [51] Chap. 7, section 3.5.
[52] Regulations on Prospecting and Exploration for Polymetallic Nodules in the Area, Reg. 34. See also Reg. 8, which provides for notification of finds by prospectors. The Regulations are available at www.isa.org.jm.
[53] Regulations on Prospecting and Exploration for Polymetallic Sulphides in the Area, adopted in 2010, and Regulations on Prospecting and Exploration for Cobalt-Rich Ferromanganese Crusts in the Area, adopted in 2012 (both available at www.isa.org.jm).
[54] See Reg. 37 of both. See also Reg. 8 in respect of finds made during prospecting. It is interesting to note that Reg. 37 makes specific reference to the finding of any *human remains* of an archaeological or historical nature, as well as objects and sites. (It seems likely that the Nodules Regulations will be revised to bring them into alignment with the two more recent sets of regulations.)
[55] The relationship between the two regimes has been little explored in academic literature to date. However, see Le Gurun, 'France' (2nd edn), pp. 85–9. (The matter is of particular interest to France in light of contracts concluded between the ISA and the French Institute for the Exploitation of the Sea (IFREMER), a government-sponsored

insight into how the relationship between these two regulatory regimes is viewed by the ISA is provided in the following statement, made by the Secretary-General of the ISA in 2002 after the adoption of the UNESCO Convention:

In the event that the UNESCO Convention enters into force, it would appear that there are two main implications for the Authority. On the one hand, in approving an application for a plan of work for exploration in an area where a finding of underwater cultural heritage has been notified in accordance with the UNESCO Convention, the Legal and Technical Commission and the Council [of the ISA] would need to take into account the existence of such finding or activity, although there is no suggestion that the mere existence of an item of underwater cultural heritage in a proposed exploration area would prevent the approval of a plan of work for exploration. On the other hand, in the event that the Authority is notified by a contractor of the finding in its exploration area of an object of an archaeological or historical nature, a State party to the UNESCO Convention may wish to invoke the provisions of articles 11 and 12 of that Convention where such object is also part of the underwater cultural heritage. It must be noted, in any event, that the rights and obligations of the contractor arise from the terms of its contract with the Authority.[56]

Although the Secretary-General of the ISA stated that 'the rights and obligations of the contractor arise from the terms of its contract with the Authority', it is clear from the discussion above that a contractor's rights and obligations may not be governed *solely* by its contract with the ISA. Where a contractor is subject to the jurisdiction of a state party to the UNESCO Convention (by virtue of the nationality principle of jurisdiction), it will find itself under a duty to report any discovery of UCH to *two* different authorities: the Secretary-General of the ISA under the mining regulations and the state party to the UNESCO Convention through its implementation of Article 11(1) of the Convention. Also, despite the reassurance in the statement that 'there is no suggestion that the mere existence of an item of underwater cultural heritage in a proposed exploration area would prevent the approval of a plan of work for exploration', provision made in the two most recent sets of regulations for cessation of exploration activities in the event of a find could be a source of concern for contractors; so might be the

organisation, for the exploration of polymetallic nodules and sulphides in the Area. For further details of contracts concluded to date, see below.)

[56] See Report of the Secretary-General of the International Seabed Authority under Art. 166, paragraph 4, of the United Nations Convention on the Law of the Sea, ISBA/8/A/5, 7 June 2002, para. 58.

prospect of a state party to the UNESCO Convention 'invok[ing] the provisions of articles 11 and 12'.

In practice, the ISA and UNESCO are already cooperating to ensure that both schemes work in harmony.[57] Once a discovery is reported, if the state of the contractor (and it is important to bear in mind that in the context of deep seabed mining the contractor is likely to be a state, or at least a state-sponsored organisation) is a state party to the UNESCO Convention,[58] it will be in a position to work with UNESCO, the ISA and any state declaring a link to the UCH concerned to determine a management plan for the site that accords with the Convention. That plan will be designed to ensure that any adverse effects of the exploration work are prevented or mitigated and that any activity deemed necessary, which will directly interfere with the UCH, is undertaken in accordance with the Rules in the UNESCO Annex. Even if the state of the contractor is *not* a state party to the UNESCO Convention (in which case there may be little that any state party to that Convention can do to 'invoke' the provisions of Articles 11 and 12),[59] it seems likely that a similar outcome will result in practice through application of the ISA's own regulatory scheme.

Between 2001 and 2010, eight contracts were concluded for exploration for polymetallic nodules. Under each of these fifteen-year contracts, exclusive rights were awarded to explore areas of up to 150,000 square kilometres in either the Clarion-Clipperton Zone in the Central Pacific Ocean, or the Indian Ocean.[60] By 2012, the number of exploration contracts had risen steeply to seventeen, including contracts for the

---

[57] It seems likely that an MOU will be drawn up between the two organisations, setting out the terms and scope of the cooperation, along similar lines to an MOU signed in 2000 between the Intergovernmental Oceanographic Commission of UNESCO and the ISA in respect of the conduct of marine scientific research in the Area.

[58] If a contractor is a consortium of states, there is clearly potential for complexities to arise in circumstances where some of the states that form part of the consortium are parties to the UNESCO Convention and others are not.

[59] A proviso to this assertion may be made in respect of UCH comprising a state vessel or aircraft, as defined by the UNESCO Convention (Art. 1(8)). Where the state of the contractor is a party to the UNESCO Convention, under Art. 12(7) it will be obliged not to undertake or authorise activities directed at the UCH without the consent of the flag state (whether or not the flag state is a party to the UNESCO Convention). Furthermore, even if the state of the contractor is not a party to the Convention, a flag state may assert a right to preclude interference with the UCH on the ground of sovereign immunity: see, generally, Chap. 4.

[60] For details, see the ISA website (www.isa.org.jm).

exploration of sulphides.[61] As is the case with respect to knowledge of the UCH resource on the continental shelf, most information in respect of UCH in the Area is likely to come from reports from those involved in activities 'incidentally affecting' UCH. In time, the operations of mining contractors on the deep seabed may lead to some remarkable discoveries.[62] As with activities incidentally affecting UCH in other maritime zones, it seems likely that – in most cases – appropriate accommodations will be reached to ensure that any adverse effects on UCH are minimised.

4. Dispute settlement

Clearly there are plenty of opportunities for disputes to arise between states parties to the UNESCO Convention. For example, the claim of one state that it has a verifiable link to a shipwreck and is entitled to be consulted as to its future management may be challenged by another state;[63] a state may rely on one of the constructive ambiguities in the text of the Convention to interpret a provision in a way that another state considers to be in breach of Article 3;[64] or a state may have concerns about the way that a coastal state is seeking to interfere with cable-laying on its continental shelf in order to protect UCH.[65]

As a matter of general international law, states are obliged to settle disputes between themselves by peaceful means.[66] The system is consensual in the sense that the means chosen will be by agreement between the parties. Usually they will seek to resolve a dispute by negotiation. If the negotiations fail, they may seek the assistance of a third party. For example, a third state may be asked to mediate or conciliate,[67] or the

---

[61] See 'ISA Council Approves Five New Applications for Exploration', ISA press release, 23 July 2012 (available at www.isa.org.jm). At the time of writing, a number of applications for the exploration of cobalt-rich crusts have also been received.

[62] For some time to come, discoveries falling within the scope of the UNESCO Convention are for the most part likely to comprise of the wreckage of ships and aircraft. In the future, space debris and even discarded mining equipment will also fall within the Convention's definition of UCH. (Telecommunications cables and pipelines, whether or not still in use, fall outside the scope of the Convention, whatever their age: see Art. 1(1)(b).) See, further, Chap. 2, section 4.1.

[63] See Chap. 3, section 4.2.2.   [64] See Chap. 8, especially section 2.

[65] See n. 32, above.   [66] See UN Charter, Art. 2(3). See also Art. 33.

[67] The distinction between mediation and conciliation is undefined. In mediation, the third party plays an active but relatively informal role in attempting to find the basis for a settlement between the parties, listening to both sides and proposing solutions. In conciliation, the role of the third party is likely to be more formal, for example it may undertake an independent investigation and assessment of the dispute and issue its own recommendation for a solution.

matter may be referred to a judicial tribunal of some sort.[68] Treaties frequently include provision for the settlement of disputes arising in relation to the application or interpretation of the treaty and the UNESCO Convention is no exception.

Article 25 of the Convention establishes what could be regarded as a three-tiered procedure for dispute settlement. The first tier is set out in Article 25(1):

Any dispute between two or more States Parties concerning the interpretation or application of this Convention shall be subject to negotiations in good faith or other peaceful means of settlement of their own choice.

In the event of a dispute arising concerning the interpretation or application of the Convention, as a starting point the parties must use a peaceful means of settlement of their own choice. Given that negotiations in good faith are the usual means of resort in the event of an inter-state dispute, these are referred to specifically. However, other means of settlement that might be chosen by the disputants include, it seems, all those generally available under international law.

If the parties choose negotiation as the means for settlement of their dispute under Article 25(1) but the negotiations do not settle the dispute within a reasonable time (the period appearing to be a matter for the judgment of the parties), Article 25(2) provides that 'it may be submitted to UNESCO for mediation, by agreement between the states parties concerned'. It should be noted that this second 'tier' of dispute settlement under the Convention is *optional* and will apply only where the parties to the dispute are in agreement that recourse should be had to this means of settlement.[69]

The third tier, set out in Article 25(3), comes into play in two circumstances only: (i) where a reasonable time has expired on negotiations and the parties choose not to resort to mediation under Article 25(2); or (ii) if mediation *does* take place under Article 25(2), but no settlement is reached. In these cases, by virtue of Article 25(3), resort must be had to the dispute settlement machinery set out in Part XV of the LOSC.

---

[68] If the parties agree to refer the matter for judicial settlement, the basic choice they have is between recourse to arbitration, or to the International Court of Justice (ICJ) based at The Hague: on both, see Churchill and Lowe, *The Law of the Sea*, pp. 450–3. In both cases, the decision will be binding on the parties.

[69] Interestingly, there is also provision for assistance from UNESCO in respect of disputes arising under the 1970 UNESCO Convention on Illicit Trade in Cultural Property: see Art. 17(5). As far as the author has been able to ascertain, to date this provision has never been used.

According to Article 25(3), the provisions of Part XV will apply '*mutatis mutandis*' to any dispute between states parties to the UNESCO Convention, *whether or not* they are also parties to the LOSC.[70]

Part XV of the LOSC contains elaborate machinery for the settlement of disputes arising under that treaty. Section 1 of Part XV sets out the general principles and provides for settlement by means freely chosen by the parties. Section 2 establishes compulsory procedures, entailing binding decisions, to which the parties must have recourse in the event that the means freely chosen by the parties under Section 1 fail to produce a settlement.[71] There is nothing to suggest that Article 25(3) of the UNESCO Convention refers only to the compulsory procedures laid out in Section 2 of Part XV and it therefore appears to refer to the whole of Part XV.[72]

The incorporation of the complex dispute settlement machinery in the LOSC into the provision made by the UNESCO Convention for dispute settlement is controversial. In part, this is because the dispute settlement machinery in the LOSC is itself controversial. Generally speaking, states are reluctant to commit themselves in advance to referring disputes to a specific form of dispute settlement and the compulsory nature of the procedures laid down in Section 2 of Part XV of the LOSC is unusual. However, robust dispute settlement machinery involving a compulsory element (whereby one party ultimately can force a binding resolution of the dispute) was regarded as essential in the context of the LOSC in light of the delicate balance of rights and duties enshrined in that treaty. It is for a similar reason that the reference to Part XV is incorporated into the UNESCO Convention.[73]

---

[70] Art. 25, paras. 4 and 5, go on to make detailed provision in this respect, modelled on equivalent provision in the 1995 Straddling Stocks Agreement. For detailed discussion of Art. 25(3)(4) and (5), see O'Keefe, *Shipwrecked Heritage*, pp. 137–40.

[71] The procedures are compulsory in the sense that they can be invoked unilaterally by any party to the dispute: LOSC, Art. 286. A state is free to choose one of four procedures: reference to the International Tribunal on the Law of the Sea (ITLOS) (an institution established by the LOSC); reference to the ICJ; or reference to one of two forms of ad hoc arbitration: LOSC, Art. 287. Section 3 of Part XV sets out a number of limitations and optional exceptions on the applicability of the compulsory procedures in section 2 to certain types of dispute.

[72] O'Keefe, *Shipwrecked Heritage*, p. 138. On the question of dispute settlement in the law of the sea, including Part XV of the LOSC, see, generally, Churchill and Lowe, *The Law of the Sea*, chap. 19; see also Klein, *Dispute Settlement in the UN Convention on the Law of the Sea*.

[73] For the negotiating history of Art. 25, see Garabello, 'The Negotiating History of the Convention on the Protection of the Underwater Cultural Heritage', pp. 170–2. It is unsurprising that a reference to Part XV was promoted by staunch defenders of the LOSC, such as Norway, France and the UK.

The reference to Part XV of the LOSC in Article 25 of the UNESCO Convention is also controversial because of its potential implications for *non*-states parties to the LOSC. At least on the face of it, Article 25 obliges states that are not party to the LOSC to be subject to the dispute settlement machinery in the LOSC.[74] Indeed, it is for this reason that Turkey and Venezuela, both non-states parties to the LOSC, voted against the UNESCO Convention.[75]

The reference to Part XV in Article 25(3) gives rise to a multitude of complex questions that would need to be resolved in the event of resort to this third 'tier' of dispute settlement, particularly the compulsory procedures in Section 2.[76] In practice, however, most disputes relating to law of the sea matters are resolved by negotiation, without the need to resort to third party procedures of any kind and it seems likely that the vast majority of disputes under the UNESCO Convention will be resolved by negotiation or by other consensual means (not least because of the complexities that would otherwise arise). Nonetheless, the availability of compulsory procedures does provide states with an ultimate safeguard for ensuring compliance with the Convention and should also provide some comfort for those states concerned that the UNESCO Convention may be interpreted in a way that runs counter to the LOSC. Furthermore, given the possibility that a dispute could arise relating to *both* the UNESCO Convention *and* the LOSC, the cross-reference to Part XV in Article 25 could ease the dispute settlement process.[77]

[74] See Art. 25(3). See also Art. 25(5). However, it should be noted that Art. 291(2) of the LOSC appears to preclude the application of Part XV to entities other than states parties to the LOSC unless specifically provided for in the LOSC: see O'Keefe, *Shipwrecked Heritage*, pp. 137–8; Carducci, 'The Expanding Protection of Underwater Cultural Heritage', p. 210 n. 361.

[75] See Statements on Vote by Turkey and Venezuela reproduced in Camarda and Scovazzi, *The Protection of the Underwater Cultural Heritage*, pp. 432 and 434 respectively.

[76] Among other things, interesting questions would arise concerning the determination of certain disputes relating to the application or interpretation of the UNESCO Convention with respect to the Area. Under the LOSC, special provision is made for the settlement of disputes relating to the exploration and exploitation of the natural resources of the Area: see LOSC, Part XI, section 5. In relation to a dispute arising under the UNESCO Convention concerning such activities (and such dispute could certainly arise: see section 3.2 above), would Part XV apply? As noted by Strati, section 5 of Part XI does not apply to disputes concerning preferential rights under Art. 149 of the LOSC; therefore it would seem that disputes concerning preferential rights in the context of Arts. 11(4) or 12(6) of the UNESCO Convention would fall to settlement under Part XV: Strati, *The Protection of the Underwater Cultural Heritage*, p. 306.

[77] See Oxman, 'Complementary Agreements and Compulsory Jurisdiction', pp. 277–307.

It is of note that the first case has recently arisen involving the submission of a dispute relating to UCH to a court or tribunal under Section 2 of Part XV of the LOSC. In 2010, Saint Vincent and the Grenadines instituted proceedings before the International Tribunal for the Law of the Sea (ITLOS) against Spain relating to the detention by Spanish authorities of the M/V *Louisa*, a vessel flying the flag of Saint Vincent and the Grenadines.[78] The applicant claimed that the detention amounted to a violation of various provisions of the LOSC, including Article 303.[79] At the time of the institution of the proceedings, both parties to the dispute were also states parties to the UNESCO Convention 2001.[80] Interestingly, after Spain drew attention to this fact, Saint Vincent and the Grenadines dropped any claim to a breach of Article 303.[81]

5. Technical implementation

A treaty of the complexity of the UNESCO Convention 2001 requires considerable organisation and oversight to ensure its effective technical implementation. However, instead of providing for the establishment of a separate international body – along the lines of the ISA – to administer the regime on behalf of states parties, the UNESCO Convention provides for an administrative structure based on states parties working directly together, with the support of UNESCO. The effectiveness of the conventional regime will therefore be dependent on substantial and sustained commitment, at a practical (and financial) level, on the part of the states parties. Among other things, they will need genuinely to embrace the principle of cooperation enshrined in the Convention and be prepared to accept compromises in order that decisions can be made with reasonable speed and efficiency.

In comparison with other recent UNESCO treaties,[82] the UNESCO Convention 2001 makes little specific provision for its technical

---

[78] See M/V *Louisa*, ITLOS Case No. 18. On 23 December 2010, ITLOS delivered an Order refusing the applicant's request for provisional measures under Art. 290(1) of the LOSC. The hearing on the merits of the case was scheduled for October 2012.

[79] For the factual circumstances in so far as they relate to Art. 303, see Chap. 7, n. 21.

[80] Saint Vincent and the Grenadines became a party to the UNESCO Convention just six days before the submission of its application to ITLOS.

[81] See Spain's Counter Memorial of 12 December 2011, para. 168, and the Reply of Saint Vincent and the Grenadines of 10 February 2012, p. 29. See also the related comment in the Rejoinder by Spain of 10 April 2012, para. 53, n. 78. All related documentation is available at www.itlos.org.

[82] See, for example, UNESCO Convention for the Safeguarding of the Intangible Cultural Heritage 2003, Arts. 4–10; UNESCO Convention on the Protection and Promotion of the Diversity of Cultural Expressions 2005, Arts. 22–4. For a discussion of the arrangements

implementation and therefore leaves much to the discretion of states parties. Article 23 provides simply that the Director-General of UNESCO 'shall convene a Meeting of States Parties within one year of the entry into force of [the] Convention and thereafter at least once every two years'.[83] The Meeting of States Parties shall decide on its own functions and responsibilities[84] and shall adopt its own Rules of Procedure.[85] The Convention affords to the Meeting of States Parties the option of establishing a Scientific and Technical Advisory Body composed of experts nominated by the states parties[86] to assist it 'in questions of a scientific or technical nature regarding the implementation of the Rules' in the Annex.[87] Article 24 goes on to provide that the Director-General of UNESCO is responsible for the functions of the Secretariat of the Convention,[88] the duties of which shall include the organisation of the Meeting of States Parties and assisting states in implementing the decisions of the Meeting of States Parties.[89]

At the time of writing, the machinery for the implementation of the Convention is still in its formative stages. However, a number of key developments have taken place.

5.1   Meeting of States Parties

The first session of the Meeting of States Parties took place at the UNESCO Headquarters in Paris on 26–27 March 2009, shortly after the entry into force of the Convention on 2 January 2009. At this session, Rules of Procedure for the Meeting of States Parties were adopted. Among other things, these set out the functions and responsibilities of the Meeting and make provision for the establishment of subsidiary bodies. The decision was taken to establish a Scientific and Technical Advisory Body, as envisaged by Article 23(4), and the Statutes of this body were adopted. Although not expressly provided for in the Convention, it was decided that Operational Guidelines that 'might contribute to a better understanding and more effective implementation' of the Convention should be drawn up.[90] It was agreed that the Secretariat would

---

for implementation of the various UNESCO treaties in the cultural field, see Forrest, *International Law and the Protection of Cultural Heritage*, pp. 415–18.

[83] Art. 23(1). An Extraordinary Meeting of States Parties shall be convened '[a]t the request of a majority of States Parties': Art. 23(1).

[84] Art. 23(2).   [85] Art. 23(3).   [86] Art. 23(4).

[87] Art. 23(5).   [88] Art. 24(1).   [89] Art. 24(2)(a) and (b).

[90] Draft Summary Record of the First Session, Doc. UCH/09/2.MSP/220/4, 15 September 2009 (adopted without amendment at the Second Session), p. 10.

prepare a preliminary draft of these guidelines, in consultation with states parties, giving priority to two specific matters: the state cooperation and consultation mechanism contained in Articles 8–13 and the appointment of coordinating states in the Area.

The second session of the Meeting of States Parties took place on 1–2 December 2009. Consideration was given to a preliminary draft of the Operational Guidelines prepared by the Secretariat and it was decided to establish an Intergovernmental Working Group to prepare a revised draft for consideration at the third session. Although not provided for in the Convention, it was resolved to establish a Special Account to provide an Underwater Cultural Heritage Fund, based on contributions from states parties and other donors. The first cohort of members of the Scientific and Technical Advisory Body was also elected. At the third session, on 13–14 April 2011, consideration was given to the composition of the Scientific and Technical Advisory Body (see below). A revised draft of the Operational Guidelines produced by the Intergovernmental Working Group was also considered and referred back to the Group for further work. At the time of writing, there is an expectation that the Operational Guidelines will be ready for adoption by the Meeting of States Parties at its fourth session in April 2013.[91]

The Operational Guidelines are of some significance. At their heart are provisions relating to a so-called 'state cooperation mechanism'. These provisions set out guidance for states parties on:

(i) reporting, notification and declarations of interest in relation to the regimes set out in Articles 9–10 and 11–12;
(ii) selection of the coordinating state and state consultations under these regimes; and
(iii) measures that can be taken by states parties under these regimes.

It is clear that aspects of this guidance have the potential to be politically controversial.[92]

---

[91] The most recent version is set out in Doc. UCH/12/WG/220/1, 17 July 2012. This working document was prepared for consideration by the Working Group at a meeting scheduled for September 2012.

[92] The Meeting of States Parties is well aware of this fact and has emphasised that the purpose of the guidelines must be to facilitate the application of the Convention, not to interpret it, or rewrite it. The most recent draft of the Operational Guidelines states that they 'can neither be understood as a subsequent agreement nor as rewriting, amending or interpreting the Convention. They merely aim to facilitate its implementation by giving practical guidance. In case of doubt, the text of the Convention prevails': Doc. UCH/12/WG/220/1, 17 July 2012, para. 22. This wording suggests that the Guidelines are not intended to have any legal status as an aid to the interpretation of the Convention

5.2 Scientific and Technical Advisory Body

The role of the Scientific and Technical Advisory Body is to 'appropriately assist' the Meeting of States Parties in questions of a scientific or technical nature regarding the implementation of the Rules in the Annex to the Convention.[93] The Rules of Procedure of the Meeting of States Parties provide that each state party may nominate an expert for election to the Advisory Body and specify that the experts shall have a scientific, professional and ethical background at the national and/or international level adequate for the task. The Statutes of the Advisory Body go on to identify as appropriate forms of background the following fields in particular: 'underwater archaeology, international law, materials science (metallurgy, archaeo-biology, geology), and conservation of underwater cultural heritage sites and/or archaeological underwater artefacts'.[94]

The Rules of Procedure of the Meeting of States Parties provide for an Advisory Body initially composed of twelve members, but with the possibility of increasing the number to a maximum of twenty-four, depending on the number of states parties. Generally speaking, the term of office for each member will be four years. The Advisory Body shall consult and collaborate with non-governmental organisations (NGOs) having activities related to the scope of the Convention, including ICUCH[95] and other competent NGOs accredited by the Meeting of States Parties. The Director-General of UNESCO shall convene a session of the Advisory Body once a year (with the option of a second session if called upon).

To date, there have been three sessions of the Advisory Body. One significant outcome of these meetings was the approval of the Manual for Activities Directed at UCH.[96]

---

and, in particular, are not intended to constitute an agreement for the purposes of Art. 31(3)(a) of the Vienna Convention on the Law of Treaties. (Art. 31(3)(a) provides that, in interpreting a treaty, account shall be taken, inter alia, of 'any subsequent agreement between the parties regarding the interpretation of the treaty or the application of its provisions'.) Whatever the final outcome, the Guidelines inevitably will be highly influential. In light of this fact, considerable attention has been paid to their drafting.

[93] Art. 23(5).

[94] Statutes of the Scientific and Technical Advisory Body, Art. 2(a).

[95] ICUCH is particularly significant because it was the body responsible for the drafting of the 1996 ICOMOS Charter on the Protection and Management of the Underwater Cultural Heritage on which the Rules in the Annex to the Convention are based: see, further, Chap. 1, section 3.2.8.

[96] The Manual is designed to assist competent authorities in their application of the Rules in the Annex (see Chap. 9, section 3.1). The approval of the Manual by the Advisory Body gives rise to questions about the intended status for the Manual as an aid to the

5.3   UNESCO Secretariat

Besides organising the Meetings of States Parties and assisting states in implementing the decisions of these Meetings,[97] the Secretariat for the Convention will also support the work of the Scientific and Technical Advisory Body[98] and play a crucial role in facilitating reporting and communication under the State Cooperation Mechanism.[99] It may also be called upon to provide mediation services in the event of disputes arising between states parties.[100] Less formally, but perhaps equally importantly, the Secretariat will play a role in promoting the Convention and furthering its objectives, including raising public awareness of the value and significance of UCH and the importance of protecting it under the Convention, and working with states parties to facilitate general cooperation and information-sharing, including in matters such as capacity building, training and technology transfer.

The Secretariat is small[101] and coping with all these tasks will be challenging. At the time of writing, it is focusing its attention on enhancing capacity building, awareness-raising and the promotion of ratifications on a regional basis.

interpretation of the Convention, given that the Rules in the Annex are an integral part of the Convention. While the approval falls short of a 'subsequent agreement between the parties regarding the interpretation of the treaty or the application of its provisions' for the purposes of Art. 31(3)(a) of the Vienna Convention on the Law of Treaties (see n. 92, above), it gives the impression that the Manual is intended to carry some authoritative weight. This does not appear to be what the authors (eminent archaeologists from around the world) intended and there is a risk that comments in the Manual may, quite unintentionally, give a misleading impression about the meaning of certain Rules, in particular those that were the outcome of political compromises (most notably Rule 2). More generally, the role of the Advisory Body in affording assistance to the Meeting of States Parties ('in questions of a scientific or technical nature regarding the implementation of the Rules') is such that the work of the Body is at times almost bound to be politically sensitive. (The resolution adopted by the Advisory Group at its third session on the funding of excavations by the pre-planned deaccession of recovered artefacts illustrates this point: see Chap. 6, n. 85 and associated text.)

[97] In accordance with Art. 24(2).
[98] See Rules of Procedure, Rule 26.
[99] It is envisaged that reporting will be undertaken electronically by means of a database accessible through the UNESCO website. Draft forms for notifications and declarations of interest are appended to the Draft Operational Guidelines.
[100] See section 4, above.
[101] The Secretariat currently comprises one permanent full-time official, assisted from time to time by temporary or part-time staff.

6. Amendment

The process for amending the UNESCO Convention is set out in Article 31. According to Article 31(1):

A State Party may, by written communication addressed to the Director-General, propose amendments to this Convention. The Director-General shall circulate such communication to all States Parties. If, within six months from the date of the circulation of the communication, not less than one half of the States Parties reply favourably to the request, the Director-General shall present such proposal to the next Meeting of States Parties for discussion and possible adoption.

In order to be adopted, an amendment will need to be supported by a two-thirds majority of states parties present and voting at the Meeting of States Parties.[102]

The requirements for the adoption of an amendment under Article 31 are more formalised than those for some earlier UNESCO treaties in the heritage field[103] and are fairly onerous.[104] The requirement for a state party (rather than, say, the Meeting of States Parties or UNESCO) to initiate the proceedings is similar to the LOSC,[105] as is the requirement that not less than one-half of states parties reply favourably to the request. However, the equivalent provision under the LOSC allows a period of twelve months for the receipt of these replies; as O'Keefe has pointed out, allowing a period of only six months to elicit positive responses from at least half of states parties is a 'substantial hurdle' to overcome.[106] Furthermore, some may regard the requirement for a two-thirds majority to support the adoption of an amendment as somewhat

---

[102] Art. 31(2). Once adopted, amendments will be subject to ratification, acceptance, approval or accession by states parties: Art. 31(3). Amendments will be binding only on states parties that accept them: see Art. 31(4)–(5).

[103] Namely, the 1970 UNESCO Convention on Illicit Trade in Cultural Property and the 1972 World Heritage Convention (see Arts. 25 and 37 respectively). Cf. the Hague Convention for the Protection of Cultural Property in the Event of Armed Conflict of 1954, Art. 39.

[104] However, it is interesting to note that essentially the same provisions are adopted by two more recent UNESCO treaties relating to culture, the Convention for the Safeguarding of the Intangible Cultural Heritage 2003 and the Convention on the Protection and Promotion of the Diversity of Cultural Expressions 2005 (see Arts. 38 and 33 respectively).

[105] See LOSC, Art. 312(1). As well as a general amendment procedure in Art. 312, the LOSC also provides for an alternative, simplified, amendment procedure whereby if no state party objects to a proposed amendment within the twelve-month period, it shall be considered adopted: see Art. 313, esp. para. 3. (Amendments relating to activities in the Area are subject to a separate procedure under LOSC, Art. 314.)

[106] O'Keefe, *Shipwrecked Heritage*, p. 150.

odd when the adoption of the Convention as a whole required only a simple majority.[107]

The amendment procedure under Article 31 applies not only to the main body of the Convention, but also the Rules in the Annex, given that they form an integral part of the Convention.[108] In light of the general nature and purpose of the Rules, particularly the fact that they are intended to represent prevailing best practice, a greater degree of flexibility in respect of their amendment may have been desirable. However, since the Rules contain politically sensitive elements (most notably Rule 2 on commercial exploitation), a tacit approval procedure for amendment of the Rules was rejected.[109]

7. Reservations

A final aspect of the UNESCO Convention meriting note is Article 30. This provides:

> With the exception of Article 29, no reservations may be made to this Convention.

This is another procedural provision which aligns the approach of the Convention with that of the LOSC. It means that when a state ratifies the Convention it will be unable to make a statement purporting 'to exclude or to modify the legal effect of . . . provisions of the treaty in their application to that State'.[110] In light of the compromises that the text of the Convention incorporates, it was regarded as important to ensure that states parties accepted the Convention as a 'package' and did not attempt to contract out of provisions they disliked.[111]

Article 30 refers to Article 29, which is the so-called 'federal clause'. This permits states with a federal system to make a declaration at the time of ratification of the treaty to the effect that the treaty will not apply to specific parts of its territory, inland waters, internal waters,

---

[107] In fact, it should be regarded as a compromise, as some states argued that a consensus should be required: see Garabello, 'The Negotiating History of the Convention on the Protection of the Underwater Cultural Heritage', p. 179.

[108] UNESCO Convention, Art. 33.

[109] For the negotiating history of Art. 31, see Garabello, 'The Negotiating History of the Convention on the Protection of the Underwater Cultural Heritage', pp. 178–9. See related comments in n. 96 above.

[110] Vienna Convention on the Law of Treaties, Art. 2(1)(d).

[111] For the negotiating history of this provision, see Garabello, 'The Negotiating History of the Convention on the Protection of the Underwater Cultural Heritage', pp. 177–8.

archipelagic waters or territorial sea until such time as conditions exist which will allow such application. In the meantime, the state concerned 'shall, to the extent practicable and as quickly as possible, promote' such conditions.[112]

[112] On this provision, see, further, Chap. 8, section 3.2, esp. n. 39.

Final reflections

In 2001, the UNESCO Convention on the Protection of the Underwater Cultural Heritage was viewed by many as a failed initiative. Although it had succeeded in resolving a number of the core areas of contention – most notably those relating to the law of salvage and commercial exploitation – a resolution of the differences of view held by coastal states and flag states on two other crucial issues eluded the negotiators. As with any initiative in the field of the law of the sea, the support of flag states is necessary before the outcome can be declared a success; in this case that support was absent. Echoing the position at the end of UNCLOS III, there was some scepticism at the conclusion of the UNESCO negotiations (in government circles and among law of the sea specialists) about whether the new treaty would come into force, or be ratified by many states outside the G-77. There was also a view on the part of some – quite possibly inspired by the example of the 1994 Agreement for the Implementation of Part XI of the LOSC – that another initiative following on the heels of the Convention might address the outstanding areas of contention.

Time moves on and it is now more than a decade since the adoption of the Convention. On 2 January 2009, it entered into force, three months after its twentieth ratification and, at the time of writing, it has forty-one states parties. While the majority of these states are G-77 members (twenty-eight of the forty-one), a number of European states have also ratified the Convention, including Italy, Portugal and Spain. The participation of these three states in the conventional regime is particularly significant from a flag state perspective. Each has a substantial maritime legacy and for this reason some understanding of the concerns of the dissenting flag states. Each has been influential in the development of the regime to date and this influence is likely to continue: if there is any risk that interpretations of the Convention will be taken that 'strain' its relationship with the LOSC, they are likely to exercise a restraining influence.[1] In the not too distant future, a broad range of states outside the G-77 may well become parties, including Australia, Canada, China,[2] Ireland and South Africa, all of whom voted in support of the initiative in 2001; they too will then begin to exert influence on the Convention's future direction.

It is inevitable that treaties are taken more seriously once they become effective internationally and begin to gather some momentum. It is interesting to note, for example, that recently there has been a change of tack in the references to the Convention made in the annual UN General Assembly Resolutions on Oceans and the Law of the Sea. As noted in Chapter 8,[3] initially the Resolutions pointedly failed to endorse the new Convention and instead urged states to cooperate in taking measures to protect UCH 'in conformity with' the LOSC. However, the Resolution adopted at the 66th Session of the General Assembly in December 2011 called upon states that had not yet done so to 'consider becoming parties' to the UNESCO Convention.[4] This indicates that there may be growing political support for the treaty in the international community.[5]

So, what of the dissenting flag states? France, Germany, the Netherlands and the UK abstained from the vote at the end of the UNESCO Conventions; Russia and Norway voted against the treaty and the USA expressed serious dissatisfaction with the text. The prospect of

---

[1] For example, the most recent draft of the Operational Guidelines indicates that Spain worked hard to ensure that the need for compatibility with the LOSC was 'hard-wired' into the text: see UNESCO Doc. UCH/12/WG/220/1, 17 July 2012.

[2] China's active interest in UCH is illustrated not only by the *Nanhai No. 1* project (see Chap. 6, section 3.4) but also by its announcement that it plans to build an archaeological research vessel to assist in the management of UCH in its coastal waters: 'China building first vessel for underwater archaeology', *Global Times*, 24 October 2012 (available at www.globaltimes.cn).

[3] See Chap. 8, section 3.6.

[4] See UN General Assembly Resolution A/RES/66/231, 5 April 2012, para. 8.

[5] For a discussion of statements made in earlier General Assembly Resolutions, see, generally, Ferri, 'The Protection of the Underwater Cultural Heritage According to the United Nations General Assembly'. It can also be noted that a Green Paper on future maritime policy published by the European Commission in 2006 encouraged Member States of the European Union to ratify the Convention: see Green Paper, 'Towards a Future Maritime Policy for the Union: A European Vision for the Oceans and Seas', Commission of the European Communities, Brussels, 7 June 2006, COM(2006) 275 final, Vol. II – Annex, p. 48.

another initiative leading to an alternative instrument to the 2001 Convention has now faded.[6] However, one of the most significant developments since 2001 was the announcement by the French Ministry of Culture in 2009 that France was preparing to ratify the Convention.[7] Despite having expressed reservations in 2001 about the Convention's treatment of sunken warships, and about its provision for coastal state jurisdiction on the continental shelf, it appears to have reached the conclusion that the broad benefits the Convention could bring with respect to UCH protection outweigh its technical legal objections.[8] In the words of the head of the French government agency responsible for underwater archaeological research:

France wishes to protect effectively all sunken heritage from pillaging, destruction and treasure hunting, wherever this heritage may be located, including international waters. The 2001 Convention is the most effective international instrument to reach this goal.[9]

In fact, it seems that France may have concluded that its concerns regarding coastal state jurisdiction on the continental shelf were unfounded[10] and that its one outstanding area of concern – the wording of Article 7(3) relating to sunken warships in the territorial sea – could be overcome by lodging an interpretative declaration upon ratification.[11] If France or, indeed, any of the other dissenting flag states ratifies the Convention this will be a major breakthrough for the initiative.

---

[6] Initially it seemed that such an initiative could have been driven by the USA State Department. However, there appears to have been a loss of interest. This may be partly because of changes in personnel, as well as recognition that the initiative could well face the same hurdles as the Titanic Agreement: political difficulties internally and a lack of political will externally. Also, there is no obvious international organisation to sponsor such an initiative.

[7] Ministry of Culture and Communications, press release, Paris, 30 October 2009. See Chap. 4, section 3.3.

[8] It is possible that activities directed at the site of *Le Marquis Tournay*, a French eighteenth-century privateer in the English Channel, may have played a part in the change of heart by France. (Litigation relating to this wreck is referred to in Chap. 5, n. 136.)

[9] L'Hour, 'An Update on France's Position Regarding the UNESCO Underwater Cultural Heritage Convention'.

[10] See UNESCO, Final Report of the Working Meeting on the UNESCO 2001 Convention on the Protection of the Underwater Cultural Heritage, London, 9 July 2008, p. 2.

[11] *Ibid.* See also L'Hour, 'An Update on France's Position Regarding the UNESCO Underwater Cultural Heritage Convention'. As pointed out in Chap. 10, there is a general prohibition on reservations to the Convention under Art. 30. However, as observed by O'Keefe, interpretative declarations may be lodged by a state 'to clarify the meaning or scope it attributes to a provision' of the treaty: O'Keefe, *Shipwrecked Heritage*, p. 148.

A factor that is capable of tipping the balance for a state with respect to its attitude to the treaty is the attitude of its neighbouring states. As discussed in Chapters 8 and 9, the regulatory and other protective provisions of the Convention are built on states working together in partnership to ensure that activities are conducted in conformity with the conventional scheme. The regime will be at its most effective when such partnerships are formed on a regional basis. There is already significant adherence to the Convention among states in the Western Mediterranean and Adriatic areas, as well as in the Caribbean. These regions may therefore be the first to benefit from its state Cooperation Mechanism.[12] In northern Europe, at present the only state to have ratified the Convention is Lithuania. However, if states such as France and Ireland follow Lithuania's lead, neighbouring states are likely to feel some 'gravitational pull'.[13]

In 2014, on the centenary of the outbreak of the First World War, maritime losses from the Great War will start to fall within the 100-year threshold for application of the Convention. As part of the general process of reflection that will take place at this time, there is likely to be heightened political interest in the status of the sunken warships of both World Wars. Unauthorised interference with such wrecks is a common occurrence: some of this interference is minor pilfering by rogue divers,[14] but there is also some incidence of industrial-scale salvaging of scrap metal and other material.[15] Some high-value wartime cargoes that have only become viable salvage propositions in recent years are also attracting interest.[16] As pointed out in Chapter 4, when taken as

---

[12] Guérin, 'The 2001 UNESCO Convention on the Protection of the Underwater Cultural Heritage', p. 3.
[13] Dromgoole, Reflections on the Position of the Major Maritime Powers with Respect to the UNESCO Convention on the Protection of the Underwater Cultural Heritage 2001', p. 5.
[14] In 2012, German heritage authorities reported that tampering with wrecks, including wartime wrecks, by trophy hunters off Germany's Baltic Sea coast, appeared to be increasing, perhaps in part because recreational diving was prohibited when East Germany was part of the Soviet Union: 'Germany tries to halt Baltic shipwreck plundering', Spiegal Online, 17 October 2012.
[15] In 2011, it was reported that Dutch vessels were ransacking three wrecks of First World War British warships lying off the Dutch coast, utilising heavy-duty claws on cranes to remove valuable scrap metal: 'British war grave shipwrecks are ransacked for scrap metal', The Times, 22 September 2011. In the same year the recovery of a bronze conning tower of the First World War British submarine G8 by a Danish salvage team was also reported: 'Concern over war grave as salvage team finds submarine from 1918', The Times, 26 August 2011.
[16] For some states with ownership interests in such cargoes, the Convention's stance on commercial exploitation could, of course, be a factor militating against ratification of the Convention: see Chap. 6, section 3.4.

a whole, the conventional regime may be seen to reinforce – rather than undermine – the flag states' position that consent must be obtained in advance of any interference with their sunken warships;[17] moreover, the principles of the Convention are well-suited for the purpose of protecting gravesites *in situ*.[18] It is therefore conceivable that states that suffered substantial maritime losses in the wars of the twentieth century may come to recognise the Convention's potential for affording protection to broad cultural values and not simply to what may be regarded as the rather esoteric values of 'history and archaeology'.

The most intractable difficulty is, and always has been, the question of coastal state jurisdiction on the continental shelf. While the UNESCO Convention does not purport to afford coastal states direct jurisdiction over UCH on the continental shelf, the constructive ambiguities in the text mean that it is open to interpretations that 'jeopardise' the balance of jurisdiction enshrined in the LOSC. In 1982, Caflisch highlighted that it was not the fear of extended jurisdiction over UCH itself that is at the core of flag state opposition to such extension, but rather the possibility that it 'might pave the way for other exceptions' – in other words, open the floodgates to creeping jurisdiction more generally.[19] It is therefore instructive to note the conclusions of a recent independent advisory report commissioned by the government of the Netherlands (notably one of the three states to express opposition at UNCLOS III to proposals for extended jurisdiction, along with the US and the UK). The Dutch Advisory Committee on Issues of Public International Law concluded that even if interpretations of the UNESCO Convention were taken that were incompatible with the LOSC, they would represent 'only a minor shift' in the distribution of competences between coastal and flag states;[20] it also concluded that the prospect that the UNESCO Convention will set a precedent leading to jurisdictional 'creep' to functions other than the protection of UCH was 'unlikely'.[21]

The difficulty of providing adequate protection to UCH located on the continental shelf stems back to the statement of the ILC in 1956 that the

---

[17] See Chap. 4, section 3.3.   [18] See Chap. 9, section 4.4.

[19] Caflisch, 'Submarine Antiquities and the International Law of the Sea', p. 17. See Chap. 1, section 2.1.2.

[20] Advisory Committee on Issues of Public International Law, Advisory Report on the UNESCO Convention on the Protection of the Underwater Cultural Heritage (Translation), Advisory Report No. 21, The Hague, December 2011, pp. 8 and 10.

[21] *Ibid.*, p. 12. At the time of writing, the Dutch government's response to the report is still awaited.

sovereign rights of coastal states on the continental shelf did not cover 'objects such as wrecked ships and their cargoes (including bullion)'.[22] This statement was taken to mean that such objects are not natural resources. It was written in the context of states claiming rights to *exploit* the resources of the continental shelf, rather than accepting responsibilities for *protecting* resources. It was also written at a time when underwater archaeology as a discipline was not yet established; when understanding of the nature and value of the underwater cultural resource was only a fraction of what it is today; and when there was no conception of the close interrelationship between UCH and marine flora and fauna.

While this pronouncement has been at the root of the problems, another statement made by the ILC in the same report may provide the most compelling argument for suggesting that the time is now ripe for reconsideration of the matter. In accepting the notion that coastal states could exercise control and jurisdiction over the continental shelf for the purpose of exploiting its *natural* resources (then a relatively new proposition), the ILC noted that such rights could affect the freedom of the seas, particularly the freedom of navigation. However, it justified any potential inroad into such freedom by saying:

this cannot be sufficient reason for obstructing a development which, in the opinion of the Commission, can be to the benefit of all mankind.[23]

The strong support expressed by states in 2001 for the general principles and objectives of the UNESCO Convention indicates that there is now widespread recognition by the international community that finding a means of adequately protecting UCH is something that will be to the benefit of humanity as a whole. The pronouncements of the UN General Assembly since 2001 indicate that there is continuing recognition of the need for urgent action in this regard and the change of tack in the 2011 pronouncement suggests that there may now be recognition that the UNESCO Convention offers the best way forward. Among states, there appears to be no disagreement that the Rules in the Convention's Annex represent the appropriate standards to apply to activities directed at UCH. The Convention takes an internationalist, rather than nationalist, approach to the UCH 'resource' – enabling, in the inimitable words of

---

[22] Report of the International Law Commission to the General Assembly, 11 UN GAOR Supp. (No. 9), UN Doc A/3159 (1956), reprinted in (1956) *Yearbook of the International Law Commission*, Vol. II, p. 298. See Chap. 1, section 2.1.

[23] *Yearbook of the International Law Commission*, Vol. II, p. 296.

Oxman, all peoples to 'drink from a single well of human wisdom and achievement', rather than 'squabbling over title to icons'[24] – and it establishes a system whereby states are entrusted with responsibility for UCH and will act as its stewards. The protection of cultural heritage is undoubtedly of much lower political priority than the economic exploitation of natural resources, but equally the implementation of the Convention's regulatory framework is likely to have relatively little impact on freedom of navigation and other high seas freedoms compared with the inroad made on these freedoms when rights and jurisdiction were conferred on coastal states with respect to natural resources.

Whether technically it would be necessary to wait for an UNCLOS IV to reopen this matter is debatable. Some would argue that this is the case, in light of Article 311(3) of the LOSC.[25] However, others would point to paragraph 5 of the same article to argue to the contrary. This provides that Article 311 'does not affect international agreements expressly permitted or preserved by other articles of' the LOSC. Is the UNESCO Convention such an agreement, in light of the 'without prejudice' clause in Article 303(4) of the LOSC? Nordquist indicates that this could be the case.[26] If this was accepted, any extension of jurisdiction over UCH on the continental shelf under Articles 9 and 10 of the UNESCO Convention could be regarded as a legitimate means of implementing the duty in Article 303(1) to protect UCH in all sea areas and to cooperate for that purpose. Indeed, this appears to have been the opinion of the Dutch advisory committee in its report of 2011.[27] While perhaps seeming counter-intuitive, this line of argument might go some small way to reinforcing the original objective of UNCLOS III: to produce 'a comprehensive constitution for the oceans that would stand the test of time'.[28] This is because it could be seen as a way of 'constraining and containing' coastal state claims with respect to UCH on the continental shelf and EEZ within the overall LOSC framework.[29]

---

[24] Oxman, 'Marine Archaeology and the International Law of the Sea', p. 372.

[25] See Chap. 8, section 2.

[26] See Nordquist, Rosenne and Sohn, *United Nations Convention on the Law of the Sea 1982*, Vol. V, pp. 161, 240, 243.

[27] Advisory Committee on Issues of Public International Law, Advisory Report on the UNESCO Convention on the Protection of the Underwater Cultural Heritage (Translation), Advisory Report No. 21, The Hague, December 2011, pp. 8 and 10.

[28] See the remarks of Tommy Koh, President of UNCLOS III, referred to in the General introduction, section 2.2, above.

[29] See Schofield, 'Parting the Waves', p. 57. Schofield points out that there are continuing pressures on this framework, especially in the areas of maritime security and environmental protection.

In 1989, in reflecting on the regime for UCH established by the LOSC, Nordquist commented:

[p]resumably, in the course of time, this incipient new branch of law will be completed by the competent international organization, above all UNESCO, and by State practice.[30]

The 'incipient new branch of law' created by Articles 149 and 303 of the LOSC has now been greatly elaborated upon by the UNESCO Convention, but it will only be truly 'completed' if and when this treaty is accepted and implemented by flag states, as well as coastal states. Ultimately, the decision taken by any particular state about whether or not to ratify the Convention will be a pragmatic one based on weighing up the benefits and drawbacks of doing so and determining what is in the best overall national interest. Over time, the balance of the scales may change.[31] In the meantime, the 2001 Convention has already had a profound impact on international thinking and practice with respect to UCH, and provides the context in which all dialogue on the subject is now conducted. For non-states parties, its very existence is likely to increase a sense of obligation with respect to the duty in Article 303(1) of the LOSC and to encourage them to seek ways of using the authority available to them under general international law, including the LOSC, to protect UCH wherever it might be located, whether on an individual basis or collaboratively. There is little reason to doubt that the USA will continue to show leadership in this respect and, given the terms of the Titanic Agreement,[32] will seek to align its approach – where possible – with the UNESCO Convention. While two parallel international legal regimes governing UCH may be in place for the foreseeable future, it seems inevitable that there will be a convergence of state practice under those regimes, based on the application of now clearly defined common principles, objectives and standards for behaviour, inter-state cooperation

---

[30] Nordquist, Rosenne and Sohn, *United Nations Convention on the Law of the Sea 1982*, Vol. V, p. 162.
[31] The 1970 UNESCO Convention on Illicit Trade in Cultural Property is a good illustration of how the fortunes of a treaty can change over time. With the exception of the USA, many of the world's major 'market states', including the UK, Japan, Switzerland, Germany, Belgium and the Netherlands, did not ratify the Convention until comparatively recently. Eventually, technical objections were outweighed by more general concerns about illicit trade. Ten years after the adoption of the 1970 Convention, there were forty-two states parties. At the time of writing, there are 122.
[32] See Chap. 10, section 2.

and, importantly, an assumption of full and active responsibility for the protection of UCH in all parts of the sea.

In 2002 one commentator expressed the view that the UNESCO Convention 'will be doomed to irrelevancy'.[33] A decade on, this seems far from likely.

Postscript: France ratified the UNESCO Convention 2001 on 7 February 2013.

---

[33] Bederman, 'Maritime Preservation Law', p. 205.

Bibliography

Adlercreutz, T., 'Sweden', in S. Dromgoole (ed.), *The Protection of the Underwater Cultural Heritage: National Perspectives in Light of the UNESCO Convention 2001* (Leiden and Boston: Martinus Nijhoff Publishers, 2006), pp. 297–312.

Alexander, B., 'Treasure Salvage Beyond the Territorial Sea: An Assessment and Recommendations' (1989) 20 *Journal of Maritime Law and Commerce* 1–19.

Arend, A., 'Archaeological and Historical Objects: The International Legal Implications of UNCLOS III' (1982) 22 *Virginia Journal of International Law* 777–803.

Aust, A., *Handbook of International Law*, 2nd edn (Cambridge University Press, 2010).

Modern Treaty Law and Practice, 2nd edn (Cambridge University Press, 2007).

Aznar-Gómez, M., 'Legal Status of Sunken Warships "Revisited"' (2003) 9 *Spanish Yearbook of International Law* 61–101.

'Spain', in S. Dromgoole (ed.), *The Protection of the Underwater Cultural Heritage: National Perspectives in Light of the UNESCO Convention 2001* (Leiden and Boston: Martinus Nijhoff Publishers, 2006), pp. 271–95.

'Treasure Hunters, Sunken State Vessels and the 2001 UNESCO Convention on the Protection of Underwater Cultural Heritage' (2010) 25 *International Journal of Marine and Coastal Law* 209–36.

Bascom, W., 'Deepwater Archeology' (1971) 174 *Science* 261–9.

Baslar, K., *The Concept of the Common Heritage of Mankind in International Law* (The Hague: Martinus Nijhoff Publishers, 1998).

Bass, G., 'Turkey: Survey for Shipwrecks, 1973' (1974) 3 *International Journal of Nautical Archaeology* 335–8.

Bederman, D., 'Historic Salvage and the Law of the Sea' (1998–9) 30 *University of Miami Inter-American Law Review* 99–129.

'Maritime Preservation Law: Old Challenges, New Trends' (2002) 8 *Widener Law Symposium Journal* 163–206.

'The UNESCO Draft Convention on Underwater Cultural Heritage: A Critique and Counter-Proposal' (1999) 30 *Journal of Maritime Law and Commerce* 331–54.

Bevan, J., *The Infernal Diver* (London: Submex Ltd, 1996).

Birnie, P., Boyle, A. and Redgwell, C., *International Law and the Environment*, 3rd edn (Oxford University Press, 2009).

Bishop, A., 'The Underwater Cultural Heritage Convention 2001' (2002) 3 *Shipping and Transport Lawyer* 18–20.

Blake, J., 'The Protection of the Underwater Cultural Heritage' (1996) 45 *International and Comparative Law Quarterly* 819–43.

'Turkey', in S. Dromgoole (ed.), *Legal Protection of the Underwater Cultural Heritage: National and International Perspectives* (The Hague, London and Boston: Kluwer Law International, 1999), pp. 169–80.

Blumberg, R., 'International Protection of Underwater Cultural Heritage', in M. Nordquist, J. Norton Moore and Kuen-chen Fu (eds.), *Recent Developments in the Law of the Sea and China* (Leiden and Boston: Martinus Nijhoff Publishers, 2006), pp. 491–511.

Boyle, A., 'Further Development of the Law of the Sea Convention: Mechanisms for Change' (2005) 54 *International and Comparative Law Quarterly* 563–84.

Boyle, A. and Chinkin, C., *The Making of International Law* (Oxford University Press, 2007).

Braekhus, S., 'Salvage of Wrecks and Wreckage: Legal Issues Arising from the Runde Find' (1976) 20 *Scandinavian Studies in Law* 39–68.

Brice, G., 'Salvage and the Underwater Cultural Heritage' (1996) 20 *Marine Policy* 337–42.

Bridge, M., *Personal Property Law*, 3rd edn (Oxford University Press, 2002).

Brown, E., *The International Law of the Sea*, Vol. I (Aldershot: Dartmouth, 1994).

'Protection of the Underwater Cultural Heritage: Draft Principles and Guidelines for Implementation of Article 303 of the United Nations Convention on the Law of the Sea, 1982' (1996) 20 *Marine Policy* 325–36.

Brownlie, I., *Principles of Public International Law*, 7th edn (Oxford University Press, 2008).

Bryant, C., 'The Archaeological Duty of Care: The Legal, Professional, and Cultural Struggle over Salvaging Historic Shipwrecks' (2001) 65 *Albany Law Review* 97–145.

Caflisch, L., 'Submarine Antiquities and the International Law of the Sea' (1982) 13 *Netherlands Yearbook of International Law* 3–32.

Camarda, G. and Scovazzi, T. (eds.), *The Protection of the Underwater Cultural Heritage: Legal Aspects* (Milan: Giuffrè Editore, 2002).

Carducci, G., 'The Expanding Protection of Underwater Cultural Heritage: The New UNESCO Convention Versus Existing International Law', in G. Camarda and T. Scovazzi (eds.), *The Protection of the Underwater Cultural Heritage: Legal Aspects* (Milan: Giuffrè Editore, 2002).

Churchill, R. and Lowe, A., *The Law of the Sea*, 3rd edn (Manchester University Press, 1999).

Clément, E., 'Current Developments at UNESCO Concerning the Protection of the Underwater Cultural Heritage: Presentation Made at the First and Second National Maritime Museum Conferences on the Protection of Underwater

Cultural Heritage (Greenwich, 3 and 4 February 1995) (London, IMO, 25 and 26 January 1996)' (1996) 20 *Marine Policy* 309–13.

Crane Miller, H., *International Law and Marine Archaeology* (Belmont, NH: Academy of Applied Science, 1973).

Davies, M., 'Whatever Happened to the Salvage Convention 1989?' (2008) 39 *Journal of Maritime Law and Commerce* 463–504.

Davies, P. and Myburgh, P., 'New Zealand', in S. Dromgoole (ed.), *The Protection of the Underwater Cultural Heritage: National Perspectives in Light of the UNESCO Convention 2001* (Leiden and Boston: Martinus Nijhoff Publishers, 2006), pp. 189–215.

Dorsey, W., 'Historic Salvors, Marine Archaeologists, and the UNESCO Draft Convention on the Underwater Cultural Heritage', paper delivered at Houston Marine Insurance Seminar 2000 (available at www. houstonmarineseminar.com).

Dromgoole, S., '2001 UNESCO Convention on the Protection of the Underwater Cultural Heritage' (2003) 18 *International Journal of Marine and Coastal Law* 59–108.

'The International Agreement for the Protection of the *Titanic*: Problems and Prospects' (2006) 37 *Ocean Development and International Law* 1–31.

(ed.), *Legal Protection of the Underwater Cultural Heritage: National and International Perspectives* (The Hague, London and Boston: Kluwer Law International, 1999).

'Murky Waters for Government Policy: The Case of a 17th Century British Warship and 10 Tonnes of Gold Coins' (2004) 28 *Marine Policy* 189–98.

'A Note on the Meaning of "Wreck"' (1999) 28 *International Journal of Nautical Archaeology* 319–22.

'Protection of Historic Wreck: The UK Approach, Part I: The Present Legal Framework' (1989) 4 *International Journal of Estuarine and Coastal Law* 26–51.

(ed.), *The Protection of the Underwater Cultural Heritage: National Perspectives in Light of the UNESCO Convention 2001*, 2nd edn (Leiden and Boston: Martinus Nijhoff Publishers, 2006).

'Reflections on the Position of the Major Maritime Powers with Respect to the UNESCO Convention on the Protection of the Underwater Cultural Heritage 2001' (2013) 38 *Marine Policy* 116–23 (dx.doi.org/10.1016/j.marpol.2012.05.027).

'Revisiting the Relationship between Marine Scientific Research and the Underwater Cultural Heritage' (2010) 25 *International Journal of Marine and Coastal Law* 33–61.

'United Kingdom', in S. Dromgoole (ed.), *The Protection of the Underwater Cultural Heritage: National Perspectives in Light of the UNESCO Convention 2001*, 2nd edn (Leiden and Boston: Martinus Nijhoff Publishers, 2006), pp. 313–50.

Dromgoole, S. and Forrest, C., 'The Nairobi Wreck Removal Convention 2007 and Hazardous Historic Shipwrecks' [2011] *Lloyd's Maritime and Commercial Law Quarterly* 92–122.

Dromgoole, S. and Gaskell, N., 'Draft UNESCO Convention on the Protection of the Underwater Cultural Heritage 1998' (1999) 14 *International Journal of Marine and Coastal Law* 171–92.

Dromgoole, S. and Gaskell, N., 'Interests in Wreck', in N. Palmer and E. McKendrick (eds.), *Interests in Goods*, 2nd edn (London and Hong Kong: Lloyd's of London Press, 1998), pp. 141–204.

Dunkley, M., 'Catastrophic Burials: The Study of Human Remains from Sunken Warships' [2011] 66 *English Heritage Conservation Bulletin* 20–2.

Earle, P., *Treasure Hunt: Shipwreck, Diving, and the Quest for Treasure in an Age of Heroes* (New York: Thomas Dunne Books, St Martin's Press, 2007).

Elkin, D., 'Case Study: HMS *Swift* – Argentina', in University of Wolverhampton/ English Heritage, Shared Heritage: Joint Responsibilities in the Management of British Warship Wrecks Overseas, International Seminar, 8 July 2008, pp. 2–13 (available at www.english-heritage.org.uk/publications).

Espósito, C. and Fraile, C., 'The UNESCO Convention on Underwater Cultural Heritage: A Spanish View', in D. Caron and H. Scheiber (eds.), *Bringing New Law to Ocean Waters* (Leiden and Boston: Martinus Nijhoff Publishers, 2004), pp. 201–23.

Eustis III, F., 'The *Glomar Explorer* Incident: Implications for the Law of Salvage' (1975–6) 16 *Virginia Journal of International Law* 177–85.

Ferri, N., 'The Protection of the Underwater Cultural Heritage According to the United Nations General Assembly' (2008) 23 *International Journal of Marine and Coastal Law* 137–49.

Firth, A., 'Underwater Cultural Heritage Off England: Character and Significance', in R. Yorke (ed.), *Protection of Underwater Cultural Heritage in International Waters Adjacent to the UK: Proceedings of the JNAPC 21st Anniversary Seminar* (Portsmouth: Nautical Archaeology Society, 2011), pp. 15–22.

Flecker, M., 'The Ethics, Politics, and Realities of Maritime Archaeology in Southeast Asia' (2002) 31 *International Journal of Nautical Archaeology* 12–24.

Fletcher-Tomenius, P. and Williams, M. 'The Protection of Wrecks Act 1973: A Breach of Human Rights?' (1998) 13 *International Journal of Marine and Coastal Law* 623–42.

Fletcher-Tomenius, P., O'Keefe, P. and Williams, M., 'Salvor in Possession: Friend or Foe to Marine Archaeology?' (2000) 9 *International Journal of Cultural Property* 263–314.

Forrest, C., *International Law and the Protection of Cultural Heritage* (London and New York: Routledge, 2010).

'An International Perspective on Sunken State Vessels as Underwater Cultural Heritage' (2003) 34 *Ocean Development and International Law* 41–57.

'A New International Regime for the Protection of Underwater Cultural Heritage' (2002) 51 *International and Comparative Law Quarterly* 511–54.

'South Africa', in S. Dromgoole (ed.), *The Protection of the Underwater Cultural Heritage: National Perspectives in Light of the UNESCO Convention 2001* (Leiden and Boston: Martinus Nijhoff Publishers, 2006), pp. 247–70.

Forrest, C. and Gribble, J., 'The Illicit Movement of Underwater Cultural Heritage: The Case of the Dodington Coins' (2002) 11 *International Journal of Cultural Property* 267–93.

'Perspectives from the Southern Hemisphere: Australia and South Africa', in Joint Nautical Archaeology Policy Committee, *The UNESCO Convention for the Protection of the Underwater Cultural Heritage: Proceedings of the Burlington House Seminar, October 2005* (Portsmouth: Nautical Archaeology Society, 2006), pp. 30–5.

Fox, H., *The Law of State Immunity*, 2nd edn (Oxford University Press, 2008).

Francioni, F., *The 1972 World Heritage Convention: A Commentary* (Oxford University Press, 2008).

Fu, Kuen-chen, 'China (including Taiwan)', in S. Dromgoole (ed.), *The Protection of the Underwater Cultural Heritage: National Perspectives in Light of the UNESCO Convention 2001* (Leiden and Boston: Martinus Nijhoff Publishers, 2006), pp. 17–41.

Gaffney, V., Fitch, S. and Smith, D., *Europe's Lost World: The Rediscovery of Doggerland* (York: Council for British Archaeology, 2009).

Garabello, R., 'The Negotiating History of the Convention on the Protection of the Underwater Cultural Heritage', in R. Garabello and T. Scovazzi (eds.), *The Protection of the Underwater Cultural Heritage: Before and After the 2001 UNESCO Convention* (Leiden and Boston: Martinus Nijhoff Publishers, 2003), pp. 89–192.

'Sunken Warships in the Mediterranean: Reflections on Some Relevant Examples in State Practice Relating to the Mediterranean Sea', in T. Scovazzi (ed.), *La Protezione del Patrimonio Culturale Sottomarino nel Mare Mediterraneo* (Milan: Giuffrè Editore, 2004), pp. 171–201.

Garabello, R. and Scovazzi, T. (eds.), *The Protection of the Underwater Cultural Heritage: Before and After the 2001 UNESCO Convention* (Leiden and Boston: Martinus Nijhoff Publishers, 2003).

Gaskell, N., 'The 1989 Salvage Convention and the Lloyd's Open Form (LOF) Salvage Agreement 1990' (1991) 16 *Tulane Maritime Law Journal* 1–76.

'Merchant Shipping Act 1995, Schedule 11', *Current Law Statutes Annotated* 1995, 21-373–21-434.

Giesecke, A., 'The Abandoned Shipwreck Act Through the Eyes of its Drafter' (1999) 30 *Journal of Maritime Law and Commerce* 167–73.

Giorgi, M., 'Underwater Archaeological and Historical Objects', in R.-J. Dupuy and D. Vignes (eds.), *A Handbook on the New Law of the Sea* (Dordrecht, Boston and Lancaster: Martinus Nijhoff Publishers, 1991), chap. 11 (pp. 561–75).

Grenier, R., 'The Annex: Archaeology and the UNESCO Convention 2001', in L. Prott (ed.), *Finishing the Interrupted Voyage: Papers of the UNESCO Asia-Pacific Workshop on the 2001 Convention on the Protection of the Underwater Cultural Heritage* (Bangkok and Leicester: UNESCO/Institute of Art and Law, 2006), pp. 110–20.

Gribble, J., 'HMS *Birkenhead* and the British Warship Wrecks in South African Waters', in University of Wolverhampton/English Heritage, Shared Heritage: Joint Responsibilities in the Management of British Warship Wrecks Overseas, International Seminar, 8 July 2008, pp. 30–44 (available at www.english-heritage.org.uk/publications).

Grøn, O. and Mortensen, L., 'Stone Age in the Danish North Sea Sector', *Maritime Archaeology Newsletter from Denmark No. 26* (summer 2011), pp. 3–8.

Guérin, U., 'The 2001 UNESCO Convention on the Protection of Underwater Cultural Heritage: References and Guidelines for Interventions on Submerged Archaeological Sites', in J. Henderson (ed.), *Beyond Boundaries: The 3rd International Congress on Underwater Archaeology, IKUWA 3 London 2008* (Frankfurt: Römisch-Germanische Kommission, 2012), pp. 3–8.

Harrison, J., *Making the Law of the Sea: A Study in the Development of International Law* (Cambridge University Press, 2011).

Hayashi, M., 'Archaeological and Historical Objects under the United Nations Convention on the Law of the Sea' (1996) 20 *Marine Policy* 291–6.

Hetherington, S., 'Discussion Paper for Review of Salvage Convention 1989 International Sub-Committee Meeting', 12 May 2010, London (available at www.marisec.org).

Hoagland, P., 'Managing the Underwater Cultural Resources of the China Seas: A Comparison of Public Policies in Mainland China and Taiwan' (1997) 12 *International Journal of Marine and Coastal Law* 265–83.

Honoré, A., 'Ownership', in A. Guest (ed.), *Oxford Essays in Jurisprudence* (Oxford University Press, 1961), pp. 107–47.

Hutchinson, G., 'Threats to Underwater Cultural Heritage: The Problems of Unprotected Archaeological and Historic Sites, Wrecks and Objects Found at Sea' (1996) 20 *Marine Policy* 287–90.

Jacobsson, M. and Klabbers, J., 'Rest in Peace? New Developments Concerning the Wreck of the M/S *Estonia*' (2000) 69 *Nordic Journal of International Law* 317–32.

Jeffery, B., 'Activities Incidentally Affecting Underwater Cultural Heritage in the 2001 UNESCO Convention', in L. Prott (ed.), *Finishing the Interrupted Voyage: Papers of the UNESCO Asia-Pacific Workshop on the 2001 Convention on the Protection of the Underwater Cultural Heritage* (Bangkok and Leicester: UNESCO/Institute of Art and Law, 2006), pp. 96–9.

'Australia' (1st edn) in S. Dromgoole (ed.), *Legal Protection of the Underwater Cultural Heritage: National and International Perspectives* (The Hague, London and Boston: Kluwer Law International, 1999), pp. 1–17.

'Australia' (2nd edn) in S. Dromgoole (ed.), *The Protection of the Underwater Cultural Heritage: National Perspectives in Light of the UNESCO Convention 2001* (Leiden and Boston: Martinus Nijhoff Publishers, 2006), pp. 1–15.

'Federated States of Micronesia', in S. Dromgoole (ed.), *The Protection of the Underwater Cultural Heritage: National Perspectives in Light of the UNESCO Convention 2001* (Leiden and Boston: Martinus Nijhoff Publishers, 2006), pp. 145–59.

Joyner, C., 'Legal Implications of the Concept of the Common Heritage of Mankind' (1986) 35 *International and Comparative Law Quarterly* 190–9.

Kang, C., 'Charting Through Protection for Historic Shipwrecks Found in US Territorial Waters: *Sea Hunt, Inc. v. Unidentified, Shipwrecked Vessel or Vessels*' (2000) 19 *Virginia Environmental Law Journal* 87–119.

Kirwan, S., 'Ireland and the UNESCO Convention on the Protection of the Underwater Cultural Heritage' (2010) 5 *Journal of Maritime Archaeology* 105–15.

Kirwan, S. and Moore, F., 'Update on Ireland and the UNESCO Convention on the Protection of the Underwater Cultural Heritage', in R. Yorke (ed.), *Protection of Underwater Cultural Heritage in International Waters Adjacent to the UK: Proceedings of the JNAPC 21st Anniversary Seminar* (Portsmouth: Nautical Archaeology Society, 2011), pp. 51–60.

Klabbers, J., 'On Maritime Cemeteries and Objective Regimes: The Case of the M/S *Estonia*', 1996 (available at www.helsinki.fi/eci/Publications/Klabbers/Estonia.pdf).

Klein, N., *Dispute Settlement in the UN Convention on the Law of the Sea* (Cambridge University Press, 2005).

Kopela, S., '2007 Archipelagic Legislation of the Dominican Republic: An Assessment' (2009) 24 *International Journal of Marine and Coastal Law* 501–33.

Kowalski, W., 'Poland', in S. Dromgoole (ed.), *The Protection of the Underwater Cultural Heritage: National Perspectives in Light of the UNESCO Convention 2001* (Leiden and Boston: Martinus Nijhoff Publishers, 2006), pp. 229–46.

Kvalø, F. and Marstrander, L., 'Norway', in S. Dromgoole (ed.), *The Protection of the Underwater Cultural Heritage: National Perspectives in Light of the UNESCO Convention 2001* (Leiden and Boston: Martinus Nijhoff Publishers, 2006), pp. 217–28.

Kwiatkowska, B., 'Creeping Jurisdiction Beyond 200 Miles in the Light of the 1982 Law of the Sea Convention and State Practice' (1991) 22 *Ocean Development and International Law* 153–87.

Le Gurun, G., 'France' (1st edn) in S. Dromgoole (ed.), *Legal Protection of the Underwater Cultural Heritage: National and International Perspectives* (The Hague, London and Boston: Kluwer Law International, 1999), pp. 43–63.

    'France' (2nd edn) in S. Dromgoole (ed.), *The Protection of the Underwater Cultural Heritage: National Perspectives in Light of the UNESCO Convention 2001* (Leiden and Boston: Martinus Nijhoff Publishers, 2006), pp. 59–95.

Leanza, U., 'The Territorial Scope of the Draft European Convention on the Protection of the Underwater Cultural Heritage', in Council of Europe, *International Legal Protection of Cultural Property*, Proceedings of the Thirteenth Colloquy on European Law, Delphi, 20–23 September 1983, Strasbourg, 1984, pp. 127–30.

Lee, K.-G., 'An Inquiry into the Compatibility of the UNESCO Convention 2001 with UNCLOS 1982', in L. Prott (ed.), *Finishing the Interrupted Voyage: Papers of the UNESCO Asia-Pacific Workshop on the 2001 Convention on the Protection of the Underwater Cultural Heritage* (Bangkok and Leicester: UNESCO/Institute of Art and Law, 2006), pp. 20–6.

Leshikar-Denton, M. and Luna Erreguerena, P., *Underwater and Maritime Archaeology in Latin America and the Caribbean* (Walnut Creek, CA: Left Coast Press, 2008).

L'Hour, M., 'An Update on France's Position Regarding the UNESCO Underwater Cultural Heritage Convention', in R. Yorke (ed.), *Protection of Underwater*

Cultural Heritage in International Waters Adjacent to the UK: Proceedings of the JNAPC 21st Anniversary Seminar (Portsmouth: Nautical Archaeology Society, 2011), p. 63.

Long, R., *Marine Resources Law* (Dublin: Thomson Round Hall, 2007).

Lowe, V., *International Law* (Oxford University Press, 2007).

Maarleveld, T., 'Drama, Place and Verifiable Link: Underwater Cultural Heritage, Present Experience and Contention', in L. Turgeon (ed.), *Spirit of Place: Between Tangible and Intangible Heritage* (Quebec: Les Presses de l'Université Laval, 2009), pp. 97–108.

'International Good Practice or a Few Comments Upon Them', in University of Wolverhampton/English Heritage, Shared Heritage: Joint Responsibilities in the Management of British Warship Wrecks Overseas, International Seminar, 8 July 2008, pp. 58–68 (available at www.english-heritage.org/publications).

'The Maritime Paradox: Does International Heritage Exist?' [2012] *International Journal of Heritage Studies* 1–14.

'The Netherlands', in S. Dromgoole (ed.), *The Protection of the Underwater Cultural Heritage: National Perspectives in Light of the UNESCO Convention 2001* (Leiden and Boston: Martinus Nijhoff Publishers, 2006), pp. 161–88.

Magnusson, R., 'Proprietary Rights in Human Tissue', in N. Palmer and E. McKendrick (eds.), *Interests in Goods*, 2nd edn (London and Hong Kong: Lloyd's of London Press, 1998), pp. 25–62.

Manders, M., '*In Situ* Preservation: "The Preferred Option"' (2008) 240 *Museum International* 31–41.

Marx, R., 'The Disappearing Underwater Heritage' (1983) 35 *Museum* 9–10.

Mather, R., 'Technology and the Search for Shipwrecks' (1999) 30 *Journal of Maritime Law and Commerce* 175–84.

Matikka, M., 'Finland', in S. Dromgoole (ed.), *The Protection of the Underwater Cultural Heritage: National Perspectives in Light of the UNESCO Convention 2001* (Leiden and Boston: Martinus Nijhoff Publishers, 2006), pp. 43–57.

McQuown, T., 'An Archaeological Argument for the Inapplicability of Admiralty Law in the Disposition of Historic Shipwrecks' (2000) 26 *William Mitchell Law Review* 289–326.

Merryman, J., 'Cultural Property Internationalism', in J. Merryman, *Thinking about the Elgin Marbles: Critical Essays on Cultural Property, Art and Law*, 2nd edn (Alphen aan den Rijn: Kluwer Law International, 2009), pp. 110–41.

'Two Ways of Thinking About Cultural Property', in J. Merryman, *Thinking about the Elgin Marbles: Critical Essays on Cultural Property, Art and Law*, 2nd edn (Alphen aan den Rijn: Kluwer Law International, 2009), pp. 82–109.

Migliorino, L., 'The Recovery of Sunken Warships in International Law', in B. Vukas (ed.), *Essays on the Law of the Sea* (Zagreb: Sveucilisna Naklada Liver, 1985), pp. 244–58.

Mohd Nor, M., 'Protection of Underwater Cultural Heritage in Malaysia: Challenges and Prospects', in J. Henderson (ed.), *Beyond Boundaries: The 3rd*

International Congress on Underwater Archaeology, IKUWA 3 London 2008 (Frankfurt: Römisch-Germanische Kommission, 2012), pp. 15–26.

Muckleroy, K., *Maritime Archaeology* (Cambridge University Press, 1978).

Nafziger, J., 'The Evolving Role of Admiralty Courts in Litigation Related to Historic Wrecks' (2003) 44 *Harvard International Law Journal* 251–70.

'Finding the Titanic: Beginning an International Salvage of Derelict Law at Sea' (1988) 12 *Columbia–VLA Journal of Law and the Arts* 339–51.

'Historic Salvage Law Revisited' (2000) 31 *Ocean Development and International Law* 81–96.

'The Titanic Revisited' (1999) 30 *Journal of Maritime Law and Commerce* 311–30.

Neyland, R., 'Sovereign Immunity and the Management of United States Naval Shipwrecks' (available at www.history.navy.mil/branches/org12-7h.htm).

Niemeyer, P., 'Applying *Jus Gentium* to the Salvage of the RMS *Titanic* in International Waters: The Nicholas J. Healy Lecture' (2005) *Journal of Maritime Law and Commerce* 431–46.

Nordquist, M., Nandan, S., Rosenne, S. and Grandy, N. (eds.), *United Nations Convention on the Law of the Sea 1982: A Commentary*, Vol. II (Dordrecht, Boston and London: Martinus Nijhoff, 1993).

Nordquist, M., Rosenne, S., Yankov, A. and Grandy, N. (eds.), *United Nations Convention on the Law of the Sea 1982: A Commentary*, Vol. IV (Dordrecht, Boston and London: Martinus Nijhoff Publishers, 1991).

Nordquist, M., Rosenne, S. and Sohn, L. (eds.), *United Nations Convention on the Law of the Sea 1982: A Commentary*, Vol. V (Dordrecht, Boston and London: Martinus Nijhoff Publishers, 1989).

Nordquist, M., Nandan, S., Lodge, M. and Rosenne, S. (eds.), *United Nations Convention on the Law of the Sea 1982: A Commentary*, Vol. VI (The Hague, London and New York: Martinus Nijhoff Publishers, 2002).

O'Connell, D., *The International Law of the Sea*, Vol. II (Oxford University Press, 1984).

O'Connor, N., 'Ireland' (1st edn) in S. Dromgoole (ed.), *Legal Protection of the Underwater Cultural Heritage: National and International Perspectives* (The Hague, London and Boston: Kluwer Law International, 1999), pp. 87–99.

'Ireland' (2nd edn) in S. Dromgoole (ed.), *The Protection of the Underwater Cultural Heritage: National Perspectives in Light of the UNESCO Convention 2001* (Leiden and Boston: Martinus Nijhoff Publishers, 2006), pp. 127–44.

O'Keefe, P., 'The Buenos Aires Draft Convention on the Protection of the Underwater Cultural Heritage Prepared by the International Law Association: Its Relevance Seven Years On', in G. Camarda and T. Scovazzi (eds), *The Protection of the Underwater Cultural Heritage: Legal Aspects* (Milan: Giuffrè Editore, 2002), pp. 93–104.

'Gold, Abandonment and Salvage: The *Central America*' [1994] *Lloyd's Maritime and Commercial Law Quarterly* 7–12.

'International Waters', in S. Dromgoole (ed.), *Legal Protection of the Underwater Cultural Heritage: National and International Perspectives* (The Hague, London and Boston: Kluwer Law International, 1999), pp. 223–35.

'Protecting the Underwater Cultural Heritage: The International Law Association Draft Convention', (1996) 20 *Marine Policy* 297–307.

Shipwrecked Heritage: A Commentary on the UNESCO Convention on Underwater Cultural Heritage (Leicester: Institute of Art and Law, 2002).

O'Keefe, P. and Nafziger, J., 'Report: The Draft Convention on the Protection of the Underwater Cultural Heritage' (1994) 25 *Ocean Development and International Law* 391–418.

O'Keefe, R., *The Protection of Cultural Property in Armed Conflict* (Cambridge University Press, 2006).

Oxley, I., 'Making the Submerged Historic Environment Accessible: Beyond the National Heritage Act (2002)', in J. Satchell and P. Palma, *Managing the Marine Cultural Heritage: Defining, Accessing and Managing the Resource* (York: Council for British Archaeology, 2007), pp. 87–95.

Oxman, B., 'Complementary Agreements and Compulsory Jurisdiction' (2001) 95 *American Journal of International Law* 277–312.

'Marine Archaeology and the International Law of the Sea' (1987–8) 12 *Columbia–VLA Journal of Law and the Arts* 353–72.

'The Regime of Warships under the United Nations Convention on the Law of the Sea' (1983–4) 24 *Virginia Journal of International Law* 809–63.

'The Third United Nations Conference on the Law of the Sea: The Ninth Session (1980)' (1981) 75 *American Journal of International Law* 211–56.

Panter, I., '*In Situ* Preservation Versus Active Conservation: Are We Prepared For the Deluge?', in J. Satchell and P. Palma, *Managing the Marine Cultural Heritage: Defining, Accessing and Managing the Resource* (York: Council for British Archaeology, 2007), pp. 59–62.

Parham, D. and Williams, M., 'An Outline of the Nature of the Threat to Underwater Cultural Heritage in International Waters', in R. Yorke (ed.), *Protection of Underwater Cultural Heritage in International Waters Adjacent to the UK: Proceedings of the JNAPC 21st Anniversary Seminar* (Portsmouth: Nautical Archaeology Society, 2011), pp. 5–14.

Polakiewicz, J., *Treaty Making in the Council of Europe* (Strasbourg, Council of Europe Publishing, 1999).

Prescott, J. and Schofield, C., *Maritime Political Boundaries of the World*, 2nd edn (Leiden and Boston: Martinus Nijhoff, 2005).

Prott, L. (ed.), *Finishing the Interrupted Voyage: Papers of the UNESCO Asia-Pacific Workshop on the 2001 Convention on the Protection of the Underwater Cultural Heritage* (Leicester: Institute of Art and Law, 2006).

Prott, L. and O'Keefe, P., '"Cultural Heritage" or "Cultural Property"?' (1992) 1 *International Journal of Cultural Property* 307–20.

Law and the Cultural Heritage, Vol. I (Abingdon: Professional Books Ltd, 1984).

Law and the Cultural Heritage, Vol. III (London and Edinburgh: Butterworths, 1989).

Roach, J., 'France Concedes United States Has Title to CSS *Alabama*' (1991) 85 *American Journal of International Law* 381–3.

'Shipwrecks: Reconciling Salvage and Underwater Archaeology', in Center for Oceans Law and Policy, Twenty Second Annual Conference, *Oceans Policy: New Institutions, Challenges and Opportunities*, 8–10 January 1998 (available at www.prosea.org).

Roach, J. and Smith, R., *United States Responses to Excessive Maritime Claims*, 2nd edn (The Hague, Boston and London: Martinus Nijhoff Publishers, 1996).

Roberts, P. and Trow, S., *Taking to the Water* (Swindon: English Heritage, 2002).

Rubin, A., 'Sunken Soviet Submarines and Central Intelligence: Laws of Property and the Agency' (1975) 69 *American Journal of International Law* 855–8.

Schoenbaum, T., *Admiralty and Maritime Law*, 4th edn (St Paul, MN: Thomson/ West, 2004).

Schofield, C., 'Parting the Waves: Claims to Maritime Jurisdiction and the Division of Ocean Space' (2012) 1 *Penn State Journal of Law and International Affairs* 40–58.

Scovazzi, T., 'The 2001 UNESCO Convention on the Protection of the Underwater Cultural Heritage', in G. Camarda and T. Scovazzi (eds.), *The Protection of the Underwater Cultural Heritage: Legal Aspects* (Milan, Giuffrè Editore, 2002), pp. 113–34.

'The Entry into Force of the 2001 UNESCO Convention on the Protection of the Underwater Cultural Heritage' (2010) 1 *Aegean Review of the Law of the Sea and Maritime Law* 19–36.

'The Protection of Underwater Cultural Heritage: Article 303 and the UNESCO Convention', in D. Freestone, R. Barnes and D. Ong (eds.), *The Law of the Sea: Progress and Prospects* (Oxford University Press, 2006).

(ed.), *La Protezione del Patrimonio Culturale Sottomarino nel Mare Mediterraneo* (Milan: Giuffrè Editore, 2004).

Soons, A., *Marine Scientific Research and the Law of the Sea* (The Hague: TMC Asser Instituut, 1982).

Staniforth, M., 'Australian Approaches to Shared Heritage: Royal Navy Vessels in Australian Waters', in University of Wolverhampton/English Heritage, Shared Heritage: Joint Responsibilities in the Management of British Warship Wrecks Overseas, International Seminar, 8 July 2008, pp. 17–29 (available at www.english-heritage.org.uk/publications).

Stemm, G., 'Differentiation of Shipwreck Artifacts as a Resource Management Tool', Association of Dive Contractors/Marine Technology Society UI 2000 Conference, January 2000 (available at www.shipwreck.net).

Stemm, G. and Bederman, D., 'Virtual Collections and Private Curators: A Model for the Museum of the Future', OME Paper 14, 2010 (available at www.shipwreck.net).

Stemm, G. and Kingsley, S., *Oceans Odyssey: Deep-Sea Shipwrecks in the English Channel, Straits of Gibraltar and Atlantic Ocean* (Oxford and Oakville, CT: Oxbow Books, 2010).

Strati, A., 'Greece' (1st edn) in S. Dromgoole (ed.), *Legal Protection of the Underwater Cultural Heritage: National and International Perspectives* (The Hague, London and Boston: Kluwer Law International, 1999), pp. 65–85.

'Greece' (2nd edn) in S. Dromgoole (ed.), *The Protection of the Underwater Cultural Heritage: National Perspectives in Light of the UNESCO Convention 2001* (Leiden and Boston: Martinus Nijhoff Publishers, 2006), pp. 97–126.

The Protection of the Underwater Cultural Heritage: An Emerging Objective of the Contemporary Law of the Sea (The Hague, London and Boston: Martinus Nijhoff Publishers, 1995).

'Protection of the Underwater Cultural Heritage: From the Shortcomings of the UN Convention on the Law of the Sea to the Compromises of the UNESCO Convention', in A. Strati, M. Gavouneli and N. Skourtos (eds.), *Unresolved Issues and New Challenges to the Law of the Sea: Time Before and Time After* (Leiden and Boston: Martinus Nijhoff Publishers, 2006), pp. 21–62.

Symmons, C., *Ireland and the Law of the Sea*, 2nd edn (Dublin: The Round Hall Press, 1993).

'Recent Off-Shore Treasure-Seeking Incidents Relating to Wrecks in Irish Waters' (2012) 27 *International Journal of Marine and Coastal Law* 635–46.

Thomas, R., 'Heritage Protection Criteria: An Analysis' [2006] *Journal of Planning Law* 956–63.

Vadi, V., 'The Challenge of Reconciling Underwater Cultural Heritage and Foreign Direct Investment: A Case Study' (2007) 17 *Italian Yearbook of International Law* 143–58.

'Investing in Culture: Underwater Cultural Heritage and International Investment Law' (2009) 42 *Vanderbilt Journal of Transnational Law* 853–904.

'Underwater Cultural Heritage and International Investment Law', in J. Henderson (ed.), *Beyond Boundaries: The 3rd International Congress on Underwater Archaeology, IKUWA 3, London 2008* (Frankfurt: Römisch-Germanische Kommission, 2012), pp. 35–40.

Varmer, O., 'The Case Against the "Salvage" of the Cultural Heritage' (1999) 30 *Journal of Maritime Law and Commerce* 279–302.

'A Perspective from Across the Atlantic', Joint Nautical Archaeology Policy Committee, *The UNESCO Convention for the Protection of the Underwater Cultural Heritage: Proceedings of the Burlington House Seminar, October 2005* (Portsmouth: Nautical Archaeology Society, 2006), pp. 23–9.

'United States', in S. Dromgoole (ed.), *The Protection of the Underwater Cultural Heritage: National Perspectives in Light of the UNESCO Convention 2001* (Leiden and Boston: Martinus Nijhoff Publishers, 2006), pp. 351–85.

Webster, S., 'The Development of Excavation Technology for Remotely Operated Vehicles', in R. Ballard (ed.), *Archaeological Oceanography* (Princeton, NJ: Princeton University Press, 2008).

Wegelein, F., *Marine Scientific Research: The Operation and Status of Research Vessels and other Platforms in International Law* (Leiden and Boston: Martinus Nijhoff Publishers, 2005).

Weinberg, G. D., Grace, Virginia R., Edwards, G. Roger *et al.*, 'The Antikythera Shipwreck Reconsidered' (1965) 55 *Transactions of the American Philosophical Society* 3–48.

Weirich, J., 'Connecting with the Past: Using Online Tools, Techniques and Partnerships to Explore Our Maritime Heritage', in J. Satchell and P. Palma, *Managing the Marine Cultural Heritage: Defining, Accessing and Managing the Resource* (York: Council for British Archaeology, 2007), pp. 79–86.

Zamora, T., 'The Impact of Commercial Exploitation on the Preservation of Underwater Cultural Heritage' (2008) 240 *Museum International* 18–30.

Index

Books in the series

Lightning Source UK Ltd.
Milton Keynes UK
UKOW06f2135060316